(v6/v4) 14/282-89

Officers of the United States Senate

EIGHTY-NINTH CONGRESS

HUBERT H. HUMPHREY, *Vice President of the United States and President of the Senate*

CARL HAYDEN, *President pro tempore of the Senate*

FELTON M. JOHNSTON, *Secretary*

JOSEPH C. DUKE, *Sergeant at Arms*

FRANCIS R. VALEO,
Secretary for the Majority
J. MARK TRICE,
Secretary for the Minority

EMERY L. FRAZIER, *Chief Clerk*

FLOYD M. RIDDICK, *Parliamentarian*

EDWARD E. MANSUR, JR., *Legislative Clerk*

BERNARD V. SOMERS, *Journal Clerk*

JOHN L. GRAVES,
Assistant Secretary for the Majority
WILLIAM BROWNRIGG III,
Assistant Secretary for the Minority

Rev. FREDERICK BROWN HARRIS, D.D., *Chaplain*

The United States Senate

EIGHTY-NINTH CONGRESS

Democrats—Roman

Aiken, George D., Vermont, 23
Allott, Gordon, Colorado, 45
Anderson, Clinton P., New Mexico, 17
Bartlett, E. L., Alaska, 84
Bass, Ross, Tennessee, 63
Bayh, Birch, Indiana, 65
Bennett, Wallace F., Utah, 4
Bible, Alan, Nevada, 18
Boggs, J. Caleb, Delaware, 73
Brewster, Daniel B., Maryland, 86
Burdick, Quentin N., North Dakota, 90
Byrd, Harry Flood, Virginia, 10
Byrd, Robert C., West Virginia, 59
Cannon, Howard W., Nevada, 57
Carlson, Frank, Kansas, 48
Case, Clifford P., New Jersey, 2
Church, Frank, Idaho, 82
Clark, Joseph S., Pennsylvania, 83
Cooper, John Sherman, Kentucky, 22
Cotton, Norris, New Hampshire, 46
Curtis, Carl T., Nebraska, 75
Dirksen, Everett McKinley, Illinois, 7
Dodd, Thomas J., Connecticut, 56
Dominick, Peter H., Colorado, 69
Douglas, Paul H., Illinois, 54
Eastland, James O., Mississippi, 29
Ellender, Allen J., Louisiana, 11
Ervin, Sam J., Jr., North Carolina, 37
Fannin, Paul J., Arizona, 67
Fong, Hiram L., Hawaii, 74
Fulbright, J. W., Arkansas, 12
Gore, Albert, Tennessee, 51
Gruening, Ernest, Alaska, 60
Harris, Fred R., Oklahoma, 97
Hart, Philip A., Michigan, 87
Hartke, Vance, Indiana, 40
Hayden, Carl, Arizona, 9
Hickenlooper, Bourke B., Iowa, 24
Hill, Lister, Alabama, 30
Holland, Spessard L., Florida, 15
Hruska, Roman L., Nebraska, 3
Inouye, Daniel K., Hawaii, 66
Jackson, Henry M., Washington, 34
Javits, Jacob K., New York, 43
Johnston, Olin D., South Carolina, 14
Jordan, B. Everett, North Carolina, 62
Jordan, Len B., Idaho, 71
Kennedy, Edward M., Massachusetts, 95
Kennedy, Robert F., New York, 99
Kuchel, Thomas H., California, 6

Republicans—*Italic*

Lausche, Frank J., Ohio, 35
Long, Edward V., Missouri, 92
Long, Russell B., Louisiana, 53
Magnuson, Warren G., Washin
Mansfield, Mike, Montana, 8
McCarthy, Eugene J., Minnesot
McClellan, John L., Arkansas, ?
McGee, Gale W., Wyoming, 91
McGovern, George, South Dak
McIntyre, Thomas J., New Ham
McNamara, Pat, Michigan, 36
Metcalf, Lee, Montana, 94
Miller, Jack, Iowa, 44
Mondale, Walter F., Minnesota,
Monroney, A. S. Mike, Oklahon
Montoya, Joseph M., New Mexi
Morse, Wayne, Oregon, 16
Morton, Thruston B., Kentucky,
Moss, Frank E., Utah, 89
Mundt, Karl E., South Dakota, 5
Murphy, George, California, 68
Muskie, Edmund S., Maine, 88
Nelson, Gaylord, Wisconsin, 81
Neuberger, Maurine B., Oregon,
Pastore, John O., Rhode Island, 1
Pearson, James B., Kansas, 41
Pell, Claiborne, Rhode Island, 58
Prouty, Winston L., Vermont, 42
Proxmire, William, Wisconsin, 7
Randolph, Jennings, West Virgin
Ribicoff, Abraham, Connecticut, 8
Robertson, A. Willis, Virginia, 32
Russell, Richard B., Georgia, 27
Saltonstall, Leverett, Massachusett:
Scott, Hugh, Pennsylvania, 19
Simpson, Milward L., Wyoming, 7
Smathers, George A., Florida, 52
Smith, Margaret Chase, Maine, 1
Sparkman, John, Alabama, 33
Stennis, John, Mississippi, 49
Symington, Stuart, Missouri, 50
Talmadge, Herman E., Georgia, 61
Thurmond, Strom, South Carolina,
Tower, John G., Texas, 72
Tydings, Joseph D., Maryland, 98
Williams, Harrison A., Jr., New Jer
Williams, John J., Delaware, 21
Yarborough, Ralph, Texas, 38
Young, Milton R., North Dakota, 2
Young, Stephen M., Ohio, 39

(Numbers refer to seating diagram on following pages.)

One Heartbeat Away

PRESIDENTIAL DISABILITY
AND SUCCESSION

One
Heartbeat
Away

PRESIDENTIAL DISABILITY and SUCCESSION

Birch Bayh

The Bobbs-Merrill Company, Inc.
Indianapolis and New York

To Marvella and Evan

Foreword

The tragic death of President Kennedy on November 22, 1963 raised—once again—the perplexing question of Presidential disability and succession.

As it happened, the cooperation of many thousands of people made possible a swift and orderly transition.

Yet many Americans were deeply troubled by the failure of our Constitution to provide for contingencies that had arisen often in the past.

Their concern was not unfounded. For the sixteenth time in our nation's history, the United States was without a Vice President. On three other occasions an American President had suffered from major disabilities that incapacitated him for weeks or even months.

Neither was their concern new. Committee after committee of the Congress had studied the problem, but there had been no action.

The problems in adopting effective succession procedures were obvious. Men held strong and widely divergent opinions as to what the order of succession should be. Furthermore, the backing of two-thirds of the House and Senate, and three-fourths of all the state legislatures was required to amend the Constitution—and that had been achieved only fourteen times in the last 173 years.

Under such circumstances it would not have been surprising for an experienced senator or representative to decline the task of trying to draft an acceptable amendment.

Senator Birch Bayh, the thirty-six-year-old junior senator from Indiana, who had been a member of the Senate for only one year and had yet to deliver his first speech on the Senate floor, thought that the time for action had come.

As chairman of the Senate Judiciary Committee's constitutional amendments subcommittee, he initiated and brought to fruition the first major alteration of Presidential and Vice Presidential succession procedures since the ratification of the Constitution.

Generating the necessary congressional and state legislative support for this task required intelligence and perseverance. It also required a willingness to listen, an ability to explain, and the skill to mediate—personal characteristics which Birch Bayh has in full measure.

This is a fascinating account of the intricate negotiations and hard work which resulted in the Twenty-fifth Amendment—and which gave the United States, for the first time, an orderly method of transition in its most important positions of leadership. It is an exciting story of a significant public achievement.

Lyndon B. Johnson

Preface

➔ The subject of Presidential succession and disability, which Senator Birch Bayh probes in this book, is a matter that has interested and concerned Presidents, congressmen, lawyers, and other scholars for many years. It is doubtful, however, that it has ever been analyzed with more political and legal reality than in the following pages. Senator Bayh (as Chairman of the Subcommittee) has provided the reader a rare insight into the problem, analysis, and solution.

The amendment itself embraces and bridges two constitutional gaps. First, in keeping with our traditional constitutional notions of checks and balances, it assures that the country shall always have a Vice President. This seems to me an important consideration, particularly when it is realized that the Vice Presidency has been vacant, for one reason or another, on sixteen different occasions—for a total of more than thirty-eight years. But the replacement provision does more than simply settle the question of succession; it additionally ensures that there will be brought into the Presidency, in case of necessity, an individual who has had full opportunity to learn much about all of the critical problems then facing the nation. In this manner there will always be available a man well prepared to carry out the job of President who will be in accord with the President's views. The President will be able to train, teach, and work with him. In short, they can develop the relationship necessary for a smooth executive transition which is so vital to the country in times of crises. The structure of this part of the amendment, to my mind, will provide a great added benefit to the nation.

The other vexatious problem handled successfully by the Twenty-fifth Amendment pertains to the determination of Presidential disability. Because of three illnesses which I experienced during my service as President, I was particularly pleased to see this matter set at rest. Fortunately, during each of these disabilities no domestic or international crises arose and therefore no constitutional crisis was invoked.

However, because this possible peril existed, Vice President Nixon and I, in consultation with the Attorney General, prior to my 1956 operation, reduced to memorandum form our understanding as to what would be the Vice President's role in the event of a Presidential disability. While such agreements existed during the remainder of my administration and the administrations of President Kennedy and President Johnson, it was recognized by all that these agreements were, at best, only stopgap solutions. It was for this reason that I personally welcomed the amendment's treatment of the disability problem.

Although it is conceivable that an unforeseeable circumstance might arise which this provision would not adequately handle, this should not shake our belief that the principals involved would undoubtedly be men of honor, men of integrity, men whose concern is the welfare of their country and not their own personal ambitions, and who could successfully bridge any gap that might arise. That presumption is made in this amendment, as it has been in other constitutional provisions. I believe it to be valid.

Let me again stress my conviction that the Presidential succession and inability remedies supplied by the Twenty-Fifth Amendment are necessary if we are to eliminate the unsatisfactory methods which had previously been relied upon to guarantee executive continuity.

To Senator Bayh and to all others whose persevering efforts are described in this book, I extend a hearty commendation for a task well performed.

Dwight D. Eisenhower

Acknowledgments

Every public official is indebted to the many whose selfless efforts crown his endeavors. And so it is with authors, those who write books instead of laws.

I am deeply indebted to my colleagues in the Congress for their understanding of a national dilemma; to the officers, staff, and members of the American Bar Association for their partnership efforts; to John Feerick for his excellently documented background material; to my staff for service beyond the call of duty; and most particularly to my wife Marvella and my son Evan who have willingly shared husband and father with the people of Indiana, the problems of a nation, and more recently with the anguish of authorship.

Contents

PROLOGUE:

A Crisis
and a Dilemma

In November 1963, a little more than a year after the people of Indiana had elected me their junior senator, I was among the many millions who were stunned by the news of President Kennedy's assassination. All of us remember what we were doing at the moment we heard of the tragedy in Dallas, and almost all of us have felt, at one time or another, the need to tell others about our own response to it. Because that tragic occurrence has a direct bearing on the story that follows, I would like to tell about my own experience of that day.

I remember the morning of November twenty-second as being an unusually busy one; not only were there the appointments, meetings, and Senate duties of the normal legislative day, but I was also preoccupied with a serious problem in my home state. It was not yet public knowledge, but I had learned from a confidential source that a shutdown was imminent at the Studebaker plant in South

Bend, Indiana. This would leave some seven thousand people job-
less the week before Christmas, and its economic impact on South
Bend and the state in general would be disastrous. During the weeks
before, as rumors of the shutdown had circulated, I had worked
with South Bend business, labor, and political leaders, trying to sal-
vage whatever we could of the situation. I had enlisted the aid of
President Kennedy and his brother, the Attorney General, and had
received assurances of sympathy and cooperation. The heads of
various departments holding contracts with Studebaker had been
sounded out on the possibility of those contracts being picked up by
some other corporation which would be willing to absorb the South
Bend facility and its employees and maintain operation in the South
Bend area. It had been rumored that the International Harvester
Company might be interested, thus I had arranged to meet in Chicago with the president of the company on the afternoon of the
twenty-second of November. To get there in time, I would have to
take a 12:30 flight out of Washington, and that meant some hectic
last-minute adjustments of my schedule.

I was to have spent two hours of that afternoon presiding over
the Senate—a traditional duty of newly elected senators of the
majority party. When I explained my predicament to the Democratic Policy Committee staff, I was assured that another junior
senator could be found to switch times with me. Next came quick
personal visits with Secretary of Defense McNamara and Postmaster General Gronouski, whose departments both held contracts
with Studebaker and who provided me with the detailed information I would need for the meeting.

I arrived at the airport with time to spare and decided to make
one last telephone call—to "touch base" with Attorney General
Kennedy. Did I still have the green light to try to keep these contracts and jobs in Indiana? The answer was yes, and armed with
his advice and assurance that he would do what he could to help us,
I boarded the plane, feeling optimistic that some good could be
brought out of what was admittedly a bad situation.

The flying weather was terrible. It was raining hard, and the
high winds buffeted us back and forth most of the way. I remember
that I held my breath as we came in for a landing. The four-engined
plane made one uncertain pass over the high-tension wires, then an-

other; on the third try we finally landed at rain-drenched O'Hare Airport. As we were taxiing toward the terminal, the intercom crackled—preparatory, I assumed, to the usual "Welcome to Chicago," and the admonition to remain in our seats until the plane had come to a stop. But instead of the stewardess, it was the pilot's voice we heard. "Ladies and gentlemen . . . I regret very much to have to tell you . . . President Kennedy has been assassinated in Dallas."

The engines were still whirring, the mechanical noises went on, but for a moment there was no human sound in the cabin. "I repeat, ladies and gentlemen . . . I regret very much to have to tell you . . . President Kennedy has been assassinated in Dallas." By then there was a slight murmur, but most of us were speechless. My first thought was "My God, he's been shot—but surely he will recover"; then, brutally, the meaning of the word "assassination" came through to me.

The line of passengers moved, as if in a trance, out of the plane and toward the terminal building. Tears streamed down the faces of many. Once inside, my reaction was that of countless other Americans when they heard the news: I went toward one of the clogged islands of telephone booths to call my wife Marvella. As I went through the motions of getting change and placing the call to our home in McLean, Virginia, recollections of President Kennedy came and went in my mind, like patterns shifting in a kaleidoscope. I had first met him during his barnstorming visit to Indiana in the spring of 1959, long before he had entered the state's Presidential primary. I had seen him again the following fall, that time in my home town of Terre Haute. It is the small, concrete details that come to mind at such times: I recalled holding my five-year-old son Evan, gaily dressed in a bright cowboy suit, high in the air, so that his outstretched hand could be clasped by the future President during a political swing through Indiana during the 1960 campaign.

During those few moments as I waited at the airport for the call to go through, more and more memories poured back, memories from the critical days of my own 1962 Senate campaign. John Kennedy had come back to Indianapolis then to give us a helping hand, and I thought of the powerful campaign speech he had made at the airport. With his characteristic flashing smile, jutting jaw, and jabbing finger, he urged my election to the Senate.

Then, the morning after the election, there had been the call from the White House. In that unmistakable New England accent he had said, "Hello, Birch, you old miracle worker, how in the world did you do it? Nobody thought you could win—especially after Cuba!" That had made Marvella and me swell with pride. Since then, we had visited the White House on several occasions. Now, with a snap of the fingers, the man who had lived there, the man for whom we had such deep respect and admiration, was gone.

These pell-mell thoughts were interrupted by Marvella's subdued voice at the other end of the line. Through her tears, she told me that the report was true. It was not just a bad dream. She had heard the first news bulletin while dictating correspondence at my office in the New Senate Office Building; at that time, the President was said to have been wounded but not killed. Marvella had decided to hurry home and get more complete news on television. As she drove down Constitution Avenue, the car radio, much to her frustration, stopped working. As she passed along Pennsylvania Avenue, however, she was momentarily reassured to see that the White House flag was still flying, that it had not yet been lowered to half-mast.

Marvella told me, too, of the frightening early reports that surrounded the assassination. There had been rumors of evidence that all top government leaders were in danger; that the Vice President had been shot; that he had suffered a heart attack. But these reports, she said, had by now been dispelled as, little by little, fact emerged out of the confused fictions that accompanied the sudden tragedy.

And Marvella told me something else, which made my thoughts go back to my arrangements to leave town that morning: When word reached the Senate floor that the President had been assassinated, the President's brother, Edward Kennedy, was the presiding officer—he had substituted for me during my absence.

Talking with Marvella, I was aware of the total lack of privacy of the telephone booth in which I was standing and was feeling somewhat embarrassed about discussing such personal matters there. I told her that I would get back to Washington as soon as I possibly could, and we said goodbye.

But when I tried to arrange for a return flight, the ticket agent informed me that the bad weather and the tragedy in Dallas would make it impossible for me to get home again until five or six that evening. His grief, I remember, made him seem to be looking through me, not at me, as he spoke. I nodded and walked away; some mechanism in the back of my mind directed me into a cab. I might as well go ahead and attend the meeting that had brought me to Chicago in the first place.

As the cab crawled through the city's streets, bleak with rain and sorrow, my thoughts turned to the tall, rawboned Texan whose shoulders would now bear the weight of the highest office in the land. When I had been a state legislator, then a prospective member of the Senate, I had read all that I could get my hands on about Majority Leader Lyndon B. Johnson and the feats of legislative wizardry he had been able to perform. No other man in modern history had been such a master of the delicate art of lawmaking; no other man had been able to accomplish more, or persuade men to work so harmoniously together toward legislative progress.

Following the 1962 election, Marvella and I had visited with him in his office adjacent to the Senate reception room. The meeting had been scheduled as a perfunctory courtesy call, for the newest member of the Senate to pay his respects to its presiding officer. The ten minutes originally allotted had flashed by; in fact, before we knew it we had been there an hour. Finally, the Vice President leaned across his desk and asked, "Do you have any plans for dinner?" Marvella and I, hardly knowing how to answer, glanced at each other. It must have been obvious what our reply was to be. With scarcely a pause, he went on, "Why don't you come out and have dinner with me? Lady Bird's shopping in New York, and I'm here all by myself. I'm sure the cook will have plenty for all of us." With that he pressed a button, picked up a phone at his elbow, and said into it: "I'm bringing some young folks home to dinner with me. Getting ready to leave right now. Be there in twenty minutes—have something ready for us when we get there."

Driving through a grief-stricken Chicago, I thought back to that first evening at the Elms: the supper in the breakfast room, the Vice President's conducting us about the spacious house, and—most fascinating of all—the long, reflective discussion of the operation of the Senate, by the man who knew more about it than anyone else. Finally, at 10:30, because the Vice President knew we were looking for a place to live we all got back into the long black limousine, and were driven past each of the houses that were for sale in the neighborhood. How many people, Marvella and I wondered later, still almost beside ourselves with amazement, had been given a house-hunting tour by such an eminent guide?

Now, I thought, Lyndon Johnson was President; he was assuming an office whose burdens were enormous even without their having been increased by the tragedy that had descended upon all of us. Like many of my fellow countrymen, I prayed—for this man as well as for his predecessor.

Yet in the midst of my misery, I reflected on the distinguished credentials of the man who was to take over the reins of government in this crisis. He had been a congressman, a senator, Majority Leader, then Vice President—over thirty years of service in the highest echelons of government. No other man had come to the Presidency with such experience. As Vice President, he had been uniquely suited to contribute to the making of important governmental decisions. Now he would be the one to make those decisions, seeking in turn the counsel of *his* Vice President. But there I sat up sharply. *There was no Vice President now!* The thoughts came flooding to my mind: I remembered the 1948 Presidential Succession Act, which provided for a line of succession in case the President and Vice President died at the same time, or in case the President died and there was no Vice President. But, at this moment, the United States had no Vice President, and to make matters worse there was absolutely *no way* to fill the vacancy in that office. For almost a hundred years, members of Congress and scholars had been trying to find a way to solve the dilemma of Presidential succession: so far they had not been able to do so.

There was a sinking feeling in the pit of my stomach as I recalled that only a month before a series of unusual circumstances had resulted in my being appointed Chairman of the Senate Judiciary Subcommittee on Constitutional Amendments—the subcommittee whose direct responsibility it was to recommend a solution to the problems of Presidential disability and vacancies in the office of Vice President. That meant, I realized abruptly, that the junior senator from Indiana had been thrust into the center of a century-old controversy, a controversy on a subject that was doubly significant now because of the terrible event in Dallas which had stunned the nation.

CHAPTER 1

Will We Ever Learn

The days passed and the problems of the nation could be put off no longer. Slowly, with laborious effort, the wheels of government began to turn once again, now under the hand of Lyndon Johnson. Each of us did what John Kennedy would have wanted us to do: We laid aside our personal grief to resume our individual tasks and responsibilities. Stunned White House aides worked along with the new President to clear up the important State business that had accumulated, new people arrived to fill administrative gaps created by the tragic disruption, and congressional, labor, and business leaders stepped forward to help.

In addition to making the government function again, two of Lyndon Johnson's most important tasks during those dark days were to gain America's confidence and to soothe the fears of a nation shaken by the trauma of an assassination. He was admirably equipped to do so—as Vice President, he had been given more

responsibility than anyone else in that office in modern times—but
the fact remained that he was working without a Vice President of
his own. There was no one to carry the burden which he himself
had borne under John Kennedy. Moreover, the new President had
earlier been close to death after a massive heart attack. No one could
know for certain how well he might withstand the physical strains
of the Presidency.

Those of us who were in Congress were well aware of this
aspect of the crisis. Editorial writers and columnists throughout
America soon began to call the matter to the public's attention.
During the first week of December, newspapers reflected the national concern over the problems related to executive continuity.
The situation was discussed at length all over America by editorial
writers, ranging over the entire philosophical spectrum.

The problem was threefold. First, Presidential succession:
When there is no Vice President, who should succeed to the Presidency? This had been dealt with by Congress on three occasions,
and the law was clear: Speaker of the House John McCormack was
next in line after Lyndon Johnson.

Second, should a means be found to fill vacancies in the office
of Vice President when they occur? For the sixteenth time in its
history, the United States had no Vice President. No human being
could perform the duties of Speaker and still have time for those
of Vice President.

Finally, Presidential disability: What if the President were to
suffer a long illness, as Garfield and Wilson had? Could the tragic
conditions that had surrounded the illness of each of these men be
prevented from reoccurring?

Concerning the recent national tragedy, what if John Kennedy
had been seriously and permanently injured—rendered a helpless
cripple, physically or mentally unable to perform the duties of
President?

The first newspaper articles concentrated mainly upon the provisions concerning Presidential succession. Public concern over who
would serve as President in the event of Lyndon Johnson's death
had been increased even more by the telecasting of his special message to Congress on November 27. During the speech, the television

cameras focused repeatedly on House Speaker John McCormack and on Senate President pro tempore Carl Hayden, both of whom were sitting on the dais behind President Johnson. Speaker McCormack was seventy-one; Senator Hayden was eighty-six. These were the two men who were next in line for the Presidency.

On December 2, the *Washington Post* summarized the sentiment of much of the nation:

> The law of succession to the Presidency is coming in for some sharp scrutiny because the country no longer has a Vice President. One reason for concern is the advanced age of the two officials who are next in line to succeed President Johnson, in case of death or disability. . . . More troublesome in some respects are the confusions and deficiencies of the present law.
>
> . . . There seems to be a widespread misapprehension that if, under this law, the Speaker should be called upon to act as President and should then himself die, the President Pro Tempore of the Senate would succeed him as acting President. But this does not appear to have been the intent of Congress. As soon as the Speaker resigned to assume the duties of the Presidency, the House would elect a new Speaker, and if the acting President should then die, resign or become disabled, the newly elected Speaker would take his place. Presumably the President Pro Tem would be called upon only if the House had no Speaker at the time the vacancy in the White House occurred, or if the Speaker were ineligible for the Presidency, but some uncertainty as to the precise intent of Congress still remains.
>
> Another serious defect in the law is the provision that the Speaker should serve as President temporarily in case of presidential disability. In order to do this the Speaker would have to resign as Speaker and as a member of the House. But he might serve for only a few days and would then be tossed into limbo with virtually no chance of regaining his post as Speaker. In these circumstances there would be great reluctance to fill a temporary gap in the Presidency, unless the Speaker and President Pro Tem should both decline and thus leave the Secretary of State in a position to fill a perilous vacuum of presidential authority. And then the Secretary of State-become-President could probably be bumped in case either the Speaker or the President Pro Tem should change his mind.
>
> The whole problem of succession to the White House needs a fresh analysis, and we hope that President Johnson and the leaders in Congress will agree upon an expert body to undertake such a study. An alternative would be creation of a joint committee of Congress for this

purpose. In any event the proposed study should be undertaken promptly. In these days of hair-trigger defense few things would be more perilous than uncertainty as to where the powers of the Presidency would lie in case of disaster or a succession of disasters.

The following day, in *The New York Times*, columnist James Reston went more directly to the point.

A few minutes after President Kennedy was assassinated the defense forces of the United States all over the world were informed and instructed to be on the alert.

No "emergency defense condition" was ordered. No additional atomic bombers were flushed, as during the Cuban crisis, but in this day of instantaneous attack nobody could be quite sure whether the assassination was the end or merely the beginning of the agony.

The nation has had too much of death lately to want any ghoulish speculation now, but this urgent signal to the troops even before Lyndon Johnson was sworn in as President indicates just how critical the problem of Presidential succession can be.

Has the Congress prepared the Presidency adequately for the possibilities of a violent age? Is the rule of Presidential succession satisfactory for these days of human madness and scientific destruction? Or do not the men in line for the Presidency—all of them, not just one or two—have to be selected and instructed much more carefully than in the past?

Then, on December 6, an announcement appeared in the newspapers that President Johnson and Speaker McCormack had entered into an agreement which would become effective should the President become disabled.

President Johnson announced today the terms of an agreement that he had made with Speaker of the House John W. McCormack on the possibility of Mr. McCormack's temporary succession to the Presidency.

Mr. McCormack began functioning today in his role as next in succession to the President by attending a meeting of the National Security Council. A Vice President is a statutory member of that body but the Speaker of the House is not.

Mr. Johnson and Mr. McCormack will follow the general outlines of a policy on temporary succession originated by former President Dwight D. Eisenhower and former Vice President Richard M. Nixon. Later, Mr. Johnson participated in a similar agreement with President Kennedy.

During those days, government officials, representatives of the news media, and interested citizens read and re-read the language of the Constitution:

> In Case of the Removal of the President from Office, or of his Death, Resignation, or Inability to discharge the Powers and Duties of the said Office, the same shall devolve on the Vice President, and the Congress may by Law provide for the Case of Removal, Death, Resignation or Inability, both of the President and Vice President, declaring what Officer shall then act as President, and such Officer shall act accordingly, until the Disability be removed, or a President shall be elected.[1]

To refresh memories, old files from the era of President Eisenhower's illness were opened, clipping boxes were searched for capsules of the meaning of the language, and constitutional scholars were telephoned for their interpretation of that meaning.

"Who's in line after McCormack and Hayden?" reporters asked. "Is a disability agreement constitutional? What happens if the President becomes disabled? Who's Vice President then?" Out of drawers, files, and reference books came information which pieced together the complex background of the problem and furnished a picture of continuity lines in cases of death or disability.

The framers of the Constitution had given the Vice Presidency little attention. The office was not created, in fact, until the closing days of the Constitutional Convention in 1787. Plans had previously been considered which would in the event of a vacancy in the Presidency place in power the President of the Senate, the Chief Justice, or a Presidential Council. Finally, however, the elected office of Vice President was proposed. The discussion centered, not upon the Vice President's role in the succession, but upon his unique combination of executive and legislative functions, and the definitions of his duties. The almost overlooked Vice President was to preside over the Senate—and vote in the event of a tie. But of much greater significance, as the course of history would prove, was the second of his two designated constitutional duties: the discharge of the powers and duties of the President in case of the latter's "Removal, . . . Death, Resignation, or Inability." The Constitution cited

[1] Art. II, Sec. 1, Clause 6.

no qualifications for the office of Vice President. However, since the original election provisions required electors to vote for two persons for President, with the person receiving the second highest number becoming Vice President, it was clear that the framers intended to place in that office a person equal in stature to the President.

Yet debates in the First Congress bearing upon the Vice Presidency made it equally clear that the office was actually held in low esteem. Franklin had referred to the Vice President as "his superfluous majesty." Some members of the House of Representatives thought his duties were so minimal that he should receive pay on a per diem basis rather than an annual salary.

The frustrations of the office are recorded in Vice President John Adams' words to the Senate:

> I am possessed of two separate powers, the one in *esse* and the other in *posse*. I am vice-president. In this I am nothing, but I may be everything. But I am president also of the Senate. . . .[2]

If there was little discussion of Presidential succession in the Convention, there was even less discussion of the question of Presidential disability. In fact, the record is bare, except for Delaware Constitutional Convention delegate John Dickinson's often-cited question: "What is the extent of the term 'disability' and who is to be the judge of it?"—a question that was not answered until 179 years later by the Twenty-fifth Amendment to the Constitution. This seems ironic, since the succession portion of the problem was an item of early consideration when the First Congress met in 1790.

The original bill presented to the House provided that an officer, undesignated in the bill, would act when a vacancy existed in the offices of both President and Vice President. But which officer should it be? The President pro tempore of the Senate, the Speaker of the House, the Chief Justice, the Secretary of State, the Secretary of the Treasury—all were suggested and discussed, without any agreement. If the President pro tempore had the Presidency or Vice Presidency foisted upon him, it was asked, would not his state be deprived of a vote in the Senate? Would he not be subject to instructions from his own state? Would he be holding two offices?

---

[2] Cited by John D. Feerick in *From Failing Hands: The Story of Presidential Succession* (New York: Fordham University Press, 1965), p. 66.

Certainly the same could be said for the Speaker. And would not the presence of the Chief Justice in the line of succession be tantamount to a commingling of judicial and executive power? Was it not also possible, it was asked, that the Vice President, because of his power of removal, could manipulate his potential successor into line if either the Secretary of State or the Secretary of the Treasury were the succession designees? The situation seemed to be futile; the House moved quietly to other matters, leaving the question unresolved.

But in the fall of 1791, the Senate did reach agreement, sending to the House a bill which designated the President pro tempore of the Senate as the person next in the line of succession. They provided, as well, that the Speaker of the House would act as President during any disability or death, in cases in which there was no President pro tempore.

The bill then moved to the House, where it was questioned whether these two should be placed in the line of succession. One of the first questions asked pertained to the word "officer." The pertinent clause in the Constitution stated: ". . . and the Congress may by Law provide for the Case of Removal, Death, Resignation, or Inability, both of the President and Vice President, declaring what Officer shall then act as President. . . ." It was argued that if the convention had considered either the Speaker or the President pro tempore "officers," they would have been appropriately designated in the Constitution. But as Elbridge Gerry of Massachusetts cogently asked, "If the Speaker is not an officer, what is he?"

The House debate continued back and forth, with motions—some successful, some not—to remove various officers from the succession line and to include others. Eventually, they voted to eliminate both the Speaker and the President pro tempore as possible successors, designating instead the Secretary of State as heir to the Presidency.

But the Senate undid the work of the House in short order; the President pro tempore and Speaker were reinstated. In that form, the bill was eventually approved by the House and signed into law by President Washington on March 1, 1792.

The first significant occurrence of the problem of succession and disability came with the death of President William Henry

Harrison on April 4, 1841. Although the events that followed demonstrated the elasticity of the Constitution, they were later to make constitutional scholars aware that what is elastic in one area may cause constriction in another. Upon President Harrison's death, the actions of Vice President John Tyler afforded a definitive interpretation of the constitutional language "In case of the Removal of the President from Office, or of his Death, Resignation, or Inability to discharge the Powers and Duties of the said Office, the same shall devolve on the Vice President." From the very first, it was clear that Tyler believed himself to be endowed, not only with the powers and duties of the Presidency, but with the office itself. Unheard of! Preposterous! Not within the purview of the checks and balances! cried Congress and the press.

But Tyler remained adamant. The first official paper placed before him to be signed contained the title "Acting President" under the prescribed place for his signature. Tyler took one look and without hesitation struck the word *acting*. It was clear that John Tyler fully intended to be President for the remainder of Harrison's term. History would prove that one stroke of the pen had removed the word *acting* from the Constitution, quite the contrary to the intention of its authors as contained in the Madison papers disclosed at a much later date. But in this fashion the Tyler precedent was born. On future occasions when a President died, the Vice President would assume the full office as well as its powers and duties.

The matter came up shortly thereafter in the Twenty-seventh Congress in the guise of a question over the wording of a House resolution: Should that resolution refer to the "President" or to the "Vice President, now exercising the office of President"? The House approved the resolution with the former wording, and it was forwarded thus to the Senate, where Senator William Allen, of Ohio, voiced a prophetic warning. If such an interpretation was valid upon a President's death, he asked, might it not be so also in cases of removal, resignation, or disability? Under Tyler's precedent, would a temporarily disabled President be permitted to return to office once he recovered, if the Vice President were to insist on keeping the office for himself? Would the Presidency then "vibrate between the two claimants"?

The constitutional language was clear that the Vice President fills a vacancy left by the removal, death, resignation, or inability of the President. In the event of death, the vacancy to be filled is permanent in nature; it must be filled for the remainder of the unexpired term. Whether the Vice President serves as President or acting President is really a matter of semantics. His position is permanent for there is no one living to reclaim the office. This is not so in the event of a vacancy caused by Presidential inability. When the President, because of various disabilities, is unable to perform the powers and duties of his office, someone has to do the job. The vacancy must be filled. The Vice President has this constitutional responsibility, but while he carries out the powers and duties of the office of President, the President—although disabled—still lives. The question raised long ago in the Twenty-seventh Congress was: Given the above circumstances, what happens if the President recovers from his disability, or claims to have recovered, and seeks to regain his office from the Vice President? If the Vice President is merely acting as President, the solution is relatively simple—the powers revert to the President. But, if the Tyler precedent takes effect in the event of inability as it did in death, the solution is much more complicated. Tyler in effect held that the Vice President does not act as President, he in fact becomes President. In the event of inability, if the Vice President is in office, then the President must be out. The country cannot have two Presidents. The insoluble question was: When the President recovers, how does he regain his office? The Constitution clearly provides the means to remove a President by impeachment, but in no manner provides for his reinstatement. According to many scholars, once the President is out of office, he is out—period!

But the Senate of the Twenty-seventh Congress stopped far short of a solution to this problem. Wishing to close the discussion, it went along with Senator John C. Calhoun, of South Carolina, who felt the matter to be academic since there was a permanent vacancy in the Presidential office which must be filled. Thus, the question was never settled, and the resolution was passed without alteration.

At the time that Senator Allen's warning went unheeded in Washington, an eleven-year-old schoolboy in Vermont, Chester A. Arthur, could have no idea what effect the Senate's reluctance to discuss the Tyler precedent would have upon himself and the country some forty years later, when President John A. Garfield was struck by an assassin's bullet. Arthur, by then the Vice President of the United States, was forced to endure an eighty-day period of uncertainty and agony while the mortally wounded President hung to life by a thread. Had Arthur been a less compassionate man, had he tried to grasp the reins of leadership prematurely, the country could have been irreparably damaged. The situation was made even more delicate by the fact that Arthur had supported Ulysses S. Grant, not Garfield, as the Republican candidate for President at the party convention. The party had included Arthur, who belonged to the Stalwart wing of the party, as a "Grant man" on the ticket only for the sake of Republican unity. Garfield's grief-stricken supporters remembered not only this, but also Arthur's having sided against President Garfield in the latter's conflict with the two New York senators Thomas C. Platt and Roscoe Conkling over a matter of patronage which resulted in both senators' submitting their resignation. And, in the light of these affiliations, the nation was even more distressed by the statement of Garfield's assassin, Charles Giteau, when he was captured: "I did it and will go to jail for it. I am a Stalwart, and Arthur will be President." In Giteau's pocket, moreover, was a letter addressed "To the White House," calling the President's death a "political necessity"; another letter, addressed to Arthur, made recommendations for appointments to various Cabinet posts. Many Garfield partisans believed Arthur was part of a heinous plot to assassinate Garfield and capture the Presidency for himself. Fortunately, Arthur's obvious distress and his exemplary conduct during the crisis soon allayed all the suspicions that linked him to the assassination. During the eighty days that Garfield lay near death, Arthur never once saw him, but was kept constantly advised of his condition by Garfield's Cabinet and staff, who did their best to keep the wheels of government turning. The only act they dared require of their injured chief was the signing of one extradition paper.

Garfield had been shot on July 2. It was not until late August, when the Cabinet members were spending long hours at the White House, that they first began to consider the possibility of Arthur's assuming the executive duties. However Arthur abruptly refused to consider such a possibility. The President's condition worsened as time went on, and the Cabinet agreed that an acting President was a necessity. They were divided, however, four to three, on what the Vice President's status would be if he actually assumed the President's duties. The majority believed that if Arthur were to perform these duties there would be no possibility of Garfield's returning to the Presidency during the rest of that term of office. At 10:35 in the evening on September 16, these deliberations were no longer relevant; President Garfield was dead.

The nation grieved for the dead President. During his struggle for life, many people had seen grim forebodings for the country in the disability crisis. Upon Garfield's death and Arthur's succession to the Presidency, the nation was to witness further weakness in its laws of Presidential succession. With Arthur as President, the office of Vice President was vacant. The 1792 Succession Act provided that in the event of Arthur's death the President pro tempore of the Senate—or, failing that, the Speaker of the House—would take the Presidential mantle upon his shoulders. However, at the moment of President Garfield's death, the Senate had no President pro tempore. When Arthur had been Vice President, his presence had been continually necessary in the Senate to break tie votes. The Republicans in the Senate had been unable to muster enough votes to elect a President pro tempore, and none had been elected. The position remained vacant. When, as President, Arthur called a special session for the purpose of electing a President pro tempore, a Democrat was elected to the office, giving the country occasion to consider the disruptive effects upon the government of a Republican President being succeeded by a Democratic President in the middle of the Republican administration's term in office. Indeed a sure formula for executive chaos!

As if the Senate muddle were not enough, at the time Arthur succeeded to the Presidency there was also no Speaker of the House. During that era the office was held only for the duration of the term the House was in actual session, and Congress was not due to reconvene for three months.

Spurred on by his own agonizing experiences with the issue of Presidential inability and succession, as they related to both his succession to the Presidency and the problems concerning his own possible successors, Arthur tried three separate times during his term of office to get Congress to take action. But other problems were more immediately pressing, and Congress refused to act. The issue did not raise its head again until 1884, when Vice President Thomas Andrew Hendricks died and President Grover Cleveland was confronted with the same vacuum in congressional succession which President Arthur had experienced. There was no immediate successor to the Presidency. Fortunately, however, this period of insecurity lasted only from November 25 to December 7, when John Sherman of Ohio was elected President pro tempore of the Senate; but the two close calls seemed to be enough to spur Congress to at least partial action.

Although they failed to make the provisions for disability that the Garfield incapacity had made obviously necessary, Congress did meet head-on the deficiencies of the 1792 Succession Act. The new legislation provided that the Cabinet officers, beginning with the Secretary of State, were to replace the congressional officers in the line of succession. Under the 1886 act, in the event that both the President and the Vice President became disabled or died during their term of office, the succeeding Cabinet officer was to act as President until the disability of the President or Vice President was removed, or until a President was elected. If Congress was not in session at that time, the Cabinet officer was to call a special session. The intent of Congress in inserting this latter provision remains unclear to this day, but there are many who believe that the act provided that the succeeding Cabinet officer was duty-bound to convene the Congress, which would then determine the need to call for a special Presidential election. The 1886 act was in effect for sixty-one years, during which time no circumstance occurred which necessitated interpreting the meaning of that provision.

The next crisis in Presidential inability began in early April 1919, when newspapers reported that President Woodrow Wilson, only recently returned from his European trip in support of a League of Nations, was suffering from influenza. To add to the growing national concern, Washington "insiders" claimed that the President had actually suffered a slight stroke and that the attack had not been his first. These rumors became more credible when Wilson returned to his duties hampered by a slight facial twitch.

Despite this physical impairment, President Wilson was determined that his plan for a League of Nations would not be defeated, although the Republican-controlled Congress was violently opposed to it. On September 3 the President left Washington for a twenty-seven-day cross-country tour designed to gather popular support for the League. During this mission there were to be twenty-six stops, with an average of one major speech and at least ten minor ones every day.

As the journey proceeded, Wilson began to have severe headaches, and the heat of the Western states aggravated his asthma. He was hoarse from trying to make himself heard during his speeches; what sleep he got came in a sitting position, which brought some minor relief from his asthma. On September 25, in Denver, the President's headache grew so severe that reluctantly he indicated he would cut short his next speech that day, in Pueblo. But true to form, the crusading President failed to do so; in fact, the Pueblo speech was longer than usual. At one point during the speech Wilson faltered, seeming to his aides to be on the verge of collapse. All that night, his headache was so bad that he could not sleep.

The next morning his aides found him sitting in his compartment fully dressed, with tears streaming down his cheeks; one side of his face had fallen and his words were nearly unintelligible. His entire left side was paralyzed. Over the President's feeble protests the tour was cut short and the train started the return journey to Washington. The press was notified that the President had suffered "a complete nervous breakdown." By the time Wilson arrived back at the nation's capital, he had regained the use of his left arm and leg and was able to perform some urgent executive business. But by October 2 his left hand was again useless. Mrs. Wilson, leaving the room temporarily, returned to find her husband unconscious. From that moment on, few people were to see Woodrow Wilson in person, and fewer still were to know the true state of his condition.

No one will ever be able to say, of the difficult time that followed, which acts and decisions came from Wilson himself, and which from those around him—his faithful wife, his jealously loyal staff, his politically conscious physician. Rumors circulated that the President was much more seriously ill than the vague official bulletins led America to believe. Though many official communiqués seemed to stress improvement, ever so slight, in the President's condition, there was no factual evidence to substantiate this information or to ease the concern of the Congress and the country. When a letter from Senator George Moses to one of his New Hampshire constituents was published, stating that the President, even if he lived, would not be "any material force or factor in anything," Wilson's physician, Cary T. Grayson, replied that "Senator Moses must have information I do not possess." Speculations and rumors continued, more vigorously than before.

Secretary of State Robert Lansing, interested only in giving some direction to the government during the President's disability, attempted to keep the affairs of the nation functioning by calling several sessions of the Cabinet. At one of these he went so far as to suggest that consideration be given to the possibility of Vice President Thomas Marshall's acting in Wilson's place. Shortly thereafter Lansing read the succession provision of the Constitution to Wilson's staff aide Joseph Tumulty. The latter rebuffed him, saying, "the Constitution is not a dead letter with the White House. I have read the Constitution and do not find myself in need of any tutoring at your hands." Tumulty continued, "You may rest assured that while Woodrow Wilson is lying in the White House on the broad of his back I will not be a party to ousting him." Secretary Lansing discussed the matter further with the rest of the Cabinet and continued to call Cabinet sessions to deal with the most urgent business of the nation. Four months later, the President would demand Lansing's resignation for assuming these responsibilities.

During the deliberations over the President's inability to perform the powers and duties of his office, the Cabinet could find no explicit solution in the Constitution's inability provision; but they continued to meet from time to time for the discussion of what press releases called "interdepartmental affairs." During those months, by hook or crook, the Cabinet maintained contact with the staff personnel, who in turn relayed advice from the President's bedroom. Vice President Marshall, who had ignored a promise by Wilson's enemies in Congress to support a move on Marshall's part to take over the running of the government, obtained whatever information he could from sympathetic Cabinet members or from the newspapers. At one point Marshall made it perfectly clear that he would not assume the duties of the Presidency without a congressional resolution of authority and the signed consent of Mrs. Wilson.

Without a hand at the helm, the League of Nations was defeated. Vacancies in government went unfilled. Twenty-eight bills became law by default. Foreign diplomats were unable to present their credentials. Becalmed, the government of the United States had come to a halt. Members of Congress proclaimed their concern for the President's health and the state of the nation. A few members went so far as to introduce proposals for dealing with the entire question of Presidential inability; but after this brief flutter of life, Congress, too, was silent.

On April 13, 1920, Wilson convened his first Cabinet meeting since the previous October. One of the participants observed:

> The President looked old, worn, and haggard. It was enough to make one weep to look at him. . . . One of his arms was useless. In repose, his face looked very much as usual, but, when he tried to speak, there was marked evidences of his trouble. His jaw tended to drop on one side, or seemed to do so. His voice was very weak and strained. . . . The President seemed at first to have some difficulty in fixing his mind on what we were discussing.[3]

Although Wilson's condition did improve to some extent, he never in any sense approached the activity of his earlier days. The nation's painful experience of this Presidential disability finally ended on March 4, 1921, when Warren G. Harding was inaugurated as the newly elected President.

In early 1945, shortly after he had been reelected to a fourth term of office, President Franklin Roosevelt died. Harry S Truman succeeded to the Presidency and the office of Vice President remained vacant. The nation was again without a second in command and President Truman, like few of his predecessors, realized the significance of this problem. He was determined to do something about it. The new President delivered a special message to Congress, proposing changes in the 1886 Succession Act. That old act,

[3] Cited in Feerick, p. 179.

he said, gave the President power to appoint his own successor, in the person of the Secretary of State. In Truman's opinion the office of the President should be filled by an elected, not appointed, official. Since only the President and Vice President were elected by the whole country, the most appropriate official to be next in line after them was the Speaker of the House, who was elected to that office by a vote of all the representatives of all the people of the country. The representatives, moreover, since they were reelected every two years, were very close to the people, and therefore best fitted to have such a responsibility. The new President's proposal to Congress would do the following things:

1. Establish the line of succession from the Speaker to the President pro tempore of the Senate, then down through the Cabinet officers, beginning with the Secretary of State.
2. Provide that if the Speaker or President pro tempore had to act as President, he would first resign from his seat in Congress.
3. Provide that if there were no Speaker or President pro tempore, the first Cabinet members who passed the necessary constitutional qualifications would serve until a Speaker or President pro tempore was elected.
4. Provide that in any circumstance in which someone other than the Vice President succeeded to the Presidency, he would hold the office only until the next congressional election, at which time a special election would be held to elect a new Presidential ticket.

During the 1945 House hearings and debates on President Truman's proposal, many of the arguments raised against the 1792 act were restated, along with new questions: Under the Article II requirements, who was an "officer" qualified to succeed to the Presidency? If the Speaker and President pro tempore were officers, what were they the instant after they resigned, as the proposed measure required them to do? Wasn't there a momentary hiatus between the time the Speaker resigned and the time he took the Presidential oath? Wouldn't the special election be cumbersome and expensive? Under the provision for that election, might not four people be President during one four-year term? And what about the Speaker or President pro tempore who resigned to act as Presi-

dent until the next election? How did they regain the congressional
post which they had left? Were they out of Congress altogether?

The House debate went on. Two participants in it, Representatives Estes Kefauver of Tennessee and Mike Monroney of Oklahoma, were later to play key roles in initiating and carrying out the
action which was to bring about a permanent settlement of the problems of succession and disability. The questions raised in the debate
were further confused by the 1946 congressional elections, which
saw President Truman's party suffer the loss of several congressional
seats at the polls. In fact, the new Congress was controlled by the
opposite party; and if the Truman proposal had been in effect, a
member of the opposition party would have been in line to succeed
him in the event of his death. Nevertheless, the President went on
pressing for congressional action.

The bill which the Senate considered was much like that debated in the House, with one definite advantage: It contained no
clause providing for a special election. There were unsuccessful
moves to alter the order of succession so that the President pro tempore might precede the Speaker, to insert a special election clause,
and to change the succession to the highest-ranking military officers
of the country. But finally, the Senate approved its bill on June 27,
1947; the House followed with its own approval. The new succession act was signed into law on July 18, 1947. A new succession law
was on the books, but the nation was no closer to solving the dangerous, double-barrelled problem of Presidential disability and Vice-
Presidential vacancies.

On September 24, 1955, like much of the rest of the nation,
Vice President Richard Nixon had read in the newspapers that
President Eisenhower, on vacation in Denver, had experienced a
"digestive upset" the previous night. But Nixon was entirely unprepared for the telephone call from White House Press Secretary
James Hagerty informing him that the President had actually suffered a heart attack. In contrast to Woodrow Wilson's bare tolera-
tion of Vice President Marshall, President Eisenhower had since
1952 relied so heavily on Richard Nixon that the office of Vice President had soared to unprecedented importance. Eisenhower had,
moreover, been concerned by the secrecy and inadequacy of procedures utilized during the illness of Wilson. Without being specific,
the President had let it be known that he preferred full disclosure

and temperate but decisive action so that the government business could continue should he experience any physical crisis.

Nixon immediately got together with members of the Cabinet and the President's personal advisors, and it was agreed that the government would continue to function through the Cabinet and White House staff. Every effort was made to reassure the world that orderliness and decorum prevailed. Richard Nixon announced that government business, as it had been defined by the President, would proceed without delay. Several Cabinet members went ahead with their plans to travel to Canada for talks on economic matters. The Vice President scheduled a Cabinet meeting for September 30 and signed several ceremonial papers on the President's behalf. In his characteristically calm manner, Attorney General Herbert Brownell assured the country that "sufficient legal arrangements" had been made "to carry on the day-to-day operation of the government."

The Vice President and Cabinet, with the assistance of Press Secretary Hagerty, Sherman Adams, and other White House aides, worked out procedures that would permit necessary Presidential acts to be performed as easily as possible. The country anxiously watched the newspapers for news of their President's recovery from what was finally termed "a moderate attack of coronary thrombosis." Moderate was described as being neither mild nor serious. By October 25, the President was up and walking; and on November 11, to the relief of the country, he was discharged from the hospital in favor of more accommodating quarters. After a convalescence in Georgia and Florida, the President returned to Washington in early January of 1956.

But later that same year, one morning in June, reporters in the White House were informed that the President "had an upset stomach and headache this morning." A few hours later, further news disclosed that President Eisenhower was suffering from an obstruction in the intestine; an exploratory operation was necessary to relieve it. The next morning, the nation read with relief that the operation had been a complete success and that within six weeks the President would be able to return to his duties. It was emphasized that no malignancy had been found and that the President's heart was in no way involved.

By July the President was in full swing again; but, as Vice President Nixon was to relate later, Eisenhower had pointed out to him that for the two hours during which he was under anesthesia, the country was without a chief executive and the armed forces without a commander in chief. In the days of Woodrow Wilson, when a full-speed locomotive was the fastest means of transportation and rifled cannon the most destructive weapon, two hours would have been unimportant; but by the Eisenhower era, the potential for world destruction was being calculated in megatons, minutes, and seconds, not in hours or days.

The President's health remained good for seventeen and a half months, until the afternoon of November 25, 1957. After returning from the chilly airport where he had greeted a visiting dignitary, Eisenhower was dictating to his secretary when he found that he was unable to express himself. The President's physician immediately ordered him to bed. He had been scheduled to attend a dinner for the dignitary that night and to address the nation on television the next. What should be done? Nixon and his aides held a hurried conference to determine how to handle the situation. During this worried consultation, Eisenhower walked into the room insisting he was all right, but at the same moment experiencing some difficulty in talking. He turned to leave, saying, "If I cannot attend to my duties, I am simply going to give up this job." Shortly afterwards Sherman Adams was telling Nixon, "This is a terribly, terribly difficult thing to handle. You may be President in the next twenty-four hours."

On the next afternoon, the White House announced that President Eisenhower had experienced a transitory small blood clot, or vascular spasm; later, it was to be described as a mild stroke. Once again, the Vice President filled the gaps which the Constitution allowed him to fill; and by December 3, Eisenhower was again immersed in the heavy load of Presidential business.

During the President's illnesses, meetings with congressional leaders had been held occasionally regarding a possible solution to the disability problem, but there had been no action. Finally the President took matters into his own hands and executed an agreement with Vice President Nixon regarding procedures to be fol-

lowed in the case of further disability. This disability plan had been
drafted under the leadership of Attorney General Herbert Brownell.
It read as follows:

> The President and the Vice President have agreed that the fol-
> lowing procedures are in accord with the purposes and provisions of
> Article 2, Section 1, of the Constitution, dealing with Presidential in-
> ability. They believe that these procedures, which are intended to ap-
> ply to themselves only are in no sense outside or contrary to the Con-
> stitution but are consistent with its present provisions and implement
> its clear intent.
>
> (1) In the event of inability the President would—if possible—so
> inform the Vice President, and the Vice President would serve as Act-
> ing President, exercising the powers and duties of the office until the
> inability had ended.
>
> (2) In the event of an inability which would prevent the Presi-
> dent from so communicating with the Vice President, the Vice Presi-
> dent, after such consultation as seems to him appropriate under the cir-
> cumstances, would decide upon the devolution of the powers and duties
> of the Office and would serve as Acting President until the inability
> had ended.
>
> (3) The President, in either event, would determine when the in-
> ability had ended and at that time would resume the full exercise of the
> powers and duties of the Office.

An identical agreement, but bearing the signatures of John F. Kennedy and Lyndon B. Johnson, was in effect on November 22, 1963.
But before then, it had become apparent to many members of Congress and legal scholars that such a measure did not constitute a definitive solution to the problem of disability.

On April 18, 1958, Senator Estes Kefauver, then the Chairman
of the Constitutional Amendments Subcommittee, had opened disability hearings before that subcommittee and presented an administration proposal, similar to the original "Brownell plan" but containing modifications that were designed to allay congressional criticism.
The original agreement had provided no means for settling any disputes that might arise between the President and the Vice President
over the state of the President's health, and impeachment was the
only way that the President could be removed—even temporarily
removed—from office in the event that he was unable to perform
his powers and duties. The new proposal provided that in the event
of a dispute, the Vice President and a majority of the Cabinet were

to submit the issue to Congress, a two-thirds majority of which could prevent the President from reassuming his office.

Senator Kefauver, the tall Tennesseean known for his coonskin cap and his crusading spirit, continued to be the main advocate of congressional reform in the area of Presidential disability. He reintroduced the proposal in the Eighty-sixth and Eighty-seventh Congresses, but he was unsuccessful in bringing the measure to fruition. Then, in 1960, the American Bar Association embarked upon an elaborate study of the entire problem. As a result, the ABA House of Delegates gave its approval to a constitutional amendment which was designated to deal with Presidential disability. Unlike the Eisenhower proposal, that of the ABA did not establish a specific procedure under which a Presidential disability might be handled. Instead, the Bar recommended that such an amendment grant to Congress the power to establish, by law, the necessary machinery which would be needed in the event the President became ill. However, no congressional action followed.

In January 1961, when President John F. Kennedy took the oath of office, concern over the problem of Presidential disability diminished. The new President was a young and vigorous man, and few anticipated that such legislation might be needed during his administration. But Senator Kefauver persisted and finally persuaded the Kennedy administration to study the thorny problem. Two years later, when the Eighty-seventh Congress convened, the country was no nearer a solution than it had been throughout the previous century. A few members of Congress continued to express their individual interest and introduced legislation in the field. In the Senate, two proposals were noteworthy. Senator Kefauver had again introduced S. J. Res. 28, a constitutional amendment of the Brownell Plan type which would contain a specific formula for dealing with the problem of disability. Senator Kenneth Keating of New York, on the other hand, had introduced S. J. Res. 35, which encompassed the enabling recommendation of the American Bar Association.

On June 18, 1963, the Kennedy administration's study was sufficiently complete for Deputy Attorney General Nicholas deB. Katzenbach to testify before the Senate Subcommittee on Constitutional Amendments, lending the support of the administration to the broad, enabling amendment—the approach recommended by the ABA and contained in Keating's S. J. Res. 35. Three days later Sena-

tor Kefauver, sensing that the chances for the enactment of his own
S. J. Res. 28 were slim after the administration's endorsement of a
contrary proposal, joined in sponsoring S. J. Res. 35 himself. Senator Thomas Dodd of Connecticut also added his name to the proposal. Thus it appeared that for the first time in history a congressional committee might favorably recommend a proposal dealing
with the problem of Presidential disability. Senator Kefauver—the
leading congressional student in the field—and the administration
had joined in support of a single approach to the problem. But on
August 10 a heart attack took the life of the tall warrior from Tennessee; with him died the best chance in over a century of setting
right a major constitutional imperfection.

Estes Kefauver had, as I knew, held a number of chairmanships
in the Senate, but most of his national acclaim had sprung from the
crime and drug investigations he had conducted as chairman of the
Judiciary Subcommittee on Antitrust and Monopoly. It was only by
happenstance that I became aware of his chairmanship of the com-
paratively small Subcommittee on Constitutional Amendments. A
short time after Senator Kefauver's death, Fred Graham, his counsel
for that subcommittee stopped at my office. Not only did Kefauver's committee chairman post remain unfilled, but the decision
had been made to discontinue the subcommittee itself; consequently,
Graham was seeking other employment. As a freshman senator, I
had been assigned to the Judiciary Committee, and I listened with
interest as Graham told me of his opinion that, because of several
important matters the subcommittee had been considering, it would
be a mistake to make it inactive. He suggested that I approach Senator Eastland, the chairman of the full committee, and indicate an interest in the subcommittee's work.

Chairmanship posts are usually held by the more senior members of the Senate. There was little likelihood that I, a junior senator
with no seniority whatsoever, might be accorded the opportunity to
serve as a subcommittee chairman. Still, the chairmanship *was* open
and the committee at that time relatively obscure. I was eager to
have an area of specific responsibility and authority, so despite the
odds against success I nevertheless decided to broach the subject
with Chairman Eastland.

Senator Eastland responded to my inquiry as I had feared; he
was, indeed, planning to close down the subcommittee. But much

to my surprise, two days later, he told me that he had changed his mind. Several constitutional matters were still pending; moreover, he saw this as a chance to give a new member of the committee some special responsibility. Therefore he had decided to keep the subcommittee active, and it would be perfectly all right with him if I served as its chairman. He made the announcement at the Judiciary Committee meeting of September 30, and the committee ratified it. It was official: I had become the new Chairman of the Subcommittee on Constitutional Amendments.

I spent the next weeks getting acclimated to the new post. Since Senator Kefauver's death, all of the staff members had, like Fred Graham, scattered with the wind and found new jobs. In addition, the space in the Senate Office Building previously assigned to the subcommittee had been absorbed by other senators. Therefore we would have to operate without staff and without facilities. To meet the temporary emergency, I assigned to Larry Conrad, a member of my legislative staff, the responsibility of establishing the future agenda for the subcommittee. Conrad and the subcommittee would operate from a corner desk of my senatorial office, in Room 1205 of the New Senate Office Building; and, because of lack of resources, little business was transacted until the shattering news from Dallas. This tragic news emphasized the importance of a vigorous committee and revitalized its existence.

On December 4, the Judiciary Committee met to consider several measures, none of which were of earthshaking importance: The agenda consisted primarily of the usual immigration cases and a goodly number of private claims against the government. Close to the end of the meeting, Senator Keating[4] requested that S. J. Res. 35, his resolution dealing with Presidential disability, be laid before the committee for its discussion. Senator Eastland agreed, and Senator Keating proceeded briefly to outline the major aspects of the measure. As I sat at my place at the long mahogany table in the Judiciary Executive Room, I found myself extremely nervous and was reluctant to impose my views on the subject under discussion. I was a newcomer to the committee and had not become accustomed to participating in the give-and-take of committee debate, even though I knew that the entire subject of Presidential disability had

[4] See Appendix, p. 359, for the members of the subcommittee and full committee, at this time; for membership during the Eighty-ninth Congress see pp. 361–362.

been dealt with at length by the subcommittee which I now chaired.

Still, despite my reluctance, during a pause in the discussion, I directed one question to Senator Keating. "Ken, I'm a bit concerned about the lack of protection afforded the President under your proposal. It's true that a constitutional amendment has to be passed by a two-thirds vote of both Houses, then ratified by three-fourths of the states. But your proposal provides that Congress may, by law, establish the procedure for determining the President's disability. Am I right in assuming this law could be passed by a simple majority of both houses—and if so, that a President could be removed for disability upon the vote of a majority, whereas he presently has the protection of a two-thirds vote in the event of impeachment? Isn't this asking for trouble at some future date?"

Before the senator from New York had a chance to reply, Senator Sam Ervin, the distinguished constitutional scholar from North Carolina, interjected: "That's exactly what's wrong with your proposition, Ken. The founders of the Constitution, in their wisdom, provided that the President couldn't be removed from office unless two-thirds of the members of the Senate felt he was unworthy to go on performing the powers and duties of President. Times are pretty smooth right now, but I don't think any of us should forget those dark days after the Civil War when Andrew Johnson missed being impeached by one solitary vote in the United States Senate. If your measure had been in the Constitution then, even though they couldn't get the necessary two-thirds vote to impeach him, all they would have needed was a majority vote to ride him out of office by claiming he was ill. We all hope and pray to God we never face such times again," Sam Ervin concluded, "but I personally would hate to see this protection removed."

As Senator Keating began to defend his position, the loud buzzer in the committee room reminded us that the Senate was in session and that further committee business was impossible unless specific authority to meet was granted by the Senate. Chairman Eastland suggested that the meeting had best adjourn.

The discussion on Presidential disability could wait until our next meeting; but Senator Keating had opened the discussion of what was to be a long and difficult debate, stretching over almost two years.

CHAPTER 2

Bases of Support

For those who live under the critical pressures of governmental responsibility, the most precious commodity is time—time to meditate, to think things out, to put problems in the right perspective. As I left the Senate Judiciary Committee on December 4 I felt particularly in need of such time, but other problems and commitments demanded my attention. The disability issue and the cogent arguments of Senators Keating and Ervin did not leave my mind, but further specific deliberation had to wait until I had a chance to give them some concentrated thought.

The chance came, unexpectedly, late the same afternoon. During a flight from Washington to Chicago, where I was to attend a function of the Indiana Society, I had been looking through a folder which outlined the past work of the Subcommittee on Constitutional Amendments and included a number of news clippings demonstrating increased interest in the problem of Presidential succession.

When I closed my eyes to think for a few moments about the activities scheduled for the following week, I could not stop mulling over the last thoughts in one *Washington Post* editorial:

> The whole problem of succession to the White House needs a fresh analysis . . . in these days of hair trigger defense few things would be more perilous than uncertainty as to where the powers of the Presidency would lie in case of disaster or a succession of disasters.

A fresh analysis? I wondered. It seemed to me that the entire subject had been studied time and time again. Committee after committee, administration after administration had investigated the problem and pondered alternative solutions. There had, it seemed to me, been ample study; the missing ingredient was action. I reached for the briefcase under my seat and began to make notes on a yellow lined pad.

What, I asked myself, should be included in the legislation? The most immediate problem was to fill the Vice-Presidential vacancy. The President should be permitted to nominate a prospective Vice President, who would then be elected by Congress. Thus, without giving the President carte blanche power to appoint his possible successor, the nation would be guaranteed a Vice President who could work harmoniously with the President. Congress, containing an exact numerical duplication of the Electoral College, could well represent the people in the election process.

My pen moved on across the pad. It was important, too, to deal with the problem of Presidential disability, and this was a real can of worms. Keating and Katzenbach were recommending the blank check enabling procedure of S. J. Res. 35, but Eisenhower and Kefauver originally preferred the specific procedural constitutional amendment. The latter, embodying the principles of the private agreements between the last two Presidents and their Vice Presidents, struck me as the best solution. The major difficulty, I noted, was in handling the delicate question of disagreement between President and Vice President on the subject of disability.

The succession should be kept within the executive branch. If both President and Vice President were killed simultaneously, the Secretary of State, then the rest of the Cabinet, should succeed to the Presidency. The Speaker was far too busy to take on the acting

Vice Presidency when there was a vacancy—or the acting Presidency when a President was disabled—and still perform his legislative duties. This change, I reflected, would be tough to get through the House, but we should try it nonetheless.

As the plane neared Chicago, I jotted down two more reminders to myself. I wanted to discuss my ideas with some legislative leaders: Majority Leader Mansfield, Chairman Eastland, Speaker McCormack, and House Judiciary Committee Chairman Emanuel Celler. I also reminded myself to get in touch with the American Bar Association, which had long been interested in the problem. It would, I hoped, supply us with valuable information on the results of its study plus influential lobbying when the going got rough.

When the plane touched down at Chicago, I got off, prepared to resume the hectic pace of my job. But that brief respite in the air had given me a firmer idea of the scope of the problem confronting us, and some notion of how to tackle it.

The second week in December was a busy one. I started to lay the groundwork for our program immediately upon my return to Washington. Early on Monday morning, December 9, three men who were to play an important role in this effort gathered in my office. There was Larry A. Conrad, the young lawyer from Muncie, Indiana, who had been my campaign manager in 1962 and who had just been given the responsibility of serving as the subcommittee's chief counsel—a position which was at the moment unsalaried and officially nonexistent. In addition, there was Bernard P. Fensterwald, Jr., chief counsel of the Subcommittee on Administrative Practice and Procedure; as a former counsel of the Constitutional Amendments Subcommittee, he had volunteered his services, urging us to get to work before some other senator took the initiative. The third man was Stephan Lesher, a young newspaperman from the *Winston-Salem Journal*. He was temporarily a member of our staff as the result of a congressional fellowship from the American Political Science Association. This fellowship allowed Lesher to spend a full year working on the staff of any congressman of his choice; when he joined mine, he had no idea that he was about to become intimately involved in amending the United States Constitution.

For the most part of that morning we discussed various aspects of the legislative activities we were planning. We were all aware that others before us had spent much time and deliberation upon the best way to solve the century-old problems of succession and disability. The disabilities of Eisenhower, the "year we had no President" during Wilson's illness, and Garfield's lingering death had not been able to stir the Congress to action. But now, for the sixteenth time, we had no Vice President. In addition, we had no tested way to deal with a severe Presidential illness. And this was a different and dangerous age. The possible consequences of inaction were so terrifying that we were determined to aim at what little chance of success there was. All of us were awed by the scope of the job that lay ahead; the chances of amending the Constitution were historically slim. Men like Keating, Kefauver, and Thomas Hennings (former senator from Missouri) had recently wrestled with the problem in Congress, but to no avail. How could a freshman senator succeed where they had not?

Reviewing possible courses of action, we first turned our attention to S. J. Res. 35. Of all the proposed solutions in the congressional hopper, this had come closest to success: It had been backed by the Kennedy administration via Katzenbach's testimony, endorsed by the House of Delegates of the ABA, and reported out of the Constitutional Amendments Subcommittee. Yet, as I had told Ken Keating the week before, I had some reservations about the measure—reservations that seemed more valid now that they had been seconded by the leading constitutional spokesman in the Senate, Sam Ervin. Senator Ervin had expressed strong opposition in the committee meeting to any measure permitting a President to be removed from office without proper safeguards. Another obvious drawback to S. J. Res. 35 was its omission of any formula to fill Vice-Presidential vacancies.

Still another fact about S. J. Res. 35 disturbed me. A constitutional amendment, to be ratified, required the support of three-fourths of the state legislatures. My eight years in the Indiana General Assembly warned me that many state legislators would be opposed to giving Congress a blank check to determine what formula should be used in dealing with Presidential disability. S. J. Res. 35 did just that. It gave Congress the authority to act, and, once the amendment was ratified, Congress could enact any formula it desired. In my judgment, state ratification would be much less of a hurdle if a specific plan could be presented to the states.

But we all agreed that the most important drawback of the "enabling" aspect of S. J. Res. 35 was that, in the final analysis, it did not actually effect a solution. For years Congress had dillydallied with the subject of disability. Each crisis in a President's health brought a new flurry of short-lived activity, which had as yet accomplished nothing. If S. J. Res. 35 were to be ratified as an amendment, further action by Congress would still be required to implement an explicit plan by law and specify a procedure for dealing with Presidential disability. I was deeply concerned with the time factor. Two or three years was the minimum time necessary to amend the Constitution. Even if S. J. Res. 35 were approved by two-thirds of both Senate and House during the Eighty-eighth Congress, it would take at least another year or two for thirty-eight states to ratify it. By that time, the traumatic effect of President Kennedy's assassination would have lessened, lulling the Congress and the people into complacency and inactivity.

The four of us decided that the approach which had first been suggested by Attorney General Brownell, and which was subsequently modified by Attorney General Rogers and Senator Kefauver, came closest to achieving the goals we believed to be important. This approach would be what we would use as the basis for our constitutional amendment. We listed three basic points: Our amendment would (1) permit a Vice-Presidential vacancy to be filled when such a vacancy occurred; (2) provide a solution to the vexing problem of Presidential disability; and (3) revise the 1947 succession statute.

We then moved on to more specific language. Our draft should state that the President would nominate a Vice President in the event of a vacancy who would assume office on confirmation of a majority vote in both houses of Congress. In the matter of disability, provisions should be made whereby the President could declare his own disability; in the event that he was unable to do so, the Vice President and a majority of the Cabinet should be given the authority to make the declaration. And if the President disputed that declaration, the controversy was to be decided by Congress, with a two-thirds vote of both houses required to remove a disabled President against his will. The entire problem of disability was fraught with controversy. Our proposal would be far from perfect, we knew, but it would come closer than any other proposal we had studied to what we believed were the important objectives.

Next we turned to succession. Even though our proposal for filling Vice-Presidential vacancies would greatly reduce the possibility of the Speaker or President pro tempore ever succeeding to the Presidency, we thought it best to make specific provision for that slim eventuality. There was, we knew, a growing uneasiness about the present succession formula. Some felt that the succession of legislative officers to the Presidency, if both President and Vice President were to die during one term of office, would violate the doctrine of separation of powers. Others thought that because of the Speaker's already heavy legislative duties it would be impossible for him to assume any of the numerous tasks which in recent history had been undertaken by the Vice President. Instead, these would be thrown back upon the shoulders of the President, adding to his already impossible burdens. Still others were more concerned with the problem of disability, and the tenuous position in which the Speaker would find himself if the President became disabled and there was no Vice President to serve as acting President. The Speaker, it was pointed out, could hardly serve as a member of Congress and still act as President. Not only would he have to resign his post as Speaker, he would also have to give up his seat in Congress. When the President regained his health and reassumed his powers and duties, what would then become of the Speaker? We thought, in view of these considerations, it would be better to restore the line of succession to what it had been before the 1947 law was enacted: The Secretary of State, followed by the other officers of the Cabinet in the order in which their departments were established, would replace the Speaker and President pro tempore in the line of succession. The succession to the Presidency would remain where it should be—within the executive branch of our government.

Before our meeting adjourned that morning, we decided on a strategy that was to prove highly important. Conrad would approach the American Bar Association to explore the possibility of enlisting its support in our effort. Inasmuch as it was already pledged to support a different type of proposal, we had little real hope that it would give us its influential backing. But we needed all the help we could get, and it was worth a try.

Conrad and Fensterwald spent that day and most of the evening working with the staff of the Senate Legislative Counsel's office perfecting the language of our amendment. Conrad later reminisced that at one point, in his attempt to cover every possible contingency, his first version of the proposed language had stretched to five or six pages. He suddenly felt that Madison and Monroe were glaring over his shoulder, for his completed version of the succession provision alone was, in first draft, longer than all the other constitutional amendments put together! Eventually, however, the language was pared down and distilled to a workable length.

On the morning of the ninth of December a press announcement was made to the effect that the Subcommittee on Constitutional Amendments was going to make a thorough study of the problem of Presidential succession and that the chairman of the subcommittee intended to introduce a proposed constitutional amendment.

Throughout the week, public concern, as reflected in the nation's press, continued to mount. Walter Lippman, in the *Washington Post*, presented a penetrating analysis of the problem:

> ... There are several very grave objections to the present [succession] law. One is that because the Congressional system operates by seniority it has provided a successor who is unprepared and unqualified to succeed. Nobody has ever given five minutes' thought to the qualifications of the man who may be the next President of the United States. Under the old law, where the next in line would be the Secretary of State, the fact that he might become President would become a great consideration in his appointment and his confirmation by the Senate. ...
>
> There is another radical defect in the present law. In our system of government it has happened many times that one or both of the Houses of Congress is controlled by the opposition party. It happened, for example, both to President Truman and to President Eisenhower. Under the badly considered 1947 law, the whole administration of the government can be transferred from one party to another by the act of one sniper.
>
> There should never be such a premium on the assassination of a President offered to criminal lunatics or conspirators to brood upon. The very thing that has sustained the country since November 22 has been the continuity of the Presidency, the undisputed accession of a completely qualified man. ...

If we arouse ourselves enough to deal firmly with the problem of the succession, we should proceed at once to repair the other great hole in our system, which is what to do when a President is incapacitated. . . .

Late in the afternoon of December 11, Conrad, Fensterwald, Lesher, and I gathered again in Room 1205 to review our progress. We carefully went over the final language which had been drafted and had been submitted to the office of the Senate's Legislative Counsel for checking. The language would do the job. We would start the wheels turning the following day.

Any legislative effort to gather support for a Senate measure usually begins with a letter from the sponsoring senator to all his colleagues, advising them of the general nature of the resolution and the date that it will be introduced, and extending a specific invitation to cosponsor the bill. When the bill is printed, the names of all senators who accept this invitation appear in alphabetical order after the name of the originating senator. Later cosponsors' names may be added on subsequent printings of the bill. Although a senator is not strictly obliged to support a measure once he has sponsored it, I had observed that any cosponsor of a measure could usually be counted on to support it in committee and on the Senate floor. Throughout that night, personal letters were typed to every member of the Senate, inviting them to join me in sponsoring the resolution. These were hand-delivered to each senator's office the following morning.

We also called a press conference that morning, December 12, disclosing for the first time the text of our proposed amendment and elaborating upon our plans to tackle the problem. The resolution was to be introduced later that day.

Up until then, time and circumstances had not permitted me to discuss the resolution's contents with Senate Majority Leader Mike Mansfield, Senator Hayden, and Speaker McCormack, as I had hoped to do. Now I tried to reach Senator Hayden but was unable to do so. A call to Mansfield's office met with better fortune, and I went over to see him.

Senator Mansfield gave me a cordial welcome and listened attentively to my explanation of the proposal's contents and objectives. He assured me that he would give the inability-succession

question his personal attention and that he would willingly cooper-
ate with us in any effort we might make to solve the problem.

Leaving Senator Mansfield's office, I crossed the Capitol hallway and entered the Senate Chamber. The Senate had just convened, and I had hoped to utilize the earliness of the hour to acquire
further support for the measure that some of us now believed to be
the country's most important piece of unfinished business.

For almost a year I had deferred to the Senate's tradition that
newly elected senators should be seen and not heard and had pa-
tiently resisted the temptation to deliver numerous speeches on
the Senate floor. This was to be my first experience of speaking on
any matter of national importance in which I would play a major
role. Now—with the time ripe, appropriate, and proper—I found
myself fidgeting with the papers on my desk and thumbing the al-
ready-worn edges of the statement I was about to read. The lights
in the chamber seemed brighter than usual, particularly over my
head, and the room seemed abnormally warm. I had what in retrospect was a ridiculous illusion that a number of persons in the gallery
were watching me and not the eloquent debate between Senators
Morse and Kuchel on a conference report of the Foreign Assistance
Act. I went on fidgeting and riffling through my papers as Senator
Morse concluded with some heated and highly uncomplimentary
remarks concerning Mr. Joe Alsop: "the most superficial, super-
egotistical, supercilious pain in the neck in the press gallery."

It was time. I got up, asked for recognition, and heard the presiding officer of the Senate, Senator Herbert Walters of Tennessee,
say, "The senator from Indiana."

"Mr. President," I replied, "I send to the desk a joint resolution,
introduced on behalf of myself and the senator from Missouri [Mr.
Long]. I ask unanimous consent that it lie over for ten days, in the
hope that we may have additional cosponsors." Senator Walters
noted the joint resolution—S. J. Res. 139—received; it was read
twice by title and referred to the Committee on the Judiciary. Then
I went on to deliver my prepared statement on the need for constitutional change to solve the inability-succession problem once and for
all.

When I had concluded my floor remarks, I went to the office
of the President pro tempore of the Senate. As always, Senator Hay-

den welcomed me warmly and listened carefully to an explanation of the goals of the proposed measure I had just introduced. It was extremely important that he not gain the impression that our efforts to change the law were designed in any way to remove him personally from the scene. He was extremely well liked; and as Chairman of the Senate Appropriations Committee he could be a powerful ally, or dangerous adversary, to any piece of legislation.

From there, Conrad and Lesher joined me; and together we walked from the Senate, through the rotunda, over to the House of Representatives. We called at the Speaker's office and asked if it would be possible to spend a moment or two with him.

Speaker McCormack ushered us into his inner sanctum, and I quickly came to the point. "Mr. Speaker, I want you to be aware of the fact that this afternoon I introduced a constitutional amendment which will deal with the problem of succession and disability. This is an extremely important problem and falls squarely within my jurisdiction as Chairman of the Subcommittee on Constitutional Amendments. I intend to study it thoroughly. But I want you to know that our desire to change the succession law is no reflection on you personally—it just seems to us to be a more practical way of dealing with a very thorny problem." John McCormack was listening attentively. "As busy as you are," I went on, "I don't see how it would be humanly possible for you to do any more than you're doing at present. Besides, by the time any amendment to the Constitution can become law, we'll certainly have a Vice President again; thus, you'd no longer be directly in the line of succession, and the measure could not be interpreted in any way as a reflection on your ability to serve as President."

The Speaker said that he appreciated my having stopped by to discuss the matter with him.

"Frankly," he said, "I have been extremely disturbed at the way some people have been batting the subject around. Just today one of those so-called lady reporters asked me if I felt I was qualified to serve as President. I told her it was too horrible to think about. I refused to talk to her about the subject."

I realized how deeply the Speaker had been hurt by some of the comments which had been made as a result of his being placed directly in the line of succession. He reached into the main drawer of his big desk, brought forth a newspaper, and tossed it to me. "Here, Birch, take a look at this. What do you say to that kind of journalism?" A newsman had editorialized:

> The country's deep concern over the Presidential succession is another stark and specific indictment of the Congress. Sophisticated Americans will live in quiet terror until the next election because they know that if President Johnson dies Speaker John McCormack will become President. . . .
>
> Speaker McCormack will be 72 in a few days, but in truth age is not his most pronounced frailty. Only the inexorable combination of a complacent Boston constituency, rules of seniority that are seldom transgressed by the House, and personal longevity could have brought him to his present eminence, where only a heartbeat separates him from the most powerful office on earth. Ability and vigor, sad to say, are found only in vestigial traces in the Speaker.
>
> It is not the law of succession that is to blame here; it is the unwillingness of the leaders of Congress to look at themselves in the clear light of reason. If the Speaker and the President pro tempore were representatives of the best that is to be found in the Congress, then the law of succession would be logical and workable, and friend and foe alike would not feel it necessary to pray nightly for the safekeeping of President Johnson.
>
> Unhappily, however, the leadership in Congress (including the chairmanship of important and powerful committees) more often than not devolves upon men whose usefulness, strength and wisdom is long past.

As I read the article, I understood the Speaker's sense of indignation over the whole matter; they certainly had been rough on him. I handed the article back.

"Mr. Speaker," I said, "That's an outright insult. It's not only in bad taste, but it's irrelevant to what the real issues are. I certainly hope you don't think that we have any feelings of this sort motivating our introduction of this amendment."

I don't think that he did take our action personally, yet we left his office with the full realization that Speaker John McCormack was in no mood to support any legislation which would give the impression that he was not qualified to perform his duties as Speaker and as a representative from the Ninth Congressional District of

Massachusetts. Truthfully, I couldn't blame him. Time would char-
acterize him as an invaluable ally in our cause; but just then he seemed
an insurmountable adversary.

From there, Lesher, Conrad, and I headed back toward our office in the New Senate Office Building to review the day's activities.
But en route we stopped by the office of Senator Richard Russell,
the wise and powerful patriarch of the block of twenty-four southern senators.

Since most of the southern senators considered Senator Russell
their leader on important legislative matters, his voice and influence
would be of incalculable importance in any successful effort to
amend the Constitution; and his advice on strategy could mean the
difference between success and failure to us. In the short period that
I had been in the Senate, I had found him to be, despite his conservative image in the northern press, not only a gentleman but a man of
unparalleled parliamentary skills. He had come to the Senate at
thirty-five, having already been governor of Georgia. As Chairman
of the Armed Services Committee, he played an important part in
maintaining our country's defenses. He was also the foremost student
of what made the Senate tick. Our stay in his office, filled with the
memorabilia of a lifetime's service to his country, lasted only about
ten minutes. Senator Russell was hospitable, but like most members
of the Senate he was unfamiliar with the intricacies of the problem
at hand. Moreover, he had recently been appointed a member of the
Warren Commission to study President Kennedy's assassination,
and he was deeply involved in this heartrending task. But before we
left, Senator Russell promised to give our proposal careful thought
and advise me of his opinion at a later date. We left a copy of the
bill with him, and as we emerged from his office the three of us felt
that an important base had been touched.

The next day, December 13, I received a call from Don Channell, Director of the Washington office of the American Bar Association. The ABA had been the foremost proponent of a solution to
Presidential disability; and although that solution, as the ABA House
of Delegates had conceived it, was entirely different from S. J. Res.
139, Channell thought a meeting between his staff and ours might
determine some middle ground, satisfactory to all.

We met the next day. Channell was accompanied by Lowell

Beck, his assistant in the Washington office, and Larry Conrad was with me. Although this first meeting accomplished little that was concrete, our discussion was the first step in a partnership that was to follow a long, tedious path to eventual success. Channell and Beck were committed to following the course of action specified by the ABA House of Delegates. On the other hand, however, I was convinced that our own proposal had more merit and was not inclined to give ground. But the meeting did prove one thing beyond question. Each of us had one common desire: to find a workable solution to a century-old problem. We adjourned after agreeing to meet again after the beginning of the New Year.

On January 2, accordingly, Channell, Beck, Conrad, Lesher, and I resumed our discussion. Channell and Beck suggested the possibility of appointing a number of recognized legal scholars to an ABA Inability and Succession Commission, which would meet and discuss the relative merits of the numerous inability-succession proposals. This struck all of us as a good idea. I had no doubt that the ABA, with its thousands of member lawyers, could be extremely useful to us at the grass roots. The major question in my mind, however, was whether the bar association could be persuaded to reverse its previous commitment to the approach of a broad, enabling amendment like Ken Keating's S. J. Res. 35. Whether or not it did so, the bar study commission could be useful. If it did adopt our S. J. Res. 139 proposal, our own efforts would have gained immeasurably. On the other hand, if the study were to disclose weaknesses and imperfections in our proposal, we needed to know what they were. In the end, perhaps, we could develop a joint effort better qualified to deal with the problem than either of the previous measures.

Channell and Beck went to work immediately, seeking reputable and influential legal scholars and practicing attorneys to serve on the study panel. We set a tentative date of January 20 and 21 for the group to meet in Washington.

In the meantime, Lesher and I went to work on a related problem: We wanted to bring our issue to focus in the mind of the general public. All previous efforts to deal with the succession-disability issue had failed as soon as national concern, awakened after a crisis, waned again with the passage of time. We wanted to maintain the public interest and support we would need for the long haul through passage and ratification of a constitutional amendment. We discussed the feasibility of interesting a national publication in our undertaking. The chances were not great, but it seemed worth the effort. The major points were outlined; and Lesher was commissioned, not only to produce a tentative first draft, but to pursue the possibility of publication with the staff of *Look* magazine in New York.

As part of the same strategy of "long-range public awareness," I held a press conference on January 9. At that time, we presented our plans for the ultimate enactment of S. J. Res. 139 to the press and, we hoped, to the nation as a whole.

During those hectic first few days of the new congress, we were also at work in another direction. Larry Conrad was delegated the responsibility of preparing the entire matter of Presidential succession for subcommittee hearings. This was the first such experience for him, in his role as chief staff man of the subcommittee; but he was not alone—the junior senator from Indiana was also plowing virgin soil.

Although we were giving considerable attention to the strategy necessary to breed grass roots support for our legislation, we still knew that the first hurdle would be the Congress of the United States. Both the House and the Senate, as any high-school civics student knows, must give a two-thirds vote to pass a constitutional amendment. We were not fooling ourselves—this would be no easy task. Only twenty-four previous amendments had run the full gauntlet of congressional approval and subsequent ratification by the necessary three-fourths of the state legislatures. The first ten of these, grouped together as the Bill of Rights, had received endorsement early in the country's history; after that, only fourteen amendments had been attached to the Constitution. We certainly had our work cut out for us, but we kept clearly in mind our most immediate goal —the approval of two-thirds of my senate colleagues. In any case, we were determined to give it the old college try.

Our early letters soliciting cosponsorships of S. J. Res. 139 soon began to pay off. By the time S. J. Res. 139 was referred to the Constitutional Amendments Subcommittee on January 17, 1964, five more senators[1] had joined Senator Long of Missouri and myself as original cosponsors. The first team of senatorial supporters numbered only seven per cent of that body. But by phone call, letter, and personal conversation, I continued our efforts to urge other senators to join the cause. Most of those efforts were met with reserve and the "let me wait and study it" response. Still, we knew that each additional sponsor represented at least a partially committed vote on final passage, so we continued our efforts to talk to each senator personally. One such conversation was with the majority whip, Senator Hubert Humphrey, who assured me that he was anxious to find a solution to the problem. Senator Humphrey had been studying the issue himself and knew its importance well.

January 20, the day that had been set for the ABA Special Study Commission on Presidential Succession and Disability, dawned cold and gray in the nation's capital. Because of the interest which had been expressed in solving this problem, Senators Hruska and Keating, Representatives Emanuel Celler and Louis Wyman, Deputy Attorney General Nicholas Katzenbach, and I had been invited to present our various views to the commission. Since I was responsible for directing subcommittee action in the Senate, and since that action was already scheduled giving a detailed argument supporting our resolution, it had been decided that I should make the first presentation—to "spread the eagle," as Hoosier defense lawyers say.

Shortly before ten in the morning, Lesher, Conrad, Fensterwald, and I made our way down Pennsylvania Avenue toward the Mayflower Hotel. The morning was cold and damp, but the environment was considerably warmer inside the Mayflower's Virginia Room. In fact, the temperature was near the boiling point. An astute group of legal minds had been assembled there; and each had his own personal ideas of how the disability and succession problem could best be solved.

This was my first chance to meet Walter E. Craig, president of the ABA, an outstanding attorney from Arizona who was soon to be nominated to the federal district bench. Without his determination and insistence that the ABA disability-succession commission

[1] See Appendix, p. 364, for a list of Senate cosponsors.

come up with a single answer, our entire efforts would have died early in the game. Craig was joined by Lewis F. Powell, president-elect of the ABA and a noted member of the Bar; he was to play an indispensible role in the late stages of the amendment's struggle for passage in Congress. Edward L. Wright of Little Rock, Arkansas, was also present; his participation, too, would later be invaluable in gaining the endorsement of the ABA House of Delegates, of which he was chairman. New York attorney John D. Feerick, author of "The Problem of Presidential Inability—Will Congress Ever Solve It?," was on hand; later he wrote a comprehensive work on the entire field called *From Failing Hands*. There was also Professor James C. Kirby, Jr., of the Vanderbilt University School of Law, formerly a counsel for the Subcommittee on Constitutional Amendments, and therefore penetratingly aware of the efforts previously made by Congress. Also present were Paul A. Freund, the noted Harvard Professor of Constitutional Law; Jonathan C. Gibson of Chicago, Chairman of the ABA Committee on Jurisprudence and Law Reform; Martin Taylor, Chairman of the New York ABA Committee on the Federal Constitution; and Charles B. Nutting, Dean of the National Law Center of Washington.

Herbert Brownell, president of the New York City Bar Association, who had served as Attorney General during President Eisenhower's disability, brought his unique expertise to the commission; as did Ross L. Malone of Roswell, New Mexico, a former president of the ABA, who had also served as Deputy Attorney General under President Truman and had been on the national scene during Truman's efforts to change the current succession law. Another former president of the ABA, Sylvester C. Smith, Jr., of Newark, New Jersey, was also present, as was Richard H. Hanson, a Nebraska attorney and the author of "The Year We Had No President."

Besides Fensterwald and representatives of my staff, staff members from the offices of Minority Leader Everett McKinley Dirksen and Senator Jacob K. Javits had been invited to participate. This was done with the clear understanding from the outset that all staff people represented a definite point of view.

After calling the meeting to order, Chairman Craig got the committee's deliberations off to a start by a brief and pertinent survey of the task at hand. When he had finished, he introduced me as Chairman of the Senate Subcommittee on Constitutional Amendments and sponsor of the most recent legislative proposal to deal with the problem of Presidential disability and succession. I had made some general notes while riding down from the Capitol and proceeded to emphasize the following points.

The first part of the general problem, and the one that had been most thoroughly discussed, was the area of Presidential disability. This had been with us since the time of President Garfield's assassination and was not much closer to solution today than it was immediately after Garfield's death. I stressed the strength of our resolution's answer to the problem. Let the President declare his own disability if he were able; if not, the Vice President, acting with the concurrence of a majority of the Cabinet, could do so instead. Under either of these circumstances the Vice President was to become acting President, assuming the powers and duties of the Presidency but not the office itself. Should there be a dispute between the President and Vice President over the disability, S. J. Res. 139 provided for Congress to solve the problem: a two-thirds vote of both Houses would be necessary to permit the Vice President to continue as acting President.

Then I turned to the other problem: how to fill vacancies in the office of Vice President. This subject had not been thoroughly discussed by Congress. Whereas the nation had gone through periods in which the President had been disabled and others during which there was no Vice President, it had not yet faced a situation in which an elected President and Vice President had both died during a four-year term of office. I tried, therefore, to stress the importance of filling a Vice-Presidential vacancy. It had taken us generations to develop the office of Vice President into that of a good right arm for the President, a prestigious and responsible job. With this development of the office, there was even more reason to keep it filled at all times. Our answer, in the event of a vacancy, was to permit the President to nominate a new Vice President, to be elected by a majority of both Houses of Congress.

Finally, S. J. Res. 139, as we had originally introduced it, would change the line of succession, in the event that both the President and the Vice President should die during the same four-year term, to the pre-1947 order, with the Secretary of State first in line fol-

lowed by the normal descending order within the Cabinet. Thereby
the Speaker and President pro tempore would be removed from the
immediate line of succession. It had been our first judgment that the
nation's best interest would be served by keeping the line of succession within the executive branch rather than commingling legislative
with executive authority.

But, I admitted to the committee, I now felt that Section 3,
which made these stipulations, should be deleted from the proposed
amendment. I suggested that the deliberations of the Bar should not
deal with this controversial problem, because the House, in my judgment, would refuse to consider any measure which might be construed as an affront to its Speaker. From past conversations with
Speaker McCormack, it was apparent to me that this section could
jeopardize all our efforts.

At the close of my remarks, members of the conference proceeded to cross-examine me—an experience that I shall never forget.
There I was, novice attorney and neophyte senator, being bom-
barded by the big guns of the legal fraternity: senior members of
the Bar like Martin Taylor and white-haired Jonathan Gibson, and
constitutional experts like Paul Freund. I had difficulty suppressing
feelings of fear. At one time when the discussion became particularly
involved, I leaned toward Larry Conrad, sitting on my right, and
murmured that I suddenly knew how Daniel must have felt when
he was face to face with the lions.

After two and a half hours of discussion, the conference re-
cessed for lunch. At that point I was obliged to leave for the airport
to fulfill a speaking commitment in Indiana. As I hurried toward
Washington National Airport, I felt extremely pessimistic. After
the going over I had just experienced, there seemed little likelihood
that the conference could reach any substantial agreement.

About noon the next day I arrived back in Washington and
went immediately to the Mayflower, eager to know what had been
going on. As I arrived, the conference was just adjourning. One
glance at Lesher's and Conrad's faces told me that the news had to be
good. They were bursting with excitement. When we had a chance
to talk, they filled me in on what had happened in the twenty-four
hours I was away.

When the conference had reconvened, Senator Roman Hruska

of Nebraska, articulate as always, had made a presentation of his view of the means for solution; afterwards he had spent some time fielding questions from the commission members. As the afternoon went on, Senator Keating, Representatives Celler and Wyman, and Deputy Attorney General Katzenbach had all expressed their views and answered the questions that were put to them.

Just as the membership of the commission represented the best of every aspect of constitutional learning, so the witness list— Hruska, Keating, Celler, Wyman, Katzenbach—had yielded the dynamics of politics and constitutional law. No lawyer could hope for a more expert congressional examination of the problem. All these men were experienced, shrewd in the politics of checks and balances, and wise in their treatment of constitutional language.

As the discussion progressed, Conrad, Lesher, and Fensterwald had continued to present the merits of S. J. Res. 139. On the other hand, Martin Taylor, doggedly determined that no specific detail would be written into the Constitution, felt that if any constitutional amendment were required it should be Senator Keating's broad, enabling version; and Jonathan Gibson over and over had expressed his opposition to any type of constitutional amendment at all.

During the course of that afternoon, a general consensus had seemed to be forming. Chairman Wally Craig and Ed Wright, followed by Herb Brownell and John Feerick, had constituted a nucleus that felt that our approach had much to recommend it. By the time the conference had adjourned for the evening, there had been considerable agreement about the general content of S. J. Res. 139. Not content to let it rest at that, Wally Craig had asked Herb Brownell, Ed Wright, Lewis Powell, and Ross Malone to his room to try to construct some final language that could be presented for the commission's consideration the following day. Finally, at three in the morning, they had arrived at what was to be a consensus adopted by the commission. The final draft was almost identical to the language of Sections 1 and 2 of S. J. Res. 139; for the most part they had simply changed a word here and a word there, sharpened the language, and clarified the intent. The controversial Section 3, however, had been dropped completely. They had felt, as I had, that no amendment with such a provision, capable of being interpreted as offensive to the Speaker of the House, could pass through the House of Representatives. One small addition had been made in order to broaden the base of support for the resolution. Language was added to Section 2 which, in the event of Presidential disability, would enable Congress to provide by law for some other body to replace the Cabinet as the group responsible for verifying the action of the Vice President in the event the Cabinet's presence in the disability provision proved unworkable. Some scholars and members of Congress had felt that the only body which could make an impartial decision concerning the President's disability was a blue-ribbon commission. According to some, this commission ought to be composed of doctors; according to others, it should contain doctors, members of the Supreme Court, and legislative leaders from Congress. This minor change in the language would leave the way open for Congress to establish such a commission to replace the Cabinet at a later date if necessary. Thus, those favoring this approach could be brought into the fold in support of S. J. Res. 139.

The Bar conference had met again that morning, January 21, for its final session. Wally Craig had presented the draft resolution he, Wright, Powell, and Malone had stayed up until early morning to forge. The conference had discussed the language in detail, and again there had been heated differences of opinion. Finally, Jonathan Gibson, who as chairman of the ABA Committee on Jurisprudence and Law Reform had studied the issue extensively, had consented to go along with the draft, laying aside his earlier opposition to a constitutional amendment because, as he put it, "I am convinced we need some solution and if we all try and hold out for our own personal plan, the result will be nothing, just as it has been for ages." Martin Taylor was never persuaded; to this day he remains convinced that the best approach was the broad, enabling constitutional amendment which would have permitted a later Congress to solve the problem by law.

By the time I returned from Indiana that noon, the conference had officially adopted the American Bar Association Consensus on Presidential Disability and Succession.[2] The first step had been taken in the longest of legislative journeys—the enactment of a constitutional amendment.

2 For text, see Appendix, pp. 348–350.

CHAPTER 3

Stumbling Blocks
and Stepping Stones

Notice of Hearings on Presidential
Succession and Disability

> MR. BAYH: Mr. President, as chairman of the Senate Judiciary
> Subcommittee on Constitutional Amendments, I wish to announce
> forthcoming hearings on Presidential succession and disability. The
> hearings are scheduled to begin at 10 a.m. on January 22 and 23, 1964,
> in Room 2228 of the New Senate Office Building.
>
> Because of the large number of resolutions already introduced—
> Senate Joint Resolutions 13, 28, 35, 138, 139, 140, and 143—we have
> attempted to confine witnesses to congressional representatives during
> these first hearings. Additional public hearings will be scheduled some-
> time in February.

With this official announcement the public was notified of our
intention to seek a constitutional solution to the succession-disability problem. As we planned it, these hearings would run for two
days in January, to sound out congressional opinion on the subject.

Then we planned to adjourn until after the meeting of the American Bar Association House of Delegates, the sole sanctioning body of the ABA, on February 17, 1964. By doing this, we hoped we would be able to reconvene with the House of Delegates' endorsement of the consensus report drafted by their special commission. With this strategy, if we were successful, our most important allies, the Bar Association officials, could testify before our subcommittee not only as individuals but with the full sanction of the Association behind them.

At precisely ten o'clock on the morning of January 22, Larry Conrad and I, armed with documents, statements, and other material, walked into Room 2228, the hearing room of the Senate Judiciary Committee. It was an impressive setting for what was, in our minds at least, the drama that was about to take place: high-ceilinged, with wood-paneled walls and heavy bronze inlaid doors, the room was spacious enough to seat approximately a hundred and fifty people. Beneath a carved wooden plaque of the Senate seal was a long horseshoe-shaped desk, elevated upon a platform. This was for the senators, and the witnesses were to sit at a long mahogany table in front of the platform.

There were some spectators, but not the mammoth crowd which I will admit we had envisioned. We had become so involved in the urgency and exigency of our work that it was hard to remember that to many others, for whom constitutional changes had no particular glamour, this was only another assault on a basically insoluble problem. Compared to many issues of the day, Presidential succession and disability had little legislative sex appeal.

The slight chill common to all high-ceilinged rooms began to be dispelled as the television lights, temporarily fastened to large bronze wall light fixtures, were tested. These lights, hot and blinding, are usually angled toward the chairman or the witness chair in Senate hearings where filming and recording are permitted. Uncomfortable as the lights may be, few senators overlook the importance of television as a vital means of communication to the "home folks" and to the nation.

Frankly, I was extremely nervous, almost to the point of fright, as I tightened my grip on my first senatorial gavel and called the subcommittee into session. This was a new experience for me, and I was surrounded by old congressional hands and constitutional experts. I began, "We are here this morning to consider the problems of Presidential succession and Presidential inability." I hoped that my nervousness did not show up in my voice; I do know, however, that whatever control I may have had over my words, I was less successful in keeping my hands from shaking.

My opening statement continued, noting background information, recent developments in the area, and the goals I hoped the subcommittee would strive to meet. Slowly I began to feel a bit more easy in the harness, and my voice and actions became a little more fluid.

During my opening remarks, Sam Ervin, a former supreme court judge from North Carolina and one of the Senate's most distinguished constitutional experts, slipped quietly in. Although Senator Ervin was soon to be appointed to the subcommittee, he was present that opening morning as a witness. Nonetheless, he exercised the senator's option of occupying a seat with the subcommittee members and took a place next to me behind the long curved committee dais. When I had finished, he whispered, "Birch, I'd like to give my statement—I've got an important Rules Committee meeting that's going on right now." I was momentarily at a loss, not being aware of the protocol procedure in such cases. Ordinarily, committee members of the majority party give their statements or question witnesses according to their rank on the subcommittee, followed by the minority committee members, also in order of their rank. Here I was confronted by the request of Senator Ervin, who technically was not a member of the subcommittee. This problem would not normally be one of earth-shaking proportions, but I was enough of a neophyte for it to seem like a major crisis. Fortunately, Ken Keating graciously bailed me out of the predicament by deferring to Senator Ervin. Struggling to regain the composure I had lost for a moment, I sat back to listen. After a few peaceful moments, I thought to myself that this business of being chairman wasn't so bad after all.

Senator Ervin's testimony criticized the 1947 succession law. He proposed, instead, a measure he had previously introduced in Congress. The ABA committee memorandum had not endorsed our original proposal to change the succession law. I, too, felt it was unreasonable to expect the House to accept the change at this time. However, succession certainly was part of the whole thorny problem.

The weakness of the present system, Senator Ervin said, was that it restricted the choice of the potential President—that is, the Speaker of the House—to House members only. "Moreover, a judgment as to who would be the best Speaker . . . might differ from the judgment as to who would make the best Presidential successor." When the Vice Presidency, or the offices of both Vice President and President, are vacant, Senator Ervin continued, a joint session of Congress should, within ten days, choose the men to fill the vacant positions. In the interim, the Presidency would temporarily be filled according to statute, as enacted by Congress.

His succession plan had several advantages, he said. It meant the potential President would be democratically selected. The need for continuity would be met, since there would always be a Vice President. "The successor to the Presidency would be chosen at a time when attention can be focused on the qualities necessary to make a good President . . . and the Congress will be able to select from all our great men, public and private, in making their choice."

Next, Kenneth Keating of New York took the turn he had ceded to Sam Ervin. Keating had long been studying the problem of Presidential disability, and he quickly plunged into a discussion of his own proposed constitutional amendment, S.J. Res. 35,[1] which was then pending before the Senate Judiciary Committee. It would do two things, he said.

"First, it would make clear that in cases of Presidential inability, only the powers and duties of the Presidency, rather than the office itself, shall devolve upon the Vice President as Acting President until the President has recovered from his condition of inability.

"Secondly, it would leave to the Congress to prescribe a method by which the commencement and termination of any inability shall be determined—and this, under Senate Joint Resolution 35, Congress can do by ordinary legislation."

According to Senator Keating's argument, his proposal had two major advantages over other proposals. It had a better chance

[1] See Appendix, p. 350.

of passage through the Congress and the state legislatures because of its simplicity, and it offered maximum fidelity. My own hunch, as I listened to my colleague, was otherwise. Perhaps it would pass the Congress, but what I had learned from my experience as a state legislator convinced me that it would never be ratified by three-fourths of the states.

Senator Keating continued his testimony by discussing his proposal to fill vacancies in the office of Vice President. Keating suggested that we "abolish the single Vice Presidential Office we have now and create two Vice Presidencies. Both Vice Presidents would be elected along with the President on a national ticket in the regular four-year Presidential elections." This, he felt, would insure that both Vice Presidents, as immediate potential successors to the President, would be of the same political party. Also, since Presidential candidates normally have a great deal to say in the selection of their running mates, both Vice Presidents would be acceptable to the President and would work compatibly with him when in office. He went on to describe the details of his twin-Vice-President plan.

> One is designated as the Executive Vice President, and would stand first in line to succeed to the Presidency in case of death, removal, or resignation of the President. The other would be designated as the Legislative Vice President. No further changes in the line of succession would be contemplated. In other words, the present succession law of 1947 could stand as is, the only difference being that a second Vice President would be interposed in the line of succession between the First Vice President and the Speaker of the House.

The Executive Vice President would have no constitutional duties at all, but would be free to take on special assignments at the discretion of the President, such as those now being given to the Vice President in order to bring him onto the highest level of executive policy circles. The Legislative Vice President would hold the constitutional powers and duties now conferred upon the Vice President, serving as presiding officer of the Senate and breaking tie votes there. He, too, would take on additional assignments at the President's discretion.

Our next witness was Senator A. S. Mike Monroney of Oklahoma. While he had served in the House of Representatives,

Senator Monroney had earned great recognition for his leadership in congressional reorganization and his interest in the Presidential continuity problem. Earlier in the month, I had discussed the problem of Presidential disability and succession with him one evening when he and his wife had joined us for dinner at our home. But despite my efforts, I had been unable to convince him that the approach of S.J. Res. 139 was the best solution to the problem. Now before the committee he stressed the need to arouse public opinion and suggested that "a bi-partisan commission, similar to the Hoover Commission, be established to study the various problems associated with the line of succession, disability, and problems of the electoral college."

At twelve noon, as Senator Monroney was finishing his testimony, the Senate bell sounded its notice that the Senate was convening. Under Senate rules, no committee or subcommittee may sit for hearings while the Senate is in session. If we were to be able to hear our last witness, we had to be excused from this rule. Conrad, who had solicited the advice of committee veterans on the do's and don'ts of conducting hearings, assured me he would get consent from the proper sources. By way of Patrick Hynes in the Democratic Cloakroom, his message was relayed to Majority Leader Mansfield, who asked the Senate's unanimous consent for our subcommittee to hear one more witness.

In the meantime, taking Larry's assurance at his word, I had called Professor James Kirby, of the Vanderbilt University School of Law, to the witness chair. Kirby had been an ABA panel member, and was a former counsel for the subcommittee under Senator Kefauver. Our only non-congressional witness during those first two days of hearings, Kirby had just happened to be in town at the time. We took advantage of his availability, for he was knowledgeable and articulate about this subject, and had a background and experience which were different from those of the other ABA panel members.

Concerning the problem of disability, Kirby expressed his strong opposition to the President's and Vice President's reliance on private agreements such as those that Presidents Eisenhower, Kennedy, and Johnson had effected. "Private memorandums and agreements can't have the force of law regardless of whether a

statute or a constitutional amendment is needed," he said. "They . . .
depend essentially on good faith for their enforcement." We were
pleased but not surprised to hear Kirby go on to argue the merits
of the disability provisions of S.J. Res. 139.

When the hearings adjourned at 1:10 p.m., I felt that we had
gotten off to a good start. Conrad and I gathered up our papers and
headed for the hearing room door. By the time we reached the hall,
the knot that had been in my stomach since I rapped the opening gavel was just about gone. My wife Marvella, who had slipped
into a front-row seat as the hearings began, joined us in the walk
back to the office. I felt certain she had shared all my moments of
anxiety. My campaign for the Senate had been very much a joint
effort, in which Marvella had done more than her share. Now,
several months later, we had shared another experience: the opening
session of the hearings which, for the first time, I was chairing. I
read in Marvella's glance a combination of pride and relief. The
first day was over.

When we reconvened the hearings the next morning, I was
the only senator on the subcommittee who was present; Conrad
was with me, as was Clyde Flynn, the Minority Counsel. Our first
witness was Senator Jacob Javits of New York. His S.J. Res. 138,
which had been introduced just before our own resolution, dealt
solely with the problem of filling vacancies in the office of Vice
President. In discussing the merits of his particular approach, Senator Javits pointed out:

> My resolution calls for the election of a Vice President from
> among the members of Congress and the President's Cabinet. These
> are the two groups relied upon in the three Succession Statutes we have
> had. . . . I think the basic policy expressed in the original constitutional
> requirement is a sound one, since it assures the election of a person
> already placed in a high position of public trust. This is particularly
> important for public confidence in such cases, when the Congress will
> be expected to act quickly. A member of Congress or of the Cabinet
> is known to the public, and therefore enables some public judgment
> to be expressed in connection with the action of the Congress.

Senator Javits' next words were unimaginably welcome to those of
us who had been living with the problem day and night and had
feared that no single solution could be agreed upon.

Now I propose, Mr. Chairman, to make a change in my resolution to make it much closer to the views of the chair, because I believe the chair has expressed and developed what I consider to be a
relatively good prescription to this whole problem. . . . And therefore
I am amending my resolution, S.J. Res. 138, to add to Section II an
additional requirement that the election by the Congress shall be made
"by and with the consent" of the President who has just taken office.

Thus, Senator Javits was the first member of the Senate to express
in public before our committee a willingness to forego individual
pride of authorship in a common search for the solution to this
difficult problem. In the past the difficulty had been, not that no one
had a solution to the problem, but that there had been so many
diverse ones. Each individual author had felt that his proposal contained the only workable solution. We had known from the outset
that we would be unable to fare better than any of our predecessors
unless we were able to create an atmosphere of give-and-take in
which the several dozen members of Congress who had already
supported one or another particular legislative approach were
persuaded to be more flexible. From a practical standpoint, it did
not matter that a great majority of Congress felt that *some* action
was imperative. All would fail unless we could get two-thirds of
the members of the Senate and House to support *one* specific proposal. Now Senator Javits had taken the first giant step along that
path.

His statement ended on a note of urgency which was soon to
be echoed by many of our colleagues: he hoped that the committee
would work unflaggingly to report out some constitutional amendment, whatever it might be. The danger, he felt, was that once the
time of crisis had passed, the work toward a solution would be
dropped. "The atomic age," he concluded, "just cannot stand our
being rudderless for any period of time on any constitutional questions or legal questions which human ingenuity can quiet in
advance."

I was extremely grateful to Jack Javits for his generosity in
moving toward our approach. He is a strong-minded man with
definite ideas of his own, and is not one to give in easily in a debate.
Perhaps, I allowed myself to think, we could take his support as a
barometer that public opinion was beginning to swing to our side;

perhaps his highly-developed intuition as a legislator made him sense that he was backing a winner. But more importantly, Senator Javits was of the opinion that our solution would do the job properly. I resolved to write him a note thanking him for giving us such invaluable backing.

Two more of my Senate colleagues, Frank Moss of Utah and Ed Long of Missouri, followed with their testimony. Senator Long had been the only cosponsor with me when S.J. Res. 139 was originally introduced; Senator Moss had joined us shortly thereafter. They had been among only a handful of supporters when S.J. Res. 139 was referred to committee, at a time when each additional cosponsor was as precious as pure gold. Both Moss's and Long's testimony contained strong, well-documented arguments that the provisions of S.J. Res. 139 proposed the best solution to the problem.

Senator Roman L. Hruska of Nebraska, who was later to become a member of the subcommittee, testified next. He expressed what was to be a continuing concern of his: that "the doctrine of the separation of powers should not be violated." Therefore he suggested that "it would be my idea, Mr. Chairman, to limit the power to make decisions as to the commencement and termination of Presidential disability to the Executive branch of the government. It could be by the Cabinet or such other body within the Executive branch as Congress may provide by law." In the months to come, Senator Hruska and I were frequently to differ about the best approach to follow; but his diligent work in helping to solve the problem and his assistance in working out the imperfections contained in the various proposals were to be a great asset to us. Our final solution may not have completely eliminated his fears about the separation of powers, but it did contain some language he was instrumental in contributing.

Senator Frank Church of Idaho, confined his attention to the need for filling Vice-Presidential vacancies. "Whenever there shall be a vacancy in the office of Vice President," Senator Church proposed, "the President, by and with the consent of the Senate, shall nominate not more than five nor fewer than two persons qualified for the office. The House of Representatives shall immediately, by ballot, choose one of these persons to be Vice President. A quorum for this purpose shall consist of two-thirds of the whole number of Representatives, and a majority of the whole number shall be necessary for a choice." I had previously discussed the problems we were studying with Senator Church, and knew that he was very much interested in finding a solution. The approach he suggested differed slightly from my own, but I hoped we could count on his support when the going got rough.

We adjourned the second day of our hearings at 12:05 p.m.; our plans were to await the outcome of the American Bar Association meeting. If the ABA ratified our proposal, we would be off and running. Our hearings would reconvene with its leaders as expert witnesses in our behalf.

In the meantime, we continued our efforts to secure additional cosponsors. My colleagues must have felt like hiding when they saw me. Time and again, I would ask them the same thing: "Have you decided to add your name to our amendment for Presidential succession and disability?"

I held one long conversation with the Majority Whip, Senator Hubert Humphrey of Minnesota. It would be a real asset to have Senator Humphrey on our side. He was one of the most eloquent men in Congress, and a real crusader for worthy causes. Later, of course, Humphrey would be even more intimately connected to the problem of Presidential disability, for he would be Vice President when Lyndon Johnson was under anesthesia during his gall-bladder removal. I was not at all surprised to learn that the senator from Minnesota had already given the matter considerable thought. He had solicited the opinions of many political scientists throughout the country, and was making his own study of the problem. The questions he asked me were both numerous and pertinent. I left his office with the knowledge that here was a man who was highly conversant with the problem, and anxious to solve it. I could only hope that his deliberations would, in the end, lead him to support our proposal.

In an effort to increase public awareness of the problem and to create support for our amendment, I had addressed letters to various legal scholars and public figures, among them former Presidents Harry S. Truman and Dwight D. Eisenhower and former Vice President Richard M. Nixon. Toward the end of January I received a call from Frank McKinney, who had been Democratic National Chairman and was now a prominent banker in Indianapolis. McKinney, a close confidant of Truman, expressed the opinion that the former President would be happy to appear and testify before the committee. I was excited by this prospect. Truman was one of the living Americans who had had actual experience serving as Chief Executive while a Vice-Presidential vacancy existed. During the crucial period at the end of the war, he had known the difficulties that faced a new President who had just succeeded from the Vice Presidency. Furthermore, he had indicated a strong interest in the problem of Presidential succession. It was his leadership that had changed the line of succession from the Cabinet to the Speaker and President pro tempore.

We quickly sent off a letter to the Truman Library in Independence, Missouri, inviting the former President to testify before our subcommittee; a few days later we received a reply, and it was brief and to the point. We would find, it said, that the whole problem had been adequately dealt with during the Truman administration—that is, by the 1947 succession law. Yet it was obvious to even the most casual student of the problems of Presidential succession and disability that President Truman's efforts had not, indeed, even considered two of the most critical problems presently before the committee. Still unanswered were the questions of what to do in the event of a Vice-Presidential vacancy, and how to handle Presidential disability. President Truman's letter, then, could do us very little good—in fact, it could actually injure us. Thus we decided not even to insert the letter into the record. It could not help us, and we did not want to embarrass the former President.

Early in February, we received a reply to the invitation we had sent President Eisenhower:

> Thank you very much for your letter of January twenty-fourth. Because of the fact that I am spending the winter in Southern California, it would be exceedingly difficult for me to appear before your committee in the near future.
>
> However, I would suggest that if the Committee would like a personal letter from me on this subject I shall be glad to send you my convictions, which have been somewhat modified since I last expressed myself publicly on this matter.

Following the receipt of this message from the former Chief Executive, I called Herb Brownell, who had served as Attorney General under President Eisenhower; he promised to secure from the former President a letter that would generally support the principles of the ABA consensus.

As we contacted potential witnesses during this break in the hearings, we kept the following criteria in mind: What was their position on the amendment? How would they express it? What would their impact be on the political and academic community? And finally, did they have national appeal—to what extent would their support gather publicity for our undertaking? This last was particularly important because, as the tragic events of Dallas faded in people's minds, we were afraid that the urgency of the problem would begin to seem less acute.

At this time, too, we were able to move our subcommittee work to new quarters—of a sort. We had been pressing the Rules Committee for working space and finally, on February 12, we were assigned a tiny, triangular room on the fourth floor of the Old Senate Office Building. The new constitutional amendments subcommittee office was a former rest room which had been equipped with office furniture and telephones. It was better than nothing, of course, but still very cramped. At the end of the year, when I presented my subcommittee budget for 1965, I invited the members of the Rules Committee to come and see the work we were doing in these tiny quarters—if they promised not to all come at once.

On February 17, I was scheduled to speak at the ABA House of Delegates meeting in Chicago. This meeting would decide the ABA's position on succession and disability, and would influence the course of our remaining hearings. The meeting meant a great deal to us, and I was nervous about the outcome of the vote. The ABA could do us immeasurable good if they supported us, and on the other hand nothing could be more harmful to our cause than a group of constitutional experts discussing constitutional law—when they were not on our side.

It had been planned that I would address a luncheon of state bar presidents, and thus have an opportunity to present a strong argument just before the voting. I knew that it would be a tight squeeze getting there, since I had been attending a British-American parliamentary conference in Bermuda, but our plans called for a razor-thin on-time arrival in Chicago. Unfortunately, our plane experienced flight difficulties. After their first panic on hearing the news, Don Channell and Lowell Beck of the ABA staff coolheadedly rescheduled my speech. When I arrived I was surprised to find myself addressing, not only the bar presidents, but a plenary session of the entire delegate body. After my remarks there was a short debate, and then the vote was called for. Sitting there with the other visiting guests, I held my breath. When the votes were tallied, the results were difficult to believe, but it was true: the ABA had unanimously endorsed S.J. Res. 139. I was jubilant; now that we had the House of Delegates behind us, the individual ABA members could come back before our subcommittee, as we had hoped, and testify in an official capacity.

Meanwhile, back in Washington, Conrad had been compiling a list of expert witnesses who could give us a broad base of testimony for our second round of hearings. Upon my return to the Capitol we checked the schedules of other subcommittee members to see which dates would be convenient for the most people. Then plans were made for the hearings to run four more days—February 24, 25, and 28, and March 5.

When the committee reconvened on the morning of February 24, 1964, we seized the advantage that the ABA action had given us, by beginning with testimony from two of the Bar Association's leaders, President Walter Craig and President-elect Lewis Powell. Craig's testimony started by outlining the contents of the consensus which, he said, had been reviewed thoroughly by the ABA Committee on Jurisprudence and Law Reform prior to its favorable recommendation to the House of Delegates. He went on to tell of the ABA's plans to conduct "an extensive nationwide educational program during the next few months on the need for clarification of procedure to be followed in the event of the President's inability and the need for providing a method in filling a vacancy in the office of Vice President." A committee of distinguished lawyers would be appointed to conduct this national program, which would begin with a conference in Washington to acquaint the leaders of national civic and professional organizations with the issue and the need for action.

Lewis Powell was next to testify. He explained in detail the reasoning behind the ABA conference consensus and gave strong support to the main emphasis of S.J. Res. 139. The problems of disability and succession, he pointed out, had been discussed through the years, but no action had ever been taken. The question now was not whether to act—everyone agreed on that—but how best to meet the need.

"It is not necessary," he went on, "that we find a solution free from all reasonable objections or which covers every conceivable situation. It is unlikely that such a solution will ever be found, as the problems are inherently complex and difficult." He concluded that it was "the hope and strong recommendation of the American Bar Association, which we know is shared by this subcommittee, that past differences be reconciled and that a solution be initiated by this session of Congress."

After Powell presented his prepared statement, he was questioned by Senator Keating, who, just prior to Wally Craig's testimony, had commented that he would be very much interested to hear the ABA's reasons for its change of position in endorsing S.J. Res. 139 instead of the broad, enabling approach of his own S.J. Res. 35. Mr. Powell now replied to that earlier comment. "Senator, I would say that in my view we may have evolved some. I do not think we have changed our mind basically." Powell admitted that when he had attended the ABA panel meeting in January, he had started out as an advocate of the Keating proposal, but after listening to the debate, "I swung around to feeling that in view of all the circumstances, it probably is desirable to include in the amendment itself self-implementing provisions to guard against the contingency that Congress may not act."

Senator Keating hastened to reply, "We are all malleable and we are all entitled to change our minds. I have no criticism of the change in position." But he continued, "I consider that the consensus evolved now differs drastically from the recommendation made by the American Bar Association twice for the enactment of Senate Joint Resolution 35."

Obviously disappointed with the way the ABA endorsement had gone, Ken Keating made it clear that his main reason for advocating the broad approach was his fear that a more detailed amendment would not be passed by the state legislatures. He was especially worried that there would be vigorous dissent over the provision outlining the manner of declaring Presidential disability. Keating was of the opinion that many state legislators would prefer a blue-ribbon commission to decide when the President was disabled, instead of the Vice President and Cabinet. The simpler the amendment, the more likely, in his opinion, was its passage by the states. Powell replied that he thought it probable that the states would follow the judgment of Congress, whichever approach was adopted.

At this point, I felt it was important to express my own thoughts, even though I was hesitant to step into what was obviously a very delicate situation. Senator Keating was thoroughly convinced of the relative merits of his proposal, S.J. Res. 35. But eventually I hoped we could secure his support for the approach of our S. J. Res. 139, if it were adopted by the Judiciary Committee. I certainly did not want to antagonize him, but neither did I want the record to intimate that by my silence I concurred in his opinion. Thus, I ventured to interrupt the colloquy between Lewis Powell and the senator from New York.

While I conceded that S.J. Res. 35 would be a first step toward solving the question of Presidential inability, I briefly pointed out that it did not deal with the problem of Vice-Presidential vacancies. I knew that the appropriate place for the two of us to debate the relative merits of the two bills was in a committee meeting, not a public hearing, but I did want to make my position very clear at that time.

The witness immediately following Powell was Martin Taylor, a member of the Bar Association conference study group and a longtime supporter of the approach of Senator Keating's S.J. Res. 35. His testimony quickly disclosed that he did not yet subscribe to the consensus adopted by the ABA conference. Taylor still felt that a broad, non-specific amendment was preferable to our proposal, which he found too complicated and thus in violation of the basic principles of constitutional law.

These principles—and the ensuing desire not to write specifics into the Constitution—were to be cited time and again in hearings and floor debate by opponents of our measure. It is generally believed that one reason our Constitution has adapted itself so well to the changes of time has been its breadth of language and its open-endedness. It is a statement of broad principles, which are then implemented by more explicit laws. However, there are a few areas in which the Constitution does specify details. My own feeling was that including specific procedures in the Constitution was important in this particular case.

The original Constitution went into great detail to describe the specifics required in establishing a procedure by which the President of the United States should be elected. Equally specific details were provided in the Constitution for the President's impeachment or removal from office. Our founding fathers realized that the powers of the Presidency were so great that they should not be subject to the political whims of a mere majority of the Congress; hence changes in these provisions required the two-thirds vote of Congress that was needed to amend the Constitution itself. The choice of a Vice President when that office becomes vacant and the possible removal of a President because he might be disabled also are part of the disposition of Presidential power. Therefore, in my judgment, it was imperative to give the transmittal of Presidential power in these instances the same protection accorded elsewhere in the Constitution.

During the next three days of our hearings—February 25, February 28, and March 5—many other distinguished legal and academic experts, including several who had participated in the ABA deliberations, testified before us. Many supported the principles of S.J. Res. 139; others, of course, opposed it in some or all of its aspects. Among the latter were some political scientists who felt strongly that no change at all should be made in the existing private disability agreement. Others put forth varying proposals of their own.

Testifying in support of our proposal were Harvard law professor Paul A. Freund, former Attorneys General Herbert Brownell and Francis Biddle, John D. Feerick of the ABA, and Professor Ruth C. Silva of Pennsylvania State University.

Professor Freund, one of the original members of the bar conference study group, contributed his academic expertise to strengthen the public record in support of S.J. Res. 139 and whole-heartedly endorsed the ABA proposal. When Senator Keating asked him whether he personally preferred a general amendment leaving specifics to Congress or a detailed plan like S.J. Res. 139, he replied, "I should find it rather embarrassing myself to go before state legis-latures with something in the nature of a blank check to the Con-gress." He also pointed out that while our proposal set up a specific procedure, it also allowed Congress to propose a different one if that seemed advisable at some later date.

Herbert Brownell, an extremely effective witness, pointed out that the real problem was not determining Presidential inability, but rather insuring that the Vice President could take over the Presi-dent's duties "with unquestioned authority" for the period of dis-ability, and that the President could re-assume office once he re-covered. During his testimony, Brownell reminded us of something that Americans, taking constitutional guarantees so much for granted, too often tend to overlook: "Ultimately, the operation of any constitutional arrangement depends upon public opinion and upon the public's possessing a certain sense of what might be called 'constitutional morality.' " Without this sense, no procedural solu-tion would be able to provide a complete answer. We questioned Brownell a long time, to have the benefit of his experience in the Cabinet during the Eisenhower administration—a period when Presidential disability was no mere possibility, but a disturbing fact. "Is it wrong," I asked him, "that the Vice President and the Cabinet working together are not what you would call completely disin-terested parties in a matter like this? The fact that the Vice Presi-dent has been timid in the past, would this be remedied by giving him a procedure which he could follow? What is your feeling about this criticism which has been expressed?"

Brownell replied:

> If I could draw on my own experience here, I was in office at the time of President Eisenhower's heart attack. This was the first time in our generation that this problem had arisen, and, of course, there was very great disturbance throughout the country as a result of it. You will recall that when there was doubt at the beginning as

to the seriousness of his heart attack, the solution, the ad hoc solution that was called upon was to have the Vice President consult with the members of the Cabinet and from time to time make statements as to the seriousness of the situation. There never came a point where the Presidential power had to devolve upon the Vice President . . . no great international crisis was involved, Congress was not in session, there were no bills to be acted upon.

I continued the interrogration: "Did you feel any great tugging between the need to be loyal to the disabled President or the feeling that you had better not be too loyal because the Vice President might in fact soon be in authority? . . . Let us know the inner feelings of the Cabinet and how it would react in the situation." Brownell replied that, in his opinion, the first basic loyalty of the Cabinet would be to the President, "and I think that is a very good thing in consideration of this proposal [S.J. Res. 139]. Because there is one thing that the people do not want. They have elected this man and the people, the majority of the people have supported him, they want him for their President and they do not want to take any chances of usurpation of power." He went on to say that the provisions contained in our proposal "would guard against any such rash action or any danger that the decision might be made by persons who are unfriendly to the President."

Another former Attorney General, Francis Biddle, followed Brownell to the witness chair. He strongly supported S.J. Res. 139's provision for filling Vice-Presidential vacancies: "After all, the President does in fact nominate his Vice President at the convention." He also said he was more inclined than not to trust the Cabinet and the Congress to act responsibly in a time of crisis. Members of the Supreme Court, he believed, should not be asked to solve the problem of disability. "It is not so much, I think, the technical separation of powers as what it does to the court psychologically. The Court has a good deal of criticism to meet. . . . To add to that burden by giving them other jobs seems to me particularly unwise."

John D. Feerick, who had been extremely valuable in leading the ABA conference toward the final consensus, did his part, as we knew he would, to help us in writing a solid legislative record. His first point was that a constitutional amendment, rather than a statute, was needed, "to eliminate all uncertainty and doubt on the question." He said the ABA panel believed that if a legislative solution were enacted, it would possibly be subject to constitutional challenge "which would come very likely during a time of inability—when we could least afford it." It was, he added, the opinion of most of the panel that the Vice President already had the constitutional power to determine inability; thus this power could not be taken from him by legislation.

He then turned to an explanation of the reasoning behind the various sections of the panel consensus. The provision for the Vice President assuming the powers and duties of the Presidency in cases of inability, but assuming the office in cases of death, resignation, and removal, would give constitutional recognition to the Tyler precedent,[2] he said.

Next, Feerick pointed out the advantages of the proposed method for allowing the Vice President, with majority approval of the Cabinet, to determine Presidential disability if the President could not or would not do so. This approach would allow the Vice President to play a role in the decision without giving him the sole power of determination. It would also enlist the participation of the Cabinet, which would be close to the President and thus likely to be aware of an inability. The ABA panel also felt the public would have confidence in the Cabinet, and that this approach would involve no violation of the principle of separation of powers.

Commenting on the panel's recommendation that Congress be empowered to substitute another body in place of the Cabinet to function with the Vice President in making disability decisions—an item that had been included to get broader support for our proposed amendment—Feerick admitted that he personally would like to keep Congress out of the matter altogether. He then refuted the main objections which were being made to the panel's consensus—that a detailed amendment would not conform to the rule that the Constitution should contain only general principles, and that it would never receive the necessary approval by three-fourths of the state legislatures. "I disagree with this position most emphatically," Feerick said. "The Constitution is quite specific as to the election of the President and as to how he may be removed. Thus, it is clearly consistent with the provisions dealing with the Presidency to em-

[2] See Chapter I, p. 15.

body the method of determining inability in an amendment." As for the question of state ratification, he felt that "to give Congress carte blanche authority to adopt by legislation any method it saw fit might have even less chance of passage." But he felt, as I certainly did, that the main difficulty about an enabling amendment was that merely giving Congress power to establish a method for determining disability was no solution in itself. "A method would [then] have to be agreed upon by Congress—and that could take years."

Professor Ruth C. Silva, the author of the book *Presidential Succession*, further strengthened our case when she discussed some of the more controversial provisions of our proposal. One objection to S.J. Res. 139 centered upon the possibility of open dispute between the President and Vice President over the former's ability to perform the duties of his office. Professor Silva believed it would be "naive" to expect a public disagreement of this sort. Moreover, our requirement for a two-thirds vote of both houses of Congress to keep the President from reassuming his powers and duties would, in her opinion, be a sufficiently heavy majority to protect the integrity of the office.

She agreed with us that the Cabinet was the proper body to act with the Vice President in specifying the President's disability, adding that "a commission would be an affront to the Presidency." The problem, she said, was not basically a medical one, but rather "political medicine." She cited as evidence the case of President Wilson, whose attending neuropsychiatrist, Dr. F. X. Dercum, had refused to declare disability, largely because of his own views on the Versailles Treaty and his opinion of Vice President Marshall— and further because of his belief that such a declaration would be bad for the patient.

Professor Silva objected vigorously to Senator Keating's proposal to elect two Vice Presidents. The electorate, she pointed out, does not really vote for the Vice President, since there is no way of voting for a Presidential candidate without voting also for his running mate. Therefore, if there were more than one Vice President, a political party would probably use the additional office for reconciling various factions of the party—thus increasing the chances that whoever succeeded to the Presidency would represent a different faction and different policies from those of the President.

Our subcommittee also, of course, took testimony from several political scientists who had strong objections to the principles of S.J. Res. 139. One of these was Professor James McGregor Burns, an outstanding author and the official biographer of John F. Kennedy. Burns, who then was chairman of the political science department of Williams College, a month earlier had published an article in *The Saturday Evening Post* called "Let's Stop Gambling With the Presidency." Burns came quickly to the point of his testimony.

In his opinion, a decision about inability could not be made by the Vice President, the Cabinet, or Congress. "Cabinet members would want to be loyal to their stricken Chief, but they would also want to support—and perhaps cultivate—the Vice President," he said. Furthermore, "the Vice President is the worst person to decide Presidential inability. Not because he would want to make a grab for power—though this is always possible—but the opposite: he would hesitate to take any action that would give an appearance of overeagerness or that might be used against him in the next election." And Congress was "a big, cumbersome body that might not be in session, a slow-moving body that would doubtless argue for weeks over the matter. Worst of all it might turn the whole question into a great public brawl."

Instead, Professor Burns proposed "a Presidential commission composed of the Chief Justice, the two ranking Cabinet members at the time (State and Treasury), the Speaker of the House, and the President pro tempore of the Senate." Each member would designate one member of a physicians' panel to report the medical facts. The commission could certify the Vice President as acting President and later restore the President to his office—or else, if necessary, certify the Vice President not merely as acting President but as full President.

"Such a commission," Burns said, "could act intelligently and authoritatively. It could be convened quickly . . . and it would have the confidence of the Nation." Furthermore, the disabled President's interests, both Houses of Congress, and the political neutrality of the Supreme Court would all be represented.

Professor Richard Neustadt, of the Department of Government at Columbia University, testified strongly against any sort of constitutional amendment to deal with the problem of disability.

"The arrangements for declaring inability now in effect" seemed to him "entirely adequate"; nor did he see any reason to vest the responsibility of declaring Presidential inability in anyone other than the Vice President. Neustadt, author of the book *Presidential Power*, based this opinion on his strong belief that there should be no interference with the Presidential prerogatives and freedom of action. He could not conceive of "any form of commission, including the Cabinet, being given constitutional power to put a President out of office, which is an interference with the practical political power of a sitting President." If any group had authority to remove the President, he said, "it would hang over the head of every incoming President," affecting his relations with every member of that decisional body.

Neustadt did reluctantly suggest a constitutional amendment to authorize the President to appoint an acting President in the event of a Vice-Presidential vacancy, with ratification by a majority vote of the Senate only. He further suggested that in his opinion a member of Congress could serve as acting President without giving up his legislative office.

On two points Neustadt was in agreement with other witnesses. He felt that no amendment or law could truly guarantee that a problem would be solved in an orderly manner unless those involved had "good will and good sense." And he believed that Senator Keating's proposal for two Vice Presidents would "multiply the difficulties inherent in the relationship."

Sidney Hyman, a well-known student of government and author of numerous works including *The American President* and the Pulitzer prizewinner *Roosevelt and Hopkins*, shared Neustadt's wariness of any legislation or amendment which would in any way weaken the President's authority. Despite the increased responsibilities the Vice President has been given, Hyman said, no Vice President is in a position "to make the yes or no decision in any great matter of state, without leave of the President." And he too stressed that no matter how carefully any proposal is framed, "the greater part of what will happen under it . . . will depend on the interplay between the constitutional morality of the nation, and the wisdom and uprightness of the chief officers of state."

Like Neustadt, Hyman believed that only the Senate, not the

House, should be given a role in filling Vice-Presidential vacancies. He was also opposed to any type of disability commission, and suggested that the discretionary power to determine disability reside in "one man who would always be the object of zealous watchfulness." That man was, in his opinion, the Vice President and only the Vice President.

After Professor Hyman had finished his testimony, I asked that a comprehensive proposal by New York's Governor Nelson Rockefeller be included in the record. Even though this proposal represented a distinct departure from our consensus, I had some regrets that it had to be presented in writing, not in person. The Governor would have been a glamorous witness, bringing to our hearings much of the press attention that I felt we needed to keep our work before the public eye. Earlier, Ken Keating, as a senator from New York, had approached me to suggest that his governor testify in person, as he was eminently qualified to do since he and his staff had given long and deep study to the problems of disability and succession.

But the situation was, I realized, a delicate one, and might have the result of making our hearings into a Republican political football. It was early 1964, and great speculation was in the air about the choice of a Republican Presidential nominee for that year's election. Senator Goldwater of Arizona, like Rockefeller himself, was a leading candidate for the nomination. Privately, I was concerned that an invitation to one potential nominee might offend senatorial supporters of the other, at a time when every bit of Senate support that we could muster for our S.J. Res. 139 was desperately needed.

To complicate things further, we had already invited Vice President Richard Nixon, himself very much a possible nominee, to testify before our subcommittee. In Nixon's case, I felt, we could hardly have done otherwise. His experiences and opinions as a former Vice President, and one who had served under a temporarily disabled President, were too valuable to dispense with.

But at the prospect of Governor Rockefeller's personal appearance, I decided we would be forced to draw the line—especially since a serious struggle seemed to be developing between the Rockefeller and Goldwater camps. Therefore, although I had great respect for the Governor's opinion and for Ken Keating's desire that he be invited to testify, and although I would have done the same thing in Ken's place, I had to tell him that the committee could not find time to schedule the Governor's testimony. Instead, we inserted into the record his written proposal, in the form of a letter to me. It began:

> Your subcommittee is taking testimony on a matter of vital concern to the American people—the urgent and critical questions of succession which would arise in the event of the death or inability of the President. . . . Based upon many years' experience in Government, I would like to comment upon the matter . . . and submit suggestions for the consideration of your subcommittee.

Based upon a proposal Rockefeller had originally made in 1960, the letter suggested that the President appoint a "First Secretary of the Government to assist the President in the exercise of his constitutional responsibility and authority in the area of national security and international affairs." The appointment should be confirmed by the Senate. The First Secretary would exercise authority as delegated by the President, be a member of the Cabinet, preside in the absence of the President and Vice President, and serve as executive chairman of the National Security Council. He would be first in line of succession after the Vice President, with the remaining members of the Cabinet after him. No Constitutional amendment would be necessary for his appointment, Rockefeller wrote, since it would be the same as creating a new Cabinet position.

Pending a permanent solution to the problem of disability by means of a Constitutional amendment, Rockefeller proposed that the present agreement be altered to provide that in case of dispute, "the beginning and ending of the President's inability be determined by the Chief Justice of the United States" after consultation with medical experts. Some authority other than the Chief Justice might ultimately be more appropriate, the New York governor admitted, but the most important thing was to agree upon such an authority in advance.

We also inserted other letters and proposals into the record.[3] Like that of Governor Rockefeller, all had obviously been the product of great study on the part of the senators and legal scholars who contributed them.

The next week began with very good news indeed. On Mon-

[3] See Appendix, pp. 360–361.

day we heard that Senator Humphrey's extensive individual study of the succession-disability problem had resulted in his decision to throw his support behind our resolution. And later that week, new support came from another area: I received a very welcome letter from Michael H. Cardozo, Executive Director of the Association of American Law Schools, stating that the Association wished to go on record as endorsing the provisions of the ABA consensus.

On Tuesday, March 3, Herbert Brownell's promise to us materialized in the form of the long-awaited letter from President Eisenhower. Fully aware of how much this could mean to us, I excitedly read through the thoughts of the former President.

> Regarding the matter of Presidential succession, I favor the law that existed before 1947 over the one now controlling, but after reflection I have come to believe that a better method of handling this matter might well be adopted.
>
> I suggest that at any time a Vice President succeeds to the Presidency he should immediately nominate another individual as Vice President to fill the vacancy with the nomination to be approved, preferably, by both bodies of the Congress rather than merely by the Senate.
>
> Should such an event occur during recess of Congress, I believe that a special session should be promptly called so that there could be no question that public opinion as represented by the Congress, would approve of the new President's nominee.
>
> The question of determining Presidential disability and the action to be taken seem to me to be more complicated. Many systems have been proposed but each seems to be so cumbersome in character as to preclude prompt action in emergency. My personal conclusion is that the matter should be left strictly to the two individuals concerned, the President and the Vice President, subject possibly to a concurring majority opinion of the President's Cabinet.
>
> A disability could be of different kinds, one caused by physical or mental illness, or another by an absence from the seat of government of such a character that would preclude Presidential decisions and action in time of emergency. Wherever possible I believe that a President's disability should be acknowledged and announced by himself. If circumstances made this impossible I think the Vice President should voluntarily step forward, announce the disability, and with the concurrence of a majority of the Cabinet, assume the Presidential responsibilities and duties. However, I believe it should be made clear that in this case the Vice President is merely an "Acting President" and would require no new oath of office and would receive no Presidential emoluments.

Reading this far in the lengthy letter, I was jubilant. We could not possibly have asked for more. Ike had come out squarely in favor of our proposal to fill a Vice-Presidential vacancy. On the problem of disability—of which he had had the direct experience which would give weight to his words—he had endorsed us one hundred per cent. That would be powerful persuasion for reluctant legislators! I went on reading—and my spirits plummeted.

> The end of the disability would be determined by the President himself upon his declaration in writing that he was ready to resume his office. Should there be any dispute between the President and the Vice President as to whether the former was ready to resume his duties and the Cabinet should agree with the Vice President, then the Vice President should continue to serve for the time being, while the matter should go to a commission comprised of the three senior members of the Cabinet, the Speaker of the House of Representatives, and the leader of the minority party in the House, the President pro tem of the Senate, and the leader of the minority party in the Senate, and four medical personnel recognized by the American Medical Association as competent in their fields and whose function it would be to advise the other members of the commission. Each member of the medical portion of the commission should be selected and requested to serve by a majority vote of the Cabinet.
>
> I should add that the chance is very remote that such a dispute might occur for the simple reason that we must assume that in these serious affairs the individuals concerned would be men of good will, concerned with the welfare of the Nation as a whole. The only possibility to be feared is that a President might become so mentally deranged that his personal convictions regarding his recovery might be logically doubted by reasonable men, thus requiring a decision of a kind that a politically and medically competent commission could make. However, again recognizing the value of public opinion, I believe that the findings of the entire commission might well be submitted to both Houses of the Congress for approval.

I had been too quick to rejoice. Here—in the area most loaded with political controversy, the occasion of possible disagreement between President and Vice President over the former's ability to perform his task—Ike had suggested a commission to solve the problem. Not only that, but the commission he proposed was made up in a more complicated way than any other that had been suggested to the committee! I finished reading the letter:

There is, of course, no completely foolproof method covering every contingency and every possibility that could arise in the circumstances now under discussion. We must trust that men of good will and common sense, operating within constitutional guidelines governing these matters, will make such decisions that their actions will gain and hold the approval of the mainstream of American thinking.

Still, I thought, after the first stab of disappointment had passed, even with his recommendation of a commission, the Eisenhower letter could be a great asset to us. After all, we *had* scored on two out of three of his recommendations; and the third was so loosely worded that it was almost impossible to imagine that it could be implemented.

Now how could we use the Eisenhower message to best advantage? That afternoon Senator Keating and I were invited to discuss the problem of Presidential disability and succession before a Junior Chamber of Commerce Leadership meeting in the Caucus Room of the Old Senate Office Building. This, it seemed to me, would be the right time to announce receipt of the letter.

After Ken and I held a spirited discussion of our differing views before the Jaycees, I closed my rebuttal by describing the contents of Ike's letter. I also mentioned, in passing, that our hearings would come to a close on the Thursday of that week, and that the last witness to appear before the committee would be the former Vice President, Richard Nixon.

But to my great embarrassment, I discovered after the meeting that Senator Keating had either never been informed, or perhaps had forgotten, that Nixon was scheduled to appear before us in two days. Ken was frantic. He was planning to attend the funeral of the wife of Robert Wagner, New York City's mayor, on the day of Nixon's appearance. Couldn't we schedule Nixon to appear another time?

We immediately got in touch with the former Vice President's office, but were told that there could be no guarantee of Mr. Nixon's appearance at any date other than the one we had decided upon. This was distressing news. I did not want to leave Ken Keating out of our plans, but Nixon's thoughts on the succession-disability issue were simply too essential to risk eliminating. Therefore, with profuse apologies to Ken Keating, we had to go ahead with our original plans; but we provided that Keating's assistant Abbott Leban be present to deliver a brief statement on his Senator's behalf just prior to the Nixon testimony. I deeply regretted the whole misunderstanding. Indeed no one could have anticipated the untimely death of Mrs. Wagner. But Senator Keating was a member of the subcommittee and one of the most devoted congressional students of the problem we were trying to solve. I thought it imperative to consult him on all our activities—and, if possible, to find some way of persuading him to throw his support to S.J. Res. 139. To be sure, he felt strongly about the merits of his own proposal; but I knew he felt even more strongly that we must arrive at some solution. In the final analysis, I hoped that he would support such a solution even if it could not be his own.

There was another area in which we lacked support so far. Up to the last day of our subcommittee hearings, no official word had been received from the Johnson administration concerning the succession-disability issue. I had addressed a letter to the President, informing him of our investigation and soliciting his thoughts, but I had also made it clear that the subcommittee would fully understand if, under the circumstances, he withheld comment at this time. Yet we *were* worried that critics of our resolution might make much of the fact that our hearings included no testimony from the top legal official in the administration, Deputy Attorney General Nicholas deB. Katzenbach.

Strange as it may seem, however, we had intentionally refrained from inviting the Attorney General to testify. During the Kennedy administration, he had been one of the leading draftsmen of the broad approach contained in S.J. Res. 35. For him to reaffirm his earlier position before our subcommittee would certainly do us no good; in fact, it could disrupt the consensus we had developed thus far. Furthermore, as Larry Conrad had learned from conversations with Katzenbach's assistants, it would be uncomfortable for the most highly placed lawyer in the nation to find himself in opposition to the American Bar Association, now that their consensus backed the approach of our S.J. Res. 139. In addition, his boss, the President, had not yet taken a stand on the complicated subject.

But the records of our hearings could not entirely ignore the views of someone so eminent and so conversant with the issue. Therefore, we decided simply to introduce into the committee record a copy of Katzenbach's June 18, 1963, testimony before the subcommittee when it was chaired by Senator Kefauver. This was done with no comment about the testimony and no mention to the press. We still hoped for some endorsement of our approach from the Johnson administration, and such an endorsement would be more difficult to come by if the Attorney General were again required to give personal testimony supporting a contrary position.

Thursday, March 5, the last day of our hearings, was a red-letter day for us. We had planned our timing as carefully as if we were staging a play. The hearing would open with our last academic witness, Clinton Rossiter, the John L. Senior Professor of American Institutions at Cornell University. While Rossiter was testifying, a special staff assistant would be at Washington National Airport, and at 10:30 would meet Richard Nixon's plane, then—complete with police escort—would hurry him to the New Senate Office Building. Upon his arrival, we intended to recess temporarily, and greet the former Vice President in my office. All the subcommittee members, as well as the press, had been notified of these plans, and when I arrived in the room to begin the hearings I found it swarming with activity. There were crowds of spectators—the way I had imagined it would be on the first day of the hearings. The witness table was bathed in the glare of floodlights. Television cameras seemed to be sprouting out of the woodwork. One of the members of the subcommittee, Hiram Fong of Hawaii, had even brought his own cameraman. As a candidate for re-election that fall, he wanted to be sure of obtaining pictures of himself with the former Vice President, who was now the titular head of the GOP.

Clinton Rossiter, author of *The American Presidency* as well as other books, proved to be an excellent witness. He delivered a comprehensive and detailed statement in two parts, one on Presidential disability, the other on Presidential succession. He began with a five-point criterion of disability: (1) the President should have the right to declare his own disability and bestow his powers and duties upon the Vice President, or the next in succession if there is no Vice President; (2) if the President is unable to declare his own disability, the Vice President should have the initiative to do so; (3) in the event of disability, the Vice President should only act as President; (4) the President should be able to recover his powers and duties at any time simply by informing the Vice President that his disability no longer exists; and (5) disability should be defined as any *de facto* inability, whatever the cause or duration, if it occurs at a time when executive action is urgently required.

Professor Rossiter then admitted that these points added nothing to the situation as it then existed. A congressional resolution or constitutional amendment incorporating these principles could "help clear the air of doubt," he said, but he himself did not like constitutional amendments, particularly any detailed law or amendment that would attempt to provide for all eventualities that might arise. He concurred with President Eisenhower's view in urging that "we think very carefully before we go beyond the President and Vice President in search of machinery to decide doubtful cases of disability." While he was willing to consider bringing Congress into the matter, he was very much against giving the Supreme Court or the Chief Justice any role. He also opposed any form of Presidential disability commission.

Indeed, Rossiter continued, in one sense, "perhaps the most important sense, the problem of disability is quite insoluble." No matter what law might be in effect, "a period of clearly established Presidential disability in any case is going to be a messy situation, one in which caution, perhaps even timidity, must mark the posture of an acting President."

At this point I interjected a question. Didn't history show, I asked, that in the situations faced by Arthur and Marshall, the Vice President had plenty of evidence to act on, and "if we had given him a good crutch to lean upon such as the Cabinet, and if we had clearly established a procedure in the Constitution, both probably would have acted?"

"I don't think Vice President Marshall would have acted in a hundred years," Professor Rossiter replied. "His one opinion was that we needed a five-cent cigar." It was unimaginable to him that Marshall could have taken over the powers of Woodrow Wilson, that "giant figure," "the first American President to have, in the best sense of the word, a jealousy of his position and prerogatives." In short, no matter how careful a law were to be drafted, Rossiter did not think that we could "plug all the holes."

He had equally definite opinions on the problem of succession, objecting both to Senator Keating's proposal for a second Vice President and to Governor Rockefeller's suggestion of a First Secretary. After enumerating several of the other methods that had been proposed to fill a vice-presidential vacancy, and giving his reasons for rejecting each, he endorsed our provision of nomination by the President and confirmation by one or both houses of Congress. Such a method, he said, would insure continuity and legitimacy. With President and Congress working together on the problem we could expect "a real display of statesmanship."

I had been listening with great interest to Professor Rossiter's well-informed testimony; but suddenly Larry Conrad was at my elbow, telling me in an urgent whisper, "Senator, we've got a real emergency! There's just been word from the airport that the fog's so bad the Nixon plane can't land. What shall we do?"

What *could* we do? There went all our careful timing. We had arranged no extra witnesses to fill any possible gap. I answered, "We'll just have to stretch the testimony out as long as we can, and hope that somehow the plane can get down soon. Make sure the airport keeps us advised so we'll know how to time things on this end."

Thus, Professor Rossiter was subjected to an unusually long cross-examination. The exchange of ideas was stimulating, and his penetrating views—often in contrast with our own—made a lively contribution to the record. Yet I must admit that during the questioning I kept imagining that I heard the former Vice President's plane, circling and circling overhead. There we all were on the ground, waiting eagerly, television cameras at the ready, press people everywhere—all powerless to do anything to help!

Finally it seemed unfair to impose on Professor Rossiter's time any longer. I thanked him for his testimony, and he was excused. Then, as a holding tactic, I decided to read into the record a letter from Dr. Paul Dudley White, the noted heart specialist who had served as President Eisenhower's personal physician during the President's critical heart attack. The pressure of his work, Dr. White said, made it impossible for him to testify personally, but he was happy to give his support to the ABA consensus: "I am in complete accord with their recommendations and I don't believe that the medical problem would be great. Naturally, as occurred when I was asked to see President Eisenhower, there is a group of doctors in charge of the patient and it is they who give the advice to the Vice President and others in the government as to what should be done medically."

By the time I finished reading the letter in its entirety, there was still no word from Richard Nixon. It would now be impossible to greet the former Vice President in my office with all the social and political amenities we had anticipated. Instead, he would have to come straight to the committee room and we would meet him there.

I hastily told my committee staff to call off the red-carpet treatment for Nixon and inform all the subcommittee members of this change in plans. We were able to round up most of them in time; but strangely enough, the word never reached the Minority Leader, Everett McKinley Dirksen. My receptionist told me later that he had arrived in my office right on schedule. Unflustered when she told him of our change in plans, he took a seat in the reception room, accepted her offer of coffee and cookies, and, in true Dirksen fashion, proceeded for the best part of an hour to regale my staff and visiting constituents with tales of his more memorable experiences in the Senate. The blow-by-blow account of his recent ulcer operation had his impromptu audience breathless. As far as we knew, he never even caught a glimpse of our star witness. There was speculation later that the wily senator's unawareness of our revised schedule was calculated to avoid embarrassing questions from the press, during an election year, about the future of the GOP and the in-fighting presently going on within the party. In retrospect this speculation seems improbable because, as Senate Minority Leader, Dirksen was always available to the press.

But while all this was going on in my reception room, things were hardly so relaxed in the crowded committee room. The spectators were getting restless. At long last, Conrad came in to inform me that the plane had landed and Nixon was on his way. Still, it would be twenty minutes or so before we could expect him to arrive. Perhaps the police escort would shave off a precious five minutes, but we were still left with nothing to do until he arrived. Television crewmen were glancing anxiously at their watches, knowing that they were already late for their next assignments. Conrad kept them informed minute by minute, hoping to hold them until our star witness arrived. I knew that Nixon's testimony could reawaken national interest, and hoped against hope that the TV boys would stay long enough to give him play on the evening news across the country.

As a last resort, I dug through my files and, slowly and painstakingly, read President Eisenhower's letter into the record, word for word. I had known that letter would be useful to us in many ways, but had certainly never thought that this would be one of its benefits.

Still no Richard Nixon! I had no more delaying tactics left. Just as I was getting ready to announce a committee recess, there was a flurry of activity outside the door. Now I *could* call a recess, but for a different reason: to give the former Vice President time to make his way through the mass of reporters and onlookers at the doorway. The subcommittee members were there to meet him; each of us formally welcomed the Vice President as pictures were taken from every angle. Finally, Mr. Nixon was conducted to the witness chair.

For the first time, I had the chance personally to see Richard Nixon in action. He was, of course, a member of the opposite political party, so that in working to help elect John Kennedy in 1960 I had, in effect, been opposing Richard Nixon. But—as we had reasoned earlier in inviting him to testify—the present occasion was a time for sober deliberation, when traditional political considerations were put aside.

And Richard Nixon made an exceptional witness. He spoke entirely without notes. Articulate and well-organized, his statement was, in my opinion, the most effective of our entire series of hearings. With his experience as Vice President, he clearly knew what he was talking about when he said:

> I would like to begin by stating that, in my opinion, the hearings being conducted by this committee are the most important hearings from the standpoint of the country that are being conducted in Washington today.

Others are more sensational, others may have greater, shall we say, political effect, but these hearings involve the future of the United States as no other hearings perhaps in recent years have.

It was only human to feel a sense of personal gratification that the former Vice President shared our opinion about the importance of the work that we were trying to do. He went on:

> . . . The time has come to remedy the constitutional flaw with regard to the Office of the Presidency itself in respect both to succession and to disability.
> I say the time has come because the American people, as a result of the assassination of President Kennedy, and as a result prior to that time of President Eisenhower's illnesses, . . . are aware of the problem. They believe that something should be done about it but the more time that is allowed to elapse between those events the less urgency for it will be felt by the American people and, of course, by the Congress to get action to deal with these problems.

Mr. Nixon first discussed the problem of succession. He reminded the committee, the Congress, and the nation of several general principles: the new law or amendment should be written "not for the problem of the moment, but for posterity"; the office of Vice President should always be filled, since the Vice President "generally is best qualified to succeed to the Presidency" by virtue of his participation in all the major executive decisions. "He is qualified to take over as President as no one else, not the Speaker, not the Secretary of State, no one else in the country, is prepared to take over." In addition, the Vice President has come to serve a useful function in government, in helping the President handle some of his many tasks. "This could not have been said perhaps even 25 years ago. But it can be said today, and clearly apart from the fact that the Vice President is the man that I think is best qualified to be President in the event the President became incapacitated."

The former Vice President went on to propose that the electoral college be reconvened in the event of a vacancy in the office of Vice President. This body, with the recommendation of the President, would select a new Vice President. I was startled at this suggestion, because I personally felt the electoral college was archaic at its best, and at its worst could be disastrous. Even at that moment I had been contemplating with my staff the advisability of introducing another amendment which would entirely do away with the electoral college and let the people of the nation choose the President by popular vote. Why, then, reinvigorate this system, to serve in the emergency situation we were studying?

The former Vice President continued without so much as a pause. The plan had its flaws, he admitted, and other witnesses during the hearings had pointed some of these out. But he went on to cite what he believed to be its merits; the electoral college, as distinct from Congress, would always contain a majority from the President's own party.

> The Congress 20 per cent of the time during the history of our country has been under the control of a party other than that of the President of the United States. It seems to me then that the electoral college has that advantage over the Congress as the elective body which will select or approve the selection of the new Vice President.

Furthermore, Nixon added, in being chosen by the electoral college, the new Vice President would take office by means of the elective process, rather than the appointive one. But whether the Vice President was approved by the electoral college or by Congress, the President should have the right to have as his second-in-command a member of his own party. I was, of course, very much pleased to learn that the former Vice President was not strongly opposed to the idea of Congress being the ratifying body, so long as the President could have some choice in the matter.

Richard Nixon then turned to the second of the two vexing problems we were considering—that of Presidential inability.

> There is a letter, a letter whose contents this committee, of course, is familiar with, written by the President of the United States to the next in line of succession, indicating what would happen and what procedure would go into effect in the event of disability.
>
> But that letter has no force in law whatever, and if an argument developed . . . a letter that the President may have written to the next in line of succession wouldn't mean anything at all, in my opinion.

Nixon went on to say that he generally approved of the proposals made by former Attorneys General Brownell and Rogers, as well as by President Eisenhower, with regard to disability; but he disagreed with the former President that a commission was the best means of resolving an argument over Presidential disability.

> In that particular case it is my belief that where the Vice Presi-
> dent, together with the approval of the majority of the members of the
> Cabinet, determine that the President is not able to take over the
> powers and duties of the office . . . and where the President declares
> that he is able to do so, that then that conflict should be decided by
> the Congress of the United States, and not by a commission.

We had Nixon on our side! None of us had known for sure what his
testimony would contain. President Eisenhower's recommendation
of a blue-ribbon commission had greatly alarmed me, and as the
former Vice President had approached the subject I said a brief
prayer that he wouldn't go along with Ike on that point. It seemed
my prayer had been answered. He went on to give his reasons:

> I take a very dim view of referring major constitutional problems
> of this type to commissions. Commissions are not responsive . . . to
> the electorate, and I believe that the Congress, with its committee
> system, could much better handle this situation than a commission.

In the event of a close commission vote as to whether the President
was or was not qualified to discharge the powers and duties of his
office, he continued, the confidence of the public would be badly
shaken, and "certainly whoever held that office would hold it under
a cloud, whereas, if that decision were made by the Congress, after
a hearing set up under the proper circumstances, then at least even
if the vote were close in Congress, it would represent a vote of the
people's representatives."

With that, Mr. Nixon concluded his extemporaneous testimony. He had done a fine job, and his response to the questions we
then put to him was equally illuminating. One of his most valuable
contributions stemmed from his personal experience of the duties
of the Vice Presidency. I tried to draw on that experience by reca-
pitulating his earlier thoughts:

> You pointed out the importance of the Vice Presidency today.
> The Vice President is one heartbeat away from the Chief Executive
> authority of this land, and the best successor to the President is indeed
> the Vice President. You pointed out also that the Vice President does
> have a job to do today. There has been some conflict as to whether
> we actually need a Vice President to perform duties to relieve the
> burdens presently resting on the shoulders of the President. Could
> we call on your experience, sir, to give us a general idea of what these
> duties are? How this constitutes an active, vigorous, working office
> today?

The former Vice President replied,

> Well, it is rather difficult to summarize the duties of the Vice President because, of course, those duties vary with everyone who holds the office. I would say that the least burdensome duty is, of course, the one that is included in the Constitution, of presiding over the Senate, and breaking tie votes.

During the eight years he had served in the office, Nixon said, he had cast, on the average, only one tie vote a year. The most important duties of the Vice President, in his opinion, were

> First, his participation in the deliberations of the National Security Council; his participation in the deliberations of the Cabinet; and then the increasingly great use of the Vice President as a trouble-shooter and as a representative of the President abroad in the field of foreign policy.

In addition, there were the specific commissions the President asked the Vice President to perform on occasion.

Mr. Nixon went on to say that he foresaw a future pattern of the President giving more and more functions to the Vice President, "because the burden of the Presidency, particularly with the foreign policy problems becoming more acute than they had been previously, are so great that the Vice President can and should be used more even than he has been in either the Kennedy or the Eisenhower administration." With this increasing use of the Vice President, he said, "the fundamental reason why the President should in effect name or have a veto power on who holds the office of Vice President is that a Vice President can only be as useful as a President has confidence in him." For this reason, he was strongly opposed to the modern practice of "ticket-balancing" at national conventions. He hoped, instead, that both national conventions would "think in terms of nominating two Presidents," bearing in mind not only that the Vice-Presidential nominees could become President, but also that they should closely represent the views of the President and be men the President could trust to carry out very important assignments.

Because of this developing stature of the office of Vice President, he continued, he was opposed to Senator Keating's suggestion that two Vice Presidents be elected; "when the office of Vice President has come to mean something, we shouldn't downgrade it." He gave an amusing example of such a downgrading through multi-plicity. At a dinner given recently in his honor, he said, the chair-man of the meeting had said that the occasion was the first time their guest of honor had been a Vice President. Then the next speaker, getting up to introduce Mr. Nixon, "happened to be the president of a major New York bank, and he said, 'Well, I can't say I am a bit impressed about the fact we are honoring a Vice President today. . . . After all, I head an organization that has 243 vice presidents.' "

After the laughter had subsided, Mr. Nixon went on to say, "Now, I know that in traveling abroad, for example, the United Arab Republic has four vice presidents. Several Latin American re-publics have two, and the moment you have more than one vice president, the usefulness of the Vice President to the nation has been greatly reduced."

With characteristic skill, Mr. Nixon had interwoven anecdote and example to make his point—a point which strengthened our own position. I was delighted with the direction his testimony had taken. The only thing that still troubled me was his reliance on the electoral college. We had had a continuous flow of testimony to the effect that the electoral college was an antiquated body, and would not be accepted by the public to choose a new Vice President. I personally agreed with this general opinion, and believed that Con-gress would be much more effective as the deciding body. Now I asked Mr. Nixon whether Congress might do this job as well; or would it become embroiled in politics at a time of national crisis?

The former Vice President replied that he had suggested the electoral college because of the possibility of the President having an opposition Congress. "Now, being quite specific, let's think of what might have happened in 1946 when the 80th Congress, with an overwhelming Republican majority, came in, when Mr. Truman was President. . . . It would seem that there could have been prob-lems there particularly where the Congress and the President were at odds." The important point, he went on, was that the Vice Presi-dency becomes vacant under one of two circumstances: when a President or a Vice President dies. "Now, when a President dies, I would say that the feeling in the country, the immense emo-tional impact at the death of a President, certainly by assassination and even by normal causes, is such that his successor would probably get broad support even from an opposition Congress." But if a Vice President dies in office, he said, "there isn't the emotional impact on the country that there would be if the President dies. In this instance, I would say that the opposition Congress factor might be a more real one, a more serious one."

But Mr. Nixon concluded on what was, to me, a cheering note: "The important thing here is not whether it is the electoral college or the Congress, but . . . to get one or the other, which is the consensus of the members of this committee and which this committee thinks will get the broadest public approval. Either solution is a great improvement over what we have at the present time and either, I think, over a period of time would work."

That ended the testimony of Richard Milhous Nixon. I came out from behind the big table and shook hands with the former Vice President. The people were crowding around, the room blazed again and again with flashbulbs, the television cameras were whirring away. He and I walked out of the committee room together, amid a babble of half-answered questions as breathless reporters scurried to keep up with us on our way out of the Old Senate Office Building. Outside, his car was waiting to whisk him away to the next step of a hectic day in the nation's capital.

As the former Vice President's car pulled away from the curb, I paused a minute to catch my breath. The tension of the last few hours had been tremendous. Now we could relax—at least enough to collect our thoughts. Then the next round in the battle to pass our amendment would begin—just as the last one had ended—in high gear.

As I walked toward the New Senate Office Building to return to my office, my thoughts drifted to the man who had just been driven away in the long, shiny black limousine. What an excellent witness he had been! Not only had he brought out the press in droves, and given our hearings greatly needed publicity—a far cry from the hours we had spent in the committee room with few spectators and no press response—but the contribution he had made to our hearings was of inestimable inherent value. He had exceeded our wildest expectations in throwing the weight of his experience and reflection behind the general approach of the ABA consensus and of our resolution.

In fact, I thought as I mulled over those six sessions of hearings that had stretched over the last month and a half, we had compiled a very good record generally. Admittedly, there had not been much public excitement. Many newspapers throughout the country still had little or no idea of the work we were doing. But the expert witnesses who had given us the benefit of their thought had, by and large, written a strong document of support for the general approach of Senate Joint Resolution 139. To be sure, there had been differences of opinion, but the great majority had carried further the ABA's efforts to create a consensus which could be accepted by a wide majority of the people. Our amendment was still a long way from being passed—longer, even, than we thought at that time —but our hearings had done much to bring us closer to that success.

CHAPTER 4

Progress
on Three Fronts

We were left with the excitement of the hearings behind us and facing the mundane reality that favorable testimony before a subcommittee was not the same thing as favorable action on the Senate floor—and that even passage by the Senate was only an intermediate goal. It would have been pleasant to bask in the glow of the satisfaction that the hearings—particularly Richard Nixon's contribution the last day—had given us; but we had a job to do, and we had no time to spare.

Therefore, the very next day, Larry Conrad and I attended a strategy meeting at the ABA offices in downtown Washington. This gathering, which included Ed Wright, Lewis Powell, Herb Brownell, Don Channell, Lowell Beck, Mike Spence, Ross Malone, and F. Joseph "Jiggs" Donahue, was noteworthy because Bill Foley, Chief Clerk of the House Judiciary Committee, had been invited as well. Thus, the meeting represented our first attempt at any liaison with the House of Representatives.

Prior to this, all our legislative efforts to gather support for our amendment had been concentrated upon the Senate. Indeed, the House had other concerns at the time. The House Judiciary Committee and its able chairman Emanuel Celler of New York had been working long hours trying to arrive at an acceptable immigration bill. No one knew how much longer they would be occupied with this problem. After that, what spare time remained on the committee agenda would be totally occupied by committee hearings and actions relating to the extremely controversial 1964 Civil Rights Act. Chairman Celler and his committee more than had their hands full.

Nonetheless, we felt we should begin to be in contact with the House, and this in the person of Chief Clerk Foley, Chairman Celler's good right arm on the Judiciary Committee. For our proposed constitutional amendment to become law, it would have to receive a two-thirds vote in the House as well as the Senate.

As the discussion moved around the mahogany conference table at the ABA office, each participant was exuberant about the Senate hearings and the strong base we had built to proceed with legislative action in the Senate—that is, until Bill Foley's turn came to speak. Our elation was quickly dampened as he laid his cards squarely on the table. There was, he told us, almost no likelihood of the House taking any action at all on our problem during this session. Our meeting closed less optimistically than it had begun, but none of us could deny that Bill Foley had been entirely realistic in his appraisal of the problem. The House committee agenda was already overloaded; perhaps more important, Committee Chairman Celler, an extremely powerful figure in the House, had been silent on his own feelings about the question. None of us, we realized, had any idea what Mannie Celler's opinion was on the matter. I told myself we had some missionary work to do in that area.

There was also the undeniable potential force of the President's influence on the Congress. When I had first written to President Johnson, soliciting his counsel and advice and informing him of our efforts to solve the problem of succession and disability, I had indicated that we were mindful of the difficulty of his position with respect to the matter of Presidential succession. There was no Vice President at that time; thus, from a practical standpoint, the President could champion no movement which would possibly be construed as an affront to the Speaker, who presently stood next in line of succession. This was especially true at that particular moment when Speaker McCormack's undiminished influence was essential in breaking the legislative logjam which had existed in the House for the best part of a year. I knew that the President's hands were effectively tied when it came to making a positive suggestion about the succession problem.

Still, I wanted to do everything possible to insure that all bases were touched at the White House. To this end, I had a long conversation with Larry O'Brien, who had been one of the late President Kennedy's closest political confidants and subsequently the legislative liaison man between the White House and Congress—a capacity in which President Johnson had wisely decided to continue using his talents. I had great respect for O'Brien's ability and wanted to be sure he was kept informed of what we were doing in the Senate. Also, master political craftsman that he was, I knew he would not overlook my emphasis on the strong base of public opinion that we were developing in support of S.J. Res. 139. I had a similar briefing session with White House special assistant Lee White, who was assigned to cover various specific areas of legislative activity at the order of the President.

The time was not yet ripe, I thought, to approach special Presidential assistant Bill Moyers, let alone Lyndon B. Johnson himself. I knew that, in the last analysis, the President would make the decision himself; but in my judgment no White House pronouncement would be forthcoming for some time. So long as Speaker McCormack remained next in the line of succession, the President would not be able to speak out. After the next election there would be a Vice President and such a legislative proposal could no longer be interpreted as an affront to the Speaker of the House, or to a lesser extent to Senator Hayden, the President pro tempore of the Senate and also chairman of the Appropriations Committee. It would be better to approach Moyers and the President closer to the time when a decision would be forthcoming. Thus, there would be less opportunity of their forgetting, and there would be no need to bother two of the busiest men in the United States more than once with the subject.

But it turned out that the President needed no congressional prompting. He was well aware that the problem needed to be solved; and, at a White House press conference on March 14, he replied to a question on the subject by saying: "I think it is important to find a way to replace a Vice President when the Vice President succeeds to the Presidency." But he carefully avoided expressing his opinion as to how this could best be accomplished and went on to say that he doubted the Eighty-eighth Congress would take any action on the subject—a statement that, given what we had learned about the feeling that existed in the House, had a ring of reality to our ears.

The *Washington Post*, in an editorial four days later entitled "LBJ and Succession," showed less patience when it commented,

> President Johnson has wisely endorsed the idea of filling the Vice Presidency whenever the position becomes vacant. . . .
> We wish, however, that the President had pressed Congress to act on the problem this year. The proposed constitutional amendment could not become effective before November when a new Vice President will be chosen at the polls. But experience has shown that unless Congress acts while the dangers of leaving the office vacant are fully apparent, corrective measures are likely to again be delayed until another emergency arises. . . .
> It is this frightening possibility that is giving the country great concern. Only a new act of Congress would remove this danger by shifting to the top of the line of succession an official, such as the Secretary of State, who would not have to resign in order to substitute temporarily for the President in case of disability. We fully understand the reluctance of the White House to ask for such a change in the law. But we surmise that the whole country would applaud a request from Speaker McCormack that he be relieved of this potential dilemma.

Despite my decision not to bother the President with this matter for the time being, I was presented with an unexpected opportunity to put in a word for our cause with the Chief Executive. Some time earlier, my Hoosier friend Ray Berndt, director of Region No. 3 of the United Auto Workers Union, had invited me to attend the National UAW Convention in Atlantic City on March 23, since a sizable delegation of Hoosier constituents was to be in attendance. Early on the morning of the 23rd, I caught a plane from Washington and then drove to Convention Hall. I was intro-

duced to the convention and had a chance to visit with a number of
Indiana delegates. Then it was time for the principal speaker, Lyndon B. Johnson. His speech was effective and extremely well received. Shortly afterward, to my great surprise, he sent me a
message by his assistant Jack Valenti that he would like me to ride
back to the airport with him, then join him in his helicopter for the
return trip to Washington. Needless to say, a senator does not receive such an invitation from the President of the United States
every day. I certainly had no inclination to turn it down.

The Presidential limousine, with police escort, made the trip
to the Atlantic City airport in a few minutes. It seemed only an additional minute until we were all aboard and off the ground. The
President and I were seated in the main section of the helicopter;
he sat on the left, in the larger of two reclining chairs, while I sat
opposite him on a long seat that ran along the right side of the plane.
He seemed very tired, and most of our conversation was limited to
political small talk. Although it was still early in the spring, the
importance of the coming election was in each of our minds. Despite
my serious reservations about doing so, I couldn't resist the temptation of bringing the President up to date on our activities in the
Senate concerning disability and succession. I reiterated what I had
said in my earlier letter to him—that I understood how awkward
his position was with respect to any change in the present succession
law. He closed his eyes and leaned back in deep thought. "I've been
following your work, Birch," he said after a moment. "But I doubt
very much if anything can be passed through this Congress. After
the election perhaps it will be different." This, I knew, was a perfectly realistic judgment, and we left it at that. During the next
few moments, as the Marine chopper buzzed over the New Jersey
and Maryland landscape, I thought of the vast responsibilities of
this man who, even sitting there with his eyes closed, could not
escape the myriad problems that demanded his attention. I had
reminded him of one more of these, and he would come to grips
with it when the time came to do so.

During March and early April, we began to formulate a dual
strategy. The passage of time, it seemed to me, was damaging our
chances on two fronts. It became clearer every day that no consti-

tutional amendment could be passed by both Houses during the Eighty-eighth Congress. Moreover, each day that went by after the Kennedy assassination diminished the public's awareness of the urgency of our work, therefore decreasing our chances for congressional action. Thus, I felt we should take advantage of every opportunity to keep the public aware of the existing danger to which our lack of adequate provisions exposed us. At the same time, we should tenaciously pursue action on the amendment in the Senate, hoping to secure passage there before the end of the session. Even though we knew that the House was not going to act, I felt it imperative to put the Senate on record before the session ended.

To help accomplish the first objective, my press assistant Steve Lesher approached NBC concerning the possibility of an appearance on the "Today" show. An invitation was tendered, which I gratefully accepted. Although Marvella and I had appeared briefly on the "Today" show shortly after our arrival in Washington, the thought of a second appearance was a bit unnerving. At 8:15 on March 16, 1964, I arrived, somewhat nervously, at NBC's WRC studios in Washington. Twenty-five minutes later Martin Agronsky and I were discussing the succession-disability problem before a nationwide television audience. Once we began to discuss the ins and outs of the amendment which had become so much a part of my life, I found that my initial nervousness disappeared without my being aware of it. Agronsky had the ability to bring out the various dangers and nuances of the critical subject in a manner which enabled me to forget the millions of inquisitive eyes which were getting their first view of a national problem.

Another important step in our efforts to maintain public awareness was an article written for *Look* magazine, called "Our Greatest National Danger." I began by citing past examples of the insignificance that had once been attached to the office of Vice President:

> . . . Theodore Roosevelt, when he was elected Vice-President, at the age of 42, was quoted as saying that he was going to Washington not to be praised, but buried. . . . And when Alben W. Barkley was sworn in as Vice-President, he began his speech this way: "Inasmuch as I am about to enter upon the discharge of duties that require four years of silence, I will be brief. . . ."

But things had changed since then, I pointed out; the Vice President under Presidents Eisenhower and Kennedy had become "the nation's chief ambassador. . . . Most significantly, however, he remains the man who is always a heartbeat away from the world's most powerful office."

> The tragic death of President Kennedy has renewed the discussion of Presidential succession and disability. There are few problems facing this nation today of more critical importance . . . yet few problems have received as little Congressional consideration.

I briefly outlined the succession laws which had been in effect since 1792, ending with the 1947 Succession Law, still in effect, which would thrust Speaker McCormack into the presidency if anything should happen to Lyndon Johnson before the next inaugural day.

> A great deal of sound and fury has been heard about Speaker McCormack's age (72) and his capabilities for the Presidency. This, as I see it, isn't the problem at all. John McCormack is an able and experienced man. The problem is, first, that we are now without a Vice-President. Second, the Speaker, the potential successor to the Presidency, is purely a member of the legislative branch of the government—not the executive branch.
>
> The Speaker already has more than a full-time job running the House. . . .
>
> [He] has neither the time nor Constitutional authority to serve as Vice-President. . . .
>
> The Speaker could be—and, in the past, has been—a member of the political party in opposition to the party of the President.

Not only was the present succession law weak in these ways, I continued, but it also made no provision for Presidential disability. The private agreements which had been initiated by President Eisenhower and Vice-President Nixon did not have the force of law:

> And what of the present situation? The Johnson-McCormack disability agreement does not answer several nagging questions: If the Speaker were forced to act as President, would he resign the Speakership? If he did, would he still be an officer of the Government, entitled under the Constitution to act as President? Would the Speaker be required to resign his seat in Congress? If he did not, how then would we preserve the separation of executive and legislative authority that is so vital to our form of government? . . .
>
> We cannot afford to gamble with the future of our nation. We must amend the Constitution to provide for a Vice-President at all

times. . . . We must amend the Constitution to answer the thorny
questions about Presidential inability.

I went on to outline the provisions of our amendment, including
the third part, which dealt with changing the traditional succession
laws and which, by the time the article appeared, we had come to
realize was beyond the realm of possibility. I ended with a call to
action:

> It is not easy to arouse widespread interest in a subject like Presi-
> dential succession and disability. But unless satisfactory corrective steps
> are taken, the danger to this nation will remain a grave and ever-
> present one.
> The stability and continuity of our democratic form of govern-
> ment are at stake. The time to act is now.

The national coverage of the *Look* article brought us an excellent
response. My office was flooded by letters supporting our cause.

Columnist Marquis Childs and *New York Times* editor Arthur Krock also gave us a hand in our efforts to maintain and stimulate national interest. Later in March, Conrad and Lesher had a long
discussion with Childs concerning the intricacies of the amendment.
A short time afterwards I had lunch in my office with Mr. Krock.
Both men responded with excellent articles stressing the importance
of finding a solution to the problem. These men were only two of
the numerous news commentators and editorial writers with whom
we discussed our efforts. Most of them were extremely helpful in
taking on the burden of maintaining public interest.

Meanwhile, we continued with our efforts to secure Senate
passage. Even though the inaction of the House would mean that a
measure passed by the Senate would die at the end of the session,
subsequent Senate passage would be much more likely if we could
get the necessary two-thirds approval this time round in the Senate.
If we succeeded this session we could introduce the amendment at
the beginning of the following session, pass it rapidly through the
upper chamber, and bring our entire effort to bear upon the House
of Representatives.

In this connection, it was vital to gain the support of the senior
senator from New York, Ken Keating. He had been more actively
interested in the problem of disability and succession than any of

his other Republican colleagues, and we knew that no constitutional amendment could possibly receive the required two-thirds vote of the Senate without support from prominent Republicans. Yet it appeared at that time that Ken and I were miles apart on the questions of filling a vacancy in the Vice Presidency and handling Presidential disability. Conrad and Lesher worked tirelessly to woo the members of Keating's staff, and we made every effort to persuade Ken to join the backers of S.J. Res. 139.

Even though some agreement with Ken Keating was precisely what we were striving for, I could not believe my eyes when I read a letter I received from him in late March. It ran to four pages and began:

> Dear Birch:
>
> You and I are in fundamental agreement that one or more constitutional amendments are urgently needed in the areas of Presidential succession and inability. We also agree that these problems are of such a high degree of urgency that arriving at a consensus and taking action on any reasonable and workable solution is more important than the exact terms of the solution itself.
>
> We have had our differences on proposed answers to the twin aspects of succession and inability. On succession, as you know, I feel very strongly that two Vice Presidents is the best answer and that, although it may be unrealistic to expect its favorable consideration in the face of qualms over its seeming novelty more than anything else, nevertheless, in the long-run I believe it would finally gain acceptance. The underlying principle of the plan, let me emphasize, is that the country needs a full-time Vice President at all times, unburdened by the duties of another office, to be ready to step into the Presidency if the occasion arises. In my judgment, your proposal, embodied in S.J. Res. 139, to fill any vacancy in the Vice Presidency through Presidential nomination and Congressional confirmation would carry out this principle and, therefore, would be a solution I could wholeheartedly support.

I read those last words again: ". . . a solution I could wholeheartedly support." Ken Keating's willingness to support our approach to the problem of filling a Vice-Presidential vacancy was the best thing that had happened to us since the beginning of our search for a solution to the knotty problem. I went on to read Senator Keating's thoughts on Presidential disability. He still felt strongly that his own proposal was the best answer to the problem:

I remain convinced that a constitutional amendment should confer upon Congress plenary power to legislate in the area. Your idea
is to spell out concrete disability procedures, with a certain amount
of built-in flexibility in the amendment itself. The nub of the difference
between our separate ways of approach is primarily in our political
hunches as to how State Legislatures would react to each. I do not
believe that this difference, which is concerned more with tactics
than with substance, should contribute in the slightest to delaying
Senate action on inability. If the divergence does in fact boil down to
political judgment, it seems to me that the full Senate itself, composed
as it is of practical politicians whose job it is to make political judg-
ments day-in and day-out, ought to be afforded a prompt opportunity
to exercise that judgment and choose between the two ways of
approach.

In other words, the senator from New York was willing to debate
our two proposals on the floor of the Senate—and to support ours,
if that was the one that was adopted! This idea of opening the question to the Senate as a whole seemed, to me, an excellent one. I still
felt that the S.J. Res. 139 approach was the best that I had seen; but,
if I couldn't sell the idea to the Senate, that approach would fail.
Such an agreement with Ken Keating seemed a practical way to
solve our differences.

The rest of the letter consisted of a detailed analysis of S.J.
Res. 139. Ken had obviously given the proposal great study, and
he made several suggestions which would tighten its wording and
clarify its meaning. One of his proposals, however, troubled me.
He reminded me of the futility of proceeding with the last section
of S.J. Res. 139—the section which, as the bill was originally introduced, would have changed the line of succession from the Speaker
of the House and President pro tempore of the Senate to the Cabinet officers. I myself had long before come to the conclusion that it
would be useless to try to get support for that approach and had
expressed my intention to delete the entire section, but Senator
Keating's suggestion ran along different lines:

> If you were to agree to the deletion of Section 6 from S.J. Res.
> 139, I, for one, would be perfectly willing to join with you in the in-
> troduction of a simple statute creating the office of Acting Vice Presi-
> dent to be filled by Presidential nomination and Senate confirmation
> under existing Constitutional authority. This would serve as an in-
> terim means of strengthening the line of succession until a modified

S.J. Res. 139 along the lines I have suggested may be approved in Congress and ratified in the State legislatures.

To my way of thinking, our effort would be seriously divided if we were now to introduce a statute on top of a constitutional amendment. In the past, no one had been able to get enough support to acquire congressional action on any one measure, let alone two. Moreover, it was conceivable that passing a statute, even a temporary one, would ease people's minds just enough that it would seem less necessary to finish the job—to do it right. I preferred to wait until the right time and enact the one major, comprehensive constitutional amendment that would settle the problem once and for all.

I re-read Keating's letter and scribbled at the bottom of its last page, "This letter is a shocker. Let's hold our breath and let Ken win this battle. I think we can afford the sacrifice." But what was I saying? "Win," "sacrifice," indeed! Ken Keating had offered to meet us more than halfway; he had paved the way for our joining forces. I immediately dictated a letter to the senator from New York:

Dear Ken:

I was pleased to receive your comprehensive letter of March 26, 1964 regarding your suggested alterations of S.J. Res. 139.

The persuasive arguments which you have advanced are well taken. As always, they reflect your intense interest and desire to gain a greater perfection in our constitutional system of government.

Having carefully reviewed your recommendations, I find myself in almost complete accord. Therefore, I am enclosing a modified form of S.J. Res. 139 which you will find encompasses all of your suggested changes except those pertaining to disability provisions in Sections 3, 4, and 5. . . .

I went on to indicate that I was eager to discuss the differences that remained between our two approaches; moreover, I immediately dispatched Larry Conrad to discuss the matter in some detail with Keating's chief assistant, Abbott Leban. The concessions that Ken Keating had made showed him to be a true statesman: he was determined to work for a solution to the problem even if its final form did not include the views he himself held on the matter.

During the next month or so we continued in our efforts to obtain cosponsors: one result of this was that Senator James Pearson, of Kansas, agreed on April 21 to cosponsor our measure. At the same time, my staff went on working out language that would meet the objections Ken Keating had raised in his letter; they were also working on plans for a definitive meeting between the Senator and me to take place sometime in May.

More assistance on the language of our resolution came from another valuable source. One day Senator Ervin of North Carolina came up to me on the Senate floor and said, "Birch, about the disability section of that resolution of yours."

"Yes, Sam? What's on your mind?" I asked.

"I was just thinking about it the other day, and I wondered whether you'd given any thought to your use of the word 'Cabinet' for the body concurring in the decision that a disability exists."

"Well, Sam, probably we didn't think about it enough," I replied, knowing that the shrewd constitutional scholar was getting at something definite. "What are your thoughts on that section?"

"You know, Birch," he went on thoughtfully, "you don't have any constitutional precedent for that. The word 'Cabinet' is never mentioned in the Constitution itself. I was just wondering whether it might be better to use the phrase 'heads of the executive departments.' Now that *is* in the Constitution, and using the same language might make your resolution a little more watertight."

"I think you've got a fine point there," I said to him. "It never occurred to us to say anything but 'Cabinet'—that's how everyone thinks of it. But you're right; why shouldn't we have the language of the Constitution behind us whenever we can?" I told him how grateful I was to him for pointing this imperfection out to me. Some might have called the change insignificant, but it seemed meritorious to me. Besides, it would be most helpful to have Sam Ervin feel that he had contributed a part to our amendment. I was hopeful that he might join us in cosponsoring S.J. Res. 139, but had not yet been able to persuade him to do so.

Leaving the Senate floor, I marveled at how tactfully the senator from North Carolina had given me the benefit of his constitutional wisdom. It was this sort of help which would eventually draft an amendment that would be as free of flaws as we could possibly make it. Sam Ervin's suggestion was eventually incorporated into the resolution that Keating's and my staff finally worked out. We were to hear reverberations later about that phrase, but I remained convinced that the logic behind the southern senator's observation was very sound indeed.

On May 14, my staff and Senator Keating's had just about completed the groundwork for our agreement. That afternoon Larry Conrad, who had been handling liaison with the New York senator's staff, informed me that we were supposed to confer with Senator Keating, his staff man Abbott Leban, and Senator Fong's staff man Don Chang the next morning. "But it looks to me," Conrad added, "that you've got to make some real decisions yourself before then."

"What do you mean?" I asked, momentarily thrown off base by the idea of still more unsolved problems. The Senate was chaotically busy at that point and things were equally demanding back home in Indiana, with speaking commitments almost every weekend. "I thought we'd already told him we were willing to accept most of his suggestions—what more is there to decide?"

"Well, yes, Senator, we have told him that. But you need to decide on exactly what specific language you want. If we don't have exact language in mind when we talk to the Keating and Fong people, we might get jockeyed out of our shoes."

I knew he was right. As he started to leave, I reached for the telephone to find out what the pending business would be before the Senate, and fired one parting order. "Larry," I said, "make a note that before either of us goes to sleep tonight we'll decide on the language." Then, thinking of the press of business before me that day, I added, "And don't let me forget."

As it turned out, Conrad and I worked until two in the morning to prepare for the conference. We knew, through Conrad's discussions with the Keating staff, that we had general agreement with their Senator; but it was no easy job to determine in our own minds what specific language could accomplish our intentions. The suggestions in Senator Keating's letter had been extremely helpful and would tighten the language of the proposed amendment; and we tried to go even beyond the suggestions of my New York colleague in consolidating the language. I was well aware that one of the major criticisms voiced against our resolution, S.J. Res. 139, was that, as originally worded, it was too lengthy.

It had been suggested that our resolution provide for a joint session of the House and Senate to elect a new Vice President who had been previously nominated by the President. In the wee hours of the morning, Conrad and I decided that since the Constitution gave no official sanction to action by a joint session of the Congress, we would not change our original provision which provided that the new Vice President be elected by a majority vote of both houses separately. This would improve our chances of passing the measure through the Senate, since a joint session would permit the more numerous members of the House to outvote the one hundred members of the Senate.

Finally, we had squeezed out all the "ands" and "thes," the commas and periods—everything that could possibly be eliminated without weakening the amendment. We had corrected minor imperfections; and we had also eliminated the entire last section, which would have changed the line of succession from the Speaker and President pro tempore back to the Cabinet officers. As the hands of my office clock approached two, we arranged our papers and closed up shop, confident that we were prepared for the critical session the following morning.

May 15 proved to be a hectic day. The Senate was keeping long hours, with the civil rights debate in full swing. One of the tactics of the filibustering southern senators was the use of the live quorum call, at which 51 senators must answer to their names if business is to proceed. To be present, everyone was obliged to break appointments, change plane schedules, and cancel or even interrupt home-state speaking engagements. That day there were five such calls, and it seemed that circumstances were conspiring against Ken Keating and me ever getting our heads together. But finally, at 4:30 in the afternoon, Larry Conrad and Abbot Leban each managed to round up his senator. The four of us, along with Don Chang of Senator Fong's office, met in the Senate lobby and sat on the large leather couches there. The setting was hardly conducive to quiet deliberation. The AP news machine was chattering away, and senators and staff members were continually passing back and forth. But to have gotten together at all that day was something of a triumph, and Senator Keating and I were both glad to have found three-quarters of an hour to discuss general strategy and some of

the more pertinent language. Our frank discussion of the nuts and
bolts of the proposed amendment accomplished a great deal. Then
we both hurried off to other engagements, turning over the final
drafting process to the staff members. Conrad, Leban, and Chang
each took away a copy of the work papers, wishing to study them
before reaching a final agreement. They met again on May 19 to
make some minor additional changes in the form of language suggested by the office of the Senate's legislative counsel.

At long last, on May 21, Senator Keating, Senator Fong, and I
arrived at a final agreement upon the language and strategy. That
agreement was reviewed with a man from the staff of Senator Dodd,
also a member of the subcommittee. We were assured that Dodd not
only would be glad to join in our agreement, but would like to
become a cosponsor of the measure. Thus, four of the six members
of our subcommittee had agreed to the specific language that should
be incorporated into S.J. Res. 139. Finally we had the necessary
majority and the subcommittee would officially report it out later.
Our strategy called for us to seek full Judiciary Committee support
of the measure in the same fashion. Then, when the resolution was
considered on the floor of the Senate, Ken Keating would move to
amend it to incorporate the general disability provisions of his
S.J. Res. 35, whose general enabling provisions he still preferred to
our more specific approach.

If his movement to amend was successful, then it was agreed
that all of us would join together in supporting S.J. Res. 139 as he
had amended it. On the other hand, if his effort was defeated, he
would join forces with us and throw his support behind the specific language upon which we had just reached agreement.

Later that day, Conrad and I went up to talk to Senator Everett
McKinley Dirksen, another member of our subcommittee and the
Minority Leader of the Senate, to let him know how our work was
going. I had really not had the chance to get to know the senator
from Illinois, except, of course, by his enormous reputation; and I
was a little nervous about going to see him. I knew I was still a very
green senator, but as we went into Senator Dirksen's office, a short
distance off the Senate floor, I will admit that I felt even greener
than usual.

As the mahogany door, with "Minority Leader" lettered upon

it in gold, swung open, we were greeted by one of the rare sights in the Capitol. Entering a small anteroom dominated by an elaborate chandelier, we looked through to a large conference table, over which another magnificent chandelier was hanging. The irregular movement of air in and out of the various doors of the office made the chandeliers tinkle constantly, like the soft music of an old-fashioned music box.

Mrs. Glee Gomien, the Senator's hospitable secretary, ushered us into the large conference room. There, poring over a mass of papers, sat the Minority Leader. We exchanged greetings, then, knowing the many other matters that awaited Senator Dirksen's attention, I plunged into the situation of the amendment, as I saw it at that time. When I paused to ask the Senator what his thoughts were on the matter, he replied, "Birch, I've just been so busy, I hardly know my own mind." However, he went on to say that he believed our approach on the replacement of the Vice President was the correct and workable one. It was his judgment that the Vice President, to serve the purpose of the office, should be selected by the President, or at least that the President should have some voice in the selection.

Senator Dirksen told us that he had not yet solidified his thinking on the amendment's disability procedures, but that he did feel concerned over the number of votes necessary for the Cabinet to remove the President. Our amendment provided that a majority of the Cabinet, voting with the Vice President, could remove the President for reasons of disability, and the Minority Leader wondered whether this would prove sufficient safeguards for the President.

Everett Dirksen pushed his chair back from his memento-laden desk and glanced at the ceiling of his impressive office. He reminded me that he had a very personal reason behind his lack of absolute faith in the infallibility of a majority. A number of years before, he had experienced some extreme difficulties with his eyesight, and his vision had begun to fail rapidly. Examination by a number of medical experts brought little consolation; time and again he was told that the only remedy was the removal of the diseased eye. Only one doctor had disagreed. "I gave the matter much thought, Birch, and no small amount of prayer," he reminisced. "Finally I decided to vote with the minority." He had won: the eye had been saved and perhaps the entire course of his life had been changed.

We were silent for a moment. Finally the Minority Leader, returning to the matter of the disability provisions of the amendment,
said that he had not yet decided in his mind what procedure would
be best. In short, he was open for suggestions.

I was encouraged, however, that he agreed that we should send
the resolution up to the full committee; he told us he would go
along with the committee decision.

We left the Minority Leader's office, returning to our own
to finish the day's work. When our earlier meeting with Senator
Keating and the others had adjourned, each office had agreed to
handle its own press distribution, and my office volunteered to
prepare a joint statement on the agreement we had reached. This
statement, which was to be released on May 23, ran to the effect that
Senators Bayh, Fong, Dodd, and Keating had joined in recommending language to deal with the problem of Presidential disability and
succession. It then gave the text of the resolution.[1]

This announcement made news. It was the first time in history that such a near agreement had been reached on this issue.
The *Washington Post* gave it extremely full coverage, beginning:

> A Senate subcommittee charged with studying presidential suc-
> cession laws favors a constitutional amendment to permit the President
> to fill a vice presidential vacancy, with approval of the Senate and
> the House.

The article went on to give the background of our efforts and para-
phrased at length the content of our resolution. It noted:

> Keating said he would seek one modification when the proposal
> comes before the full Senate. This, he said, would be to authorize the
> Congress to determine by statute the procedures under which a Presi-
> dent would be declared unable to discharge his duties and the method
> by which he would regain the full powers.

I was jubilant that we had gotten so far. The bargain with
Senator Keating represented a gamble on my part, to be sure, but
I felt it was a calculated one. Any amendment, after all, would be
better than none; and I would rather have seen Ken Keating's proposal written into the Constitution than to have left things as they
stood at that time. I also felt that our approach had many things
going for it. The Bar Association was on our side, and the "blank

[1] See Appendix, pp. 352–353.

check" argument against Senator Keating's proposal would weigh heavily with states' rights senators. There was, moreover, the psychological fact that a bill reported out of committee always has a certain advantage over an amendment coming from the floor. Majority members who are not themselves directly involved with a measure will usually trust the chairman of the subcommittee, feeling that he has been able to give the subject the time and study which their other concerns have not afforded them.

Thus, in agreeing to gamble with Ken Keating, I knew that we had much more to gain than to lose. If his own amendment were defeated on the floor, we could then count on his positive support of ours.

Furthermore, Conrad's conversations with the Keating staff led us to believe that Ken really had little hope of his own proposal coming out on top, and that the agreement was, in a sense, a strategic withdrawal on his part—the old "if you can't beat them, join them."

Yet I wanted to be sure that my hunch about the difficulties of state legislatures' passage of a "blank check" amendment was an accurate one. None of us had any actual proof of how either plan would be accepted by the various state legislatures. I had my opinion, and Ken Keating had his. Was there anything positive we could do to prove that our theory was right—or, for that matter, to find out in time that it was wrong?

Larry and I were mulling it over in my office; we had been discussing it for more than an hour. Finally, I said, "I'll tell you what to do, Counselor. Let's prepare a personal letter to each Speaker and President pro tem of the fifty state legislatures, describing as accurately as we know how the relative merits of Keating's proposal and mine. Then let's ask them to be very frank with us and give us their judgment about which of the two plans would have the best chance of acceptance in their particular legislature."

Steve Lesher had just come into the office as I made this suggestion. "Senator," said Lesher, "that may be a great idea but it's loaded with dynamite. Right now you have a theory on how your proposal will be accepted by the state legislatures. No one knows for certain whether you're right or wrong, but at least it makes good sense. I think you can sell it from a logic standpoint. But just what happens if we take a poll and a majority of the legislators think Keating's plan would work better in their states? What do we do then?"

"Yes," Conrad concurred, "what *would* we do if that happened? Would we publish the results of our poll? I suppose," he added, "if it didn't come out in our favor we wouldn't have to say anything about it."

"Well, boys," I said, after thinking for a moment about what they had said, "it's chancy either way you play it. But I personally think it's a risk we have to be willing to take. As to what we'll do if the results prove we're wrong, well, we'll cross that bridge when we come to it. In the meantime, Steve, let's get out a press release stating publicly that we're going to poll the state legislative leaders —that will lend more credence to whatever results we obtain. I certainly don't intend to go on the floor of the United States Senate supporting an argument from a poll that my colleagues think is a phony—we could really get shot out of the water that way. If we make it public now and the results are favorable later, we'll be the stronger for it."

"In the meantime," I concluded, "you fellows can say a little prayer that the results turn out as we think they will."

CHAPTER 5

No Hand
at the Helm

After the American Bar Association's House of Delegates meeting in February, we knew that we could count on the support not only of ABA leaders such as Wally Craig, Lewis Powell, and Don Channell, but also of rank-and-file members of the organization all over the country, to help us create the environment of public concern that was so necessary to the passage of our constitutional amendment. It was imperative that the people in the precincts be kept aware of the problem. The grassroots membership of the ABA was doing an invaluable job in stimulating this awareness.

As part of this program, the Bar Association had planned a Conference on Presidential Inability and Vice-Presidential Vacancy to be held in Washington on May 25. This was to be a truly national forum; civic, business, labor, and government leaders from all over the country had been invited to attend. A panel discussion was scheduled for that morning, and I was to be one of the participants.

111

This forum would be followed by lunch, and the ABA had managed to persuade Dwight D. Eisenhower—a citizen with no small amount of experience with the problems Presidential disability could create —to be the luncheon speaker.

The program was scheduled to begin at ten-thirty; but Walter Craig had asked the panel members to gather earlier in his room at the Statler Hilton for an orientation session. Conrad, Lesher, and I arrived there shortly after nine.

The moderator of the panel, Leroy Collins, former Governor of Florida and at that time president of the National Association of Broadcasters, was in the hotel room, as were former Attorney General Herbert Brownell, who had already been of great help to us at the hearings of our subcommittee, and Edward L. Wright, the chairman of the House of Delegates of the ABA. These latter two had been instrumental in the ABA's efforts from the beginning of our contacts with that organization. The other member of the panel, Congressman Emanuel Celler, had not yet arrived. It was he who was the unknown quantity to us. As chairman of the House Judiciary Committee, he had to be considered an indispensable cog in any efforts to amend the Constitution. All of the other panelists more or less knew each other's views: we all backed the ABA consensus and our amendment, S.J. Res. 139. But we did not really know what Mannie Celler's ideas were on the succession-disability problem, or what he would say when his turn came to speak.

Ed Wright, Herb Brownell, Lewis Powell, Wally Craig, Conrad, Lesher and I, and the other panel members all discussed the ground rules of the meeting and the format which the morning's program would follow. Late in the briefing session, Mannie Celler arrived. But the discussion continued to be entirely about the form of the meeting, not its substance. By 10:30, when we all went downstairs to the Congressional Room of the Statler Hilton, we were none the wiser about the direction Celler's remarks were to take.

As President Walter Craig began by welcoming the 750-odd opinion leaders who had gathered there that morning, I thought how successful the Bar Association had been in getting together such an impressive audience. From the panelist's table at one end of the room, where I was sitting, I looked into the crowd and could recognize many notable personalities. I was also pleased, for different reasons, to see two other familiar faces in the front row—my wife, Marvella, and my father.

President Craig's introductory remarks outlined the immediacy of the problem and the purpose of our gathering.

> Since the death of President Harrison in 1841 and the assumption of the Presidential office by Vice President Tyler, the Congress has failed to solve the problem. Since 1960, the American Bar Association has consistently urged the Congress to act. In January of this year, a conference of scholars on this subject, law professors, legislators, and bar leaders was held here in Washington at the instance of the American Bar Association. The conference reached a consensus. That consensus has the official approval of the American Bar Association. The Senate Judiciary Committee is ready to act. The Senate cannot accomplish the desired result alone. We need your help. You, as representatives of leading national organizations, with your respective memberships, can perform a great service to your country by actively engaging in this effort.

Governor Collins, as panel moderator, was the next to speak. He provided a dramatic example of the impossibility of escaping the problems of succession and disability, problems that did "not arise from the age or physical condition of any particular President, at any given moment," but "spring from the inescapable fact of human frailty." Governor Collins reminded his audience that he had served as permanent chairman of the Democratic party's last national convention, and thus had participated closely in the nomination of the late President Kennedy.

> All of the following men were very closely and intimately involved in the work there in Los Angeles: Paul Butler, the Democratic Party Chairman; Honorable Sam Rayburn, the Speaker of the House; Philip Graham, publisher of the *Washington Post*; Senator Kefauver of Tennessee, the Vice-Presidential nominee of the preceding convention; Senator Kerr of Oklahoma; and Congressman Clarence Cannon of Missouri, who served as Parliamentarian. And all these, every one of them, along with Senator Kennedy, the Convention's nominee for President, have since been brought down with little or no warning, and almost all in the summer or fall of their years.

Governor Collins introduced the first member of the panel, Herbert Brownell. As usual, the former Attorney General launched into his topic with telling effectiveness, using his descriptions of the disabilities of Presidents Garfield and Wilson to highlight the urgency of our need to solve the problem of Presidential disability. Knowing what had happened during these critical periods, he said, would make it easier to "visualize what chaos could ensue and how our country could be damaged in this atomic age" if, during a period of disability, no machinery existed defining when and how a successor assumes the President's powers and duties. Brownell described President Garfield's lingering eighty-day decline.

> His mind was clear for the first days of that period. . . . But later he was unconscious and it was reported that he suffered from hallucinations during the last days. . . . Moreover, he was physically unable to discharge the duties of his office during a substantial part of that 80-day period. There was a serious crisis in our foreign affairs, yet the Department heads transacted of necessity only such routine business as could be transacted without the Presidential supervision.

To make the problem worse, Brownell continued, public opinion was sharply divided over how state business should be managed during Garfield's disability: The *Boston Evening Transcript*, for example, defended Secretary of State Blaine's conduct of public affairs, but the *New York Herald* branded the Secretary's conduct a "usurpation."

Next he described in detail the tumultuous period that followed Woodrow Wilson's stroke. These examples, he believed, illustrated "the need for having a means of supplying an active President during periods of Presidential inability." But, he continued:

> The belief that a Vice President actually becomes President, rather than Acting President, during the disability has, as a practical matter, made the Vice President unwilling to act to administer the Government when a President is incapacitated. And it is probable that in any future crisis concerning Presidential inability, the same conflicts and opinions that occurred in the Garfield and Wilson cases would then arise.

Such conflicts and uncertainty, under contemporary circumstances, could "very well jeopardize the country's safety and stability."

The private agreement between each President and Vice President since 1956, Herb Brownell emphasized, was only a "temporary stopgap," and "could be challenged legally if actually acted upon." He concluded,

> . . . the history of the Presidential inability problem up to date
> amply demonstrates the need for an amendment to the Constitution
> to furnish a permanent solution to the problem and to eliminate the
> risks of doubt and confusion as to our national leadership in time of
> crisis.

It was the next member of the panel, Congressman Emanuel
Celler of New York, whose remarks I had been particularly eager
to hear. I listened intently as he began.

> The Judiciary Committee has been wrestling with this very
> vexatious problem for a great many years. In fact, their deliberations
> go back to the year 1920. I remember myself participating in many
> discussions on the matter commencing in 1940. But we could never
> come to any resolution, for the simple reason that when you had three
> Congressmen discussing this matter, you had 17 different opinions.

I joined wryly in the general laughter; I was coming to know all
too well how true this remark was. Congressman Celler went on to
summarize congressional activity from 1792 through 1957, then
reminded the forum that "in the present Congress there is now
pending before the Judiciary Committee of the House twenty-two
proposals relating to Presidential succession and inability; five of
them are in statutory form, and the remaining seventeen are proposed constitutional amendments." He continued,

> It is my opinion that over the years the study and the consideration
> which have been afforded to this problem has resulted in the distilla-
> tion of many of the facets and shades of a very intricate and complex
> legal question, so that there appears to be a growing consensus of
> opinion that the proper application must be by way of the root of a
> constitutional amendment.

So the chairman of the House Judiciary Committee believed a constitutional amendment was necessary to solve our problem! This
was welcome news.

Mannie Celler went on to say that the general agreement of
the ABA conference of last January was "closely aligned to my
own thinking as well as my legislative proposal on this issue of
inability." On the related question of succession, considered by the
ABA conference, "I recognized the vital importance which now
attaches to the office of Vice President of the United States. I am
in complete agreement with the members of that conference that

the office of Vice President should be occupied at all times. There should be no gap."

At that point, I breathed a little easier and glanced down at Don Channell, who was sitting toward the left side of the front row. He returned my look of relief. It seemed as if Mannie Celler was in agreement with the Bar Association proposal. If he did, indeed, support the approach of S.J. Res. 139, we would have gained a powerful ally. I listened intently as he continued:

> While I have not reached a final conclusion as to the best method to provide for the filling of that office in the case of removal, resignation or death or by succession to the office of the Presidency, I am respectfully suggesting here today a method to fill such a vacancy.
>
> I propose that the succession act be amended to provide, as did the 1886 act, for succession to the office of the Presidency for the various heads of the executive departments in the same order as provided in that former statute. Since the members of the Cabinet are selected by the President, and are subject to Senatorial confirmation, I believe this proposal is most consistent with the basic principles and practices surrounding the filling of the office of Vice President. We are all cognizant of the fact that it is the Presidential candidate who selects, for all intents and purposes, his running mate, his Vice President, just as he selects the members of his Cabinet. Since Cabinet members are confirmed by the Senate, I see no need to have either a joint session or the Senate itself confirm or approve the individual Cabinet member who would be in line under the succession act to assume the office of Vice President.

Again I glanced at Don Channell, and I read in his face the same surprise that I was feeling. The powerful chairman of the Judiciary Committee concluded his remarks:

> I offer this suggestion in the form of a constitutional amendment at this time with no pride of authorship, and I would gladly solicit any and all views and opinions on that suggestion.

I had certainly not expected this. A constitutional amendment, removing the Speaker of the House from the line of succession, had been proposed by a committee chairman from the House itself. We in the Senate had already decided that such an open affront to the Speaker would never meet with approval in the lower chamber. Would the Speaker of the House indeed accept such a plan? Would the entire House accept it?

Congressman Celler had, I reflected, come close to approving the Bar consensus plan. But, on the other hand, he had mentioned no specific thoughts on disability; and his 1886 succession plan was hardly a substitute for filling the Vice Presidency while we still had a living President. Clearly we had some proselytizing to do in the House, and Congressman Celler was the place to start. I thought of his closing remark: "I would gladly solicit any and all views and opinions. . . ." Well, I thought, we would certainly be glad to share ours. Surely if Mannie Celler recognized the need to find a solution to the problem, we could come to some agreement!

I was the third of the four panelists to speak; the topic I had been assigned was "A Solution to the Problem." I began by pointing out the significant role that the Bar Association had played in our efforts to date, then attempted to outline the specific proposal we were now considering. S.J. Res. 139 was not, I admitted, a perfect solution, but it had gained wider agreement than any other proposal before it. Congressman Celler's suggestion would solve the succession problem only if both the President and the Vice President died or left office. Ours, I pointed out, attempted to solve two additional problems: that of keeping the Vice Presidency filled at all times and that of determining Presidential disability. After outlining the specific provisions of our amendment and giving our reasons for advocating them, I concluded with a statement on how we planned to proceed:

> We hope to be able to move this through our Judiciary Committee as soon as the business of the Senate permits. And we look forward to working with Chairman Celler and our colleagues in the House.
>
> I will close by saying we have not dealt with either one of these problems for 190 years. We have been very fortunate. And I ask your help, on behalf of all of us who are extremely interested in solving this problem. Let's not continue to take a chance with the very foundation of our constitutional form of government.

The closing panelist was Ed Wright, chairman of the ABA House of Delegates. As Governor Collins said in introducing him: ". . . the next question that naturally comes is how can you help to obtain the support, the interest and activity necessary to meet this need?" Ed Wright answered this effectively by issuing a "Call to Action."

... As individuals we can inform ourselves of the facts and acti-
vate our respective associations, unions, and trade groups to galvanize
into action and completely destroy the inertia that has gripped this
country for 175 years.

I propose four things specifically. One, appoint interested and
dedicated committees to inform themselves of the problem, with a
view of distributing to all of your membership the problem and the
possible solutions.

Two, energize the news media, all forms, into publicizing the
problem.

Three, be active on the speaker's forum on the subject. And,
parenthetically, I will say the American Bar Association is prepared
to send speakers.

Four, communicate with the members of Congress. All seemingly
agree that we can lay to rest these dreadful questions best by a constitutional amendment. This requires the cooperative effort of the
members of Congress and 38 States. We cannot say to Congress, "This
is your job," because it is not. It is our job. Let's finish it while we
are all acutely aware of the great need.

During the brief question-and-answer period which followed,
a question from the audience caused Chairman Celler to shed a
little more light on his succession proposal. First, he would change
the line of succession to the Cabinet. Since Cabinet members are
appointed by the President and confirmed by the Senate, Celler
said, there would be no need to have the intervention of the electoral college or Congress. He pointed out that Article II, Section 5,
of the Constitution provides that Congress has the right to determine succession. "I think," he went on, "there is ample Congressional authority for a simple statute that the Members of the Cabinet shall advance and in the event of a vacancy in the Presidency,
the Secretary of State . . . shall become the Vice President of the
United States."

Congressman Celler's proposal troubled me. It went entirely
counter to what we had heard again and again from the constitutional scholars who had testified in our hearings that we *did* need
a constitutional amendment in this area. Yet from a practical standpoint, I felt it would be impossible to pass any resolution through
the House that was not in accordance with the Judiciary Committee chairman's views. Well, we would just have to wait and see
what the future held.

Following the question-and-answer period, the meeting adjourned. Several of us gathered together with members of Congress and bar officials in a small reception room for conversation before the luncheon. Here, for the first time, I met former President Dwight D. Eisenhower. During my brief chat with him, I thanked him for his thoughtful letter to our committee and tried to stress what an important contribution his presence made to our program that day. He was personable and congenial. I shortly excused myself, knowing that most of the people in the room also wanted to pay their respects to the former Commander in Chief.

I spotted Wally Craig halfway across the reception room; catching his eye, I elbowed my way toward him. When I arrived at his side, I casually took his arm drawing him slightly away from the rest of the group around him. "Walter," I whispered in his ear, "do you have any idea what President Eisenhower is going to say this noon?"

"No, Birch, I haven't. Why?"

"Well, maybe I'm just jittery, but I'm afraid he might repeat that suggestion of his about a disability commission—you know, what he proposed in the last paragraph of the letter he sent to the committee. If he comes up with that idea again at this late date, our goose may really be cooked."

"I'll tell you what let's do," said the president of the ABA after a minute, "We'll go over and see Herb Brownell. He's the one who's been talking to Ike, and if anyone can answer your question, he can."

The room was filling rapidly, but we caught a glimpse of Brownell across the room. He was sipping a before-lunch drink and chatting with Senator Keating—two fellow New Yorkers discussing, I imagined, the future of the Grand Old Party.

Walter Craig and I, apologizing right and left, shoved our way through the increasingly dense crowd until we were in a position to nudge the former Attorney General into a nearby corner. "Herb," Wally Craig asked him without any hesitation, "have you talked to President Eisenhower about what he's going to say?"

"Is it possible," I elaborated, "that he might make a pitch for adding the disability commission that he presented in his letter to the subcommittee?"

Brownell took another sip of his martini. "Frankly, I don't know," he said. "I don't know that anybody knows. When you sent up that distress call after you got his letter, I called him again, one weekend when he was in Palm Springs, and made a hard pitch on the whole disability problem. I stressed how important his help would be, and I also gave him my thoughts—as strongly as you can give your thoughts to a former President—about the whole commission idea. I told him I thought it would create a real problem for everybody."

"But you haven't heard from him since, Herb?" asked Craig.

"I'm afraid not," answered Brownell. "But why don't we go talk to him right now?"

During our conversation, the room had begun to empty as the guests went to their places at lunch in the main dining room. At first we could see Ike nowhere. Finally, searching desperately, we found him standing by himself outside the reception room. Quickly we joined him, glad to have a chance to put in a plug for our approach before it was too late.

While the former President listened attentively, I quickly summarized the main proposals contained in S.J. Res. 139. Craig followed up with a capsule version of the grassroots support that the ABA was generating for the proposal; and finally, Herb Brownell took the bull by the horns and cited some of the opinions expressed before our subcommittee about the dangers of disability commissions. We had made our pitch, as strongly as we knew how, and waited eagerly for Dwight Eisenhower's response. But just at that moment some obviously well-meaning ABA officials, eager to get the luncheon under way and the principal speaker seated, interrupted us. We were literally dragged off into the dining room and put in our separate positions at the head table. We would have to wait for the speech, after all, to see if our last-minute plea had had any effect.

The lunch itself seemed to drag by. To this day I have no idea what was on the menu; and my conversation with Senate Minority Whip Tom Kuchel, on one side of me, and Lewis Powell, on the other, was probably far from stimulating. The only thing I could think about was what Ike was going to say.

Finally lunch was completed, and the visiting dignitaries at

the head table were introduced. One of these was Senator Carl
Hayden. We felt that his attendance was particularly important.
The newspaper coverage of the succession issue, right after the
Kennedy assassination, had made our position, with respect to both
Speaker McCormack and, to a slightly lesser degree, Senator Hayden, a very delicate one. Wally Craig, whose father was a close
friend of Senator Hayden, had told me earlier of his personal plea
to the venerable Senator to attend, stressing the need for unity and
the lack of animosity on our part and that of the ABA. After being
assured that it was neither a full-dress occasion nor one which
would demand that he speak, the Senator had accepted. He had
then gone on to reminisce to Craig about the time when he, as a
congressman, had told Vice President Marshall, "Tom, Woodrow's
not well." Now, as Senator Hayden was introduced, I thought with
awe that here was a man to whom Wilson's disability was a personal and concrete memory, not history as it was to the rest of us.

Then the thirty-fourth President of the United States took his
place behind the rostrum, facing the 750 assembled guests. He spoke
without notes. That morning, he began, we had heard our subject
discussed "from the standpoint of very able lawyers." But the
former President of the United States was not going to discuss the
legal aspects of the problem. He did what he alone could do: "I'm
going to discuss it from the standpoint of a patient."

> I have a personal approach to this whole problem because three
> times, while in the Presidency, unforeseen circumstances reminded
> me that I might be one of those people found with a disability to carry
> on my duties.

The former President first discussed the problem of succession. He "firmly agreed" with the consensus of the ABA that in
the event of the Vice President succeeding to the Presidency, he
should immediately nominate another Vice President, subject to
ratification by both Houses of Congress.

Such an arrangement, he said, "not only settles the question
of succession . . . but it assures that there will be brought into the
Presidency, in the case of necessity, an individual who has had full
opportunity to know all about all of the critical problems then facing the country." It was, he felt, especially important for the Vice

President to be in on the deliberations of the National Security Council, so that he could be prepared to act as President in the field of foreign affairs.

Next, Ike turned to the problem of disability. "First of all," he said,

> I will relate to you several personal experiences. One morning at 2 o'clock I had a pain, and the doctors came. . . . The next thing I knew I was under an oxygen tent. But from that moment on, I never felt the slightest pain, the slightest difficulty. I thought this was something that happened to other people—not to me. And I wondered why.
>
> . . . The doctors kept me practically incommunicado for almost a week, . . . the doctors did keep the newspapers away from me. Later they told me this was so I wouldn't be reading about my own illnesses and what they were saying to the press. Some of these things were actually embarrassing, I assure you.
>
> Now, what I'm getting at is that within one week thereafter I began picking up the load, and within a matter certainly of three or four weeks was carrying to the full the essential burdens of office, although I still was in the hospital.

The President went on to tell of his two other serious illnesses in office; then he summed up:

> Now, though in each of these three instances there was some gap that could have been significant—in which I was a disabled individual from the standpoint of carrying out the emergency duties pertaining to the office—I was fortunate that no crisis arose.

A disability, he went on, was not necessarily something physical. It could be as simple a matter as the President's being temporarily out of communication—"let us assume that a President is flying across the ocean and his telephonic communication with the West is far less than satisfactory"—at a time when an important decision had to be made. Because of the importance of immediate action, he said,

> I personally believe the only individual who can make the decision that a President is disabled and cannot for the moment carry out his duties is the Vice President of the United States. I think he could not be excused if he should fail to accept that responsibility, act upon it, according to his best judgment, because by the nature of his duties he is the only individual who can make the decision and do it in time.

Then the former President went on to the touchy question of what to do if there were a disagreement as to disability. Assume, he said,

> There is a quarrel about this, that the President, being a little bit wacky, thinks he can take back the job but that the Vice President and, let us say, the majority of his Cabinet thinks that he is not capable under the circumstances—and I think the chance is remote that this would occur—regardless of the method determined by the Congress by which this question would be resolved, it is no longer an emergency. Someone is still there operating as Acting President, and with everything going on as before. Therefore, there can be plenty of time to resolve the matter, whatever ritual that the Congress may decide. Unquestionably such a plan would include some kind of expert medical and probably psychiatric advice.

But not, I began to realize, the commission I had feared the former President would advocate! Herb Brownell's phone call or our last-minute plea—who knows which?—seemed to have borne fruit. The President went on to point out, as many had before, that no law or amendment could foresee every single possibility; instead, we had to assume that the men involved in any future crisis would be "men of honor, men of integrity, men whose concern is the welfare of their own country and not of their own personal ambitions." He concluded:

> And I believe, trusting in that and with the kind of law that would stand behind the Vice President who would be protected thus from the charge that he had operated rashly or without authority, I believe that we can solve this thing, not next year or in two or three years, but now. I do not believe that it's quite as intricate as we make it. But it does mean, as I say, that we do believe that all of us, of all parties and of all levels of government, have as our first thought and concern, the United States of America.
>
> And, if we do that, I think all of the other problems kind of recede in their immediacy, their urgency and in their, you might say, crisis-type of complexion and they become resolvable by people of good will—that is, good Americans.

The General received a standing ovation. He had highlighted the problem from a personal viewpoint as no other American could, and he had thrown his prestige and the mystique of his personality behind our efforts. Truly we had made great progress that day.

As I took a cab back up to the Hill, I thought that things could not possibly have worked out better. The ABA had chosen an impressive guest list. These influential men, I hoped, had been moved to action by the appeals of the panelists. And Ike, especially, had fired the audience, and through the press the country at large, with the urgency of working out a solution to the problems of Presidential succession and disability. He had given us personal evidence of three occasions in recent history when our government had no hand at the helm. The former President had given us a real boost. We seemed, at the moment, to be very well off; and we had our friends at the Bar Association to thank for it.

CHAPTER 6

First Step
Up the "Hill"

From the hotel I went straight back to my office. Now, I thought—still coasting on the exhilaration of the morning—we could really begin to roll.

We had gone to some pains to schedule a subcommittee meeting for the next day, May 26. The Senate was still embroiled in hotly contested debate over the 1964 Civil Rights Act. Because of the deep involvement of many of the senators in this issue, it had been difficult to get together the quorum of our subcommittee members which was necessary for officially reporting S.J. Res. 139 out of subcommittee. But a week earlier, Conrad and I had been able to get promises from Senators Dirksen, Keating, and Fong to meet at ten on the morning of May 26, long enough to take official action on the measure.

When I got back to my desk following the ABA conference that afternoon of the 25th, I immediately picked up the phone and asked to be connected with Senate Judiciary Committee Chairman James Eastland who, with Senator Dodd, made up the remainder of our subcommittee.

"Hello, Birch," the soft drawl of the Mississippi senator came over the line, "what can I do for you?"

"Mr. Chairman, I just wanted to remind you of our subcommittee meeting tomorrow," I replied. "I hope we can get this matter of Presidential succession and disability cleared up and get a bill reported out of committee. As you know, the ABA has thrown its support behind us, and it certainly would be a big help if Jim Eastland were fighting for us in the trenches when the time comes."

"Birch, I doubt very much if I can be there for your meeting. But I'll tell you what. You take my proxy and vote it any way you see fit. Will that be all right?"

"Fine, Mr. Chairman," I answered. "I'll report back to you tomorrow on our results."

"That's not necessary, Birch," he replied. "You're chairman of that subcommittee."

It looked as though we were set for the next day's action; however, later that afternoon I had a call from Minority Leader Dirksen.

"Birch, I'm terribly sorry, but we've had some unexpected developments on this civil rights bill; and there's no way in the world that I can be there at ten tomorrow morning. Could we do it the following day? I checked my calendar, and I can promise you I can make it then. What do you say?"

"Everett, we won't have a quorum without you. Ten the following day will be fine with me, but let me check with the rest of the troops. I'll call you back."

It was getting too late in the day to reach anybody. I picked up the phone. "Larry, get on the phone pronto and check with Keating's and Fong's offices. See if we can reschedule our hearing for ten o'clock day after tomorrow."

By half-past six that evening, we were momentarily back in business; our meeting had been put off for twenty-four hours. But Lady Luck's smile was a fleeting one—at half-past eight the next evening, Larry Conrad called me at home to say he had just learned that Senator Fong, this time, would be unable to attend our meeting the next morning. The senator from Hawaii suddenly had become involved in a crisis with the Appropriations Committee, which had, earlier that day, made drastic cuts in the funds allocated for his state's East-West College. At that very minute, several Hawaiian educators were en route by jet to Washington, and Fong felt duty-bound to be with them the next morning when they pleaded their case before the Appropriations Committee—which was to convene precisely at ten o'clock.

"Well, Larry," I said, "let's shoot for eleven and hope by then we can get four warm bodies together for a quorum, for just long enough to pass our resolution out of subcommittee." Later that night, Conrad called back: The new time was all right with both Fong's and Keating's offices. I personally called Senator Dirksen, who said he would try to drop by long enough to make up a quorum.

The next morning, Conrad and I were in the Judiciary Committee room well in advance of the eleven o'clock meeting hour. Senator Keating arrived first, then Senator Fong, who had just come from the Appropriations Committee. We were all accompanied by our staff assistants—an informality that we allowed ourselves in our small subcommittee, where often staff members as well as senators contributed to the discussion. We all began a general discussion of the problems raised by our amendment, more or less killing time, knowing that we still lacked the quorum we needed to conduct official business. Finally Senator Dirksen arrived. The scheduling difficulties of the past couple of days had made me acutely aware that everyone was very busy, so I promptly put the question.

"Gentlemen," I said, "I suggest that we report Senate Joint Resolution 139 to the full Judiciary Committee for consideration. I'll be glad to so move, unless someone else would like to do so."

Senator Dirksen discussed for almost ten minutes how badly we needed a solution, recounting his past experience in the Congress when the problem had been discussed before. He would, he said, be happy to join in voting to report the bill out of the subcommittee; but he wanted it plainly understood that he reserved the right to offer amendments at a later date.

Ken Keating followed, and in two minutes' time summarized the terms of his previous agreement with me. He would be glad to vote "aye" to pass our resolution out of subcommittee, but he felt duty-bound to seek to amend the disability provisions in accordance with those contained in his S.J. Res. 35 when the whole matter was discussed on the floor of the Senate.

Hiram Fong, one of the early cosponsors of S.J. Res. 139, declared that its provisions were the best that we could come up with. "Mr. Chairman," he continued, "I would be honored to move that the Subcommittee on Constitutional Amendments forthwith report Senate Joint Resolution 139 to the Judiciary Committee for appropriate action. Mr. Chairman, I do so move."

Ken Keating seconded Senator Fong's motion, and on a unanimous voice vote the motion was carried. I had been holding my breath, and I now let it out very, very slowly. We had gotten over one more hurdle.

Before adjourning, I asked for and received the subcommittee's permission to call Senators Eastland and Dodd and add their votes to the 4–0 vote the resolution had just been accorded. This was actually a formality; I already had Senator Eastland's proxy, and Senator Dodd was a cosponsor of S.J. Res. 139. But at that moment I didn't want to take anything for granted.

Then, as we began to push back our chairs to get up from the big mahogany table in order to return to the civil rights battle on the Senate floor, Ken Keating said, "Mr. Chairman." We all paused, and I wondered what Ken was up to. With twinkling eyes and a little smile, he continued, "Since we have so promptly dispatched one important piece of legislation and since we all have plenty of time, I would like to suggest that the subcommittee turn to the consideration of the noncontroversial prayer amendment." He was referring, of course, to what would soon become known as the Dirksen Amendment, one of the most controversial items before the Congress in a number of years. The amendment would later, when Senator Keating was no longer in the Senate, demand long hours of toil and tribulation, hearings and harangue, within our subcommittee. But Senator Dirksen, not to take his colleague's good-natured ribbing without rebuttal, now straightened up in his chair. Shaking his head in righteous indignation, he turned to his colleague from New York.

"Why, Ken," he said, his deep resonant voice filling the small committee room, "before I would want to enter into any discussion on the prayer amendment, I would first have to talk with the Chief Justice—and then, of course, with God."

In more than one sense, that broke up our meeting.

The next step was to prepare a subcommittee report, tracing the historical background of the problem, outlining how S.J. Res. 139 would deal with it, and concluding with individual views which stated the divergent opinion of Senator Keating. It was Larry Conrad's responsibility, for the most part, to prepare this report, and, by early June, he and I had gone over it and had shown the draft to the other subcommittee members for their approval.

But before we could get it printed to present to the full Judiciary Committee, I was temporarily removed from the scene by an unexpected disability of my own. On June 9, at the personal request of Senator Edward Kennedy, I was scheduled to deliver the keynote speech at the Massachusetts Democratic Convention, which was being held in Springfield. Ted Kennedy and I had planned to fly up together, early on the afternoon of the 9th, but were detained in Washington waiting for the final vote on the civil rights bill. Thus by the time we left the Capitol we were quite late, and even more so leaving Washington National airport with Ted Kennedy's aide Ed Moss, my wife Marvella, and Edward Zimney, a commercial pilot. A number of thunderstorms had developed in southern New England and a dense fog developed as we neared Barnes Field, the airfield near Springfield where we were scheduled to land. In our efforts to get through the fog, we crashed to earth in an apple orchard two and a half miles short of the runway.

Our pilot was killed instantaneously. Senator Kennedy, Marvella, Ed Moss, and I were all rushed by ambulance to Cooley Dickenson Hospital in nearby Northhampton.

Ed Moss, who had been in the copilot's seat, lost his battle for life around six o'clock the next morning. Marvella and I were fortunate. Our fastened seat belts in all probability saved our lives, and it took only a few days in the hospital and several weeks of recuperation at home for us to be almost as good as new. Ted Kennedy was not so lucky. He narrowly escaped death, and faced many months during which he heroically fought to recover from a broken back and numerous other injuries. Fortunately, he too would in time be able to resume his duties in the United States Senate.

The tragic accident which delayed our efforts to advance S.J. Res. 139 only served to increase my determination to succeed in solving this problem involving death and disability in the executive branch of the government. For during the period of my recuperation, I had many hours to give thanks that all of us had not perished in a pile of wreckage in that apple orchard. Such a narrow escape from meeting one's Maker has an extremely sobering effect. How relatively insignificant is each human being's existence, compared to the broad horizons of history and the universe! The young senator, brother of the slain President; the junior senator from Indiana and his wife; a personable senate aide, father of three children; a pilot who had more than ten thousand hours of flight experience—each of these five human beings had recently been only one heartbeat away from tragedy. And only three had survived.

Presidents, kings, heroes and rogues—all are only mortal. Why should the leadership of our country hang by such a thin and fragile thread? I was now even more determined that it should not.

During my own disability our efforts to solve the problems of Presidential disability and succession slowed to a walk. But Conrad and I kept in close telephone contact and we decided that he should go ahead and have the subcommittee report printed. Thus the amendment and the report were reported to full committee on June 23.

The next Judiciary Committee meeting I was able to attend was on August 4. We started off by considering and disposing of the usual number of individual bills and private claims. When those were finished, I spoke out from my place at the end of the long committee table. "Mr. Chairman, I move that the committee consider Senate Joint Resolution 139."

I had never been more nervous. Conrad, Lesher, and I had put weeks of study into the report. With the two of them serving as devil's advocates, I had tried to think of every question that might possibly be asked and prepare what I hoped was an appropriate response to each. Yet, as I waited for Chairman Eastland's reply, I felt that the committee table stretching between us was a hundred yards long and that the room was as narrow as a coffin. Finally, after what seemed an eternity, Chairman Eastland agreed. S.J. Res. 139 was now the pending business before the committee.

"Is there any discussion on the bill?" the Chairman asked.

"Mr. Chairman," I answered, "briefly, Senate Joint Resolution 139 would do the following. . . ." I gave a quick outline of the provisions of the bill, after which Senator Keating stated his own opinion and repeated the terms of our agreement. Then Sam Ervin made one observation, half in jest.

"The trouble with your proposal, Ken, is that it doesn't show the same good judgment as my own." As the committee members laughed, the North Carolinian proceeded, in a more serious vein, to describe his own proposed amendment, which dealt with succession to the Presidency and filling a vacancy in the office of Vice President. He had described this plan during our subcommittee hearings; briefly, it specified that when the Vice Presidency, or both Presidency and Vice Presidency, were vacant, a joint session of Congress would choose who should fill those offices. In the ten days before this choice had to be made, the office of President would temporarily be filled, according to a statute enacted by Congress.

Chairman Eastland obviously wanted to reconcile the differences between his committee members and be fair to all of them. Faced with these differing opinions, he suggested that all three proposals—mine, and those of Senators Keating and Ervin as well—be presented to the Senate. "Let's report them all out," he said, "and let the Senate decide."

My heart began to sink. Surely it was within the committee that the choice should be made. Nor were my spirits raised when Senator Roman Hruska, who had not ventured a word during the previous discussion, interrupted, "Well, if we're going to do that, I want mine reported out too."

I did not want to seem overaggressive, but I felt that something had to be done. We were dangerously close to falling into the same trap which had doomed disability legislation for the best part of a century. The past practice had been to report out everything and act on nothing. Junior senator or not, I wasn't going to sit still and let that happen this time if I could help it. For the first time in my year and a half in the Senate, I interrupted the discussion that had been going around the committee table. Much to my surprise, I found that I was even raising my voice.

"Mr. Chairman! Your Subcommittee on Constitutional Amendments has held extensive hearings on the subject which is presently before the full committee. By unanimous vote, it reported out Sen-

ate Joint Resolution 139. This proposal has the enthusiastic endorsement of the American Bar Association. With all due respect, I must
suggest that we would do a grievous wrong to report out all of the
measures which have been introduced on the subject of disability
and succession!"

I stopped for a brief moment to catch my breath, then continued: "If we do this, Mr. Chairman and my colleagues, we will be
right back where we started. Nothing will be done, and we'll be
sitting like a dead duck waiting for tragedy to strike our country
again."

As I spoke, Chairman Eastland had slipped quietly out of the
room, summoned by an emergency telephone call; John McClellan,
the racket-busting senator from Arkansas, had taken over as temporary chairman. But I felt much too strongly about what I was
saying to wait for Senator Eastland's return. "Mr. Chairman," I
said, now addressing Senator McClellan, "if it's appropriate, I move
the committee report out Senate Joint Resolution 139 as it has been
reported by the Subcommittee on Constitutional Amendments. If
any of our colleagues desire to make changes in its content, they
may seek to amend its provisions when the matter is discussed on the
floor of the Senate."

For a full minute, the committee room was silent. I sat back,
still a little surprised at my own temerity. Finally, Senator McClellan
said that in his judgment the motion was in order. Was there, he
asked, any further discussion?

"Mr. Chairman." Everett McKinley Dirksen, the distinguished
Minority Leader, was seeking recognition. What now, I wondered!

"I have no objection to the proposal made by my friend from
Indiana," began Senator Dirksen, to my great relief. "In fact, I'll
be glad to second his motion with the understanding that, if and
when the matter reaches the floor of the Senate, I, or any of the rest
of us who wish to do so, will have complete freedom to seek to
amend the measure as we see fit."

"Is there any further discussion?" asked the senator from Arkansas. "Are there any objections to the bill?" I waited anxiously.

"The Chair hears none," stated McClellan, "and the measure
is reported favorably to the Senate. Is there further business to come
before the committee?"

There was not, and the committee meeting adjourned. Larry Conrad, who had been given special permission to be present to assist me during the discussion of the amendment, helped me to scoop up the numerous papers we had brought with us.

"Nice job, Senator, nice job," Conrad said, looking almost as pleased and surprised as I felt. We left the committee room and promptly proceeded to our office on the first floor. We called a quick staff meeting to share the good news with all the people who had helped us with the measure, and promptly telephoned Don Channell at the ABA to let him share our feeling of success.

Later in the afternoon, Conrad, Lesher, and I had a chance to rehash in greater detail the committee meeting that morning. I confessed to the others that I had been plain, old-fashioned scared—scared that my first major presentation before the committee would not be sufficient to get the job done—scared that the committee would not accept the resolution.

The other thing, I admitted to them, was that I was surprised that the committee battle had been won so easily. I had been thinking about this to myself, earlier in the afternoon. We were, after all, dealing with an amendment to the Constitution of the United States; yet the entire committee debate had occupied scarcely fifteen minutes—although it seemed like living, eternal hell to me while it was going on. None of the really big guns in the committee had been turned on me. Why? Why had I escaped so easily? Was it because all the members of the committee were aware of the importance of enacting legislation on inability and succession? Well, perhaps. But wasn't there a more practical reason? I now began to think aloud.

"Boys, we were pretty lucky this morning. I'd like to think we got off easy because I completely hypnotized the committee with my eloquence and logic, but I know better. I'd like to think it was because all of them were sold on the fact that Senate Joint Resolution 139 is the only right solution, but we all know that some of the committee members have very definite thoughts of their own on the matter. I'll tell you what it was, or at least what I think it was, that got us through with so few hitches this morning."

I paused. "Come on, Senator," said Steve Lesher, "don't leave us up in the air. Give us the word!"

"I'm convinced you'll not find a more conscientious group of

men than the ones in that committee this morning," I continued.
"They're a bunch of sharp cookies, and they don't have to take a
back seat to any lawyer in this country. They know all the laws of
the land inside and out—some of them were making laws when I
was born. You'd think that they'd go over anything that was to become part of the Constitution with a fine-toothed comb. You'd
think they'd check every word of it, every clause, every sentence.
But this morning they didn't. Why?"

Conrad and Lesher waited.

"Well," I continued, "there's only one reason I can see; and
when you stop to think about it, it makes real sense. They don't
think our precious amendment *is* going to become part of the
Constitution, so why should they waste a lot of effort on it?"

"You mean," said Conrad, amazed, "that all our efforts are
going to go down the drain, just like everyone else's have? You
don't think we're going to make it?"

"No, Larry, I don't mean it just that way. I don't think we're
going to make it now, that's all. What I mean is this. Each of us in
that room knew full well that there's almost no chance of the House
getting to Senate Joint Resolution 139, or any similar resolution,
this session. Didn't you tell me just the other day that you'd be
willing to bet the House wouldn't even hold hearings on it this
session?"

"That's sure the way Bill Foley made it look," replied Conrad.

"That's what I mean. We're not the only ones who have that
feeling. My colleagues on that committee have been around a lot
longer than we have. They have a pretty good idea of when something is going to pass both Houses and when it isn't. So why waste
precious committee time on it? There'll be plenty of chances to
have another crack at it next session."

Although it eased my mind to tell Conrad and Lesher what
had been going through my thoughts, I realized that it was a pessimistic note to end what had been more or less a victory meeting.
Conrad and Lesher both looked as if they had lost a few pints of
blood, and I felt sorry to have dampened their spirits so badly. As
they got their things together to leave, I fired one last thought at
them.

"Now listen here. You fellows don't need to rush out of here feeling sorry for yourselves and go off and drown your sorrows. I don't have to tell you that Rome wasn't built in a day. We didn't expect an easy job, or a quick one, when we took on the job of amending the Constitution. But just remember this. Even if we have to fight this committee battle again next year, today was important. We got that amendment out of committee for the first time. Things are moving now, and every step forward is one we don't have to take again. Every time we get a senator to vote for us now, the less apt he is to vote against us next time the same measure comes up before him."

By August 13, Conrad and the committee staff had prepared a comprehensive committee report on S.J. Res. 139. It contained the same general provisions that the subcommittee report had contained and included the individual views of Senator Hruska as well as those of Senator Keating. Thus, S.J. Res. 139 was reported to the Senate and was now on the Senate calendar. The fate of S.J. Res. 139 in the Eighty-eighth Session was in the hands of the gods—and the leadership of the United States Senate. All we could do was circulate to each senator a copy of the hearings and the report, plus a staff compilation which briefly stated the views of each witness appearing before the subcommittee.

Meanwhile, we were making slow but important progress with individual senators. One day I was riding up in the Capitol elevator with Senator Jacob Javits, who two months ago had given us one of our first rays of hope when, before our subcommittee, he had indicated his willingness to alter his own proposed constitutional amendment on the subject, to bring it closer to the terms of ours. Now, as we walked toward the Senate floor, he took me by the arm. "Say, Birch," he said, "I've been thinking about that constitutional amendment of yours. It's so close to what I've been proposing, I can't see anything to be gained by each of us going our separate ways. If you don't mind, I'd like to become a cosponsor with you."

"If I don't mind?" I said incredulously. "Jack, you know what a big asset to us your support would be. I'll see that the desk clerk lists you as a cosponsor this very afternoon!" Arm in arm, we went through the door onto the Senate floor, and to our seats on opposite sides of the Chamber. I suddenly realized, as I sat down, that I had completely forgotten why I was there. For a quorum call? A vote? If so, on what? All I could think of was that Jack Javits was now on our team—not only was there another Senate sponsor for our S.J. Res. 139, but there was one fewer opposing measure to divide the support. I could only hope our luck would remain that way.

That same week, after a full Judiciary Committee meeting which had to do mostly with immigration problems and private claims, I paused for a moment to chat with North Carolina's Sam Ervin. We exchanged a bit of small talk, and I was about to leave when Sam brought up our amendment problem. "One other thing, Birch—I've been intending to call you. That amendment of yours on succession—I've thought a lot about it, and I think that your solution for choosing a Vice President is about the best we can work out. I personally would prefer the Congress to make the choice alone, but I can see why you included the President too. The more I think about it, the more I think that's a pretty good compromise and the best we'll be able to come up with."

I held my breath. The distinguished lawmaker added, "I'm concerned about the problem of disability. Nobody has a perfect solution to that, but I suppose your solution is about as good as any. The important thing is that we get something on the books."

"Sam, that's one of the best things I've heard in months," I told him. "Does that mean," I ventured, "that I could list your name as a cosponsor?"

"Sure enough. I'll be glad to help out any way I can. It's high time we solve that problem!"

I left the committee room and found Larry Conrad waiting to discuss some other subcommittee business with me. "Pinch me, pinch me, Counselor," I said, grinning incredulously.

"What's the matter, Senator?" He asked.

"It's really not much," I said, playing it for all I could get. "I just had a nice little visit with the distinguished senator from North Carolina."

"Oh? What was on Sam's mind?"

"Well, he seems to be determined to make more work for me."

"What do you mean?" Conrad asked me, really puzzled by that time. "What's he up to?"

"You may not believe it, but as soon as the Senate goes into session this afternoon, I'm going to have to walk all the way over to the floor, seek recognition from the presiding officer, and add Sam Ervin's name as a cosponsor to Senate Joint Resolution 139."

Conrad stared at me for a long moment, speechless. Finally he said, "You're kidding, Senator. What did he *really* say?"

"Larry, darn it, I can jest with the best," I answered, not able to keep up the facetious tone any longer, "but I can't kid about this. Sam's on board, and you know what that means!" Neither of us said anything else as we walked down the stairs and through the brass doors of the New Senate Office Building. Outside, hot summer sunshine bathed Constitution Avenue. We waited a moment for the street light to change, then crossed the street to the Old Senate Office Building, still not saying a word, not daring to voice our new-found optimism—yet we couldn't resist taking the steps up to the entrance two at a time. When we reached the landing and started to go inside, I paused for a moment and glanced toward the dome of the Capitol Building, clearly visible above the leaves which crowded the branches of the elms across the street. The sun seemed to be reflected more brightly than usual from the dome of the national edifice, and I thought as we went inside that moments like this one compensated for all the tribulations of life in the Senate.

Conrad and I were no longer able to conceal our elation. We both knew how important it was to have Sam Ervin on our side. He was the man to whom all the southern senators—the largest single bloc of voting strength in the Senate—looked for advice and counsel on constitutional matters. His support, we knew, could well mean a successful resolution to a legislative impasse that had already existed for the better part of a century.

I thought it might be worth it, at about that time, to make one overture toward 1600 Pennsylvania Avenue. So one morning I put in a telephone call to my friend Bill Moyers, reminding him that our measure was awaiting action in the Senate and needed to be passed. But Moyers told me what I knew already: even if our measure passed the Senate, there was no chance of its passing the House.

It was true. We were in August of the 1964 campaign and everyone was anxious to adjourn. By the last week of the month, no Senate action had yet been taken on S.J. Res. 139. I was really not surprised. At the end of every session the calendar becomes crowded with important measures, especially the anxiously awaited appropriations bills which are given priority over everything else as they are reported out of committee. But despite my pessimism, I felt that nothing could be lost by trying. So, in those closing days of August, I checked in periodically with Majority Leader Mike Mansfield, asking if it were possible for him to use his influence to get the Senate to act on our measure.

"Birch," the Majority Leader told me at one point, "even if your measure passes the Senate, there's no chance whatsoever of its passing the House."

There could be no arguing with this fact. "But, Mike, if we pass it in the Senate this session," I reasoned with him, "then the way will be clear for introducing it again next session and passing it through the Senate quickly. That way we can focus all our attention on getting action in the House. Neither House has ever passed legislation to deal with this. If we could just get Senate action this session it would be a great morale booster. It would maintain our enthusiasm and impetus to get the final job done next year."

Knowing how busy he was, I took leave of the Majority Leader, feeling a bit guilty for taking up even a few minutes of his valuable time. Mike would give us a break if he could, I thought. But the chances were very, very slim—one in a hundred, or perhaps even one in a thousand.

But sometimes even long odds pay off. About eleven on the morning of Monday, September 28, my secretary buzzed me on the intercom: the Majority Leader was on the phone wanting to talk to me. I quickly picked up the phone on my desk, wondering what it was all about.

"Birch, this is Mike. We want to bring up your constitutional amendment today. Can you be ready?"

I couldn't quite believe my ears. "What time will *you* be ready, Leader?"

"Well, the morning hour should take until about one o'clock. Can you manage that?"

"Yes, sir. I'll be ready by one, and if you need me before that, I'll be here in the office. And, Mike—thanks a million!"

"That's all right, Birch," he said, "that's important business." A click at the other line ended the conversation. In his characteristically plain-spoken and businesslike manner, the senator from Montana had told me that he had done what he had promised to do. Now it was up to me.

Up to the time of the phone call, I had gradually been forcing myself to accept the idea that the session would close without any congressional action on disability and succession. Thus I had not yet taken the time to think out what I would do if S.J. Res. 139 did actually reach the floor. Now, I found myself with two hours to prepare for debate on an amendment to the Constitution of the United States.

The thoughts were exploding inside my head. This was to be the first major floor debate in which I had participated during my almost two years in the Senate. As a freshman senator, I had tried to "go slow." I knew that the sure way not to get along in that great body was to give the appearance of being a young upstart who knew all the answers. Up to this time, then, I had purposely avoided numerous prolonged speeches on the Senate floor; I had tried to listen and learn. But now my apprenticeship was coming to a close. In less than two hours, I was going to make my debut by trying to convince my Senate colleagues to support an amendment to the Constitution!

I picked up the phone and buzzed my secretary. "Virginia, get Lesher and Conrad! We're going to amend the Constitution this afternoon!" Then I tried to call home. I wanted Marvella to know just what I had gotten myself into; I would feel a lot better if she were in the gallery silently providing me with moral support. She was not at home; but I finally located her and she promised to be in the gallery at one o'clock.

When Lesher and Conrad rushed in, we quickly decided on the major points I should cover during my presentation; clearly, there would be no time for a prepared statement or for press releases. Besides, I do not like to speak from a prepared text; I would make my presentation from some hurriedly prepared notes on index cards. Clark Norton, my legislative assistant, joined us, and for forty-five minutes we tried to anticipate what might be expected from opponents of S.J. Res. 139 and how best to answer them. Then, at 12:15 we left the office and walked out into the fall sunshine and proceeded over to the Capitol Building.

Suddenly I remembered the agreement I had reached with Senator Keating; he was to be given the opportunity to present his amendment when the matter was discussed on the floor of the Senate. Senator Hruska, too, had certain changes he had wanted to present in the form of amendments during floor debate. Thus, when I arrived at the Senate floor, I immediately sought out the Majority Leader and told him of these commitments. Preoccupied with a hundred other problems, he wasted no words: "Well, get them over here then. If we don't take care of this matter today, you may not get another chance before adjournment." I dispatched Lesher and Conrad to hunt out the two senators, then went to my desk in the Senate to make final preparations for the ensuing debate.

Much to my chagrin, I soon learned that Senator Keating was campaigning for reelection in New York and that Senator Hruska had a speaking engagement in Nebraska. Now what to do? "Let's telephone them long distance," I told Conrad. "We've got to get an okay from both of them or we can't go ahead. I've promised we'd give them a chance to be heard on this matter. If they won't release us from our commitment, we just won't be able to do it today."

Meanwhile, the sparsely-populated Senate was considering the Reserve Officers Bill, which had been held over from Friday. I looked up to the gallery: Marvella had just taken a seat in the front row of the family section. She shot me an inquisitive glance; in reply, I shrugged my shoulders wryly. At the moment, I had no idea what the future held.

At about one-thirty, while I was in conversation with the Majority Leader in the well of the Senate, Conrad sent word that both Ken Keating and Roman Hruska had given us the green light. We could go ahead.

Senator Mansfield sought recognition from the presiding officer, who at that moment was Senator Daniel Brewster of Maryland. "Mr. President," the leader said, "I move that the Senate proceed to the consideration of Calendar No. 1317, Senate Joint Resolution 139."

The presiding officer gave the standard reply: "The Joint Resolution will be stated by title."

The Chief Clerk read: "A joint resolution (S.J. Res. 139) pro-

posing an amendment to the Constitution of the United States relating to the succession to the Presidency and Vice Presidency and
to cases where the President is unable to discharge the powers and
duties of his office."

While this was going on, I had moved to the Majority Leader's
seat on the front-row aisle. It is usual, when a specific measure is
being considered, for the senator who is most involved to handle it
on the floor. Thus, both as chairman of the subcommittee and as
sponsor of the bill, I was floor leader from that time on. A small
chair for Larry Conrad had been squeezed in next to mine. One of
the few times staff members are permitted to sit on the Senate floor
is during debate when it is necessary for them to be close at hand
in order to furnish information as required.

With my heart in my mouth, I stood up. "Mr. President," I
began, "I invite the attention of the Senate to a proposal involving
a great degree of gravity." I continued,

> The recent publication of the Warren Commission Report has
> reawakened in our minds, if indeed that was necessary, the tragic
> events of last November in Dallas, when the President of the United
> States was assassinated. Tragic as was the passing of this man, and as
> were the diabolical events which led to his demise, more tragic, indeed,
> will be his passing if we do not use that unfortunate set of circum-
> stances to understand and overcome an imperfection in our system of
> government which is made evident, once again, by the laws and con-
> stitutional provisions relating to the offices of President and Vice
> President of the United States.

I then set out the problems which confronted us. Briefly, they were
two in number. First, we have no method of filling a vacancy in
the office of Vice President. Sixteen times in our history we have
been confronted with such a vacancy. Eight Presidents have died,
seven Vice Presidents have died, and Vice President John C. Calhoun resigned from the nation's number-two office to return home
to South Carolina and run for U. S. senator. For periods totaling more
than thirty-seven years, the country has had no second-in-command.

The second problem before us was the lack of an effective
means of dealing with presidential disability. President Wilson was
out of commission for well over a year, Garfield lay at death's door
for eighty days, and Dwight Eisenhower had three serious ill-

nesses. Still there was no way to let other hands perform the duties of the Presidency while the Chief Executive was unable to do so.

These problems had to be discussed in detail and their final ramifications placed before the Senate. I turned to the problem of Vice-Presidential vacancies by pointing out that the office of Vice President, itself, had gone through a period of development "perhaps to a greater degree than any other office in the history of the country." Starting with John Adams' description of it as "the most insignificant one that the invention of man had contrived," it had developed to its significant position today as the second most important office in the land. In recent times, Vice Presidents have performed highly important missions for their Presidents. By virtue of the roles they have been given in Equal Employment Opportunity, the National Aeronautics and Space Council, and the National Security Council, they have been involved in the most important issues of the day.

In the final analysis, the most important qualification for a Vice-Presidential candidate is his ability to fulfill the office of President if tragedy should strike. In his unique capacity as "understudy" to the President, the Vice President is well qualified to do just that. Thus "reason dictates that we take steps to assure that the nation shall always have a Vice President."

I then moved on to discuss the second problem, that of Presidential disability. Why has so little been done, said, or written about the course of action our government should follow when the President is unable to perform the powers and duties of his office?

> The provision for impeachment is clearly written into the Constitution. It has been implemented on but one unfortunate occasion in the history of our country. Yet, there is not a word, not a hint about what is meant by the inability of a President. There is no clue as to the method of determining disability, who would make such a determination, what would happen once the determination was made, how the period of inability would be terminated, and whether the President would then resume his office or simply lose his position. These are some of the vexing problems which are presented by the superficial manner in which Presidential inability is referred to—on only one occasion, and by only one word, in the entire Constitution of the United States.

We have had several narrow escapes when the country stood still and courted disaster during those occasions when the President of the United States was ill. Presidents are only human beings. When would the next such occasion confront us with disaster? "It seems to me that history has been trying to tell us something," I said; ". . . the time has come when all of us had better listen."

In our hearings several arguments had been presented which stressed reasons for not supporting an amendment or pointed out other ways of solving the problem. These points had to be dealt with effectively in the floor debate, and I quickly moved to the first of them. Professor Richard Neustadt, of Columbia University, had expressed the opinion that the private agreement on disability, first entered into by Eisenhower and Nixon and subsequently endorsed by their successors, was sufficient to do the job. No legislation was needed. Professor Neustadt was an extremely capable political scientist, but I strongly disagreed with his contentions. The Eisenhower-Nixon agreement, I said, had made a positive contribution.

> It was the first time that anything concrete had been proposed in this area. But such informal agreements are unsatisfactory as permanent solutions. Both Mr. Eisenhower and Mr. Nixon were among the first to say so. Such agreements depend on good will between the President and the Vice President. They do not have the force of law. They could be subjected to serious constitutional challenge. They open the door for possible usurpation of power from the President.
>
> . . . The one thing we must press for is an orderly transfer of power. Whatever procedure is established, it must be generally accepted by a majority of the people. It seems to me that a private agreement would not enjoy the confidence of the public, as would the measure which I hope will be enacted by this body.
>
> These questions can be solved by amending the Constitution. Some say they could best be solved by statute. Many distinguished lawyers disagree. But what most lawyers do agree upon is that if a reasonable constitutional doubt exists, the best method to eradicate any doubt is to amend the Constitution.

In other words, when in doubt, why take chances? Play it safe and be sure! Perhaps the private agreement would suffice, or a law might close the breach. But the preponderance of legal opinion suggested that both of these remedies were insufficient. A constitutional amendment was needed. This should end all doubt. Certainly no one could dispute the constitutionality of a constitutional amendment once it had become a part of the Constitution itself.

S.J. Res. 139 was just such a constitutional amendment. Not only did it provide a Vice President at all times and furnish machinery for determining Presidential disability procedures, it also represented the consensus of many who had previously sponsored proposals of their own. There was a real need to emphasize this broad base of support existing for our amendment; I proceeded to do so.

> I express my gratitude to the long list of cosponsors—which now lists some 32 Senators. . . . This is good evidence of the fact that Senators today are willing to compromise, even though they have their own ideas on the best way to achieve the end we all seek.
> . . . There is no pride of authorship in Senate Joint Resolution 139. Rather, there is the desire that Senators on both sides of the aisle support the resolution.
> Some 13 different proposals were submitted to our committee. Half the Senators who sponsored the various resolutions have now joined in cosponsoring Senate Joint Resolution 139. I believe it is fair to say that we have come as far as we can in obtaining a consensus which I hope this body will accept.

During my presentation, I had noticed that Sam Ervin, our new ally, had come into the back of the room and seated himself at his desk in the far right-hand side of the Chamber, about two-thirds of the way back. Now he arose and addressed the Chair:

> Mr. President, I should like to ask the Senator from Indiana a set of questions in order to point out what is involved in the problems he has been discussing unless the Senator wishes to complete his statement first.

I replied that I would be more than happy to yield and went on to express my gratitude to the senator from North Carolina for having been one of those who had "led us down the road to a consensus," despite his previously favoring a proposal of his own.

Senator Ervin, taking the floor, was quick to return the compliment: "On my own behalf I should like to state that the person who is primarily responsible for bringing these problems as near a solution as is possible today is the able and distinguished Senator from Indiana, who has worked tirelessly on the problems." Then he picked up where I had left off, outlining the method we proposed for filling a Vice-Presidential vacancy. He went straight to the heart of one of the subjects of controversy. Who should choose the new Vice President? Should the task fall solely to the Congress, as the representatives of the people? Senator Ervin thought not.

> . . . There were those who feared that if the selection were made solely by Congress, it might happen that Congress would have to exercise such power at a time when it was controlled by one political party, whereas the White House might be controlled by the other political party . . . and there would be friction between the person designated as Vice President and the President. . . .

The senator from North Carolina continued his argument by pointing out that in the event that the Congress appointed a Vice President of a different party, who subsequently was forced by tragedy to succeed to the Presidency, there would be a lack of continuity between the two administrations. In fact, great confusion, even chaos, could result at a time of crisis when the nation badly needed stability. Yet, he went on, many people including himself felt strongly that the selection of a person to fill a Vice-Presidential vacancy should be made by the representatives of the people in Congress. How could this be accomplished without risking the possibility of political turmoil between the nation's two top executives? In his opinion, the proposed amendment did just that. The President made the nomination and would surely choose a Vice President with whom he could work. The Congress would make the final choice. They would, in actuality, elect the new Vice President.

The senator from North Carolina continued, couching his probing remarks in the form of questions addressed to me, even though his very manner of asking the question, in many cases, served to answer it. What he was doing was masterfully writing into the legislative record questions which might be asked later— by a nation, a court, or a Congress—should circumstances require the implementation of the legislation we were discussing. The courts have stated that where the language of a proposal does not clearly state its intent, they will look to congressional debates, committee reports, and particularly the statements of sponsors of the legislation, to surmise what that intent must have been. By directing these questions to me and letting me answer them as I saw fit, Senator Ervin was determined to make crystal clear my intention, as sponsor of the Resolution, and the intention of Congress when acting upon what might, one day, be the Twenty-fifth Amendment to the Constitution of the United States.

Senator Ervin next turned his attention to the almost forgotten first section of our proposal, which specified that "In case of the removal of the President from office or of his death or resignation, the Vice President shall become President." This section was designed to remove all doubt about a Vice President's status in the event that he was forced to succeed to the Presidency. As Sam Ervin pointed out, it would deal with

> . . . the ghost that has troubled some constitutionalists since the death of William Henry Harrison, about 1 month after "Old Tippecanoe and Tyler, too" were elected, respectively, President and Vice President of the United States. As the Senator knows, there has been an argument among some scholars and some constitutional lawyers ever since John Tyler assumed the office of President on the death of William Henry Harrison, as to whether or not the Vice President who comes to the office under those circumstances is really the President or whether he is merely the Acting President. I think this is a fine provision in the proposed joint resolution, because it would lay to rest the constitutional ghost that has been stalking to and fro in America ever since that time.

As the colloquy with Senator Ervin proceeded, I noticed that Senator Mike Monroney of Oklahoma had taken his chair in the back row of the Senate. Senator Monroney, one of the Senate's leading exponents of governmental reorganization, had testified before our subcommittee. From that testimony, as well as from our private conversations, I knew that Mike had definite thoughts about how best to deal with the problem that we were discussing and that he was by no means happy with all the provisions contained in S.J. Res. 139.

Now, as Senator Ervin and I ended our discussion, the senator from Oklahoma addressed the Chair: "Mr. President, will the Senator yield?" Of course I would be glad to yield, and the senior senator from Oklahoma proceeded to present his own views on the problems of succession and disability. Senator Monroney emphasized the shortcomings of the present line of succession, as well as those of any proposal which gave to Congress the sole responsibility for filling a Vice-Presidential vacancy. He, too, was well aware of the ramifications of having a President of one party and a Vice President of another. If we follow such a plan, he said,

> . . . we jeopardize continuing control of a government which has been elected for a 4-year period by putting it through the speakership of the House, because every 2 years control of the House is subject . . . to change by the voters of the electorate. . . . Automatically to have this change would create a rather difficult political situation in the management and operation of the country, right at a time when the Nation was suffering from the shock of the death of its Chief Executive. The change at this period of time, would be most unwise from the point of view of party control and would be upsetting to the general authority of the Government.

Any proposal to fill the office of Vice President, the senator from Oklahoma contended, should insure that the man being chosen to fill the vacancy be as responsive as possible to the wishes of the people. Thus, he suggested that the people themselves should be permitted to elect their own successor, by providing that

> . . . at the time of the election, a first and second Vice President should be nominated and voted upon by the people in the regular election of President. . . . this would be an expression of the entire electorate of the United States, and thus bless the office or ratify the offices of first Vice President and second Vice President with the vote and the acceptance of the entire electorate.
>
> I recognize the fact that the joint resolution must be a compromise; but I question one bit of the philosophy in the selection of the successor by the nomination of one man, placing in the supreme line of authority over 180 million Americans one man chosen absolutely by the President, by sending the nomination to Congress, and saying, "This is my man. I choose him for my successor."

Thus it was Mike Monroney who, in his extremely logical way, was putting forth the "two Vice President plan" on the floor for the first time. He went on to substantiate his opinion that this plan would be the best way of insuring continuity in the executive branch:

> . . . I would appreciate having the comment of the Senator from Indiana on this theory, which has been supported by a large group of people. . . .
>
> I wish the distinguished chairman of the subcommittee to understand that I appreciate the diligent work and the compromise that have been necessary to introduce this joint resolution. It was necessary

to act. Even though the joint resolution does not comport with my hopes and feelings that two Vice-Presidential candidates would be better, it is still a subject on which Congress must take action. Therefore, I intend to vote for the joint resolution that is now before us. However, I wish that it had been possible to provide for this contingency by having the nominations voted upon in the general election and ratified by the entire public, rather than by Congress alone upon the recommendation of the President.

Before I could reply to the senator from Oklahoma, Sam Ervin was again on his feet, seeking recognition. Without hesitation, I yielded to my colleague from North Carolina. Senator Monroney had, he said, raised a point that merited grave consideration, but

> . . . there are other problems . . . in this field. I introduced a resolution to amend the Constitution to take care of one of them which was pointed out by the tragic assassination of President Kennedy. . . .

His own proposition, he went on, would have dealt with the problems raised by the possibility of the simultaneous deaths of the President and Vice President. However, Ervin pointed out that this proposal, as well as Senator Monroney's and others, "simply went beyond the scope of the area which a majority of the subcommittee. . . and a majority of the full Committee on the Judiciary, thought that Congress and the country would accept in a single amendment."

> . . . The underlying thought, which I believe to be absolutely sound, was that every proposal additional to filling vacancies in the Vice-Presidency and coping with Presidential inability would cause some loss of support in the subcommittee, the full committee, the Congress, or the country at large, and thus endanger the prospect of any accomplishment.
>
> For this reason, the subcommittee eliminated my proposal . . . and the proposal of the Senator from Oklahoma. It was not because the members of the subcommittee felt that the proposals did not merit consideration, but because they felt that if they added these additional proposals to a joint resolution to remove defects in the existing Constitution, their action would jeopardize the possibility of securing favorable action on two essential changes which everyone conceded must be made.

Senator Ervin illustrated his point with one of Aesop's fables. A dog carrying a bone in its mouth was crossing a stream on a small bridge.

Looking down, the dog saw its own reflection in the water. Thinking another dog was beneath him, he opened his mouth to grab the bone the other dog was carrying, and in so doing lost his own. "I believe," concluded Senator Ervin, "that story illustrates the reason the subcommittee did not go any further than it did. . . . The subcommittee recalled the fable of the dog, and knew that if it tried to get too many additional bones it would lose the ones it was attempting to carry across the legislative stream."

At this point Senator Leverett Saltonstall, the distinguished senior senator from Massachusetts, asked recognition. As one of the earliest sponsors of S.J. Res. 139, Senator Saltonstall had been extremely helpful to us. Now, the wise elder statesman from the Bay State stated his wholehearted support for the provisions of our resolution.

> I feel that this proposed amendment satisfactorily resolves the present ambiguity of Article II, Section 1, of the Constitution relating to Presidential succession and disability. Although we cannot foresee every eventuality that might befall our Government, I think this makes adequate provision for the uninterrupted conduct of our Nation's affairs.
>
> With the election of a President and Vice President in November, we shall once again have passed through this dangerous period when we have a vacancy in the Vice-Presidency—a situation we have encountered 16 times in our history. However, we should not let this opportunity pass to resolve the situation once and, hopefully, for all time. Since 1792, when the first succession law was passed, this matter has been disputed. The proposal now before us is the result of exhaustive study and numerous committee hearings. It has the support of state and national bar associations as well as distinguished constitutional lawyers from all over the country. I urge my colleagues to consider this amendment carefully, and to take favorable action on it so that at last we may have a clear and definite constitutional policy on these twin problems of Presidential succession and disability.

As Senator Saltonstall was speaking, another early cosponsor, Senator Fong, entered the still very empty Chamber. I had earlier asked Larry Conrad to get all our strong early supporters to be on hand. What this debate would involve was anyone's guess; but I knew that the vocal support of men like Ervin, Saltonstall, and Fong might well mean the difference between success and failure— not only this time through, but the next time our measure came up in the Senate, as we now knew it would have to next session. In addition, these prominent Republicans, speaking out for us, would greatly lessen the chances of our resolution falling prey to a straight party-line vote later.

Senator Fong's statement was also an unqualified endorsement of the provisions of our measure.

> We must not gamble with the constitutional legitimacy of our Nation's executive branch. When a President or Vice President of the United States assumes his office, the entire Nation and the world must know without doubt that he does so as a matter of right. Only a constitutional amendment can supply this necessary legitimacy.

Larry Conrad's telephone calls seemed to be paying off. By now Senator Bible of Nevada had entered the Chamber. Another early supporter of S.J. Res. 139, he strongly refuted, point by point, the arguments against our provisions to fill a Vice-Presidential vacancy.

> To those who argue against congressional confirmation, I would point out that we are talking about the choice of a man who may himself become President—a man normally elected by the people. The people must retain a margin of control in this choice, and congressional confirmation provides this.
>
> To those who argue that Senate confirmation alone would be adequate, I must point out that we are dealing with an elective office, not an appointed one as in the case of a Cabinet officer. Both Houses should have a vote.
>
> To those who propose giving the choice to the electoral college, I would point out that this body, except in a Presidential election year, is not subject to the direct will of the people. Nor is it constituted to perform the complete function of nominating and electing a Vice President.
>
> To those who argue that this proposal contradicts existing constitutional provisions, I would point out that the order of succession set out by the Constitution is not changed. All that this proposal contemplates is the continuance of the Vice Presidency. In the event of vacancies in both the Presidency and Vice Presidency, the Speaker of the House remains the next in line to succeed.

Senator Bible went on to a strong defense of the disability provisions of our measure and terminated his remarks on a very practical legislative note:

> . . . I know that no single proposal will ever satisfy everyone. But I believe we have at last confronted and met the problem. I believe at

last we have presented the most workable and acceptable solution. It seems to me that now we must act without further delay in view of the possible consequences of inaction. We have no other responsible choice.

After thanking the senator from Nevada, for his intense interest and co-operation over a period of months, I went on to discuss some questions Senator Monroney had voiced earlier, concerning his proposal that two Vice Presidents be elected. He had asked me to explain why this proposal had not been adopted by the committee. This was a valid question and one that deserved an answer. First, in my judgment, further division of the executive power would result in "a reversal of the trend of the past several years toward recognizing the Vice President as an important, significant office." No sooner had the Vice Presidency become a prestigious office in its own right than it would be bisected by such a proposal.

Second, I felt that "when there is a sole repository of Executive power in the Presidency, to the extent that secondary sources of authority are established, the chances of confusion and turmoil are created." Often, I pointed out, the President and Vice President may not agree on certain issues. The existence of a second Vice President would involve a further possibility of disagreement as well as possibly "a vying between the two Vice Presidents for a favored position with the President."

Finally, I pointed out that for a number of years the two political parties had tried to reconcile various geographic or philosophical interests in choosing the Vice-Presidential nominee. In recent years, there had been a tendency away from this practice and efforts were made to get the best man for the position. But if another Vice President were added, it might bring about a resumption of this tendency to use the post to "round out the ticket." There would be an even greater temptation to choose the Vice-Presidential candidates on the basis of what regional, religious, racial, ethnic, or philosophical support they could bring to the ticket. I was not so naive as to ignore the necessity of wise political decisions, but surely the most important criterion in choosing a Vice-Presidential candidate was his possession of the qualities that would allow him to give able service, God forbid the necessity, as President of the United States.

I continued discussing the points the able senator from Oklahoma had raised.

> The Senator pointed out that if the President makes the nomination, it is not too different from making it in the convention. The Senator pointed out that the man to be appointed by the President and subsequently chosen by the Congress would not get the stamp of approval of the entire electorate. I would prefer that he did. I think the other matters I mentioned, in view of the conflicts involved, override this latter factor. If Congress is to choose the man nominated, it will certainly consider this a serious responsibility and act as the voice of the people. What better opportunity is there for the people to express their wishes than through those who serve in Congress?
>
> One suggestion made was that the electoral college be convened, since it is already part of the constitutional system, and that the college meet to determine who the President and Vice President shall be. I for one feel that that would be a terrible solution. It would fall far short of having the confidence of the people. It is surprising, but nevertheless a fact, that very few Americans know any one member of the electoral college. To have the electoral college choose, out of the clear sky, someone who had not been on the ticket, who had not made speeches over the country, would not tend to gain the confidence of the people.

Senator Monroney agreed that the electoral college system would not be the proper vehicle for deciding the question of Presidential succession; but he was still troubled by the possibility of a Congress controlled by a party opposed to that of the President, which might succumb to the temptation to play politics with the choice of a Vice President. This was, I conceded, certainly a possibility. I confessed to my friend from Oklahoma,

> This is something I wondered about in my own mind. As the original sponsor of this measure, I gave that matter considerable thought. . . .
> . . . Let us bring our minds back to last November, December, and January. The most impolitic thing would have been for someone in public life to play politics to be a successor to Lyndon Johnson as Vice President. At that time, with the death of the national leader fresh in the minds of the people, the last thing a member of Congress would do would be to play politics; there would be a recognition of the right of the people to make a choice and have a voice.

Senator Monroney and I continued to debate our separate views of the subject, and then Senator Ervin again joined the debate.

... The Senator from Oklahoma put his finger on why the joint resolution has some provisions in it, and why it does not have other provisions in it, when he referred to the numerous compromises that had to be made in order to get any kind of resolution to the Senate floor. I believe my observation will be illustrative of the point the Senator from Oklahoma is making.

I could hardly suppress a smile of admiration for Sam Ervin's rhetorical mastery. Somehow, by "illustrating" Mike Monroney's fleeting reference to compromise, Sam was managing in actuality to refute the senator from Oklahoma's own objections. Senator Ervin listed in detail the various views which had been held on the matter of succession and disability, stressing, once again, that he himself had originally been an adherent of one of them.

Fortunately, he went on, "the subcommittee did not follow the pattern which has been followed by those who advocated changes in the electoral college system." He cited, as parallels to our situation, the three main schools of thought on electoral college reform and said that they had been unable to reconcile their differences. He concluded,

> I believe that one of the greatest accomplishments for which the Senator from Indiana and the other members of the subcommittee deserve credit is the fact that they did not insist upon their respective views as being the only permissible ones, but, on the contrary, laid aside all pride of individual authorship and the human quality which one's friends call firmness and one's enemies call obstinacy, and sought a broad area of agreement. As a result, they have brought forth a most workable joint resolution which will take care of two defects in the Constitution, by providing a practical method for filling vacancies in the office of Vice President and a sound method for determining when presidential inability exists.
>
> I thank the Senator from Indiana again for his fine work. I also wish to tell the Senator from Oklahoma that I am much impressed by the wisdom of his observation, as indeed I always am when he speaks.

Next, Senator Frank Church of Idaho rose to speak. Frank and Bethine Church had become our close personal friends since Marvella and I arrived in Washington. Earlier in the afternoon, as the debate was continuing, I had gone to the back of the Chamber to take a seat next to my good friend from Idaho. I didn't hesitate to put my concern on the line: "Frank, I know full well you have some reservations on our resolution. I'd be the last one to tell you that you should desert your proposal. But from a practical standpoint, we've sifted and sorted, we've compromised and combined, to the point where we finally have a package that has more support than anything else that's been proposed so far. I'm afraid if we don't pass it this time, we'll have lost our best opportunity to deal with this problem that you and I and so many others have been worrying about. Frank, if you can see your way clear, I need your help. I need your vote."

I felt I could say no more and went back to the center of the Senate, still uncertain of how the senator from Idaho would respond to this plea. He had long recognized the need for finding a solution to the problem and had testified before our committee in support of his own proposal to deal with the matter of Vice-Presidential vacancies. Now, as he rose to talk, I wondered whether my words would have any effect on his position.

> . . . As the Senator from Indiana knows, I have some reservations with respect to the proposal finally reported by the committee. Specifically, I have felt that it would be preferable if the President were to nominate a panel of at least two, but not more than five, candidates, so that the role of Congress might be a more significant one, in the final selection of the new Vice President.

After asking that an article he wrote for the *Progressive* magazine setting forth his personal views be inserted into the record, Senator Church went on.

> . . . Mr. President, despite the difference between the position I have taken and the conclusion reached by the committee, I nevertheless feel that the committee proposal is highly meritorious, and that the need to remedy the deficiency that now exists in the Constitution is so great that it is incumbent upon Congress to move forward in the best way that is open to it. Therefore, I shall vote for the joint resolution, in the hope that it may stimulate interest in this matter, and in the expectation that early next year Congress can move ahead toward submitting to the States an amendment to the Constitution, thus rectifying this serious weakness.

I was extremely gratified that Senator Church had spoken out as he did. Men like Church and Monroney, and all the others who possessed views different from my own and yet were willing to put them aside for the sake of getting a rapid and equitable solution to the problem, were in a large measure responsible for our ultimate success.

Senator Javits, who also had foregone his personal solution and joined us in cosponsoring S.J. Res. 139, spoke next, stressing the importance of our task.

> . . . I hope that although the Senate is not too busily attended today, and this debate will have been consummated in a relatively short period of time, people will not overlook the portentious decision which we shall make for the future of American Government.

Senator Javits was followed by Senator Hart of Michigan, a fellow member of the Judiciary Committee, who also emphasized the importance of the problem and the critical necessity of finding a solution to it. Next, Senator Pearson of Kansas joined in the debate.

> Mr. President, the legislative measure now before us is of great importance to both the stability and tranquillity of this Nation. The electrified rapidity of events which occurred last November riveted attention to the necessity for an effective Presidential succession and disability arrangement.

Following Jim Pearson's closing remarks I took the floor once again to express my thanks to the senator from Kansas. As I was doing so, Senator Mansfield, who had been observing much of the debate from the wings, came onto the floor from the cloakroom and proceeded into the well of the Senate, directly toward me. Without interrupting my remarks, he whispered in my ear, "Vote. Vote. Vote. Vote!"

The wise and observant Majority Leader had seen many worthwhile pieces of legislation talked to death; he had a keen sense of when the situation was right for favorable floor action. I was prompt to take his advice and bring the debate to a close. The acting President pro tempore moved the bill on to the final reading and stated, "The question is on the engrossment and third reading of the joint resolution."

Before the vote, Senator Mansfield rose to his feet to compliment all of those who had played a part in the progress of the proposed amendment.

> I believe this is a momentous and historic occasion. I am delighted that so many of our colleagues on both sides of the aisle have joined

with the distinguished junior Senator from Indiana, and, under his
leadership, I am delighted that the proposed joint resolution is now on
the verge of passage. It is a foundation which will set well in the building of this Republic.

Despite the Majority Leader's admonition to wind things up, I
could not resist a few more words. Niceties are commonplace on
the floor of the Senate; some are sincere, others are utilized to ease
the tensions of heated controversy. But, in those closing moments
of my first senatorial debate, I could not have meant more sincerely
what I said:

> Mr. President, if I may take one final moment I would like the
> Senate to know that none of this could have taken place without the
> continuing interest and assistance of the distinguished Majority Leader.
> During the last two historic years, when the Congress has been faced
> with a multitude of pressing, often delicate, problems, and has been
> confronted with a number of delays, the distinguished Senator from
> Montana has never lost sight of the significance of this issue now before
> us. Now, when all of us are anxious to complete our business, he has,
> nonetheless, seen to it that we take the time to debate and act on this
> issue. I thank the Senator. It is just one more example of his statesman-
> ship and devotion to the good and welfare of our Nation above all
> other considerations.

Thereupon the acting President pro tempore put the question,
"Shall it pass?" There were ayes from the floor. He paused for a
moment and then continued: "In the opinion of the Chair, two-
thirds of the Senators present and voting having voted in the affirmative, Senate Joint Resolution 139 is passed."

By then I felt a little numb. The final passage had been almost
anticlimactic, with very few senators on the floor. No roll-call vote
had been requested or taken. But we had done it. Our resolution
had been passed, by unanimous consent, in the United States Senate. We had made one more step down the long road toward
amending the Constitution.

Or so we thought. The following day, shortly after the Senate
convened at twelve o'clock, Larry Conrad dashed, wild-eyed, into
my office. He had just received a frantic call from John Graves, the
assistant secretary for the Senate majority, saying, "Larry, get your
boss and get over here fast. Senator Stennis is here, and he's filed a

motion to reconsider yesterday's vote on your constitutional amendment. For crying out loud, hurry!"

I was speechless with disbelief. Without a word, Conrad and I
ran out of the office, across to the Capitol, up the steps of the
Senate, past the elevators, and through the swinging doors into the
Senate Chamber. Sure enough, Senator Stennis had introduced a
resolution to reconsider the previous vote on S.J. Res. 139.

It was certainly possible to do such a thing. The presiding
officer had simply asked, "Shall it pass?" and in this case it had been
noted that in his opinion two-thirds of the senators had carried it.
The normal procedure, to foreclose further or later discussion, is
for someone who favors a proposal to move to reconsider the vote
just taken. The sponsoring senator then moves to lay the reconsideration motion on the table. If the tabling motion is successful,
as is usually automatically the case, the bill is passed beyond recall.

But in the excitement of my first presentation in the Senate,
I had neglected to arrange for this simple parliamentary move, without which, under Senate rules, any vote can subsequently be opened
on a motion to reconsider. Senator Stennis had now done just that.
But why? I was hot enough to explode.

"What's he trying to do?" I asked John Graves furiously.
"Why is Stennis trying to shoot us out of the water?"

"Senator, you'd better talk to him. He said something about
its being bad business to establish a precedent of amending the
Constitution with only nine senators present."

I turned away and strode toward the Senate cloakroom to find
John Stennis. It looked to me, just then, as if the senator from
Mississippi were purposely trying to defeat S.J. Res. 139. I was
angry enough to fight, but I was also puzzled. This action was completely out of character for John Stennis, who had been very kind
to me and was generally very courteous in his dealings with all of
his colleagues. Why this potshot taken for no reason? When I
found the senator from Mississippi, I tried to conceal my boiling
emotions.

"John, what's the idea? We've been working on this matter
for over a year. Now that we've passed it, you make this motion.
It will jeopardize everything we've done."

The senator from Mississippi got up from the large brown

leather chair in which he had been sitting. Ignoring the poorly concealed anger in my voice, he said genially, in his pleasant southern baritone, "Hello, Birch! Say, I'm glad you came over here. I've wanted to talk to you about that vote yesterday. I should have called you on the phone."

"Now, Birch," he continued, "as I see it, we'd be setting a bad precedent if we amended the Constitution by unanimous consent. We ought to require a roll-call vote. That way, in the future, if some court or some future congress looks back on our action, they can see that the entire Senate was in favor of it, not just a handful of senators who happened to be there when the question was put."

I began to see the light. "In other words, John," I said, "you feel it really strengthens our position to have a roll-call vote? Then we'd have proof positive that two-thirds of the Senate does support the proposed amendment—is that what you mean?"

"That's right," Stennis said. "I don't know of any constitutional amendment that's ever been ratified by unanimous consent. Maybe one has," he added tactfully, "but I have no recollection of it, do you?"

"No, John. The more I think of it, the more I like your idea. In fact, I'll be glad to join in your motion if you want me to." Ten minutes ago, as Larry and I had rushed furiously over to the Senate, I certainly never dreamed I would be saying *that*.

"Fine, Birch," was the reply. "In fact, I'll tell you what we ought to do next session. You and I ought to get together and go before the Rules Committee to establish a Senate rule that would require a two-thirds roll-call vote on any proposed constitutional amendment. I don't think any Senate rule covers that now, and I think we ought to see to it, together."

"That's fine with me, John," I answered. "Now let's go ahead and accept your motion; then we can get that roll-call vote."

Without further ado, Senator Stennis and I went back into the Chamber. The presiding officer then put the question of S.J. Res. 139 for a second time.

After Senator Stennis took the floor to explain the reasons for his motion, Senator Mansfield defined the vote, but cautioned against reopening the question for extended debate since that would take up valuable time that was needed in the Senate for other things.

After some bargaining between Stennis and Senator Mansfield, it was agreed that a vote would be taken no later than four o'clock that day. Senator Stennis had asked for the vote to be postponed until half-past three the following day, but the Majority Leader was pressing to vote while we could be certain of getting a quorum.

Senator Stennis and I alternately took the floor. It was important for me to make it clear that I was in complete agreement with the senator from Mississippi on the question of precedent that was involved here. The discussion was brief. When the final tally was announced, the vote was sixty-five ayes, no nays. I went over to Senator Stennis and shook his hand.

"John," I said, "I certainly appreciate your interest in this whole thing. I apologize if I was hot under the collar for a minute."

As Conrad and I left the Senate and headed back to our office, he said, "Well, Senator, you just made a record that's not likely to be equaled."

"What do you mean?"

The committee counsel grinned. "I don't suppose there's ever been another senator who's succeeded in passing two constitutional amendments in less than twenty-four hours."

He stepped back to avoid the playful swing I took at him. As we went into the office building, I said, "You know, Larry, John Stennis really did us a favor there. First of all, he's right—it's mighty poor business to amend the Constitution by a vote of nine senators." I was remembering my feeling of anticlimax the day before, when the voice vote was taken. "Not only is he dead right on that, but now we have sixty-five members of the United States Senate on record as favoring Senate Joint Resolution 139—as it is! I grant you next session's a new ball game. We'll have to do this all over again, and I think it's going to be harder than it was this time. But be that as it may, each of my colleagues who voted yes today is going to have a lot of explaining to do if he votes no next year. In other words, sixty-five to zero means a lot more to us than the consent of nine anonymous senators."

Thus, legislative action on S.J. Res. 139 came to an end. Upon passage by the Senate, the resolution was referred to the House Judiciary Committee, which was to be its permanent grave.

On October 3, 1964, Congress adjourned *sine die;* and the

second session of the Eighty-eighth Congress came to a close. Not having passed both Houses, prior to adjournment, S.J. Res. 139 was null and void. It took its place with the dozens of other measures which had been unable to make their way through the difficult catacombs of the Congress. But S.J. Res. 139, I felt, was more of a phoenix than a dead duck—and it would, if I had anything to say about it, spring out of the ashes with new vitality.

CHAPTER 7

We Could Not Ask
for More

On November 2, 1964, a landslide victory propelled Lyndon B. Johnson into a new term as President of the United States. Along with him, Hubert H. Humphrey of Minnesota stepped into the Vice Presidency, which had been vacant for the 344 days since the assassination of President Kennedy. The fact that the country now had a Vice President removed much national anxiety about the question of Presidential succession. On the one hand, this lessening of concern might make our job more difficult. But from our point of view it was also an advantage for tactical reasons. The fact that the Speaker of the House was no longer one heartbeat away from the presidency greatly eased the difficulties of obtaining House passage of our disability and succession measure.

In early December, we resumed our campaign to win legislative support for what had been introduced a year ago as S.J. Res. 139, but which would now be reintroduced as Senate Joint Resolution 1.

Larry Conrad persuaded Bud Ast, the Senate Bill Clerk, to reserve this more auspicious title for our new effort which would begin on the first day of the next session.

We sent out letters to all senators urging that they cosponsor our new resolution. It was, we emphasized, identical to the one passed in the Senate sixty-five to zero—with the absent senators who were announced as voting for it bringing the proponents to eighty-five. To the senators who had supported us before, that was all we needed to say. To those who had not voted before, we stressed the heavy support the bill had received the first time. Because of a clerical mix-up, we realized too late that the letters, unfortunately, had been sent to *all* senators who were currently serving, including those who would not be around in the new session to give us the support we requested. Thus we had a wry note from Senator E.L. Mechum, of New Mexico, who had been defeated by Senator Montoya in November, saying he would like to help but that under the circumstances it was impossible. I wrote him back apologetically, thanking him for his past support and saying I knew he would understand that secretaries would never be adequately replaced by machines. We were fortunate in the potentially more embarrassing case of Senator Keating. Abbott Leban, closing up his office, returned our letter to us instead of forwarding it.

About that same time, we called a small conference with Don Channell and other members of the American Bar Association, to plot our strategy in the next session. We discussed the idea of approaching Chairman Celler of the House Judiciary Committee, hoping to persuade him to join us by introducing a parallel measure, House Joint Resolution 1, which could proceed in the House at the same time as ours in the Senate. Thus, the Bayh Amendment could become the Bayh-Celler or the Celler-Bayh Amendment.

"It doesn't matter what we call the thing," I told the bar officials. "Let's just get it passed!"

The meeting ended with a decision that the obvious person to approach the Judiciary Committee Chairman was a fellow New Yorker, Herb Brownell. Herb had already been invaluable to us, and we relied on him to use his tact and influence on Mannie Celler, who could spell success or failure for our efforts in the House.

Just before Christmas, Herb called to say that he had had a

long and fruitful conversation with Mannie, who had agreed to introduce H.J. Res. 1 in the House of Representatives. This was some of the best news we could have received. Emanuel Celler was a strong committee chairman; he had the warm respect of his colleagues and maintained close control and supervision over his committee. If Chairman Celler was backing our proposal, the odds were more strongly in its favor now than they had ever been before.

That same week, Conrad and I decided it was time to strike a blow for our amendment at the White House. The press was full of various legislative items which were being considered by the new Johnson-Humphrey administration, and I thought it imperative that succession and disability be placed high on the list of priorities. The time had come, then, to go straight to the top. I had been reluctant to bother the President before, when our chances of obtaining final passage had been extremely slim. Now we could no longer afford to wait. If we were not successful in the coming session of Congress, with the memory of Dallas already fading, our efforts would go the same way as those of all our well-intentioned predecessors.

So, throwing caution to the wind, I called White House assistant Jack Valenti and made an appointment to see the President personally on the tenth of December. At 11:25 A.M. I presented myself at 1600 Pennsylvania Avenue. After only a short wait, I was ushered into the circular office which served as the focal point for all our major national and international problems. Here was the seat of power of the United States. Upon the shoulders of the man who worked here rested an awesome concentration of responsibility.

The President greeted me and motioned me to sit on a couch across the room from his massive desk; he took a seat in his rocking chair just to my left and ordered coffee for us both over a White House phone. As he did so, I looked around me—at the colored pictures of his wife and daughters, and the memorabilia he had acquired during his more than thirty years of public service.

By the time the coffee arrived, the President had made two phone calls, one to a staff aide and one to the Secretary of Defense.

He picked up his coffee cup, sat back in the rocking chair, and turned to me, saying, "Now, Birch what's on your mind today?"

As briefly as I could, I outlined my thoughts concerning the need for action on the problem of succession and disability. The American Bar Association, I emphasized, was creating strong grass-roots support for our measure; and for the first time in history one House of Congress had taken action on the matter. Now, I said, the election of Vice President Humphrey made it possible for the House to take action without appearing to insult its speaker.

The President, who had been listening intently, motioned me to pause for a moment as he punched one of the numerous buttons on the nearby phone panel. "My hand is giving me some trouble again. Let's see if another of those massages will help." Four days earlier a small growth had been removed from his right hand. It had been minor surgery, of course, but had increased public speculation and concern over the problem of Presidential disability. The medical technician came in, applied lotion to the back of the President's hand, and began to massage it gently. The President turned toward me again. After a moment's hesitation, I called his attention to the press speculation which even such a small injury had evoked, remarking that even something so minor was a matter of considerable concern to the entire nation.

The President urged me to go on. "Birch, what does your resolution do? How would you deal with the problems?"

I quickly summarized the way we had provided for the President and Congress together to fill a Vice-Presidential vacancy, then reviewed the three-point program for dealing with Presidential inability.

The medical aide went out, and Lyndon Johnson folded his hands under his chin. Looking down at his knees, he slowly and silently rocked back and forth for a moment. Then he looked up.

"Birch, talk to Bill Moyers about this; Bundy, too. I know it's a problem that needs to be solved, and you'll have a lot better chance of solving it now that we've had an election. You talk to those fellows and let them have your thinking. Then we'll see what can be done."

I rose, thanked the President, and bade him good-bye. Bill Moyers' outer office was to the left as I went out of the President's office. On an impulse, I stuck my head inside the door and asked his secretary if her boss was around. I was in luck; he was on the telephone, but would be with me as soon as his call was finished. After a little wait, I was ushered into the office of the President's good right arm. He sat in the far corner of the room, behind a desk which contained, in neat stacks, some of the most important problems that confronted the nation. Bill and I had become close friends since we had been in Washington; but beyond my personal admiration and affection for the man, what mattered at this moment was that Bill D. Moyers was the White House aide whose advice was very highly valued by Lyndon Johnson. If Moyers' enthusiasm could be enlisted behind our efforts on the inability-succession problem, it would be second only to the support of the President himself. I gave him the same brief rundown that only minutes before I had given to the President. As I finished, Bill leaned across the desk to offer me a long, slender cigar. "No thanks, Bill," I said. He took one, lit it, and leaned back in his chair propping his feet on the corner of the desk.

"Frankly, Birch," he said, "we're just now trying to put together some generalized thoughts on the State of the Union message. Would it be any help to you if the President mentioned succession and disability?"

"Any help?" I exclaimed. "Just like sterling on silver, Bill, that's all!"

"Well, for now let's keep this conversation between us. But we'll see what we can do; I don't think the President's made up his mind definitely on it yet. Did you say," he went on, "the boss told you to see Bundy?"

"That's right, Bill. Do you have any thoughts on what my approach to him ought to be?"

"No. I'd just tell him what you told me. We'll try to work something out. I'll tell you what, Birch, why don't you check with us right after the first of the year and remind me? I'll let you know as soon as anything's decided."

I thanked him and left. It looked as if I had talked to Bill Moyers just in the nick of time, at a moment when the President and his staff were hard at work preparing a program to present to the new Congress.

McGeorge Bundy's office was on the lower floor of the White House. I stopped by, hoping my luck would hold out; but he was out of the city and would not be back until the following week. His secretary arranged an appointment for me to see him on his return.

I arrived the next week at the appointed time and had a lengthy conversation with the Presidential aide who served as Lyndon Johnson's advisor and trouble shooter on a wide variety of subjects. He had been close to President Kennedy, and he seemed equally to have the confidence of the new Chief Executive. Only recently, he had returned from a personal Presidential mission in South Vietnam, and the first part of our conversation dealt, in some detail, with this visit. Like other members of Congress, I was greatly concerned with the events in that part of the world and was glad to have the chance to get Bundy's first-hand view of recent events.

Finally, we changed the subject, and I plunged into the main reason for my visit.

"Mac, the President asked me to stop by and talk with you about our proposal to deal with the problems of Presidential succession and inability."

"How do things stand now on that, Birch?" he asked.

I gave him a blow-by-blow account of our past efforts. He asked numerous questions, mostly about what I thought we could expect from the Congress, and he indicated that he had already discussed the matter with Attorney General Katzenbach. From the tone of his voice as well as from the content of his questions, I could sense that he was wary of creating any system which might possibly remove the power of a duly elected President.

I did not want to monopolize too much of his time and so excused myself shortly after that. But as I left his office, I had the impression that I had not quite sold him on the provisions of our resolution. Not that he had seemed to be convinced that any proposal could do the job better; but his statement that he had discussed the matter with the Attorney General made me wonder if Katzenbach had been trying to convince him to follow the enabling approach of Senator Keating's S.J. Res. 35. The Attorney General had supported such a proposal in his testimony, and, by all indications, still preferred it to the specific proposal embodied in our amendment. The Attorney General, I reflected, could be a powerful adversary. Indeed, he was the nation's number-one lawyer.

At the end of the year I put in another call to Bill Moyers, reminding him that he had wished me to jog his memory about the inclusion of a statement on succession and disability in the State of the Union message. "Bill," I said, "if you hadn't wanted me to take you up on that invitation to bother you, you shouldn't have made it."

Our brief conversation concluded with Bill's assurance that they still had us in mind and that he would do everything he possibly could to see that a clause containing some reference to succession and disability was included in the message.

The calendar turned, and we were in 1965. On the second of January, two days before the President was to give his State of the Union message to a joint session of Congress, I received a call from Ramsey Clark, who at that time was serving as a White House assistant. Ramsey, son of the distinguished Supreme Court Justice Tom Clark, was an extremely able and personable man. Moyers had asked him to explore my thoughts on the succession and disability matter and, needless to say, I was not at all bashful about expressing them to him. I stressed the great benefit which could be derived, particularly in the House of Representatives, from the President's indicating by way of the State of the Union message that he considered our problem to be an important one.

"Ramsey, we passed this matter once in the Senate, and I think we can pass it again. But frankly, my friend, I'm not sure about the House. Last session they were jittery because of the Speaker's feelings. I don't think they will be this time, but we can't afford to take any chances. If the administration comes out for our program, that will be a significant step toward House passage. If they act, we'll be home free."

"We'll do what we can, Birch," replied Ramsey Clark, "but it'll have to be brief. They're sifting and sorting like mad down here right now. Everyone's trying to get his pet project included in the President's message, and we have to fight like the devil for every additional word—but I'll do my best."

The State of the Union message was to be delivered in the House chamber at nine o'clock on the evening of January 4. At half-past four that afternoon, Ramsey Clark was on the line again.

"Birch," the young Texan's voice came over the phone, "I told you I'd let you know how we were progressing on this. I'm as near certain as I can be that we're going to have a passage you'll be happy with. I wanted to check it out with you. Could you listen?"

"Are you kidding, Ramsey? Fire away!"

"All right, here it is," said Clark. " 'I will propose laws to insure the necessary continuity of leadership if the President should become disabled or die.' Birch, that's the best we've been able to do so far. What do you think of it?"

"Ramsey, I think any mention at all will be great. We just need to be able to emphasize to the members of Congress that the President wants this problem solved. And I think it's important for him to remind the country as a whole that we have some unfinished business to take care of in this area."

After gratefully saying good-bye to Ramsey Clark, I reminded myself that mention of our problem was still not a certainty. Yet, I could not help feeling great optimism at the turn of events.

That night I was sitting in the back row of the House as the joint session was called to order. The House Chamber was crammed. Not only were the members of both Houses of Congress there, but all of the ambassadors, members of the Supreme Court, and Cabinet had also been seated. There were not enough seats to go around. Some people were finally being seated on temporary chairs set in the back of the aisle; others had to stand behind the brass railing at the back of the chamber. The galleries, too, were packed.

The session had been called to order at 8:45. At nine o'clock the doorkeeper, William M. ("Fishbait") Miller, announced: "The President of the United States."

The President's address covered many subjects from the traditional problems of international intrigue to the burning domestic problems. He chose this forum to announce his plans to establish the Great Society. The President talked about the need for eliminating waste, saying, "I will soon report to you on our progress and the new economies we plan to make." Each major point that he made was interrupted by applause. I was hanging on every word, but I must admit that I was not the most disinterested of listeners.

Every time Lyndon Johnson mentioned a different topic I thought that the odds against ours being included were a little greater. With each new sentence we were further along in the message without any mention of succession and disability.

I was beginning to think that we had lost our battle with the word-printers down at the White House. The President went on: "Even the best of government is subject to the worst of hazards. I will propose laws to insure the necessary continuity of leadership should the President be disabled or die. In addition, I will propose. . . ."

He had mentioned our problem! Those eighteen words were like nuggets of the purest gold. With them, we could approach each member of the Congress with a definite assertion that the President of the United States recognized the urgency of the problem and wanted it solved.

Although we considered that the President's reference to inability and succession in the State of the Union message was a major victory for our amendment, others did not see it that way. A few newspapers were quick to interpret the phrase "I will propose *laws*" to mean that the President would seek to introduce a statute, not a constitutional amendment, to deal with the problem. My own feeling was that there was little indication that that might happen. What did trouble me, however, was the strong influence of Attorney General Katzenbach, who favored a constitutional amendment, but one which followed the enabling approach of the former S.J. Res. 35. Despite one statement after the other to the press, stating my optimism, it was a little unsettling to realize that none of us really knew exactly what the President's reference had meant.

The House stayed in session that night after the President was escorted out, and Judiciary Committee chairman Celler introduced H.J. Res. 1 at that time. Our version, S.J. Res. 1, would not be introduced until two days later, when the Senate first convened.

In the meantime, we were waging an all-out campaign to acquire cosponsors for our measure before it was introduced. I was urging all of my colleagues to join in our efforts. We were deviling them—in person, over the telephone, and through the mails.

I wrote personal letters to each senator and buttonholed those I happened to run into, seeking their cosponsorship. Our staff kept the phone lines busy with calls to legislative assistants in the senators' offices: "My senator says he needs your senator's help. His support can be the difference between winning and losing—can we add his name as cosponsor?"

I felt that strong cosponsorship was vitally important. It was true that a cosponsor of a measure had, and often exercised, the right to oppose it later; this would be especially true for a constitutional amendment, where no vote would be cast without a great deal of reflection. Nonetheless, a cosponsor would be much more likely to vote for the bill than to vote against it, thus backing out of his original commitment. By January 5, we had acquired fifty-four cosponsors.[1]

On the morning of January 6, we were still making phone calls to those senators who had not yet come on board. We had arranged for the Bar Association people to bombard the more reluctant senators with requests to cosponsor; and, as usual, the ABA was extremely efficient in this enterprise. Thus, Conrad's last-minute call to the office of the venerable senior senator from Virginia, Harry Byrd, produced surprising results. His bewildered legislative assistant told Conrad, "I don't know what it is, but the lawyers are all over us. Put us down as a cosponsor."

On the other hand, Conrad was less successful when he talked to a legislative aide of Senator John Tower, the junior senator from Texas. "We're not sure of the Senator's feelings," the aide told Conrad, "but we think he favored the 1886 law." Conrad had a hard time concealing the disgust in his voice as he hung up the phone. "Eighteen eighty-six? What the devil could you expect? Somebody ought to tell those people we're living in the twentieth century!"

"Cool down, Larry," I told him. "You know that's Tower's aide talking, not Tower. No senator can keep up to date on everything."

Undoubtedly our ability to say that the administration favored action on the problem helped in getting cosponsors. Also, there was a tendency to snowball—our dwelling upon one senator's cosponsorship often persuaded another senator to join us. But most important, I think, was the fact that every member of the Senate

---

[1] See Appendix, p. 365, for the full list of cosponsors.

began to realize that for the first time in history there was a chance —a good chance—of getting something done on the problems of succession and disability; and they wanted to lend a hand in getting the job done. Be that as it may, by the time S.J. Res. 1 was introduced on the afternoon of January 6, we had acquired seventy-two cosponsors.

On January 13, Larry Conrad met with Mrs. Bess Dick, a House Judiciary Committee assistant and close advisor of Congressman Celler. It was becoming increasingly important to coordinate the efforts of the two Houses and try to minimize any friction or competitiveness which could develop. Such friction was unlikely, I thought, on so important an issue which both Houses were obviously eager to solve. Yet it is natural for the members of each chamber to feel that the activities of their own body are more important than those of the other. Therefore, the closer liaison, the better.

After the meeting, Larry promptly sought me out in the Capitol doctor's office, where I was receiving ultrasonic treatment for a strained back muscle that was still troubling me after the airplane crash. Mrs. Dick from House Judiciary, he told me, had proposed that the House should be the first to take action on the bill during the new session, since the Senate had passed S.J. Res. 139 already. This information troubled me. I called Senator Mansfield then and there to get his thoughts on Mrs. Dick's proposal. The Majority Leader felt that the Senate should not hold off; rather, it should get to work as quickly as possible, making our measure an early order of business.

That, of course, was my feeling too. Still in the doctor's office, I called Don Channell and Lowell Beck at the American Bar Association office to tell them about the potential timing problem. We agreed that much unnecessary controversy could arise over this sort of jockeying for position. I asked Channell and Beck if they could try to spread some oil on these troubled waters, and they promised to do some diplomatic lobbying for Senator Mansfield's contention.

On the way back from the doctor's office, Conrad and I, along with Steve Lesher who had joined us, paid a call on the Majority Leader. It took exactly two minutes to find out that he stood by his earlier opinion.

"Birch, it's your bill. If I were you, I'd take it on through."
Without further ado, we said good-bye and left. The die was cast:
We would proceed with our original plans to have the Senate act
as rapidly as possible. At no time did we suggest that the House
await our action. Rather, we felt that both sides should take parallel
action on the problem as quickly as possible.

I felt resolute that we were doing the right thing, but fortunately our decision to move full-speed ahead was not, as it turned
out, put to the test. By the next day, when Larry Conrad again
talked with Mrs. Dick, she did not seem at all concerned about
which House acted first. I thought to myself, three cheers for Don
Channell's powers of persuasion!

On January 14 we were joined by an important cosponsor,
Robert F. Kennedy, the new junior senator from New York. As
the former Attorney General—the nation's highest judicial official
—Bob Kennedy would be a significant part of our movement. He
commanded great respect in the Congress, on his own merits as
well as for his closeness to the former President.

On January 22, two days after Lyndon Johnson and Hubert
Humphrey were inaugurated, S.J. Res. 1 was referred to the Subcommittee on Constitutional Amendments. We had asked that it
remain at the desk where it was introduced, pending the addition of
new sponsors, so that the names of those who had joined since
January 6 would appear on the first printing of the bill.[2] Now we
could start Senate action in earnest.

Late in January, the American Bar Association gave us further
help in implementing our desire to work effectively with the House
by sponsoring a luncheon meeting. It was held in the House Hearing
Room, and Chairman Celler and the ranking Republican committee
member, William McCulloch, led the House delegation. I was the
sole representative from the Senate. Don Channell, John Feerick,
and other bar officials rounded out the guest list. We hoped that
this luncheon would not only help us to achieve closer liaison with
the House, but would also get us some publicity, thus keeping our

[2]This can no longer be done. On the recommendation of Senator Dirksen, a
new rule makes it necessary for all cosponsors to have been acquired prior to the
time of introduction. Additional new cosponsors after that time must be added by
specific motion from the Senate floor.

amendment in the public eye. The press was well represented, and reporters were given ample opportunity to get the joint views of both Chairman Celler and myself on the subject. We had good coverage and were glad of it. Perhaps interested citizens across the country, reading the story and seeing the pictures, would write their congressmen on the subject, thus keeping the legislators aware that the public was still concerned over the problem.

We still received no word from the White House concerning what proposal the President might make to the Congress. He had said that a message was forthcoming; but, not knowing its content, we all were silently apprehensive that it would recommend an approach contrary to the groundwork we had laid in support of our amendment. We were not sure what we could do about this; in my judgment, another formal approach to the Administration seemed inadvisable at the moment. But an opportunity was presented in an unexpected fashion.

On January 24, Don Channell gave a cocktail party at his Virginia home, in honor of Lewis Powell, Walter Craig, and ABA president-elect Ed Kuhn. I was unable to be present, having committed myself to join some of the many Indiana constituents who were still in town following the inauguration festivities. But fortunately, both Conrad and Lesher were free to accept Channell's hospitality. The next morning, when I saw them at the office, they both had an I-know-something-you-don't-know look on their faces.

"Morning, boys," I said, "how was the party?"

"Oh, well," said Lesher, grinning broadly, "I guess it was all right as those things go."

"Have you ever stopped to think," said Conrad, equally gleeful, "how much time people waste going to parties? Why, we could have been here in the office, working to get something done on our amendment, instead of standing around in some Virginia living room making small talk."

"That's right," said Lesher. I was getting more and more intrigued; but they were obviously enjoying themselves and weren't going to disclose their little secrets until they were good and ready.

"What a bore!" Conrad continued. "All that meaningless chit-chat. What possible importance could there be in making conversation with, say, Ramsey Clark?"

I began to see the light. "Clark was there?" I asked. "Okay, boys, that does it. Drop the act. Did you get a chance to talk to him?" Knowing Conrad and Lesher, I was sure they would have moved heaven and earth to put in a word for our amendment with the White House aide.

"We absolutely cornered him," said Lesher. "I just hope he wanted to talk about Presidential succession and disability, because if he didn't, he was out of luck."

"It turns out that he's the one who's been assigned the responsibility of coming up with a positive proposal for the President to endorse," said Conrad. "He wasn't sure, when we talked to him, what it was going to be—whether the President would accept our proposal or come up with something new."

"That's what I was afraid of," I said. "So we're still back where we were before?" I was disappointed that this, after all, had been the substance of Conrad's and Lesher's excitement. It was good to know where we stood, but it seemed the ground under our feet wasn't all that firm at the moment.

"Not exactly, Senator," Conrad hastened to add. "We lobbied hard for our own proposal, and we pointed out the flaws in every single alternative approach that Clark suggested. As you know, I thought earlier that Attorney General Katzenbach was in there pitching for the old S.J. Res. 35 approach, and there's still no evidence that he isn't."

"That's too bad, Larry," I answered. "Katzenbach's an important man. He's the Attorney General and he's a good Attorney General, and his influence on something like this would be enormous."

"Yes," said Conrad, "but we really kept at Clark. We told him how important it was, if the amendment was to be passed, for it to stay within the general boundary of the Senate and ABA consensus. We told him that this approach had the Senate's backing and the support of the ABA, not only at the top level but at the grass roots."

"He still didn't seem to be buying," continued Lesher, "so we started talking about the importance of getting a proposal which would pass, not only the two Houses of Congress, but the state legislatures as well. I told him about the results of the poll—"

"The poll!" I exclaimed. It had completely slipped my mind that months before, we had written the state legislative leaders to ask their opinion on which measure would be more easily passed in their particular states. "You mean the final results are in?" I asked Conrad. "What've you been doing, Counselor, keeping that information for a rainy day?"

"Well, no, not the final results," Conrad replied. "It's taken a long time to get in touch with all those people. Some of the letters must have been forwarded to their homes, or maybe just ignored. But we've heard from twenty-nine states so far; and all but two of them favored our approach, just as you thought they would."

I was elated. I had, I must admit, half expected that the results would be in our favor. Still, we had known that this was a gamble, and an expensive one to lose. We would really have been in hot water if the poll we ourselves sponsored had showed that our hunch was wrong.

"Anyway," said Lesher, eager to get on with the story, "Ramsey Clark rose to the bait. He wanted to know who exactly it was we polled, what kind of response we got, and what the results were. We told him that you'd really put it on the line—that you wanted to know how the legislators felt so that if you were wrong you could find out about it. I told him, as things stood now, it was twenty-seven to two in our favor. He was really interested. He asked us if we were sure—if the results were authentic."

"I'm afraid that irritated me a little," admitted Conrad. "I told him I hadn't bothered to call in a handwriting expert to verify the signatures, but that we did have all the letters in our files. He asked if he could see them himself, and I told him he'd have to wait until eight thirty this morning."

"What are we waiting for, boys?" I answered. "It's nine o'clock already. Let's get that correspondence over to the White House, pronto!"

"Right, Senator, right," Conrad answered. They both prepared to get started; and as they left, I said, "Looks to me like you fellows have done a good night's work. Congratulations—and many thanks!"

The correspondence with the state legislative leaders went off to the White House, in care of Ramsey Clark, that morning. We can never know, of course, how much of a role those poll results played in the final White House determination; but they might well have weighed heavily. Lyndon Johnson had thirty years of law-making behind him. He would be well aware of the inadvisability of recommending that Congress endorse a proposal which could not be supported by the state legislatures when it was their turn to act.

Four days later, on January 28, my secretary informed me that Bill Moyers was on the line.

"Hello, Birch," the familiar voice came over the wire, "I just thought I'd let you know that the President's message on succession and disability is on its way to the Hill."

This was it, I thought. "What did you do to us, Bill?"

"What did we do to you? We endorsed you, that's what!"

"The heck you did! Well, I'll be darned!" I was dazed with relief. Bill was busy, and we cut our conversation short—but those few words had been music to my ears. I called in Conrad and Lesher to tell them the good news; though they shared my excitement, they were still a little doubtful. After all they had been through on the amendment and from what they had seen of Ramsey Clark's doubts, they were not going to let themselves believe the President's message supported us until that message was signed, sealed, and delivered.

I was more optimistic, especially after a second telephone call, from Ramsey Clark, conveyed the same information.

At four o'clock that afternoon, our hopes were confirmed. I was on the Senate floor, waiting excitedly for the message to be delivered in the ceremonious manner I had seen so often before; but this time the well-known formalities had more meaning to me than I ever thought they could have.

John Graves, the Assistant Senate Secretary for the Majority, was called out of the Chamber and a moment later returned to usher in Mr. John Ratchford, one of the President's secretaries. Seeing the two men standing at the back of the Chamber, Floyd Riddick, the Senate Parliamentarian, set the formal ceremony in motion by quietly informing the presiding officer, that day Vice President Humphrey himself, that there was a message waiting from the President.

At the first available opportunity the Vice President rapped his gavel and ordered, "The Senate will suspend to receive a message from the President of the United States."

Then, from the back of the Chamber, Mr. Graves, bowing, echoed, "A message from the President of the United States."

"Mr. President," said Mr. Ratchford, also bowing.

"Mr. Secretary," responded the Presiding Officer.

"I am instructed to deliver a message in writing by the President of the United States."

Thereupon Mr. Ratchford handed the envelope bearing the President's seal to Mr. Graves, who in turn carried it up to the Parliamentarian. Mr. Riddick took it and broke the Presidential seal. At that point the Senate could resume its business. The President's message would be referred to the appropriate committee, in this case, of course, to the Judiciary Committee.

I hastily secured a copy of the message and sat down in the Cloakroom to see what it contained at long last.

> *To the Congress of the United States:*
> In 1787, Benjamin Franklin remarked near the conclusion of the Constitutional Convention at Philadelphia, "It . . . astonishes me, sir, to find this system approaching so near to perfection as it does. . . ."
> One hundred seventy-eight years later the relevance of that Constitution of 1789 to our society of 1965 is remarkable. Yet it is truly astonishing, over this span, we have neither perfected the provisions for orderly continuity in the executive direction of our system, nor, as yet, paid the price our continuing inaction so clearly invites and so recklessly risks.

The President summarized the periods of our history when the "conspicuous and long-recognized defects in the Constitution relating to the office of the Presidency" had been most apparent: those times when we had been confronted with a disabled President or a vacancy in the office of Vice President. He went on to say that he felt it was "the strong and overriding will of the people today" to eliminate these imperfections in our constitutional system; "I am, accordingly, addressing this communication to both Houses to ask that this prevailing will be translated into action. . . ."

My eye raced on to the discussion of Presidential disability. We were, Lyndon Johnson emphasized, presently "all but defenseless against the probability of a President's incapacity by injury, illness, senility, or other affliction." Then I read:

... On September 29, 1964, the Senate passed Senate Joint Resolution 139, proposing a constitutional amendment to deal with this perplexing question of Presidential disability. ... The same measure has been introduced in this Congress as Senate Joint Resolution 1 and House Joint Resolution 1. The provisions of these measures have been carefully considered and are the product of many of our finest constitutional and legal minds. Believing, as I do, that Senate Joint Resolution 1 and House Joint Resolution 1 would responsibly meet the pressing need I have outlined, I urge the Congress to approve them forthwith for submission to ratification by the States.

The President of the United States *had* endorsed us. Those were the magic words we had been waiting for. I moved down to the President's thoughts on Vice-Presidential vacancy. An echo of those terrible first days during which Lyndon Johnson had assumed the Presidency was in his words:

Indelible personal experience has impressed upon me the indisputable logic and imperative necessity of assuring that the second office of our system shall, like the first office, be at all times occupied by an incumbent who is able and who is ready to assume the powers and duties of the Chief Executive and Commander in Chief. . . .

. . . For this reason, I most strongly endorse the objective of both Senate Joint Resolution 1 and House Joint Resolution 1 in providing that, whenever there is a vacancy in the office of Vice President, provision shall exist for that office to be filled with a person qualified to succeed to the Presidency.

Later I would go back and re-read the message in detail. Much later I would be intimately involved with the third part of the President's message, that containing his proposal on reform of the electoral college, which was to become a major concern of our subcommittee. But in the excitement of the moment I skipped down to the last paragraph:

Favorable action by the Congress on the measures here recommended will, I believe, assure the orderly continuity in the Presidency that is imperative to the success and stability of our system. Action on these measures now will allay future anxiety among our own people, and among peoples of the world, in the event senseless tragedy or unforeseeable disability should strike again at either or both of the principal offices of our constitutional system. If we act now, without undue delay, we shall have moved closer to achieving perfection of the great constitutional document on which the strength and success of our system have rested for nearly two centuries.

It was true. I was holding the President's message in my hand, and he *had* endorsed our proposal down to the last period. This man, who had been propelled into the Presidency under tragic and chaotic circumstances, had had for those first difficult months no Vice President to share the heavy load of responsibility. He had been Vice President himself, and he knew what the job could mean and how important it was. More than most Americans, he knew also, by way of a nearly fatal heart attack, that life hung by a very thin thread. Nor could he help but be aware, as President, that the heartbeat of the entire nation, its economy and its people, coincided in great part with his own. Living, in effect, every day under the shadow of the very constitutional imperfections we were trying to correct, the President had succinctly and effectively stated his reasons for believing that our measure should be written into the Constitution.

We could not have asked for more.

John Tyler knew that politics, as much as nature, abhors a vacuum. The U.S. Constitution was ambiguous about Presidential succession, but when William Henry Harrison died on April 4, 1841—one month to the day after taking his oath of office—Tyler was immediately sworn in as President. This succession became known as the "Tyler precedent," and it established the legitimacy of the Vice President's succeeding to the higher office.

On November 21, 1899, Vice President Garret A. Hobart of New Jersey died of heart disease at 55. The nation was without a Vice President for 15 months, until William McKinley and Theodore Roosevelt were inaugurated as President and Vice President on March 5, 1901.

Six months later, at 2 A.M. on September 14, William McKinley died in Buffalo of a stomach wound inflicted by a mad youth, Leon Czolgosz (*above*), at the Pan American Exposition on September 5. McKinley was the 5th chief executive to die in office. Eight Presidents have not survived their terms of office. Four died natural deaths: Harrison (1841), Taylor (1850), Harding (1923), and Franklin D. Roosevelt (1945); four were assassinated: Lincoln (1865), Garfield (1881), McKinley (1901), and Kennedy (1963).

The Bettmann Archive

Following a controversy with President Andrew Jackson over states' rights and nullification, John C. Calhoun resigned from the Vice Presidency in December 1832 to enter the Senate. He is the only Vice President to have resigned; seven others have died in office, as have eight Presidents. The Vice Presidency has been vacant 16 times, for periods totaling more than 37 years.

Perhaps more tragic than death, and more dangerous to national stability, has been prolonged Presidential disability. John Garfield lay helpless for nearly 80 days after being struck by an assassin's bullet. Woodrow Wilson (*below, with Mrs. Wilson*) was paralyzed for the better part of 16 months, and Dwight D. Eisenhower suffered three serious illnesses during his eight years in the White House.

Wide World

Wide World

On April 12, 1945, Franklin Delano Roosevelt died of a stroke in Warm Springs, Georgia. Never before in our history had the Presidency changed hands in the midst of such a crisis.

Wide World

During his eight years in office, President Dwight D. Eisenhower was temporarily disabled three times. Before his operation in 1956, he and Vice President Richard M. Nixon agreed in a memorandum on Nixon's role during the disability. The arrangement between the two, although better than nothing, was at best a stopgap measure. It served the cause by pointing directly to a weakness in the Constitution.

(Opposite page) Harry S Truman was sworn in as President by Chief Justice Harlan F. Stone in the Cabinet Room on the day of Roosevelt's death. In 1952 Winston Churchill told Truman, "I must confess, sir, I held you in very low regard then. I loathed your taking the place of Franklin Roosevelt. I misjudged you badly. Since that time, you, more than any other man, have saved Western civilization."

The tragedy of November 22, 1963, forced the Congress to recognize the necessity of facing the problems of Presidential disability and succession. Senate Joint Resolution 139 was introduced by Senator Birch Bayh on December 12, 1963.

A major step toward an amendment: The American Bar Association sponsored a Conference on Presidential Inability and Vice Presidential Vacancy at the Statler Hilton in Washington, D.C., on May 25, 1964. Left to right: Herbert Brownell, former Attorney General; Emanuel Celler, U.S. Representative from New York; Leroy Collins, former Governor of Florida; Senator Birch Bayh; and Edward L. Wright, Chairman of the House of Delegates of the ABA.

The author and Senator Everett Dirksen at the Senate hearings (January 22–March 5, 1964) on Senate Joint Resolution 139. The Minority Leader's support, during the final legislative battle on the Senate floor on July 6, 1965, constituted a giant step toward passage of the measure.

President Lyndon Baines Johnson officiates in a White House ceremony witnessing the ratification of the Twenty-fifth Amendment to the United States Constitution on February 23, 1967. Standing, left to right: Congressman William McCulloch; Senator Birch Bayh; Senate President pro tempore Carl Hayden; Vice President Hubert H. Humphrey; Congressman Emanuel Celler; Speaker of the House John McCormack. Seated: Lawson Knott, General Services Administrator, and President Johnson.

CHAPTER 8

The White Heat
of Publicity

On January 29, the day after the President's message was delivered to the Senate, our subcommittee met in Room 2228 of the New Senate Office Building to hold hearings on S.J. Res. 1. This was in the Eighty-ninth Congress. It had been precisely one year and one week since I first nervously took the Senatorial gavel in that same room to open the hearings on S.J. Res. 139. Much had happened since then. A landslide election had indicated the nation's desire that Lyndon Johnson stay in the office to which he had so tragically succeeded. The election had also given the country the security of having a Vice President once again. Another result of the election was reflected in the membership of our subcommittee: Kenneth Keating, the long-time advocate of legislative reform in the area of disability, had been defeated. We had two new faces, those of Joe Tydings, the newly elected senator from Maryland, and Roman Hruska, the veteran senator from Nebraska.

The status of our proposed amendment had changed greatly too. Since that day when I opened the 1964 hearings, it had acquired the support of the American Bar Association, of the Senate—both by its unanimous passage as S.J. Res. 139 in the last session and by its healthy number of cosponsors already this session—the support of such distinguished and influential personalities as Richard Nixon and Dwight Eisenhower, of a majority of the state legislative leaders, and now of the President of the United States. We had, I thought, a workable amendment by now—one with a good chance of passage. We had worked long, hard hours to arrive at what we believed to be the most reasonable solution. We knew its strengths; we also knew its weaknesses. But we still wanted to make sure our S.J. Res. 1 would hold water under every possible contingency. As I opened what I hoped would be the single day of subcommittee hearings, I stressed our willingness to accept divergent opinion, but also tried to indicate the strong consensus we had behind our joint resolution.

> . . . We are here this morning to consider the various problems connected with Presidential inability and filling vacancies in the Office of Vice President. . . .
>
> Prior to proceeding with the witnesses, I think it would be wise to note one or two ground rules. . . . We are going to emphasize in this hearing views from those who differ in part or entirely from the consensus which has developed over the past year on this issue. We are not trying to railroad anything or gag anybody. Our first witness this morning is the new Attorney General of the United States. He is going to be followed in turn by some outstanding individuals who will express either . . . support or dissent. I want anyone to feel free to testify, especially those who want to oppose the proposal on which we have a broad consensus, Senate Joint Resolution 1. . . .
>
> It may not please everyone. No law can. But it is a proposal that would safeguard the Nation against interruptions in the continuity of executive authority. The fact that 76 Senators are cosponsoring Senate Joint Resolution 1 does not mean that all of us have agreed to every comma and semicolon. What it does mean is that all of us have agreed to compromise on one point or another in order to achieve consensus.
>
> Problems of presidential inability and filling vacancies in the office of Vice President will never be solved if we in the Congress are naive enough to believe that there is a perfect solution that meets all conceivable contingencies. If we attempt to do this, we run the grave risk of formulating a rigid and inflexible proposal that may well create more problems than it solves.

Then I introduced our star witness, Nicholas deB. Katzenbach, whose nomination to the post of Attorney General had been sent to Congress scarcely twenty-four hours earlier:

> The first witness was previously the Assistant Attorney General in charge of the Office of Legal Counsel under President Kennedy. He became Deputy Attorney General when Mr. Justice White was named to the Supreme Court. He became Acting Attorney General when the now Senator Kennedy resigned. Yesterday he was given the great honor which he so richly deserves of being nominated for the office of Attorney General by the President of the United States.
>
> This introduction is not sufficient to properly portray the fine legal record of the first witness, but Mr. Attorney General, let that suffice for now, if you will. My apologies and we are happy to have you with us.

As the Attorney General made his way to the witness table, I was struck by the thought that his position at the moment was a rather difficult one. A year and a half before, when the subcommittee was headed by the late Senator Kefauver, he had testified in support of the provisions of S.J. Res. 35, which had been endorsed by the Kennedy administration. Now the situation was entirely different. The new administration, of which he was the chief legal official, had endorsed our S.J. Res. 1, which was directly opposed to the plan he had previously favored. In that sense, I had been partially responsible for the circumstances now requiring the Attorney General to change his stand, and I felt some guilt about putting him into that uncomfortable position. But he handled it magnificently.

After introducing Mr. Norbert Schlei, Assistant Attorney General in charge of the Office of Legal Counsel, Katzenbach went straight to work:

> I am privileged to appear before this subcommittee in support of Senate Joint Resolution 1. . . .
>
> The subcommittee may recall that in 1963, I testified on several proposed amendments to the Constitution relating to cases where the President is unable to discharge the powers and duties of his office. Last year the subcommittee continued its efforts and approved a bill identical with Senate Joint Resolution 1 which was passed by the Senate. Since the subcommittee has already made a comprehensive study of this matter, I shall do no more today than to state fairly briefly what we understand Sente Joint Resolution 1 proposes to do and what the Department's views are respecting it.

Turning his attention to the problem of Presidential inability, the Attorney General went through our resolution section by section. Then, in his capacity as the nation's top legal officer, he proceeded to help us write a record which would clearly state the intentions of the subcommittee, pointing out those places where our intentions might be misconstrued. Inevitably, he told the subcommittee, some aspects of the resolution might seem ambiguous in certain situations; thus, to "assist in minimizing any such ambiguity, I would like to set forth the interpretations I would make . . . in several difficult areas so that the subcommittee may have an opportunity to consider whether clarification is needed." He began by citing long-standing precedent for his assumption that the phrases "majority vote of both Houses of Congress" and "two-thirds vote of both Houses" meant, respectively, a majority and two-thirds vote of those members in each House present and voting, assuming a quorum to be present. After several similar clarifications, he turned to what was to become a major theme that morning, namely, under what circumstances the Congress would act to remove a President who was considered unable to serve by the Vice President and a majority of the Cabinet.

> . . . I assume that the language used in section 5 to the effect that Congress "will immediately decide" the issue means that if a decision is not reached by the Congress immediately, the powers and duties of the Office would revert to the President. This construction is sufficiently doubtful, however, and the term "immediately" is sufficiently vague, that the subcommittee may wish to consider adding certainty by including more precise language in section 5 or by taking action looking toward the making of appropriate provision in the rules of the House and Senate.

Then, summing up his views on our provisions for disability, the Attorney General very frankly and directly set forth his own change of position:

> In my testimony during the hearings of 1963, I expressed the view that the specific procedures for determining the commencement and termination of the President's inability should not be written into the Constitution, but instead should be left to Congress so that the Constitution would not be encumbered by detail. There is, however, overwhelming support for Senate Joint Resolution 1, and widespread sentiment that these procedures should be written into the Constitution.

The debate has already gone on much too long. Above all, we should be concerned with substance, not form. It is to the credit of Senate Joint Resolution 1 that it provides for immediate, self-implementing procedures that are not dependent on further congressional or Presidential action. In addition, it has the advantage that the States, when called upon to ratify the proposed amendment to the Constitution, will know precisely what is intended. In view of these reasons supporting the method adopted by Senate Joint Resolution 1, I see no reason to insist upon the preference I expressed in 1963 and assert no objection on that ground.

I might add, Mr. Chairman, it would be a courageous man who would take issue with 75 Senators.

The Attorney General proceeded to a brief discussion of our provisions for filling Vice-Presidential vacancies: "In my opinion, S.J. Res. 1 embodies a highly satisfactory solution to this problem." He concluded his statement:

I understand that 47 State legislatures will be in session this year. Given the opportunity, I believe that many of these State legislatures will be able to ratify the necessary constitutional amendment if Congress acts without delay. I earnestly recommend such action.

There followed a lively session of cross-examination by members of the subcommittee. The Attorney General handled himself like a master.

In an effort to write a more complete record and take advantage of his legal expertise, I asked him a few brief questions. I wanted, especially, his complete thinking on something which still bothered many of us: Were we establishing a legal formula by which the Vice President could conspire to initiate a coup d'état and purge the President? Had we given the President enough protection to allow him to make unpopular decisions without fear of usurpation? The Attorney General replied that he thought we had that problem reasonably solved, especially if "it is further clarified so that there must be quick action after which or without which the matter is decided and the President 'immediately' resumes his powers and duties."

There were two ways, he pointed out, to handle the problem of who held the Presidential power during a disagreement on disability. The first was that which we proposed, for the Vice President to continue to act, with Cabinet support, until Congress declined to support him, with the President thereupon resuming his powers and duties. Or else, the President could resume his office merely upon his declaration, whereafter the Vice President and majority of the Cabinet would contest his ability; if they were supported by Congress, then the Vice President would reassume the Presidential powers and duties.

I replied that two considerations were present here. One was to make sure that we did not have, "even for a short period of time, a disabled President acting as President" and making decisions that could be harmful to the country. The other consideration was to provide a means of quickly settling the questions of Presidential inability. If Congress could not decide this immediately, the legally elected President should have his powers and duties restored to him.

Senator Dirksen, who had to leave soon, asked two brief questions of the Attorney General. Might it be advisable, he asked, to limit the President's possible choice for a new Vice President to members of Congress and heads of the departments of government? This would still be a broad field from which to choose, Katzenbach replied, but he did not believe the choice should be limited at all. The Presidential candidate customarily has a free hand in choosing his running mate—even though that freedom may be "governed by a variety of considerations within the party." I stepped in momentarily to point out that Senator Dirksen's limitations would exclude state governors; with some understatement, the Attorney General replied that "it would be in the interest of ratification not to eliminate the Governors"—a contention with which I was in complete agreement.

The second question of my Illinois colleague was whether the choice of a new Vice President should be made by a majority or a two-thirds vote. A two-thirds vote, he pointed out, was used for the more critical matters. The Attorney General expressed the opinion that a two-thirds vote might give an opposition party abnormal power in determining who would be Vice President, thus leading to an undesirable delay in filling the office.

Senator Roman Hruska of Nebraska was next to assume the role of interrogator. Two aspects of the approach of our resolution had troubled him for a long time. He was concerned that we not "clutter up the Constitution" with procedural detail and that our amendment not lead to violation of the principle of separation of powers. Hruska, an astute attorney, pursued his point with great determination and detail, focusing his questions upon the word "immediately."

> ... Now, it is all right to depend or to think that one depends upon the good faith of Congress ... but it has been suggested by scholars in the field that there are such things as unlimited debate in the Senate. ... I doubt very much that our feelings of sympathy in this matter would prevent someone from saying, "let us have hearings and expert testimony. Let us have a full discussion on this subject, so that the public may be informed."
>
> Now, do you think "immediately" will encompass that sort of thing?

The Attorney General replied that he did not think so; rather, the word expressed a sense of urgency. "I think it is extremely difficult to know what word you put in," he added, "unless you put in a specific time limitation," which, as he said before, he did not consider a good idea. It might, he pointed out, take several days to acquire the medical opinions to arrive at such a decision; "I frankly, Senator, am at somewhat of a loss to say how it could be better expressed than the word 'immediately.'" Senator Hruska replied with some asperity,

> I am sure the words you have just uttered will be greeted with great joy and anticipation by those who will seek to define legislatively "immediately" as meaning 90 days. Because if we are going to have a situation here where we will put a word into the Constitution and then say "It is competent for the Congress to define that word anyway it wants to," I say we are making a shambles out of the Constitution.

Picking up the Attorney General's admission that "immediately" was difficult to define, either by the Court or by the Congress, my colleague from Nebraska cited the possibility of the President's having a mental or nervous disorder, in which case data might take a long time to gather.

> That is the sort of thing we run into when we do two things. When we get into procedural details in the constitutional amendment, and when we violate the separation of powers. You say that it is difficult to put in words and to put in language something that would be acceptable and workable. I have a solution for it. ... Briefly it is this: If that power is kept within the executive department where it belongs,

and exercised by the heads of the executive departments, we immediately dispose of the time element in very satisfactory fashion. If those department heads will not go along with the Vice President and say that the President is not able to proceed, then ... the President resumes his office. We have the matter resolved from the standpoint of time. Would you have any comment on that, Mr. Attorney General?

Those who thought Congress should play a role in determining Presidential disability, replied Mr. Katzenbach, "are adopting a philosophy that says that the elected representatives of the people would better give the sense of the people, at least in confirming that executive decision." Moreover, such an arrangement would prevent the possibility of a coup d'état—a possibility I had questioned the Attorney General about earlier—since a Vice President seeking to depose an unpopular President would need to control Congress as well as the Cabinet. He continued,

> On the separation of powers point, Senator, I don't believe that this procedure amounts to a violation of that principle as I understand it. It is already provided in the Constitution that Congress shall decide this procedure in the event of an inability of both the President and the Vice President . . . that Congress get into the picture of selection processes in the Constitution.

Senator Hruska disagreed. Our approach, he said, would put "one branch in a dominant position over the other. . . . The Congress would be in a dominant position over the President. . . ."

"I could take mild issue with that if I could, Senator," replied the Attorney General.

> . . . all that Congress can do is to affirm a decision that has already been made in the executive branch, because the majority of the Cabinet have already supported the Vice President. So that the only participation of Congress in this it to . . . protect, I suppose, against a coup d'etat here, to say, "These fellows have tried to take over and we do not think they ought to." So I do not think they are dominant.
>
> Congress cannot initiate. Congress cannot get rid of the President here, except on its own process already contained in the Constitution for impeachment.

The determination to impeach a President, responded Senator Hruska, was a question of policy; the determination of disability, one of fact. "Those that are policy in nature should be decided by the Congress . . . [but] . . . with reference to a factual determination

on the physical or the mental capabilities of a serving President, it
would be a question for the executive branch to decide." Here I
brought up the point that impeachment, in addition to being a policy
decision, was a question of fact as well—"Did the President actually
do what he is accused of doing?"—and the Attorney General remarked that the converse was also true:

> I would think that a question of this importance, Senator, could
> scarcely be regarded as a purely factual question. There are all kinds
> of gravest considerations of policy involved in the determination that
> Congress would make—the whole question of the confidence of the
> country, the confidence of the world.
> . . . I would think that was a policy decision, . . . a policy question
> of the highest order. I would think it would be extremely important to
> know, in the event that a Vice President was taking over the offices,
> that he had the support in that determination of two-thirds of each
> House of Congress.

But if only sixty-three senators, rather than sixty-seven or two-
thirds, voted that the President was unable to serve, argued Senator
Hruska, "what becomes of your consensus . . . in the eyes of the
Nation and the world?" That situation, replied the Attorney General, was "inherent in the problem, not in the procedure here." Nor
did he believe that a Vice President would take such a question to
Congress without being absolutely assured he would have overwhelming support.

> If there was that kind of doubt . . . that you could not muster a
> two-thirds vote, then I do not think that the issue would ever be put.
> . . . I consider the process as a safeguard against usurpation, which is
> what I think it is intended to be. . . . I think the practice would end up,
> any time it is submitted, with the Vice President being supported. Be-
> cause it is such a horrible situation to imagine, for him as well as for
> the country, that I do not think it would ever be submitted except in
> the clearest kind of situation, where he had in the usual processes of
> politics the assurance that that was going to be backed up by a majority
> or by two-thirds of each House.

Senator Hruska's questioning continued along the same lines;
before the subject was finally dropped, I could not resist interjecting
one observation myself.

> . . . I just wanted to state for some of us who have studied this, as
> the Senator from Nebraska has, that we differ with him as he very

articulately expresses his point of view. But just to rephrase what the Attorney General said, it is our feeling that this business of removing the legally elected President of the United States for any cause is of such a serious nature that we do not want the Vice President or Cabinet or any other group to have the responsibility for doing it. The final determination, we feel, must be made by the representatives of the people. If there were some way we could get the people themselves to make this decision, I would say more power to this. But we have found no practical way of doing this.

Only when the Congress, as the legally representative body of the people, says, "Mr. President, you are unable to carry on the powers and duties that were given to you, this great mandate that was given to you by the people," are we willing to say that he should step down.

Now, certainly the Senator from Nebraska feels equally strong about it and I appreciate his opinion. He states it very well.

Our cross-examination of the Attorney General was drawing to a close; I asked him to clarify one more point. If Congress were ever called on to judge a President's ability to perform the powers and duties of his office, it would, I knew, be a difficult decision for each member of that body. They would need all the facts they could get. Thus, I asked Katzenbach.

Could you state specifically whether you think, as we use the word "immediately," that this would still permit Congress to make a reasoned, intelligent judgment, and to take what time is necessary to get this evidence—to hear this testimony?

The Attorney General replied that he thought there would be time for such judgment. The difficulty might lie on the other side, that Congress might not act with the greatest expedition. "I think that is what you are trying to tell them to do," he said. "There is no word that you can use that completely resolves that problem. I do not know what 'immediately' means, except it means as soon as you can darn well do it."

Would this indicate, asked Senator Hruska, that Congress could inquire of members of the President's family and medical experts? Could they also debate the issue? Yes, replied the Attorney General.

"Reasonable debate?" "How much debate?" The senator from Nebraska and I asked almost simultaneously.

That was impossible to answer, replied Attorney General Katzenbach. "I would think that on this kind of an issue, the amount of debate that would be required would be really very, very limited in order to make a judgment."

This ended the testimony of Attorney General Katzenbach. As he left the witness chair, I thought how very helpful he had been, bringing before the subcommittee his legal expertise and his logical and systematic reasoning in support of the provisions of our measure.

Next Senator Hiram Fong of Hawaii, one of the original sponsors of S.J. Res. 1, delivered a statement in strong support of our measure.

Senator Hruska's statement followed that of Senator Fong. By and large, my colleague from Nebraska repeated the objections that he had discussed with the Attorney General and presented as a substitute to our S.J. Res. 1 the provisions of his own S.J. Res. 6. Hruska stressed that

> Some would advocate spelling out the procedure for determining inability within the language of the proposed amendment. I disagree. The logic of locking into the Constitution those procedures deemed appropriate today but which, in the light of greater knowledge and experience may be found wanting tomorrow, escapes me.
>
> The preferred course would be for the amendment to authorize the Congress to establish an appropriate procedure by law. . . .

However, he continued, there should be "one fundamental limitation" imposed on this authority given to Congress; otherwise that body "might adopt a procedure that would violate constitutional doctrines of the most essential character," especially that of the separation of powers. "Some of the pending proposals on presidential inability," he continued, "illustrate how seriously the doctrine can be impaired if care is not exercised."

> This is the rationale behind the limitation contained in Senate Joint Resolution 6 which provides that the executive branch shall determine the presence of and termination of the inability of the President. . . . Stated another way, Congress must be prohibited from prescribing a method which would involve either the judicial or the legislative branch of the Government.

Senator Hruska also requested that we insert two statements into the record: a *New York Times* comment on a report of the Committee for Economic Development, which suggested "a shift in the main burden of responsibility for declaring a President's disability from the Vice President to the members of the Cabinet," and a *Washington Post* editorial reinforcing Senator Hruska's doubts about the meaning of the word "immediately."

By then I was beginning to feel that things might get out of hand; I had hoped to keep the hearings to a single day. Although we did want to keep open minds and hear all dissenting opinions, I also thought it was time to stress the consensus we had achieved on S.J. Res. 1 and the damage that could be done to all of our efforts to find a solution if we continued to talk the problem to death as had been done in previous Congresses. Thanking my colleague from Nebraska for including the editorials in the record, I commented that such newspaper attention had made "substantial contribution to discussions like those we are participating in here . . . , where we have divergent views expressed, particularly as they are expressed as articulately as my friend from Nebraska expresses his." But, I continued, the problem of succession and disability has gone unsolved for almost two hundred years now. Why has it not been solved?

> . . . The answer is not that Congress has not studied it, that Congress has not made proposals. Quite to the contrary. The answer is . . . that we have had so many different proposals and a refusal or reluctance on the part of the proposers to sit down and work out an agreement which we admit is not perfect, but which is better than no solution at all.
>
> That, I think, is why we have had so much discussion on Senate Joint Resolution 1. . . .
>
> I know the Senator realizes the need for give and take in the legislative process, yet the goal must be gotten to in the best way we possibly can. I felt compelled to make this statement to the Senator. If he wants equal time, he may fire away.

"I have already had equal time, Mr. Chairman," Senator Hruska replied. "We understand the process of legislation, I am sure." He continued,

> I do feel that this time the Congress will speak on the subject, make a determination among the various views and submit the amendment to the States for ratification. In loyalty to the practices I feel important, I do feel a necessity in presenting this view. I thank the chairman for his tolerance.

My colleague from Nebraska and I understood each other. I had great respect for Roman Hruska's sincerity and legal astuteness.

The point he had been pursuing was, I knew, one about which he felt strongly; he had given great thought to the problem which confronted us. But I had wanted to make it clear to him that we, too, had studied the problem in great detail; we were, for example, thoroughly familiar with the editorials which had been inserted into the record and with the objections which underlay them. We had not arrived lightly at the solution we were proposing. It was, I thought, the most workable one we could get; and I was determined to make a maximum effort to enact the consensus we had so painfully worked to achieve.

We proceeded to the next witness before the subcommittee, Senator Jack Miller of Iowa. Senator Miller had introduced S.J. Res. 15, which dealt solely with the problem of succession and provided that, in the event of a vacancy in the office of Vice President, the President should nominate a Vice President with the same party affiliation as his own, and this nomination should subsequently be confirmed by a majority vote of both Houses of Congress in joint session. This arrangement would solve the potential problem which arose when the President and Congress were of opposing parties. The resolution concerned succession alone, Senator Miller said, because he thought it unwise to join together in one single amendment provisions dealing with both disability and succession. Miller was concerned that joining the two together would lead to the entire amendment's being opposed by legislators who were against one or the other of the provisions it contained.

Our next witness was Marion B. Folsom, who had served as Secretary of Health, Education, and Welfare under President Eisenhower, and was presently chairman of the Committee for Improvement of Management in Government, which had been created by the Committee for Economic Development. Like the American Bar Association, the CED had given thorough study to the problems of succession and disability. Its report to the President had been the subject of the *New York Times* editorial Senator Hruska had just introduced into the record. Mr. Folsom outlined the CED proposal, which differed at several points with the ABA-endorsed S.J. Res. 1:

> First, we believe that Congressional confirmation of a Presidential nomination to fill a vacancy in the Vice-Presidency should be through a joint session of the two Houses, requiring approval by a majority of all Senators and Representatives present and voting. . . .

We favor this method, as opposed either to confirmation by the Senate alone, or to approval by the two Houses acting separately, for three primary reasons: (1) The joint session corresponds to voting strength State by State, in the electoral college; (2) action—pro or con —would be more expeditious than could be expected through separate consideration by the two Houses or under normal Senate procedures; and (3) the Senate and the House of Representatives might be in disagreement, with unfortunate effects. We acknowledge that formal action in joint session would require establishment of rules of procedure for that body but this would seem to be a relatively simple problem.

Second, we believe that the initiative in determination of an undeclared presidential inability should lie with the Cabinet and not with the Vice President. In other words, we feel that such determination should be by the Cabinet, the Vice President concurring as was provided in the amendment as passed by the Senate last year. . . .

Third, we are much concerned that the Nation avoid any possibility of doubt, dispute, or delay concerning termination of any conceivable presidential inability. That is why we urge that this matter also be decided by the Cabinet, subject only to presidential concurrence. . . .

The principle of separation of powers among the three branches of government appears to us to be eminently sound. We cannot agree that it is wise to place a conceivable future difference of opinion between President and Vice President over the termination of a presidential inability before the Congress for decision, especially if the result is to depend on two-thirds majorities in both Houses.

. . . Under the language previously proposed, it would be possible for a President to terminate his own disability, against the judgment of the Vice President supported by the entire Cabinet and a unanimous vote of the Senate, if only one-third of the House of Representatives were to agree with the President.

Summarizing his argument, Mr. Folsom said:

. . . if the committee finds that they get better agreement on your resolution, we certainly feel that you should go ahead and pass the legislation as it is without any changes. But we do feel . . . it would be improved with these three somewhat minor differences.

As I listened to Mr. Folsom's statement, I had been thinking that although many of the differences between the Committee for Economic Development proposal and ours were perhaps irreconcilable, one distinction seemed to be more imaginary than real.

"May I ask a question or two, please?" I said when the former

Cabinet member had finished. "In that portion dealing with disability, there seems to be a little difference between who should have the initiative." I went on to cite the wording of the CED proposal:

> The authority to decide that Presidential inability exists should be placed in the hands of the Cabinet, in consultation with the Vice President or other successor. Any such decision should be by a majority vote of the Cabinet, the Vice President concurring.

But the CED report, I pointed out, went on to say, "Upon the initiative of any member or of the Vice President."

"Now, how do you reconcile that?" I asked.

Mr. Folsom replied,

> . . . The Cabinet members can bring it up, or the Vice President can bring it up, and we say we ought to have a majority of the Cabinet, with the Vice President concurring. In other words, we do not want to leave the initiative entirely with the Vice President. If he wants to bring it up, fine, but we also want to have an opportunity for the Cabinet to bring it up, because we do find in past practice that the Vice President never wanted to bring it up. . . . It is a very difficult position for the Vice President to be in.

I did not think there was any need to explore this discrepancy any further.

"I was interested," Mr. Folsom then commented, "to see the Senator from Nebraska agreed pretty much with our position on this." Indeed, I replied, with a smile at my colleague from Nebraska, it seemed to me that I detected "the fine hand of the Senator from Nebraska" in parts of the CED proposal. But the Senator from Nebraska vigorously denied the implication I had made in jest, when he commenced to question Mr. Folsom.

> . . . Needless to say, the Senator from Nebraska thinks your report is of high quality and of great merit. However I would suggest there has not been direction by this Senator in the formation of this report. . . .

Senator Hruska went on to say that the business of the joint session lent added strength to the approach of his own S.J. Res. 6,

> which says that all procedural matters—this matter of what rule and what parliamentary procedure should be used—are left to legislation by Congress. The merit in this case is, that if actual practice would show that the separate sessions of each House would be an impracticable situation, then we could change it by statute.

Mr. Folsom commented that, although his committee had read S.J. Res. 6, they felt that their province was not wording but policy; "we did not want to get involved in detailed language of legislation."

At the end of Mr. Folsom's appearance before our committee, I wanted to set the record straight on one point. Mr. Folsom had referred to his experience with the Eisenhower administration as an example of the difficulty of the Vice President's taking the initiative in declaring Presidential inability. I remarked,

> I would like to make one reference to the conference held here last spring, again under the auspices of the American Bar Association. I was very interested to learn President Eisenhower's opinion of this business of who should take the issue. He came out with the flat statement that he thought the Vice President could not escape this authority, that constitutionally it was his, that he thought no one else should have it. . . . But if we thought someone else should be, he thought we ought to go along and give the Cabinet ratifying or confirming authority.

Mr. Folsom was followed by another former member of the Eisenhower Cabinet, Herbert Brownell. The former Attorney General, appearing as chairman of the ABA's Committee on Presidential Inability and Vice Presidential Vacancy, inserted into the record a statement on behalf of ABA president Lewis F. Powell, Jr., who had been unable to appear in person. Then, after making a brief statement of his own, Mr. Brownell indicated that he would be happy to answer questions.

Herb Brownell was, as usual, highly articulate and very helpful. He had been in on the ABA study from the beginning, and I wanted his thoughts about some of those contentions that had been made by opposing witnesses.

I first asked him about CED's preference for a joint session of Congress, as compared with the individual sessions called for by the ABA and our resolution. He replied that the ABA had proposed separate meetings of both Houses "in the belief that it would speed the consideration of the matter and eliminate some of the procedural difficulties that might arise." This method, moreover, was "more usual and . . . a little more orthodox."

I then turned to the problems surrounding the word "immediate," which had been discussed earlier. I did not want to put words into his mouth, I said, but as far as dilatory tactics are concerned

... would you say it is fair to feel that public opinion, plus the good faith of the Members of Congress, would prevent the possibility of a Senate filibuster, for example, or one House being in control of the opposite political party to the President?

Herbert Brownell replied,

I listened to some of the questions and answers earlier in the session this morning, any number of which seem to revolve around that question. . . . But I think that is perhaps unrealistic because we must picture the kind of situation that would be involved if this question ever arose. It would be a national crisis and not only the eyes of the United States but of the world would be focused on this particular thing.

I think our public officials always rise to their best heights at a time of crisis of that kind and, therefore, I would think with the overwhelming backing of public opinion for a solution of any crisis to having an orderly government, the Congress could be counted upon, without any question, to do its part.

He went on to point out that in "over 90 per cent" of the situations in which a President might be disabled, he would be able to resume the powers and duties of his office at any time that he certified he could do so. Thus, the problem of a disagreement which would then involve congressional participation would be most extraordinary. Under those circumstances, the President

... would not be likely to resume the duties of the office unless he was pretty sure that he had public support, that he had congressional support, that he had the support of a majority or practically all the members of his Cabinet. It would be such a reckless thing for him otherwise. It would only be in a situation . . . where he was mentally unbalanced, or something of that sort, which would be very obvious to everyone when you consider the white heat of publicity that beats upon the White House. In that kind of a situation, it follows almost automatically that there would be strong insistence on the part of the public and the leaders in the Congress to see that he did not come back. Therefore, I do not visualize long hassles involved in this. . . .

I think that there would be overwhelming opinion one way or the other that would demand immediate action.

For a particular solution that is in here, the language, "immediate," we in the American Bar Association do support the language of the present Senate Joint Resolution 1, and we believe that this principle should be kept in mind.

Next, Dean Sharp, counsel with Senator Dodd, appeared before our committee to present a statement by Senator Dodd, who was unable to be present. The senator from Connecticut stated his support of S.J. Res. 1, of which he was a cosponsor, and ended with a call for action:

> I feel that the time for study is long past. Of course, there may be technical changes in the proposed amendment. Nevertheless, it is now time for prompt action, as an impressive majority of my colleagues, and fellow Americans will agree.

Subsequently, Representative Willard S. Curtin of Pennsylvania appeared very briefly to ask that his statement in support of his own House Joint Resolution 129, involving the establishment of a Presidential Inability Commission headed by the Chief Justice of the United States, be inserted into the record. We did so and thanked him for taking the time to come over from the House to contribute to our discussions.

Justice Michael Musmanno, of the Supreme Court of Pennsylvania, next appeared to present a statement. He, too, had proposed a constitutional amendment, S.J. Res. 34; but in the light of the President's message endorsing ours, he was withdrawing his provision that "Presidential inability be decided by the combined Judiciary Committees of the House and Senate of the Congress," in favor of the provisions of our resolution. He also suggested, in light of the previous colloquy over the meaning of "immediately," substitution of the word "forthwith," which seemed to him to indicate more urgency. "I know that in the military they very rarely use the word 'immediately.' You are supposed to be acting forthwith, as soon as the order is given."

Another feature of Justice Musmanno's proposed amendment was the transfer of the Vice Presidency from the legislative to the executive branch of the government; the duties of the Vice President would be those assigned to him by the President. The Vice Presidency was no longer the nondescript office it was in John Adams' day, he said.

> We have here the extraordinary case where the office has outgrown the temple of the Constitution, so that the occupant must work outside in the cold and the wet of unconstitutional authority.
> I respectfully submit that the roof and the walls of the Constitution be extended to fully enclose the powers which we know should and must be inherent in the Vice-Presidency. Thus the Vice President will

be enabled to toil untrammeledly, with all his wonderful energies and talents, in projecting forward at all times, at the side of the President, the beautiful destiny of this beloved and great Nation of ours.

The subcommittee next heard testimony from Professor Robert Deasy of Providence College. Professor Deasy was of the opinion that the verbal or written agreement between President and Vice President was still the most desirable arrangement. He echoed the earlier suggestions that a second Vice President be elected. He did seem to be reconciled to the fact that "more than likely—and I would certainly acquiesce in it 100 per cent—the amendment as proposed here in Senate Joint Resolution 1 will pass." But he wanted to go on record that "I do not think . . . we should be hasty"; and he went on to put our activities last session in an unusual light:

> The urgency of legislation is still obvious but there is no longer the aura of "panic" legislation. This could well have been ascribed to any legislation passed before January 20 of this year and may I speak with some authority when I say that historians would have been the first to say this in future years if anything untoward would have happened.

It was now well past lunchtime; but, as I had announced earlier, I intended "to go ahead as long as there is a witness who desires to discuss and present his views on the matter." Now it was time to hear our final witness, Martin Taylor, chairman of the Committee on Constitutional Law of the New York State Bar Association and one of the original members of the ABA disability-succession panel, which had met thirteen months earlier in the Mayflower Hotel. To my knowledge, he was the only member of that distinguished group who had opposed the consensus provisions down to the eleventh hour.

Now, in his testimony before the committee, Mr. Taylor said that "everyone approves of" the provision to fill Vice-Presidential vacancies. But why, he asked, was the period between the election and the inauguration not provided for as well? I replied, as I had replied to others that morning who wished additional provisions to be included within our amendment, that

> . . . constitutional amendments being what they are, requiring two-thirds of each House plus three-fourths of the legislatures, are difficult to pass.

It would be best, I thought, to deal with such problems in separate resolutions. The more we cluttered up the proposed amendment with added details, the more we risked increased opposition.

Then Martin Taylor proceeded to his main point of contention. He disapproved of our writing specific details into the Constitution. He cited Chief Justice John Marshall "that only a broad enabling power should be given in the Constitution, not implementation, not detail." This was, of course, the point that my colleague from Nebraska had dwelt upon time and time again. In my judgment it was time that a strong statement go into the record citing our reasons for having given Congress the specific duty to determine disability. Thus, before Mr. Taylor went on, I interjected my thoughts on the matter.

> May I say . . . on this matter of intertwining the executive and legislative power, I, for one, feel this should be avoided if at all possible. But do you not feel, Mr. Taylor, that we have sufficient precedent in the 12th amendment in which Congress itself ends up electing a President under certain circumstances if neither candidate or no candidate gets a majority of the electoral vote? Then Congress makes the determination of who the Chief Executive shall be.
>
> Also, in the impeachment proceedings, we not only bring in both Houses of the Congress, but bring in the Chief Justice of the Supreme Court to preside over this proceeding. Does this not act as a precedent, that there are specific times? . . .
>
> I am concerned about this business of bringing in the Congress but it seemed to me and to my colleagues who have joined us, this is a matter of the greatest possible moment, the removal of the President of the United States from office—temporary disability, true. But should not we allow the elected representatives of the people themselves to have the final say so in the event we get into that small percentage of circumstances where you have disagreement between the President on the one hand and the Vice President and majority of the Cabinet on the other?

Mr. Taylor conceded that in one sense our proposal was "an expression of policy . . . that might meet general approval," thus he was in agreement with me; "I was only being somewhat technical about it as a matter of constitutional law."

But it was not just a question of satisfying people, I replied; rather, it was a question of getting the best possible solution. "Maybe they would be satisfied with the best result," said Mr. Taylor, obviously wanting to close the discussion. "I do not know."

Taylor went on to discuss the potential hazards in terms of delay at a critical moment—for example, "bombers coming over the Potomac"—while President, Vice President, Cabinet, and Congress tried to decide whether the President was able to reassume the duties of his office. Moreover, he went on, what if the Congress did not back up the Vice President and Cabinet, furnishing the two-thirds majority to keep the Vice President on as acting President?

That would be unfortunate, I replied.

> . . . It would not be a desirable situation. This, as I have pointed out repeatedly, and will point out again, is a situation for which there is no perfect solution. This one particular case where you have a President fighting openly with a Vice President and the majority of the Cabinet is a rather unfortunate situation, undesirable to say the least.
>
> But . . . it is going to be an unusual Congress that does not go along. It would be an unusual Vice President and majority of the Cabinet that would get themselves in that position.

The hour was getting late, and Martin Taylor sought to conclude his remarks, saying, "Instead of arguing your questions, let me congratulate you on your success to this point and hope that you have further success."

"I must admit," I replied, "the conversations I have had with you here and that we have had both privately and publicly have done a great deal, not only to stimulate my thought processes, but have helped us to arrive at a decision. I appreciate your coming."

"Thank you, sir," said Mr. Taylor, as he left the witness chair.

I inserted some further statements into the record and advised the committee, that although there were those who had suggested the record should remain open for a while during the House hearings, I would leave it open only a few more days for further statements.

> Let me say that I share Professor Deasy's admonition that we should not act in panic. I do not think that any of the discussions we have had to date or intend to have will be indicative of a panic situation, but I do think there is a sense of urgency. . . . I do not intend to hold additional hearings unless there is a compelling reason that I do not foresee.
>
> If there is no further testimony, the hearings will be forthwith closed. . . .

It was 2:40 in the afternoon. We had proceeded for over four and a half hours without a break. But we were now finished. The

hearings had not been lengthy, but they had certainly been pro-
vocative. As we had hoped, numerous specific questions about
wording as well as about policy had been directed to the committee.
We were now in a better position to review the specific wording of
S.J. Res. 1, in an attempt to refine our amendment into the best one
possible.

Three days later, the subcommittee met in the Senate Judiciary
Committee room. Not every senator was in full accord with the
specific wording contained in S.J. Res. 1. Nevertheless, by unanimous agreement, we voted to send to the full committee the identical
resolution which had passed the Senate the year before.

Later that very afternoon, Majority Leader Mansfield telephoned. "Birch, how are you coming along on succession and
disability?"

"We just referred Senate Joint Resolution 1 to the Judiciary
Committee this morning, Mike," I answered. "The next step is to
consider it in full committee. I'm not sure when the chairman in-
tends to hold the next meeting, but I'll do my best to see that it's
considered at that time."

"Do that, Birch. We ought to act on your measure as soon as
possible. It's important in itself, and this is a good time to act on it.
We're early in the session, there's not much legislative activity, and
we can give your amendment the consideration it deserves. Later
the calendar will get crowded, and things will be a little more
difficult."

When the Majority Leader left the line, I flashed for the operator and asked her to connect me with Senator Eastland's office.

"Mr. Chairman," I said, "I haven't had the chance to brief you
on our last subcommittee action. As you know, we were scheduled
to meet this morning. Well, we did meet, and we've passed on to the
full committee the same succession–disability resolution that the
Senate passed last fall. I guess the next step is consideration by the
full committee."

"Birch," Senator Eastland replied in his southern drawl,
"Mike's been asking me about that. He's anxious for us to take it
up as soon as possible."

"If there's any way I can help," I said, "I'll be glad to do it."

"I've called a Judiciary Committee meeting for ten o'clock Wednesday morning, Birch. If it's all right with the committee to take up your resolution then, it's all right with me, too. Will you be ready?"

"I'll be ready, Mr. Chairman," I answered, "and thanks very much."

By 10:20 that Wednesday, February 3, a quorum of the Judiciary Committee was present, and Chairman Eastland called the committee to order. After we had disposed of several perfunctory measures, the chairman looked down the long conference table at me.

"Gentlemen," he said, "Senator Bayh has a measure dealing with succession and disability that he'd like to bring before the committee."

"Thank you, Mr. Chairman," I said and began my presentation. I got no further than the third sentence, however, before I was interrupted by a voice from the far end of the table, on the minority side. It was the senator from Nebraska.

"Mr. Chairman," said Roman Hruska, "if the Senator from Indiana will yield, I should like to point out to the Committee that S.J. Res. 1, with which the Senator from Indiana has worked so diligently, seeks to amend the Constitution of the United States. This is important business, as the members of the Committee know. However, Mr. Chairman, we are now asked to discuss this subject, and yet the hearings which have recently been held on the resolution have not been printed. I personally have some amendments that I want to present to the committee, and I know other committee members may have amendments too. It seems to me that we should not consider the matter until the hearings have been printed and distributed, so that we may all examine them carefully."

Technically, of course, my colleague from Nebraska was right. Normally it is not good legislation to consider a measure before the hearings on the subject have been printed and distributed. However, it seemed to me this was an exception: we were not plowing new ground. Nothing had come out in the second set of hearings that had not been disclosed in the first, the printed transcript of which had been available for a long time. We were studying a bill identical to the one that had been passed sixty-five to zero in the previous session. I wondered if Roman Hruska really wanted to

study the printed hearings or to a gain a little additional time to prepare a defense. I personally thought we should act—the sooner the
better.

"Gentlemen—Roman—the Majority Leader has been after me
to consider this matter," I said. "Mike thinks it is important, and so I
have asked the Committee to consider it now. What the senator from
Nebraska says is true. The hearings have not been printed in final
form. But we did receive three copies of a first print last night. I'm
sure our Committee counsel can make those available to as many
of the committee members as desire to study them." I looked over
at Larry Conrad and he nodded. "But more importantly," I went
on, "the Committee doesn't need to be reminded that the problem
of succession and disability is a serious one. The issue was discussed
by this Committee last year. In fact, the resolution before the committee now is the same measure which this Committee considered,
passed, and referred to the Senate floor, where it was agreed to by a
vote of 65 to nothing. It seems to me that the presence or absence
of printed hearings is not as important as the prompt consideration
of this measure. However, as I said a moment ago, I shall see that
our subcommittee counsel personally delivers a draft of the hearings to the senator from Nebraska, and to any of the rest of the
committee who may want one."

I paused for a moment and, hearing no objection from any of
the committee members, continued with my brief review of the provisions of S.J. Res. 1. When I had finished, Senator Hruska took
up the debate. Basically, he told the committee, he was in accord
with the provisions of our resolution and sympathetic with the need
to solve the problems toward which it was directed. But then the
senator from Nebraska outlined for the committee the feelings he
had expressed repeatedly in our hearings. He was opposed to writing specific procedural language into the Constitution and he was
concerned that the doctrine of separation of powers was violated
by bringing Congress into the decision of determining Presidential
disability.

"For example, I invite the Committee's attention to the use of
the word 'immediately' in Section 5. . . . Just what does 'immediately' mean? How fast will we be required to act and still follow
the command which would then be in the Constitution of the

United States which tells us we are to act 'immediately'?" The senator from Nebraska went on, reiterating the arguments he had dwelt on during the subcommittee hearings.

Senator McClellan, the second-ranking member of the committee, joined the discussion. "Well, gentlemen," he said, "I have not studied this matter carefully, and amending the Constitution is serious business. I trust the subcommittee has studied the matter thoroughly. Of course I would be happy to have the subcommittee hearings when they are printed—but frankly, gentlemen, I don't know when I will have the time to read them in detail. If we have to act quickly on this matter, I just won't have the time. I have my own committees to chair and my own hearings to concern myself about."

I was grateful for Senator McClellan's reasonableness and, above all, his realism. It is simply a fact of congressional life that no single senator can be up to date on all the background and individual details of every committee issue. This is, in a sense, the function of subcommittees, which can give detailed attention to a narrower field. We had hoped that, with all the preparation we had made and the support we had gained, the rest of the committee would trust us to have worked out the most feasible solution possible. Yet each member has the right to explore, in depth, all matters before the Committee.

"Now if 'immediately' appears to be bothering the Senator from Nebraska," continued Senator McClellan, "why don't we change the wording, and instead of 'immediately' use the words 'proceed to'? In other words, instead of 'Congress shall immediately decide the issue,' it would read, 'Congress shall proceed to decide the issue.' "

This was obviously a well-meaning effort on Senator McClellan's part to iron out the difficulty and expedite our action on the amendment. But, even though I was not adamant about the specific language of the bill, I did feel that giving way on this particular word might change the broader meaning. Most of the language had been put there to do a specific job, and we had by then been over every word so thoroughly that I felt we knew better than anyone the import of the phraseology upon which we had finally decided.

"John," I said, "we are trying to convey a real sense of urgency here. Now, to me, 'immediately' comes closer to conveying a sense of urgency than anything that has been suggested. I should also point out to the committee," I added, "that we looked to the language of the Twelfth Amendment as precedent." We had been living with the problem for so long that I was able to cite from memory that amendment's provisions for the procedure used in counting the electoral votes and electing the President:

> ... The person having the greatest number of votes for President, shall be the President, if such number be a majority of the whole number of Electors appointed; and if no person have such majority, then from the persons having the highest numbers not exceeding three on the list of those voted for as President, the House of Representatives shall choose immediately, by ballot, the President."

"And so," I concluded, "it seems to me that if we use 'immediately' in describing how to elect a President to office, it is appropriate to use the same language when determining whether he should be removed from office."

At that point, Senator Ted Kennedy, who was sitting immediately to my left, joined the discussion. "Mr. Chairman, it certainly seems to me that 'immediately' conveys a real sense of urgency. With all due respect to the Senator from Arkansas, 'immediately' conveys a much greater sense of urgency to me than his suggestion, 'proceed to,' does."

"Well," Senator McClellan conceded, "I am certainly not wed to the words 'proceed to.' I haven't studied this matter carefully; I was just trying to be helpful. The Senator from Nebraska is concerned about 'immediately,' but personally, 'immediately' sounds all right to me."

"Perhaps," suggested Chairman Eastland, "a good middle ground might be 'immediately proceed to decide.' "

Senator Ervin remarked that in legal language "thereupon" has a particular meaning. "Why not use the language, 'Congress shall thereupon decide the issue'?"

I still believed that "immediately" conveyed the sense of urgency for which we were searching. Racking my brains for something upon which all the individual senators could compromise, I suggested, "Personally, I see nothing wrong with 'Thereupon, Congress shall immediately decide the issue.' "

Senator Javits of New York, a new member of our committee, spoke up. "Gentlemen, I agree with my colleague from Massachusetts, Senator Kennedy, and with the original statement of the author of S.J. Res. 1, that 'immediately' conveys the urgency we are looking for."

At this point, Senator Hruska again broke into the conversation. Since the hearings had not been printed, he repeated, the entire matter should lay over for a week. "Am I right," he asked the chairman, "in assuming that the Committee rule under which any member of the Committee may ask that a pending measure lay over for a week still applies?"

"Well, that's right, Roman," replied Chairman Eastland. "You know the rules. But gentlemen, as I said a minute ago, the Majority Leader has been after me to consider this matter so that he can put it on the calendar. Now Senator Hruska has a right under our rules to have this matter lay over a week. But"—and Jim Eastland turned toward the senator from Nebraska—"isn't there some way that we could put this over today and consider it tomorrow? Why don't we meet tomorrow at ten o'clock with the understanding that we'll vote on this matter at eleven?"

After a moment's thought, Senator Hruska agreed. "I'll be glad to abide by the wishes of the Chairman."

"Well, then, gentlemen, are there any objections? Can we have a unanimous consent agreement that the Committee will consider this matter and vote no later than eleven o'clock tomorrow morning?"

There was no objection, and the committee meeting was adjourned. Conrad and I gathered up the arsenal of material we had brought along—files, statute books, excerpts from constitutional language, court cases—whatever we might need to answer a particular objection or document a particular point.

As we left, I was feeling fairly glum. I knew that Roman Hruska and the others who had offered suggestions were as sincere and as strongly concerned about getting the best form of amendment as we were. But I also felt that much of the discussion was the product of the Committee members' first thoughts on the subject. It seemed to me that if they had lived with the problem for as long as we had and had had the exposure to every possible argument, every possible viewpoint, that the ABA conference and the sub-committee hearings had given us, what first struck them as the best solution to the problem would not, in the long run, seem quite so convincing. But then, that was my responsibility as subcommittee chairman—to do a little selling.

"Remember how easy it was in committee last year?" asked Conrad, reading the thoughts which must have been written on my face.

"I felt like a fish in a barrel in there," I admitted, "with every-body shooting at me. I was afraid this would happen. Before, the committee members knew there wasn't the slightest chance of get-ting Senate Joint Resolution 139 past the House and actually mak-ing it a part of the Constitution. This year they know it's for real—and it looks like they have blood in their eyes."

The subcommittee staff spent the rest of the day making pho-tostatic copies of the printer's print of the hearings. They then contacted the offices of the various committee members, giving them the opportunity to study in detail the testimony that had been given during the hearings. By the end of the day, only two mem-bers of the committee had accepted the offer.

I was in my place at the end of the long table by 9:45 the next morning. One by one, the members of the committee drifted in. By a quarter after ten, with the arrival of Senator Dirksen, we had enough members to constitute a quorum. Chairman Eastland called the committee to order, and Senator Dirksen immediately asked for the floor.

"Mr. Chairman, I have prepared here a little amendment or two to the proposed resolution, and I would like to ask Mr. Flynn to distribute them to you so that I can propose them formally." Clyde Flynn, the Minority Counsel for the Subcommittee on Con-stitutional Amendments, began to hand around the material. I tried to conceal my surprise at this new development. Since Senator Dirksen was the ranking minority member, it was to be expected that he and the Minority Counsel would work closely together. But Flynn was also a member of our subcommittee staff—yet until that moment, I had had no inkling that the minority had any amend-ments to propose.

But when I looked down at my copy of the Dirksen amendments, I was even more startled. The "little amendment or two" ran to two single-spaced typewritten pages.

I felt that our efforts were really being undermined. If this last-minute effort succeeded, it would gut the entire resolution, leaving little more than a group of meaningless and jumbled words. I knew that Senator Dirksen was introducing his amendments with every good intention; but I knew equally well that whoever on his staff had prepared those amendments had not bothered to give much study to the expert testimony which we had accumulated in page after page of our hearings.

The committee began to debate the proposals of the senator from Illinois. By the time the hands of the clock reached 10:45, Chairman Eastland reminded us that we had unanimously agreed to vote on the resolution at eleven o'clock.

"Well, Mr. Chairman," said Senator Dirksen, "we're debating a constitutional amendment. I have before the committee a series of amendments each of which I think the committee should consider. Could we change that time to 11:45?"

"Is there any objection?" asked the Chairman, glancing around the table. "All right, then, we'll vote at 11:45."

"Well, gentlemen," Senator Dirksen continued, "as I have had a chance to review the provisions of S.J. Res. 1 and hear the committee debate my amendments, I am prepared to suggest that Sections 1 and 2 are completely agreeable to the Minority."

I pricked up my ears at the last word. "Minority," when Senator Fong was one of the original cosponsors of our resolution? When Senator Javits was with us, and it looked as if Senator Scott would join us as well? I thought, and certainly hoped, that the senator from Illinois was using the phrase to give a little more weight to his proposals. The last thing I wanted was to put our resolution into a majority-versus-minority context—not when we needed a two-thirds vote in the Senate to pass. But I did not think that the issue was in any real danger of turning into a partisan one. We had worked hard to keep it from becoming that.

"Mr. Chairman," I said, "since the distinguished Minority Leader has no objections to Sections 1 and 2, I respectfully suggest that for the sake of time we could make more rapid progress if we consider S.J. Res. 1 section by section, voting on each. If that is agreeable to the Chairman and to the committee, I would like at this time to move that the committee accept the provisions of Section 1 as they are before us in the draft resolution."

"Are there any objections?" asked Senator Eastland. "The Chair hears none; Section 1 is approved."

Senator Ervin immediately followed suit: "Mr. Chairman, I move that we adopt the provisions of Section 2 as they are in the draft resolution before us." Again there were no objections, and the section was adopted. We were two-fifths of the way through— I knew, however, it was the easiest two-fifths.

We moved to the discussion of Section 3, the draft of which read as follows:

> If the President declares in writing that he is unable to discharge the powers and duties of his office, such powers and duties shall be discharged by the Vice President as Acting President.

"To whom," asked Senator Hruska, "is this declaration in writing by the President going to be addressed? The Vice President? How will we really know that the letter was actually sent? What's to prevent the Vice President from coming up with such a letter at some critical time in history—say, finding it in his desk drawer or his coat pocket?"

This point struck me as well taken. Senator Javits suggested that the declaration should be sent to the Congress, in the same manner that all Presidential messages are sent.

"But, Jack," objected Senator Dirksen, "what if the Congress is not in session? To whom should the declaration be addressed then?"

Senator Hruska suggested that the writing should be transmitted to the presiding officer of both Houses of Congress.

"But suppose Congress is not in session?" repeated Senator Dirksen. "Suppose the Speaker of the House is out whale-hunting and I have a Presidential declaration that I have to deliver to him? Does that mean I have to run him down, wherever he is?"

Senator Ervin brought his legal experience to bear on the point. "Any reasonable construction would hold that if the President's declaration was written to the office of the Speaker and accepted by his staff there, that this would constitute constructive delivery under normal legal terminology."

Another five minutes of debate on Section 3 slipped by. Senator Hruska, who had been writing furiously on the yellow pad in front of him, interrupted the debate to suggest wording that made a good deal of sense to me. It read:

> Whenever the President transmits to the President of the Senate and the Speaker of the House of Representatives, his written declaration that he is unable to discharge the powers and duties of his office, such powers and duties shall be discharged by the Vice President as Acting President.

I quickly moved that the committee accept the language suggested by Senator Hruska. There were no objections, and Section 3 was agreed to in that form. Now we were three-fifths of the way there.

We then moved to the discussion of Sections 4 and 5. Here, Senator Hruska vigorously protested the violation of the doctrine of separation of powers, and Senator Dirksen strongly argued that we should return to the approach of S.J. Res. 35 rather than write specific details into the Constitution. At one point, when the committee debate was raging, Ted Kennedy turned to Larry Conrad, who was seated between us at the far end of the table, and said, "We have no business trying to amend this here, after you people have worked on it so long in subcommittee."

The debate became more heated. I searched for some language that might reconcile our differences. My consternation must have been obvious, for at one point Joe Tydings of Maryland, a new addition to our committee, leaned over from where he was sitting on my right. "Stick to it, Birch," he said, "we can beat them! Don't give in; we've got the votes." I murmured a heartfelt thanks to him. His encouragement raised my spirits, but I did not share his confidence. I began taking a mental poll of how the committee members who were present would probably vote. In my judgment, at that moment, it would have been nip and tuck.

Suddenly, Chairman Eastland was saying that Senator Robert Kennedy, former Attorney General, thought that the resolution should require two-thirds of the Cabinet to go along with the Vice President before the President could be declared disabled. There was a flurry of debate on this point; then to bring it to a head, the Chairman moved that we change the Cabinet requirement from a majority to two-thirds. "Bobby thinks this is important."

A knot tightened at the pit of my stomach. I had never before flatly opposed a motion of the Committee Chairman—but someone had to do it now.

"Mr. Chairman," I said, "with all due respect to the position of our distinguished Chairman, I think that two-thirds of the Cabinet is not necessary. In fact, I think it would be far less desirable than the majority which has been recommended by the ABA Conference and which is contained in S.J. Res. 1. We want to have a proposal that will work. It is conceivable that even if a President was obviously disabled, one third of his Cabinet, for one reason or another, would be afraid to vote him out of office, even temporarily. A majority seems to me to be ample safeguard against the Vice President taking over on his own. Still a majority of the Cabinet is not such a large requirement that a few members can arbitrarily block the decision.

"With all respect to our distinguished Chairman," I concluded, "I would have to oppose the two-thirds motion."

Chairman Eastland put the question. I held my breath; to my surprise, the motion failed. The debate continued. In an effort to bring the matter to a final vote, I accepted a minor amendment here and there. Thus, Sections 4 and 5 would conform to Section 3 in that all written declarations would be directed to the Speaker of the House and the President of the Senate—Senator Hruska's change which, I felt, strengthend the resolution. I also agreed to substitute for "immediately decide the issue" the phrase "immediately proceed to decide the issue," a change which incorporated the opinions of three individual senators and in no way altered the real meaning or lessened the sense of urgency.

It was a quarter to twelve, then twelve o'clock; but the debate went on. The Senate was now in session, and technically any member of the Senate who had wanted to object to our continuing to meet could have done so. At a quarter past twelve Senator Ervin moved that the committee favorably report out S.J. Res. 1 as amended. I hastened to second his motion, but to no avail; the debate continued.

Senator Hruska was still voicing his concern over the inclusion of Congress in the decision on Presidential disability. I could only repeat what I had said in the committee hearings: Congress was included in the bill because they were the personal representatives of the people, and no President should be removed from office against his will without the people having a voice in it. The inclusion of Congress here, I asserted, was no different, and no greater violation of the "separation of powers" doctrine, than the inclusion of Congress in the impeachment proceedings and in the election provisions of the Twelfth Amendment.

By half-past twelve Senator Dirksen was as strongly convinced as ever that the right approach was that of former S.J. Res. 35. "Why put all these details into the Constitution?" he asked. "Let's just enable Congress to pass a law dealing with the specifics of this at a later date." But Sam Ervin, in his characteristic manner, countered with a parable.

"That reminds me," he said thoughtfully, "of the fellow walking down the road on a rainy day when he saw a man fixing the roof of his house. 'How come you're up there in such a bad rainstorm fixing your roof?' he asked. 'Why don't you wait until it stops raining?' But the other fellow answered, 'It don't leak then.'" Our laughter did a great deal to ease temporarily the tension of the debate.

The clock on the committee room wall showed 12:45. For a moment all of the participants seemed to pause for breath at the same time; the voice of the chairman came from the far end of the table.

"Gentlemen," he said, "I'll have to vote with the Chairman of the subcommittee." Until that moment, I had not been certain what Chairman Eastland would do on final passage, although he had been most cooperative with us at all times. His words were music to my ears. Senator Ervin inquired whether his earlier motion to vote was still before the committee.

"That's my understanding, Sam," answered the chairman. There was another momentary pause. "Senator Ervin's motion is before the committee," he continued. "Are there any objections?"

Again I held my breath.

"The chair hears none. The Resolution is adopted."

I must have slumped in my chair with relief, but friendly slaps on the back from Ted Kennedy and Joe Tydings, on either side of me, jolted me upright again. The Judiciary Committee adjourned, and most of the members hastily went their ways to attend their other duties.

Roman Hruska and I, along with Larry Conrad and Bob Young of the Judiciary Committee staff, stayed on to check and double check the language. Next, Larry and the subcommittee staff painstakingly drafted the committee report. Twenty-four hours later, they had it ready to submit to Senators Hruska and Dirksen for the inclusion of the individual views the two senators had so vigorously expressed in committee.

Now that the furor was over, I realized how important it was that our resolution had experienced such a thorough going over by the committee members. We were, after all, trying to amend the Constitution—not a matter to be taken lightly. When the full Committee on the Judiciary favorably reported S.J. Res. 1 to the Senate floor, the resolution had been given all the attention and close scrutiny that a constitutional amendment deserved.

CHAPTER 9

Open Season
on Senators

The same week that S.J. Res. 1 was reported out of the Judiciary Committee, the House of Representatives began to take action on the succession-disability problem. H.J. Res. 1 had been introduced in the House by Congressman Celler, and the House hearings would be held by the full Judiciary Committee, rather than a subcommittee as we had done in the Senate. Thus Chairman Celler hoped to move more quickly and to focus more public attention upon the problem. I had been invited to be the lead-off witness on the first day of hearings, February 7. My feelings about appearing before the House committee, and especially in such a prominent role, were, to say the least, mixed. On the one hand, I knew that if anyone from the Senate was to present our views to the House, I was by then the obvious one to do so. On the other hand, I had heard from several of my Senate colleagues that it was always "open season on senators" at House hearings, and naturally I had no particular desire to be a sitting target.

However, when I talked over the problem with Don Channell and other friends at the American Bar Association, they agreed with Chairman Celler that since I was the leading congressional advocate of our particular solution to the problem, it was appropriate for me to be the first witness. I could have ducked the whole question by sending a written statement. Yet despite my trepidations, perhaps it was necessary for me to be present—if the House committee was going to be shooting at our resolution, I wanted to be there in the trenches defending it.

At ten o'clock on the morning of February 7, Larry Conrad and I arrived at the House Judiciary Committee hearing room. My anxiety was not decreased by Chairman Celler's opening remarks, which stressed the scope and importance of the job he and his House colleagues faced.

"Today, the full committee of the House Committee on the Judiciary initiates hearings on 32 proposals relating to the problem of Presidential inability. We are confronted with one of the most difficult problems that has ever challenged a Congress. It is a problem which has existed since the adoption of the Constitution and on more than one occasion it has been a stark reality." I swallowed hard. Thirty-two resolutions, and I, after only two years in the Senate, was there in support of just one among them! As Conrad and I went to the witness table, I noticed that Attorney General Katzenbach and his assistant Norbert Schlei were in the audience. Although I was unaware that the Attorney General had been called before the committee to testify, this was obviously the case. It struck me as inappropriate that a member of the Cabinet should be forced to wait while I addressed the committee. So, before I began my prepared statement, I suggested to the chairman that, if the Attorney General wished to go first, I would be glad to follow him.

"Mr. Attorney General, do you want to embrace that invitation of the Senator?" asked the chairman.

"No, Mr. Chairman, I think Senator Bayh has been burdened by this for a long time and I would be happy for him to go first."

The chairman nodded to me. "Proceed, sir."

We had prepared a long, detailed statement concerning the

provisions of S.J. Res. 1 as it had been reported out of the Judiciary Committee. Certain changes had been made, and I felt that it was important for the House committee to know the reasons behind these changes. I did not, however, want to read the statement in all its detail. Instead, I felt that the best strategy would be to give the committee a personal and extemporaneous summary. Therefore, I merely asked permission to introduce the statement into the committee records.

During my summary, I tried to impress upon the House committee how much study and preparation had previously gone into the phraseology of S.J. Res. 1. A similar measure, I said, had been passed sixty-five to zero in the Senate last session. But even more important was the need to find a meeting of minds which would gather sufficient support to get congressional passage of a single measure dealing with the problem and subsequently secure the necessary ratification by the state legislatures.

There was no perfect solution to "this rather complicated and vexing problem," I admitted; but "our efforts have been directed at finding the best proposal possible. Each has been willing to give and take a little bit on his idea in the true legislative process to come up with the best solution we could find—which would certainly be better than none at all." The extensive hearings; the scrutiny which our committee had given the measure, and which the House committee would give it; the study by the American Bar Association—all these, I said, would guarantee that "we don't find a hit-or-miss solution."

I advised the House committee that since its introduction, S.J. Res. 1 had been altered by action within the Senate Judiciary Committee. During two years of executive sessions, we had closely scrutinized the bill and made some changes which, I felt, improved it. "I do not believe that any of the changes deal with the substance of the resolution," I said; rather, they were perfections in the language "which will make the meaning and the intentions easier to perceive."

Then I proceeded to a section-by-section summary of the provisions of S.J. Res. 1. The ranking Republican member of the committee, Congressman William McCulloch of Ohio, had introduced a resolution which provided for a ten-day limit on congressional debate over Presidential disability. I felt that I needed to deal forcefully with this matter, knowing my Senate colleagues, particularly those from southern states, would be violently opposed to inserting any such limitation, since free debate had long been a tradition in the Senate.

"One of the problems that has been discussed not only by our committee but at some length in the news media is the problem of a time limitation. How quickly should Congress act? The distinguished ranking minority member of this committee has suggested there should be a 10-day time limitation. There have been other time limitations suggested. Some of the news media have suggested the use of the word 'immediately' is too vague. . . ."

"I must say the feeling of my colleagues in the committee," I went on, "was quite the contrary. They felt that the use of the word 'immediately' could well be too restrictive . . . might even imply a decision without any debate whatsoever." For this reason, I told the House committee, we had finally decided to amend the paragraph to read "Congress shall immediately proceed to decide the issue"—a phrase which "would more clearly imply that the process of determination could include calling witnesses and the like. Nevertheless, the word 'immediately' means forthwith, quickly, and with the greatest of dispatch. Now this committee, in its judgment, can determine whether this gives too much leeway or not."

Another change the Senate committee had made, I continued, concerned the provision under Section 3 for the President to transmit a written declaration of inability to the Speaker of the House and the President of the Senate. This, we felt, would be "sufficient constructive notice for the transferral of power," yet would involve only a short time lapse.

I admitted next that there had been disagreement within the Senate over the concept of the separation of powers. "I would like to point out I am a strong adherent to the separation of powers doctrine," I said; but "I would like to also point out that our forefathers have found it expedient and wise to include in the body of the Constitution itself, as have subsequent amendments, certain commingling of the various branches." I cited the veto power of the executive over the legislative branch, the confirmation power of the Senate, the role of the House in deciding a Presidential election if no candidate received a majority of electoral votes, and the impeachment provisions, which involved the House, the Senate, and the Chief Justice of the Supreme Court. "I feel it is necessary," I concluded, "to bring Congress into the picture because I don't want the powers which have been given to the President by all of the people to be taken away from him without the representatives of the people having a voice."

That ended my extemporaneous statement. Even though I had been bracing myself for the questioning of the House committee members, I was unprepared for the rigorous questioning that followed. The rest of the morning, and much of the afternoon, I found myself in the center of a bull's-eye of controversy. The congressmen on the committee were determined to have their questions answered. This was their responsibility, and while I was under fire I could only try to console myself with the fact that we were writing a detailed record which could provide the basis for determining legislative intent if some future generation needed to look to our testimony.

Congressman Byron G. Rogers of Colorado was the first questioner. "In the event that the President should name a Vice President, and the Congress . . . did not confirm that designation, would the Speaker of the House then assume the duties of the President in the event of vacancy?" he asked.

I replied that although this was a possibility, it was, in my opinion, an unlikely one. "Our feeling is that in a time of national tragedy such as a death of a President where the Vice President succeeds, or where the Vice President himself dies—the country is in no mood to tolerate political chicanery in the appointment of a Vice President and I don't think this would be the case." I soon regretted my words.

"You think it is political chicanery," echoed Congressman Rogers, "if you in your judgment as a Member of the United States Senate, should feel a man is not competent to be a Vice President or President? Don't you think it is your duty to vote against him and if you vote against him you call that political chicanery."

"No," I admitted. "But I think in most—"

"Well, aren't you at the same time advocating and saying that you as a Member of the Senate and I as a Member of the House, if we should vote against that, that we are not exercising our best judgment?"

I quickly realized that I was going to have to watch my words very, very carefully. "First of all, Congressman, perhaps the use of the term 'political chicanery' was not a good one."

"Well."

"But," I continued, "there is the possibility of a political power struggle going on and this is one possibility." I went on to say that normally the President would be able to rely on the members of his own party to support his Vice-Presidential nominee. "In the event the opposite party controlled the Congress, then I feel that the effort to play politics with this appointment would be prevented by a strong voicing of public opinion."

Congressman Rogers changed the subject. "Do you see any political implications that might arise due to the fact we are removing a Speaker of the House of Representatives as a possible successor to the office of President in this amendment?"

"No, sir, I don't."

"You feel Members of the House would go right along and think that their prerogative of passing legislation where the Speaker is the one in succession—that that removal meets with their approval and they wouldn't hesitate to approve it on account of that?"

"You, sir, could speak better to this question than I," I answered.

"Senator, may I interject?" asked Congressman Celler, who proceeded to point out that our amendment would not really interfere with the present succession line, which would come into being only if both the President and the Vice President were to die. In that case, the chairman said, the Speaker would succeed to the Presidency, as was presently specified in the succession statute.

"Will the gentleman yield for one observation?" asked Congressman Robert T. Ashmore of South Carolina. "Did your committee consider the situation that might arise in the case where the President should nominate or name the Speaker of the House as Vice President? Then the Congress refused to confirm the Speaker of the House. Where are you then?"

"You would probably be in a rather unlikely situation," I replied with some understatement.

"The Speaker of the House would take over anyway, wouldn't he?" Ashmore inquired.

It would, I pointed out, take two deaths to get the Speaker into the picture; both the President and the Vice President would have to be taken before the Speaker succeeded to the Presidency. "This would be the case if the nominee for Vice President was not confirmed by the Congress and the President died."

Congressman Herbert Tenzer of New York spoke up. "Mr. Chairman, would the gentleman yield?"

But Congressman Ashmore went on, "Well, does your bill provide if the Congress should refuse to confirm the person the President has named, then would the President be authorized to submit another name?"

"Yes, sir," I answered, "and another, and another, and another." But I added, "I think we have to assume we are dealing with reasonable men. They would give reasonable consideration to the name submitted by the President. If Congress doesn't approve, another name would be submitted."

"Would the gentleman yield?" repeated Tenzer.

"I yield," said Ashmore; but before Tenzer could continue, Congressman Basil Whitener of North Carolina, wearing in his lapel the red rose which was his trademark, began to fire questions at me.

"I would like to ask the Senator," he began, "if it is the feeling of his subcommittee that a constitutional amendment is necessary to accomplish this purpose."

"Yes, sir; we feel a constitutional amendment is necessary."

"Now, Article II, Clause 5, Section 1 says that 'in Case of the Removal of the President from Office or of his Death, Resignation, or Inability to discharge the Powers and Duties of said Office,' " Mr. Whitener continued, " 'the Same shall devolve on the Vice President and the Congress may by Law provide for the Case of Removal, Death, Resignation, or Inability both of the President and the Vice President, declaring what Officer shall then act as President and such Officer shall act accordingly until the Disability be removed or a President shall be elected.' "

"As the Congressman undoubtedly knows," I replied, "there has been a considerable amount of debate over whether a constitutional amendment was in fact needed because of the very wording he just read to the committee. Because there is sufficient debate, some doubt, we felt it would be safer—to be absolutely safe—to put a matter like this in the bedrock law of the Constitution so there cannot be a court test at some moment of crisis as to the constitutionality of this provision."

"I gather from the questions these gentlemen ask," remarked Mr. Whitener, "that the amendment you now propose also raises questions so it doesn't seem likely we are going to eliminate legal questions."

"But we would eliminate constitutional questions if it is the Constitution, would we not?" I parried. Whitener was not convinced.

"It seems to me this language is abundantly clear," he said, again referring to that of the Constitution. "The only thing that I can see you make clear in this that is not clear in the present Constitution is that you take away from the Congress the right to move without the intercession of the President in making this determination. Under this proposed amendment, the Congress, it seems to me, will have to sit here and wait until the President makes a move whereas without this amendment and going under the present language of the Constitution, the Congress on its own motion makes this decision."

"Well, the Congress, of course, has not made its own motion," I replied, "and there is a considerable amount of division of opinion as to whether it does have the constitutional authority to do so in this particular case—in the case of disability. There seems to be almost unanimous agreement that Congress does not have the power to appoint a new Vice President, which is the second part of this amendment. This would require without a doubt a constitutional amendment."

"I think that's clear," Whitener agreed, "that the present language does not apply to the Vice-Presidency, but if this situation arises that we are talking about, the dual death—the Vice President and the President . . . we either have the constitutional authority to do what you would propose to do in this amendment to the Constitution or we didn't have the authority to do what was done when we put the Speaker in the third position. Isn't that correct?"

"In the case of the Speaker, we are dealing with the death of both officers and the Speaker does take over as President."

"Or inability," added the congressman from North Carolina. The problem of inability, I said, was something else again. In the event the President is disabled and the Speaker has to serve, "we hope this is a temporary divestiture of the powers and duties of the office."

"Well, may I ask you one other little question?" asked Congressman Whitener. Then he continued, zeroing in on the language "A majority of the heads of the executive departments," which we had used, at Sam Ervin's suggestion, to designate the Cabinet. "Now, in your prepared statement which I glanced at, you and our chairman in his statement just seemed to assume that that meant members of the President's Cabinet. Now, what legal authority do you have for saying that the words 'a majority of the principal officers of the executive departments' means members of the President's Cabinet?"

"This has been the general interpretation put on this language," I replied.

"By whom?" Whitener persisted.

"As it has been used in the past," I answered. I added that our report had made our intent abundantly clear.

But he was not to be swayed. "Now, let's take the Department of Defense," he said. Would the principal officers of the Navy, Air Force, and Army departments be part of this group?

No, I replied, the Department of Defense had superseded those departments, whose heads did not sit in the Cabinet. "The logical interpretation is that the heads of the executive departments are the principal officers of the executive departments. This is the Cabinet."

"If the gentleman would excuse me, why did you not say the members of the President's Cabinet?" Whitener asked.

"The terminology 'Cabinet' has never been used in the Constitution. The term 'executive departments' has, and in the report we define this as the Cabinet, making this interpretation very clear. It was our desire that the language of the amendment be consistent with that of the Constitution itself."

"Of course, when that was used in the original Constitution," Whitener retorted, "they didn't contemplate several departments we now have. I think that putting it into the report would not obviate the hazard any more than language that has been put in many reports to which courts have paid no attention in the past. The language should be clear in the amendment itself."

As I was about to answer, Congressman Rogers broke into our discussion, asking about an entirely different subject. "May I back up and inquire about your Section 3. You say if the President declares in writing he is unable to discharge the powers and duties of the office, such powers and duties shall be discharged by the President as Acting President. Well, now—"

"By the Vice President," I corrected.

"Now, if someone should show up with a letter presumably signed by him would that give the President or Vice President the authority to assume the office under this amendment?"

We had, I told him, changed the wording for just that reason. "You can no longer show up with a letter. It has to be written, a written declaration which has been transmitted to the President of the Senate and the Speaker of the House, and certainly so—"

"That isn't what I construe Section 3 to mean," Rogers disagreed. "Suppose the Vice President . . . says, 'I got a letter from the President. He says he is not able to perform these duties. Therefore I am acting as President.' Now, is there anybody in a position to stop him from acting?"

"First of all, I want to repeat once again. Apparently, I did not make it clear. The committee was sufficiently concerned about the Vice President coming up with a letter in his pocket . . . that we changed the wording of the section to which the Congressman referred."

Before Congressman Rogers could continue his argument, Congressman Harold D. Donoghue of Massachusetts entered the discussion. "Would the gentleman yield? Let us assume the President becomes mentally incompetent. If the President declares in writing that he is unable to discharge his duties, if he is mentally incompetent, what value should that writing have?"

"Well," I replied, "if he is mentally incompetent, whether the value of the writing was in question or not, I think it would be incumbent upon the Vice President and Cabinet under Section 4 to assume the powers and duties of the office as if there were no writing from the President."

Congressman Tenzer re-entered the questioning and moved to another line of attack. We had been discussing Sections 3 and 4. Tenzer now brought us back to Section 2, which we had been discussing when he had unsuccessfully tried to capture the floor from Congressman Ashmore. Under our amendment, he asked, "would it not be clear that if the President made a nomination for Vice President and if both Houses of Congress did not approve, then the President would make another nomination before the Speaker of the House would succeed?"

"Yes, sir," I replied, "of course, the Speaker of the House does not succeed at all, unless there is a double death."

"That is," said Tenzer, "both President and Vice President."

"Yes; yes," I said.

"That is what I want to make perfectly clear. Another nomination would have to be made," said Tenzer.

"They would have to die simultaneously in a catastrophe?" Mr. Donoghue chimed in.

"Yes," replied Tenzer.

"Would the gentleman from Colorado yield?" asked Congressman Celler. He then returned to Congressman Whitener's earlier contention that a statute would be preferable to a constitutional amendment in solving the disability problem. To rebut this contention, he read aloud a statement that former Attorney General Herbert Brownell had made when he appeared before the House Judiciary Committee in 1957.

I must admit that I was as glad for a chance to draw a few peaceful breaths as I was of Chairman Celler's enlisting the aid of the Brownell statement to prove that a constitutional amendment was necessary. We had gone back and forth from subject to subject so rapidly that I had the feeling of being at a tennis match, trying to follow the ball back and forth—or was I perhaps the ball itself?

As Chairman Celler concluded, Mr. Rogers began to question me again. "Senator, turning to Section 4, as amended, it says, 'Whenever the Vice President and a majority of the principal officers of the executive departments'—let's stop there. Who do you envision as being principal officers of the executive departments?"

"The President's Cabinet," I repeated.

"And when you use it in that term you only intend to have the President's Cabinet?"

"That is correct, sir."

"And none other?"

"Yes, sir."

"If in the future," Rogers elaborated, "we should create an office of Cabinet of Humanities as an example or of Natural Resources and so forth, each one of these would be a member of the Cabinet who would be in a position to act. In other words—"

"That is correct," I said.

"Any Cabinet officer created under the act of Congress would be in a position to act."

"That is correct. Yes, sir."

"You and I recognize that these positions are at the pleasure of the President and subject to confirmation of the House—or of the Senate," Rogers added. "Now . . . suppose that a majority of the officers should arrive at a conclusion that the President is unable to perform the duties of his office and he learns of it, and he immediately discharges all of them, accepts their resignations—then where are we in your constitutional amendment if he says you no longer are a member of the Cabinet hence you cannot say that I can't perform the duties of the office. What would happen in that case?"

"This is one of the contingencies for which it is very difficult to find a positive solution," I replied. I proceeded to cite a similar possibility: the Vice President might take over the powers and duties of the Presidency with the consent of a majority of the Cabinet, and then as Acting President proceed to fire the Cabinet members who had voted against him. This, too, might happen, I said; and yet "we don't want to put a Vice President in a situation as Acting President where someone dies on the Cabinet and he doesn't have the authority to replace him."

"No, but here the point is this," insisted Rogers, "that the man selected for the Cabinet position, the men selected for the Cabinet positions are those the President has trust in and he expects honor from them. He's not likely to look with favor to them if they pass a resolution saying you are no longer competent. They are turning on the man who made their position possible. Do you think that is the proper body to make this determination?"

"Yes, I do, sir," I answered, "for the reason that I feel that the body that works the closest with the President, that is most familiar with his capability, should have the opportunity to make this determination with the Vice President, who, I think, has the inescapable constitutional responsibility of participating."

"Isn't there a safeguard," inquired Chairman Celler, "because you say, 'or such other body as Congress may by law provide'?"

"Now, Mr. Chairman, that's true," admitted Rogers.

"That body could be the body of physicians, the Supreme Court or what have you. That is the safety valve, isn't it?" the Judiciary Committee chairman asked me.

"Yes, sir," I replied, "and that's—"

"Would the gentleman yield?" asked Rogers. But I went on to explain that that was the very reason we had allowed Congress to designate another body: "We don't know what the future is going to reveal to us."

"Senator," interjected Congressman Peter Rodino of New Jersey, "I don't want to seem facetious. Let's consider this possibility. . . . What provision do we make here, or is there any provision intended to be made if after the assumption of the Vice President of the powers and duties of Acting President . . . the then Acting President becomes disabled?"

"We have not provided for this contingency," I told him.

"May I follow through?" Rogers asked; but before he could further elaborate his point, Mr. Rodino continued.

"Is there the likelihood, especially in this day and age, when we hear so much of the seriousness of heart attacks and other serious ailments that suddenly strike, or again the question of mental competency—" in short, could it not be that both the President and the Vice President could become disabled? "And if we are going to now amend the Constitution I think we should weigh this question and make some provision."

"I think that it is wise for the committee to weigh it and I think it is a question well put," I replied. But on the other hand, "the reason we did not include it was that the more complicated you make a constitutional amendment, quite frankly, the more contingencies for which you provide, the more difficult it is to get it passed . . . What we tried to do is to provide for the most likely eventualities and hope we can get it through, feeling we would have most of those things covered."

As I was going on to give other examples of contingencies that were not included for this reason, Chairman Celler brought us back to an earlier problem. "Would the gentleman yield for a moment to clear up a point with reference to . . . the resignation of a member of the Cabinet that might gum up the works?" He pointed out that after the Vice President and Cabinet members had submitted their written declaration, "if the member of the Cabinet resigns or is fired . . . , he has made a decision. What happens after he makes his decision could not operate retroactively . . . so that I think your question and the answers that were given should be clarified so that it makes no difference whether the Cabinet officer resigns after he has made his written declaration."

This brought Congressman Rogers back into the fray. "But the point I tried to emphasize," he protested, "is not only that, but naturally if a man . . . is President . . . certainly he is going to have at least one loyal member among the Cabinet say a meeting is necessary to determine whether he should continue to be President. He might take action before they get this written declaration. That's the point I am trying to emphasize and I want to follow through on the other problem as presented here." What would happen, he continued, if Congress substituted for the Cabinet a commission composed, for example, of five psychiatrists, five members of the House, and five members of the Senate? "Could Congress enact such a law and designate such people to make these determinations and immediately upon that determination being transmitted to the Speaker of the House of Representatives and the President of the Senate, that that immediately removes the President from his position?"

"With the consent of the Vice President, yes, sir, the Congress could," I replied. Mr. Rogers and I threw this point back and forth for another moment or so. Our discussion was cut short by Mr. Whitener, who, I had noticed, had been busily thumbing through a copy of the United States Code during the last few minutes of our colloquy.

"Would the gentleman yield?" he asked. "I notice you and our chairman keep referring to members of the Cabinet and I don't want to belabor this point, but you say a majority of the principal officers of the executive departments and no one questions that Congress has the right to create executive departments, I assume. Now, I just quickly looked here at Title 5, Section 1 of the United States Code, and it says that the provisions of this title shall apply to the following executive departments. First, the Department of State. . . ." Mr. Whitener went down the list, reading the names of the various Cabinet departments. ". . . Department of Health, Education, and Welfare," he concluded.

"Then," he said, "when we go to Title 10, Section 101, relating to the Defense Department, and from this in subsection 6, quote: 'Executive part of the Department,' unquote, means the executive part of the Department of Defense, Department of the Navy, or Department of the Air Force as the case may be at the seat of the Government.

"And then when we look at Title 42, Section 201, Subsection (e), we find the Congress defining 'executive department' as follows. . . ." I was beginning to feel almost nostalgic about the good old days when a relatively simple controversy had raged in the Senate over the use of the word "immediately."

"Now, in 5 minutes," Congressman Whitener said, "I have found these definitions of executive department in existing statutes. . . . It seems to me that you have opened up greater opportunity for litigation and contention by the use of that language and that if you mean the Cabinet you should say the Cabinet. There are probably other conflicts. I am sure the learned Attorney General when he appears will tell us other definitions of the executive department to be found in the United States Code."

"I will merely say," I answered, "that whatever language is used, the intention should be made clear that we are talking about the President's Cabinet, his official family. I, for one, think that the language—"

"Or such other body as Congress may designate," broke in Mr. Whitener, "and if Congress—"

"The Congressman is talking about the use of the words 'executive departments,' " I said firmly, "and I admit this other is in there. It is in there for the purpose we discussed but when you are talking about the principal officers of the executive departments I, for one, think it is clear we are talking about the President's Cabinet."

"Would the gentleman yield?" asked Congressman Charles Mathias of Maryland.

Simultaneously, Congressman Arch Moore of West Virginia chimed in. "Why do you object to putting it in? Why do you object to using Cabinet?"

I was beginning to feel as if I were being shot at from all sides. "I have no specific objection to putting it in, except that—" Then I turned to Chairman Celler, hoping that with his help we might end the discussion once and for all. "Mr. Chairman," I was almost appealing to him, "if I may clarify my reason again. The reason it was put in is the word 'Cabinet' was not used in the Constitution. The words 'members of the executive department' are."

"If I may interrupt." It was Congressman Moore again. "The gentleman from North Carolina picked out three or four instances in which the phrase 'executive department heads' has been used which certainly should lead you to the conclusion there could be some confusion somewhere. Why would it not be best to designate who shall have this responsibility to determine the incapability or capability of the President to handle the affairs of his office?"

"I have no objection if the committee wants to change the wording," I repeated. "I might say the distinguished senior Senator from North Carolina was the one most vehement in his feeling against putting additional language in the Constitution that has no precedent so long as we make it clear. If you gentlemen don't think this is clear, we ought to take further steps."

"Senator Ervin feels this is sufficient," I continued, "I do, too. But if the committee differs, I think it should be made abundantly clear whether in the proposal, in the reports, or whether in the discussion on the floor, that we are talking about the President's Cabinet. We don't want the head of Soil Conservation Service or the Veteran's Administration or someone else to be brought into this determination. We are talking about the President's Cabinet, the people who sit with him."

Mr. Whitener, to whose North Carolinian loyalties I had hoped to appeal by citing Sam Ervin on this issue, responded. "May I say this? Senator Ervin is one of my most distinguished constituents and one of the most able lawyers to be found." But still Whitener was of the opinion that the language was ambiguous.

Then, in a complete change of direction, he continued. "In Section 2 you use the wording, 'confirmation by a majority vote of

both Houses of Congress,' and then go on again in Section 5, . . . line
5 of page 3, 'If the Congress determines by two-thirds vote of both
Houses,' do we mean actually a majority of the members of the
House of Representatives or a majority of the members present and
voting? Do we mean two-thirds of the members of the House of
Representatives or two-thirds of the members present and voting?"

"This is one question that was asked of the Attorney General,"
I replied. "It is his opinion, and it was our intention, that we prescribed a majority of the quorum or two-thirds of the quorum as
prescribed by the rules of both Houses. The Attorney General was
of the opinion we have adequate precedent so that whenever we talk
about a majority or two-thirds we are talking about a majority of
the quorum which is necessary to conduct the business in the first
place."

"The House when you have 218," put in Mr. Rogers, who had
been listening silently for some minutes. "If there are 218 present,
two-thirds of them vote. That meets the requirement?"

"Is that what you mean?" asked Mr. Rodino.

"That's what we mean," I replied, scarcely knowing at whom
to direct my answer. "That is the way it has always been construed."

"I thank the gentleman for yielding," said Congressman Mathias as he finally was granted the floor, after waiting for over five
minutes of questions from others. His question brought us back to
the discussion of what constituted the Cabinet, which I thought we
had finally laid to rest.

"Going to the question of the gentleman from North Carolina,
the use of the phrase 'majority of the principal officers of the executive departments' and relating this to the term 'Cabinet' because
these are not necessarily parallel terms, today I believe that the
Ambassador of the United Nations sits with and is a member of the
Cabinet. . . . I understand some other executive officers, including
the head of the poverty program, Mr. Shriver, is also sitting as a
member of the Cabinet. Would it be desirable as a matter of policy
that people of this sort who have close contact with the President
and who are constantly in communication with him be included in
the generic term, 'the Cabinet,' though they are excluded by the
language that has been used so far?"

"I personally do not think they should be included," I replied, although I agreed that there were arguments on both sides. "We are talking about the chief executive offices of this country, which I think exclude the United Nations or the poverty program."

"Will the gentleman yield?" asked Congressman Celler. He, too, must have been eager to put an end to this line of questioning, for he continued: "I think we find the words 'executive departments' in another part of the Constitution. In Article 2, Section 2, of this language it says:

> The President shall be Commander in Chief of the Army and Navy of the several States, when called into the actual service of the United States; he may require the Opinion, in writing, of the principal Officer of each of the executive Departments.

"What did the Founding Fathers mean," Congressman Celler continued, "when they used the term 'executive departments'? I imagine they must have meant the members of the Cabinet so called when they used that term. . . ." But if the Chairman of the Judiciary Committee had hoped thereby to settle the matter, he was mistaken.

"The point is—" began Rogers.

"I should like to ask this question," interjected Congressman McCulloch. "Is the Atomic Energy Commission an executive department of the Government? Would the principal officer of the Atomic Energy Commission be one clothed with authority under this proposal? And I refer specifically to the section of the Constitution which the gentleman just read."

"If you are asking me," I replied, "I would say 'No.' "

"First of all," McCulloch persisted, "the Atomic Energy Commission is not an executive branch of government? Do you make that conclusion?"

"Not in the last degree, it is not," I replied with some caution. "Not in the highest degree. It is a subsidiary branch. It is not a department but a commission."

Chairman Celler stepped in again. "I think we are going to have the Attorney General appear here subsequently. I think he might give us some enlightenment on this matter. I think it should be clarified because there are undoubtedly some doubts in the minds of a good many present." Undoubtedly, I thought, as the Judiciary Committee chairman continued. "I think there should be some precise language so that there is no ambiguity whatsoever. I think you would agree?"

"I agree," I said.

To my relief, we moved on to other matters. Chairman Celler returned to the question of possible usurpation of Presidential power. "I think the gentleman from Colorado reading something about Section 3, whenever the President transmits to the President of the Senate—no—Section 4 whenever the Vice President and so forth . . . he then shall succeed and become Acting President.

"I think the gentleman from Colorado feared there might be some ambitious Vice President who might want to usurp power," the chairman observed. Did we not have a safety valve, he asked me, in that such an ambitious Vice President, once he became Acting President, could be impeached? As I was about to reply, Mr. Rogers broke in.

"I am sure, Mr. Chairman, we have had many ambitious Vice Presidents in the past and I anticipate we will have many in the future; but the point is this. To place in the hands of a few individuals the power to upset what the people of the United States have done in electing a President by the whim of a signature which may or may not be genuine, it goes a long way. That's the thing that I'm emphasizing."

"The answer is impeachment," repeated Chairman Celler.

I tried to clarify the issue. "You can think of all sorts of eventualities, but in Section 3 which the gentleman referred to first, this is a voluntary procedure . . . which the President voluntarily submits to. Now if someone shows up with a written letter and says, 'Look what I got from the President,' and the President comes on television the next instant and says this is a forgery—"

"Yes, but under this," said Rogers, "suppose as suggested by the gentleman from Massachusetts that he is actually insane and the ambitious Vice President knows that he is insane and—"

"I would think if he is insane, we better get him out of there."

But Rogers was not daunted. "Suppose he is insane and somebody through trickery got him to sign it or suppose that he is unable to even sign it. Then . . . if he shows . . . up with the letter, then immediately the Vice President takes over. Now, the point is, that I think it is dangerous to put in the hands of a few people the right to upset what the majority of the people in this country has determined."

"The final right, if I may say so, is not in the hands of a few people, but in the vote of two-thirds of the House and Senate," I reminded him. Mr. Rogers and I continued to throw this question back and forth for a while, with Congressmen Celler and Rodino interjecting their thoughts occasionally. Finally, Mr. Rogers yielded to Congressman Richard Poff of Virginia.

"Mr. Chairman," Poff began, "may I say I think we should all recognize candidly what hasn't yet been articulated; namely, that the Celler-Bayh proposal or the Bayh-Celler proposal is the end result, the precipitant of a long process of distillation and filtration in which many hands have played a part. I say this because I want to emphasize that this is not a carelessly drawn measure and I say that because I am anxious to see that expeditious action is taken at this session of Congress on this vitally important matter."

Congressman Poff's words would have been welcome at any time. At that stage of the game, they were virtually music to my ears. Finally someone was acknowledging the long hours of study and the careful weighing of alternatives that were behind our measure, rather than peppering it with questions that seemed, to me at that harassed moment, more to pick it apart than to explore its meaning. I gratefully sat back to listen to Poff's next words. But my relief was temporary, for his next words were not so encouraging.

Congressman Poff continued. "Now having said that, however, I think it is important that we not do anything precipitously, that we not do any rash acts which all of us and future generations may regret. To illustrate what I mean by that, I call attention to the fact that most legal scholars thought that the Senate bill had been refined to its highest state of polish and yet the Senator has brought with him what is described as the text of Senate Joint Resolution 1 as reported by the Judiciary Committee on February 4, 1965, and most of his testimony has been addressed to changes that have been made.

"Now, I suggest that the fact that the Senate committee was able to discover the need for changes demonstrates that this committee should be careful in dealing with the subject and that we should not in any way be foreclosed in our examination of the subject." Here we go again, I thought, steeling myself for the further interrogation which was to follow.

"We always welcome your scholarly inquiries," said Chairman Celler at the close of Poff's preparatory statement.

"The gentleman is most generous," replied Poff. "I shall not testify as I previously intended. Perhaps I can make my points in my interrogation."

"Birch, old boy," I thought to myself. "Just remember that you chose to be here this morning. This was your baby, and you wanted to be here defending it. Well, here you are, and you're getting no more than you should have expected."

Poff began his questioning; he brought up one point of which we were to hear much more later. Had we, he asked, considered a time limit for the two separate acts provided for in Section 2—the nomination of a new Vice President and the action by Congress on that nomination?

"When you put a time limit in the Constitution," I asked, "then, what happens if a sequence of unforeseen events prohibits the President from adhering to this time limit? Then he is in violation of the Constitution." The glare of publicity and public opinion on the President, I continued, would insure that the matter would be taken care of judiciously and quickly.

Even so, replied Congressman Poff, we should recognize that there might be situations in which the President would play politics and not nominate quickly. Therefore, he asked, would I object if the adverb "promptly" were inserted to modify the verb "nominate"?

"I have no objection to the word 'promptly,' " I answered. "I hope your committee doesn't spend as much time with the word 'promptly' as we did on debate of the word 'immediately.' "

What about his second point, asked Poff; should there be a time limit within which Congress had to act on the nomination?

"I feel as far as time limitations are concerned throughout in a constitutional amendment," I replied, "it would be better to . . . trust the President and Congress to use their good judgment as to what would be reasonable." Some names submitted by the President, I pointed out, might not be controversial at all; in other cases there might be good reason for rather prolonged consideration.

Congressman Celler added that such a determination might well take longer if the Congress were dominated by a party other than that of the President. I agreed.

"Mr. Chairman"—Mr. McCulloch was speaking—"will the gentleman from Virginia yield for this observation?"

"Yes," said Mr. Poff.

"I would like to say that while the Vice President is Acting President, even though the Congress may be in adjournment, under the Constitution he would have the right to convene the Congress and in these days of fast transportation it doesn't take too long for the Congress to convene"—I realized, with a start, that he had somehow gone from the provisions of Section 2, concerning the choice of a new Vice President, to the disability provisions of Section 5—"and quick, certain, effective, dynamic leadership may justify such an action and that, by the way, is one of the reasons why I said we had to discuss a bit further some of these proposals."

Congressman Celler returned to the provisions for selecting a new Vice President. "In answer to the question by our distinguished ranking Republican member that 10 days may elapse between the nomination and the confirmation, suppose that the Congress does not act within 10 days?"

"Mr. Chairman," said McCulloch, "I might answer that question if the chairman will permit."

"Yes, sir."

"The legislation that I proposed provided that under Section 5"—we had gone from Section 2 to Section 5 again, I noted almost dazedly—"the President shall forthwith thereafter resume the duties of the Presidency." I stepped in at this point to observe that all sorts of unforeseen events—nuclear disaster, to name one horrible example—might keep Congress from determining within any time limit.

"Mr. Chairman." Congressman Whitener was seeking to gain the floor.

"Mr. Chairman, if I may recapture the floor," urged Poff.

"Just one question," Whitener insisted. "Senator," he said to me, "earlier I made some reference using the expression members of the President's Cabinet. I think now, perhaps, I understand more fully the problem in looking at Corwin on Constitution of the United States. I find this statement. 'The Cabinet as we know it today, that is to say, the Cabinet meeting, was brought about solely on the initiative of the first President and may be dispensed with on

Presidential initiative at any time being totally unknown to the Constitution.'

"I do note," Whitener continued, "there was a study made by the Attorney General, 36 Opinion, Attorney General, April 12–16, 1929, on the history of this proposition. I am just hoping it possibly will be available."

I must admit that at that moment I did not share his hope.

"Has the gentleman concluded?" asked Mr. Poff.

"Yes, sir; thank you very much."

Mr. Poff resumed his line of inquiry. Before, he said, he had been talking about Section 2; "now, I want to shift to Section 5, if I may." He went on to discuss his own version of that section, which proposed a ten-day time limit for Congress to make the determination of whether a President was disabled. I continued to state my opposition to putting any specific time limits into the Constitution.

The morning wore on, a short lunch break intervened, and the interrogation continued into the afternoon session. Finally I noticed that Attorney General Katzenbach had returned to the hearing room. Again, I was embarrassed that he should be sitting through my testimony while awaiting his own turn.

"If I may ask the committee, I will be glad to return any time you may have other questions," I said. "In deference to the Attorney General, perhaps I should yield to him."

"I think you have been very, very patient," Chairman Celler replied.

At that point, after having spent the past few hours on the defensive with others directing the line of questioning, I felt it important to summarize briefly the major points that *I* thought were important. "May I make one statement in summary, please?" I said and then continued.

> First of all, I want to thank the committee for its penetrating questioning. I only hope that some of my answers served to shed a little light on this complex question. The main barrier, I want to emphasize, to our ability to find a solution has been the fact that so far we have had so many different opinions that we have never been able to come close to a consensus. Now we have, it seems to me, arrived at a situation where the chairman of this committee, the chairman of our subcommittee in the Senate, 76 of my colleagues in the Senate, the American Bar Association, and others are joining in this consensus. This in no

way precludes this body from making improvements to the consensus, but I would ask you to consider once again the impossibility of finding perfection and the gravity of the situation which now exists in which we have no answer whatsoever.

I think for a number of years with a carrier pigeon being our most rapid means of communication and the caisson being one of the main implements of armed warfare, we didn't have quite the problem. But now we can destroy the world as we know it in minutes. So we ought to take a second look at our individual views. We want to get an answer.

I appreciate the fact that the questions indicated you wanted to get an answer too, and my colleagues in the Senate want to work closely with you. Thank you for your studied approach and I will be glad to return if you want me to.

Although I felt I had been in the House committee room forever and had been given as thorough an interrogative going-over as I had ever had, in the long run I was glad to have been given the opportunity to appear. I could only hope that my presentation had stood up under the relentless fire it had received. When my colleagues had told me that in the House it was always open season on senators, they had certainly not understated the case.

The House Judiciary Committee hearings went on for ten days, until Wednesday, February 17, and ran to 292 printed pages of testimony. The committee's investigation had been extremely thorough—a fact which, as I left the hearing room, I was in a good position to know.

CHAPTER **10**

Second Step
Up the "Hill"

On the night of February 17, 1965, the lights in my office burned past midnight. We had learned that S.J. Res. 1 would be the pending order of business in the Senate the following day.

It was not the cheeriest of settings for a cramming session. We were in the process of moving to a better office, and all that day chairs, desks, and filing cabinets had been moved from our office in the New Senate Office Building across the street into Room 304 of the Old Senate Office Building. By evening, only my own desk and chair and a big couch were left in the office I had occupied for more than two years. Also left behind were the books, files, records, and papers we were using that night in an attempt to anticipate every conceivable question that might face us in the Senate debate the next day. Perched where they could on what remained of the office furniture were Larry Conrad, Steve Lesher, my legislative assistant Clark Norton, and my administrative assistant Bob Keefe.

We went over and over the various contingencies which might possibly confront us the following day. Finally, at one o'clock in the morning, realizing that we were confronting the law of diminishing returns, we stacked all the books on the couch in readiness for the next day and wandered homeward for a few hours' sleep.

Conrad arrived first the next morning and found—to his great surprise—that the couch was completely empty. The files, the papers, the huge annotated and bound copies of the U.S. Code and the Constitution—all were gone. We checked with our office manager, Patty Rees, who was arranging the new office, hoping against hope that they had been moved across the street during the night, but they had not. Finally Jerry Udell, another assistant, traced the material to the Senate waste area, to which our carefully prepared documentation apparently had been consigned by an overzealous cleaning woman. Had it not been for the bound books, which someone had saved and put on a shelf, we would never have known what happened to any of our material. Conrad began to catalogue what was lost, hoping that he could find copies of some of the material; at the same time Udell and Lesher sifted desperately through the bales of trash in the Senate basement. Bale upon bale was opened; and scrap by scrap most of the files were reassembled. The only papers we were unable to find or could not duplicate were the letters which we had received from state legislative leaders in response to our poll. It turned out that some bales of paper had gone out during the night, by train, to Baltimore; Conrad even tried to trace them there, but to no avail.

Despite this depressing beginning, Conrad and I were in the Chamber, ready to do battle, by the time the Senate convened at noon. We made a quick check with the Senate clerk, who informed us that Senators Cooper, Hruska, and Thurmond had all introduced amendments to our resolution—amendments which they intended to present when it came up for debate. I went to my seat in the next-to-the-last row at the right-hand side of the chamber and listened for a while to some of the colloquy that was going on during the morning hour. But I was finding it difficult to sit still. I began to wander about the Chamber, talking briefly to various senators who had previously volunteered to give us their support and volunteering to answer any questions they might have on the amendment.

As I meandered about the Senate floor, I suddenly noticed that Senator McCarthy had gone over to the Republican side of the aisle and was sitting next to Senator Dirksen with whom he was deep in conversation. "There's trouble," I thought to myself. Earlier that week, Senator Dirksen had held a press conference, during which he had expressed dissatisfaction with some of the provisions of our amendment. I knew that he was planning to introduce an entire substitute, the provisions of which were very similar to those of Senator Keating's S.J. Res. 35. Ironically, the Senatorial confrontation between Ken's approach and mine was apparently going to take place after all, even though Ken was no longer a member of the Senate. Then, a day or so later, Senator McCarthy, again in a press conference, had indicated his own concern with the provisions of S.J. Res. 1, saying that the problem of disability could best be solved by statute, not by constitutional amendment. I had worried a good deal over the possibility of Senator McCarthy's opposition. He had been a professor of sociology and economics before coming to the Senate and was one of the leading members of the Senate's liberal bloc.

Now, seeing the two senators in a huddle, I mused that not every measure would find Eugene McCarthy and Everett Dirksen on the same side of the fence. From a purely arithmetical point of view, this could spell big trouble for us. If McCarthy could engender significant opposition among my liberal colleagues while Senator Dirksen sought defectors from those in the Republican ranks who had previously supported S.J. Res. 1, we would have a very hard time getting the two-thirds vote we needed for passage. As I watched them uneasily, I was convinced that they were plotting the demise of S.J. Res. 1 and the first legislative effort of the junior senator from Indiana. Finally I pulled together enough nerve to amble nonchalantly down to the well of the Senate and over to the Minority Leader's desk, in the front row, the first seat left of the center aisle. I was about to suggest, as a jocular opening gambit, that it was a violation of Senate rules for two senators to conspire against a third so early in the afternoon; but Everett Dirksen beat me to the punch.

"Why, hello, there, Birch. Gene and I were just sitting here having a little visit and wondering if there was any truth to the

rumor that's going around that you've decided to accept our substitute to your resolution when it comes up this afternoon."

It took me a moment to see the gleam in Everett's eyes and the
barely concealed smile on Gene's face. My leg, I realized, had just
been given a healthy pull. "Why no, Everett," I said, "I just can't
imagine where that rumor could have originated." I did not try to
hide the facetious tone of my voice: if such a rumor did exist, I
knew good and well who had originated it. "Frankly, Everett," I
went on, "I just thought I'd stroll over and tell you and Gene how
happy I was to hear that you had both decided to make a speech
in favor of S.J. Res. 1 when we call it down this afternoon. I just
wondered whether you'd like to speak early or late in the debate."

The Minority Leader had decided the jesting had gone on long
enough. "Well, Birch," he said seriously, "we couldn't very well
do that even though neither of us wants to oppose you."

I leaned over and slapped both Dirksen and McCarthy affec-
tionately on the shoulders. "Well, to tell you the truth, boys," I
said, "this senator's still wet behind the ears, and he certainly isn't
looking forward to confronting two of the Senate's wisest spokes-
men on his maiden voyage in Senate debate!"

"Never forget, Birch," replied Eugene McCarthy, "that Everett and I would both trade our seniority and all that wisdom you
talk about for your youth and vigor."

As I turned away to leave I said lightly, "Well, fellows, when
I was a young boy on the farm, my grandfather always told me to
leave the tailgate on the wagon down so it'd be easy to jump on.
Just remember, as far as I'm concerned the tailgate of our wagon
is down—and you fellows are welcome on board whenever the
spirit moves you." But I did not feel so lighthearted inside. "Birch,
old boy," I told myself as I walked up the center aisle toward the
rear of the Chamber, "I guess you found out what you wanted to
find out, and it isn't good news. With Everett Dirksen and Gene
McCarthy determined to oppose S.J. Res. 1, it won't be smooth
sailing." Conrad, who had been watching our little exchange from
the leather couch in the back corner, came over to me as I got back
to my seat.

"What did you find out, Senator?"

"Well," I retorted, "what we've been reading in the papers is apparently true. The boys are out to try and scuttle our boat." And then I told him a related bit of news which I had picked up earlier from Don Chang in Senator Fong's office. "The word is that Dirksen's going to argue that Attorney General Katzenbach doesn't really support our resolution—that he was only forced to testify in its favor because of pressure from LBJ. Dirksen's argument is that Katzenbach still favors the S.J. Res. 35 approach, which will be incorporated into the Dirksen substitute. After all, that was the position he supported before the committee in 1963."

Conrad paused for a moment, then looked at me hard. "Senator, you don't suppose the Attorney General really *is* behind the scenes in the Minority Leader's little cabal, do you?"

"Why hell no, Larry, where did you get that idea?"

"Well," the Chief Counsel continued, "I've just been going over his testimony before the Senate and, at one point, when he referred to his previous support of S.J. Res. 35, he then proceeded to say he *saw no reason to oppose* S.J. Res. 1. Well, I can see how a canny operator like Dirksen could take this remark and twist it around our necks, to the effect that while Katzenbach doesn't oppose S.J. Res. 1, what he *really* supports is the Dirksen approach—in other words, S.J. Res. 35."

"I don't think so, Larry," I said. "At least, I certainly hope not. Anyone with half a brain cell who bothered to read his testimony before the Senate—and even more so before the House—just has to come away with the opinion that he strongly supports S.J. Res. 1."

"I know that, boss," Conrad countered, "but how many senators are going to have the chance to read the whole of his testimony? What if Dirksen only reads bits and pieces of it?"

"Well, old buddy," I said, "I don't think Ev Dirksen would do that. But just in case, there's just one way to handle that kind of skulduggery. Call the Justice Department, right away, and tell them we've got to have a letter from Katzenbach—and we've got to have it now." Without another word, Conrad headed for a telephone. In a couple of minutes he was back.

"I talked to Katzenbach's assistant, Norb Schlei. He says they'll see what they can do."

"See what they can do? Well, you call them back and tell

them that we damn well need that letter, and then give Ramsey Clark a call at the White House and tell him about the predicament we're in. We've got to turn some screws down and turn them down in a hurry." I was becoming more convinced by the minute that the situation was desperate.

As Conrad headed back toward the phone, I went over to Mike Mansfield to see when our debate would start. Other matters, he told me, had intervened, and it was now his feeling that the debate on S.J. Res. 1 would probably not start before late that afternoon at the earliest, and probably not before the next day. He went off to confer with some staff personnel and other senators, then motioned me to join him again.

"Birch, here's what we'll do. As soon as the Gold Reserve Bill is finished, I'll move that the Senate proceed to consider your amendment. That'll make it the pending order of business. Then we'll go ahead and take care of some of these other matters; when we're through with them, your measure will already be before us."

As the minutes ticked by, it became increasingly obvious that Mike Mansfield's prediction was accurate: Debate on the amendment would almost certainly not start that day. However, we did have some welcome words of support in remarks delivered on the Senate floor that afternoon from Senators Smathers and Bartlett, who had anticipated that the resolution would come to a vote that day. Senator Smathers stressed the need for a constitutional amendment and warned against eleventh-hour attempts to amend our resolution in order to give Congress a "blank check." Senator Bartlett, urging acceptance of our resolution and reviewing its progress in the last session as S.J. Res. 139, was kind enough to say,

> I thank the Senator from Indiana for his efforts on behalf of Senate Joint Resolution 1. He has done an astounding thing: In his first term, he has studied one of the most delicate and most troubling problems of our day, and has found for it, here in the Senate, a well nigh unanimously supported solution.

But I was not at all confident about the unanimity of that support as I headed back to my office around two o'clock. I resumed doing what I had been doing for the past two days: personally calling my colleagues in the Senate to solicit their support for S.J. Res. 1. If they had any questions or reservations, I tried to answer them. For faithful supporters of the measure, I needed only to remind them that we were in for a tough struggle and needed them behind us. Conrad, Lesher, Norton, and I devoted the next twenty-four hours to such telephone calls, making it clear to senators and staff members that we would not accept the Dirksen amendment. I did not know how widespread that rumor was, but it obviously existed; and I was determined not to lose a single Senate vote on the misconception that I had decided to go along with the Minority Leader.

One person whose presence and support I felt to be particularly vital was the senior senator from North Carolina. Sam Ervin was an eloquent debater, and his authority on constitutional matters was readily accepted by a great many of his colleagues, particularly those from the South. Especially in the light of the combined opposition of Senators Dirksen and McCarthy, I felt we needed Senator Ervin's advice about how to handle the debate. Larry Conrad, however, had learned from Ervin's administrative assistant, Jack Spain, that the Senator was home in Morgantown, North Carolina. He had not been feeling well for the past several weeks, and his staff had conspired to get him to take a rest. This period, between Lincoln's and Washington's birthdays, was usually one of little activity in Congress, and it had seemed a good time for him to escape the Washington pressure cooker for a while.

Naturally I didn't want to do anything to injure Sam's health, but I did feel that his presence might well make the difference between success and failure to us. I called Spain and put my cards on the table. "If it's at all possible, Jack, I'd certainly feel better with Sam on the floor when the debate is going on tomorrow."

"Tell you what, Senator," replied Spain, "I'll call him in Morgantown and report back to you right afterward."

Within fifteen minutes, I had Jack Spain's assurance that Senator and Mrs. Ervin were willing to leave immediately by car, if necessary. By driving late and starting early the next morning, Sam Ervin could be in Washington by about half-past noon. "Should I advise my boss to make the trip?" asked Jack.

I was now certain that S.J. Res. 1 would not be debated until the following day. Immediately I called the Majority Leader and told him of the situation with Sam Ervin; as always, Senator Mansfield was highly cooperative. He would call the Senate into session the next day at noon; with a short morning hour, debate on S.J. Res. 1 should not get started until 12:30, by which time Sam could be there.

I quickly called Spain back with the news. Then I put in a call to Sam Ervin in Morgantown to express my heartfelt thanks for his unselfishness in cutting short a badly needed rest to give us a helping hand.

By early Thursday morning, February 19, there was still no letter from Attorney General Katzenbach; reports persisted that Senator Dirksen was going to use his previous position to cut us down. It was absolutely vital that we have a restatement from the Attorney General himself of his support for our approach. Time was running out. I picked up the telephone and called Ramsey Clark at the White House.

"Ramsey, for heaven's sakes, what's happened to our letter from Katzenbach?"

"Birch, I'm sure there's no problem. I relayed your request to Justice yesterday evening."

"No problem? Ramsey," I said, "in just about three hours Dirksen's going to be shooting at us. Any ammunition that arrives after the battle's been lost isn't going to do much good."

"Okay, Birch, I'll double check." I knew Ramsey would do anything he could, but was equally certain that at this stage of the game we could leave no stone unturned. Again I asked the Capitol operator to get me the White House; this time I wanted to talk to Jack Valenti, a close assistant of the President and a personal friend of mine. I hoped that a word from him would guarantee our letter.

When Valenti's friendly voice came over the line, I quickly filled him in on our plight. Then, as if it were an afterthought, I said, "Jack, I hesitated to bother you, but after all this amendment has been endorsed by the President and is part of his program. I'd hate like the very devil to see us lose it at this late hour."

"I'll check it out, Birch," replied the Presidential aide.

"That's good enough for me," I answered, feeling reassured.

No one will ever be certain who was responsible, but by half-past eleven that morning a special Justice Department courier arrived with a letter from the Attorney General. I breathed a sigh of relief as I read it; he had given us exactly what we needed.

I understand that recent newspaper reports have raised some question as to whether I favor the solution for the problem of presidential inability embodied in Senate Joint Resolution 1, or whether I prefer a constitutional amendment which would empower Congress to enact appropriate legislation for determining when inability commences and when it terminates.

Obviously, more than one acceptable solution to the problem of presidential inability is possible. As the President said in his message of January 28, 1965, Senate Joint Resolution 1 represents a carefully considered solution that would responsibly meet the urgent need for action in this area. In addition, it represents a formidable consensus of considered opinion. I have, accordingly, testified twice in recent weeks in support of the solution embodied in Senate Joint Resolution 1.

After proceeding to highlight the testimony he had given on January 29 before our subcommittee, the Attorney General concluded: "In view of the above, there should be no question that I support Senate Joint Resolution 1."

I felt much better about the coming ordeal. The letter would allow us to rebut, once and for all, any inferences which might be made during the debate that the Attorney General's support of S.J. Res. 1 was only lukewarm.

At noon the shrill buzzer sounded in my office to indicate that the Senate was going into session; Conrad, Lesher, Norton, and I went over to the Chamber. I told the Majority Leader that I was ready to go.

"You're in the batter's box, Birch, as soon as we dispose of the morning business," he replied. As I walked toward the Democratic cloakroom to make last-minute preparations with my staff, I was surprised at my own nervousness. "Think how you'd feel," I told myself, "without that letter from the Attorney General."

"Any news from Senator Ervin's office?" I asked Larry Conrad.

"I checked with them this morning," he replied, "and the latest word is that the senator is on the road now. He ought to arrive soon after the morning hour."

"Let's hope so," I said, as I walked back into the Chamber. Finally, at 12:45 the morning business was over. We were on.

As I was about to begin my presentation, I tried to quiet my nerves by telling myself that I had, after all, been through all this before; nothing I had to say was any different from last time. But, in the back of my mind, I knew that there *was* a difference. We were playing for keeps now, and from the subcommittee hearings on, the whole atmosphere had been different. However easily things might have gone last session, I knew this time no one was going to give us a free ride.

"Mr. President, and Members of the Senate," I began.

> ... on December 1, 1964, the President of the United States had a small growth removed from his hand. The Nation wondered. On January 23, 1965, Americans awoke to learn that during the night the President had entered the hospital with a cold. The Nation, and, indeed, much of the world worried. But we were fortunate on both of those occasions.
>
> Today we have a strong, forthright, and vigorous President of the United States. I might also add that we are fortunate today because we have an able-bodied and vigorous Vice President of the United States. This was not the case in the sad months following November 22, 1963.

I went on to review the background of the nation's problems in the areas of Presidential succession and disability, quoting from historians' studies, newspaper reports, and eyewitness accounts to give a sense of the chaos that might again confront us if we failed to act on the problem. Then I came to the issue at hand:

> Senate Joint Resolution 1 is an effort to guarantee continuity within the executive branch of Government. It is designed to provide that we shall always have a President or Acting President physically and mentally alert. Second, and of equal importance, it is to assure that whoever the man will be, there will be no question as to the legality of his authority to carry out the powers and duties of the office.

Lastly I gave a brief summary of the provisions and goals of our proposed amendment. I had purposely avoided a long detailed statement. I have never been comfortable reading from a prepared text, and on this occasion I knew very well that there was no point in giving the full content of S.J. Res. 1; the ensuing debate would expose the very nuts and bolts of our resolution to the detailed examination and criticism of the foremost legislative experts in the world. Only the next few hours would tell if the structure we proposed was built soundly enough to stand up under such scrutiny.

My expectation that the full fury of Senate debate would

shortly be raging about my head was soon fulfilled. Senator Hruska threw out the first challenge; the articulate senator from Nebraska expressed, not for the first time, his concern about putting specific details into the Constitution. His preference for an enabling amendment was, of course, one in which he would soon gain a formidable ally when the Minority Leader proposed his amendment.

After Senator Hruska spoke, the tempo of the debate increased during a spirited exchange between Senator Ellender of Louisiana and me. The senior senator from Louisiana believed, as had some scholars whose testimony we had heard earlier, that article II of the Constitution already gave Congress the power to determine the problem of disability. I contended that this was not, in my opinion, the case. Senator Ellender cited the relevant constitutional passage:

> In Case of the Removal of the President from Office, or of his Death, Resignation, or Inability to discharge the Powers and Duties of the said Office, the Same shall devolve on the Vice President . . . and the Congress may by Law provide for the Case of Removal, Death, Resignation or Inability, both of the President and Vice President, declaring what Officer shall act accordingly, until the Disability be removed, or a President shall be elected.

"The Congress has the right to do all those things now," asserted Senator Ellender. "I am wondering if Congress does not now have the authority to do everything that is proposed in the joint resolution we are now considering except providing for ways and means to select a Vice President."

I told the senator from Louisiana that, although some senators did indeed believe Congress had this power, others did not. The great weight of testimony we had heard supported the latter contention. "We feel we should resolve any doubt whatsoever. . . . Why take a chance? Give the power by a constitutional amendment."

I went on to call Senator Ellender's attention to "two very small words" in the passage he had just read aloud. What did our constitutional fathers mean, I asked, when they said "*the same* shall devolve"? Did they mean the Presidency itself, or the powers and duties of the Presidency? The Tyler precedent took care of this problem when the death of a President was concerned, I said. When a President dies, the Vice President assumes both the office and its powers and duties. The President cannot reclaim his office. But what about cases of disability? If it is impossible to separate the powers and duties from the office itself, as men from Henry Clay to Harry Truman have said is the case, under the present language, then "Once the Vice President has taken over from a sick President, it is impossible for the President to resume his office." But the senator from Louisiana was not convinced. I tried to persuade him.

"I should like to ask the Senator from Louisiana to go back to the language immediately prior to the point at which he started reading the last time," I said. "I think we must look at each word individually. In part, the section states, 'and the Congress may by Law provide for the Case of Removal, Death, Resignation, or Inability, both of the President and Vice President. . . .' There has been a considerable amount of opinion that Congress could not provide relief by law unless both the President and the Vice President died." The first succession statute, I went on, was passed in 1792, when many of those who attended the Constitutional Convention were in Congress. "If that had not been their interpretation, . . . they would have provided for other contingencies that would not have required both the President and the Vice President to be out of the picture before Congress could act."

"As I recall," replied my colleague from Louisiana, "Congress did provide, without Constitutional amendment, for a succession to the office."

"But only in the event both the President and the Vice President were involved," I reminded him, ". . . we are now dealing with only one of them being removed—for disability."

Still Senator Ellender was not to be convinced that a constitutional amendment was necessary. In fact, I felt that this was the same philosophical concern which underlay Senator McCarthy's support of the Dirksen proposal.

I tried another line of reasoning. If we utilized a statute to solve the problems raised by Presidential disability, I said, this statute would be met with all the uncertainties of a court test, at a time of crisis when its provisions were required to be implemented. "Should we not reconcile this doubt once and for all by inserting in the Constitution an amendment which would provide for these contingencies?"

Senator Ellender pointed out that "we may have a court test on the very language which we are now discussing." But I countered that one could hardly question the constitutionality of a part of the Constitution.

"I am referring to an interpretation of the provision. . . . The language could be tested for a determination of its meaning."

"That is correct," I said. But in the case of a statute, "it would be necessary to test not only the intention . . . but also its constitutionality. We feel that there is sufficient doubt to warrant placing an amendment in the Constitution."

At that moment, the gold-trimmed mahogany doors in the back of the Chamber swung open, and Senator Ervin hurried in. His face was flushed; clearly the long drive had been difficult for my friend and committee colleague.

"There's Sam!" I said to Conrad, who was seated on a temporary chair next to me. "Thank God he's here." It suddenly occurred to me that Sam Ervin would probably have better results than I in dissuading Senator Ellender, his fellow southerner, from opposing a constitutional amendment. I had thought of Sam as a trump card; perhaps it was too early to play that trump, but I decided to take the risk. I said to Senator Ellender,

> There is another reason for dealing with the problem by constitutional amendment. The distinguished Senator from North Carolina was one of the strong proponents of this theory in the Committee on the Judiciary. He said that by dealing with the problem of disability by constitutional amendment, certain guarantees of Presidential protection could be provided. For example, a two-thirds vote is required by Congress before the President can be removed. But if it were left to Congress to specify by law what formula should be followed, that could be done by a majority vote. I believe that would afford insufficient protection for the President.

Moreover, I thought the senior senator from Louisiana should be aware of the important efforts that had gone into arriving at the consensus which S.J. Res. 1 contained. More than thirty proposals on the subject were before the House this year, I pointed out, and our Senate colleagues had been equally prolific. "If there is any reason why we have not solved this problem, it is not that we have not given it much thought, but that we have been unable to reach an agreement or consensus around which we could rally a two-thirds majority."

I continued, "At the risk of taking the copyrighted story of my friend, the Senator from North Carolina . . . I think an Aesop fable which I heard him relate in his own inimitable manner very adequately describes our problem." I proceeded to repeat Sam Ervin's dog-with-the-bone story, which he had so handily used to help bring the Senate debate to a vote the previous session. Then I looked straight at the back of the Chamber toward my colleague from North Carolina. By now he would have had time to catch his breath, and I knew that Sam Ervin hadn't made the long, hard drive back from Morgantown to sit idly by while his Senate colleagues debated this problem. I was not disappointed.

"Mr. President, will the Senator yield?" asked Sam Ervin. I gladly did so. "In addition to the Aesop fable about the dog with the bone," Senator Ervin began, "a very apt adage is that 'Too many cooks spoil the broth.'" He continued,

> A multitude of amendments were offered along this line in seeking to take care of the situation. I introduced an amendment myself. I thought it was rather good. But I think the reason why we have progressed as far as we have in this matter is that the Senator from Indiana recognized that too many cooks can spoil the broth.
>
> If we try to get everything to accord with our own notion, we get nothing. The Senator has recognized the need for clarification of a constitutional question. As a result of his fine example in that respect, other members of the Subcommittee on Constitutional Amendments and members of the full Committee on the Judiciary have been influenced by his example and have sacrificed their individual views in an attempt to get some proposal that would recognize the problem. . . .
>
> I was interested in the colloquy engaged in by the senior Senator from Louisiana and the Senator from Indiana a moment ago with reference to the power of Congress. Does not the Senator from Indiana agree with the Senator from North Carolina that it would devolve upon Congress to designate the succession to the Vice-Presidency, and then to the Presidency, that necessarily we cannot designate individuals, but would have to designate the occupants of the particular offices, as we have always done in times past?

I said that this was correct. In the past, the Congress had not specified that Mr. X or Senator Y should succeed to the Presidency if both the President and the Vice President should die. Instead,

Congress had specified that whoever holds the office of Speaker of the House or Secretary of State or President pro tem of the Senate at that future time should succeed to the Presidency.

The senator from North Carolina then turned to emphasize the element of protection provided for the President within the language of S.J. Res. 1. Before a President can be removed from office, he pointed out, "a majority of the members of the Cabinet must take action, and that action is subject to review by Congress."

I sought to reinforce his argument.

> In essence, this action would have to be taken twice by the Vice President and Cabinet. . . . They would make the declaration that the President was unable to perform his duties. He might make a declaration that he was able to do so. Then two-thirds of the Congress would have to affirm that action. That is more protection than is given to a President in the event of impeachment, because it takes only a two-thirds vote of the Senate and a majority of the House to impeach. . . .

The senator from Louisiana then took the floor and turned to another field of questioning. If you placed such confidence in the members of the Cabinet and their ability to act, he asked, why did your joint resolution provide for some other body to pass upon the matter? I explained that we had so provided "as a result of the consensus for which we have striven."

> . . . If the Cabinet approach proved unworkable, Congress could provide another body. . . . At any time the Congress felt that the Cabinet was serving as an arbitrary obstacle to what was in the best interests of the Nation, namely, the President was obviously deranged, yet the Cabinet would not cooperate with the Vice President—I suppose it could . . . attempt to establish another body.

Just then, Everett McKinley Dirksen came slowly through the big swinging doors and down the center aisle. He stood by his chair near the well of the Senate, across the aisle from the Majority Leader's post where I was leading the debate on the resolution. At the first pause in the colloquy with Senator Ellender, he came over to me and whispered, "Birch, why don't we bring up that resolution of mine now? I won't be able to debate it right now, but we can make it the pending order of business and debate it in a few minutes." I realized that I had never seen the Minority Leader look so fatigued. His face looked aged and weary; and his unmanaged hair, which usually added such character to his appearance, now seemed to augment his ashen pallor. I was alarmed.

"Everett, we'll handle this any way that's convenient for you. Frankly, you look like you're under the weather. Shouldn't you see a doctor?"

The Minority Leader struggled to reassert his forceful baritone, but failed. "Birch, I feel like the very devil himself is working on me. I want to slip back in my office and eat a dish of custard and maybe take a pill or two. I know I'll feel better then. I can get back here and we can get on with our business."

I yielded to the Minority Leader and he submitted his amendment, numbered 33, advising the Senate, "It is actually a substitute for the entire proposal that comes from the committee." He made his way back up the aisle and out through the rear of the Chamber. "There goes a sick man," I thought, watching him. I didn't think I could even stand up if I felt that bad, let alone do battle on the floor of the United States Senate.

Following Senator Dirksen's departure, Senator Milward Simpson of Wyoming was recognized by the chair. He made a strong statement in support of our measure, of which he had been one of the early cosponsors. It was comforting to see that one of the older, more conservative members of the Senate was not going to follow the Minority Leader; perhaps it would be true of other members of the GOP old guard.

Next Senator Tydings, a fellow Judiciary Committee member, made a brief statement rebutting some of Senator Ellender's objections. He was followed by Senator Fong, another early sponsor and a member of the subcommittee, who made a strong statement supporting the provisions of S.J. Res. 1. Afterwards, Senator Leverett Saltonstall summed up his colleague's remarks.

> What the Senator has said in substance is that Congress should act now on this subject, that it should act by constitutional amendment, and that the constitutional amendment should be specific in its terms rather than general, in order to leave future actions in future Congresses to supplement it.

We were very fortunate that Leverett Saltonstall, one of the solid pillars of the United States Senate, had at an early state of our deliberation indicated a genuine willingness to assist in our efforts toward constructing and actually passing our constitutional amendment. Having the support of a man of his stature was an immeasurable aid in providing the bipartisan support we needed so desperately. Apparently he had not been swayed by the Minority Leader's position.

Senator Hugh Scott of Pennsylvania, another leading Republican and a few years earlier the party's national chairman, spoke next. "Mr. President," he began. "I rise in support of Senate Joint Resolution 1." I had been holding my breath. Now I let it out with a sigh of relief. Scott, too, was not going to be dissuaded by Dirksen. The senator from Pennsylvania continued: "Let me say, for my part, that I shall support the proposed Dirksen substitute for Senate Joint Resolution 1. . . . However, if the Dirksen amendment should not be adopted, . . . I would then, as a cosponsor, support Senate Joint Resolution 1." My spirits fell. I had been wrong. One of our cosponsors had been wooed and won by the Minority Leader; how many others, I wondered, would there be? I did not yet know how extensive or effective Senator Dirksen's missionary work among his Republican colleagues had been, but there was obviously cause for concern.

During the last half hour of the debate, the new junior senator from New York, Robert Kennedy, had been standing now and then behind his desk in the back row on the majority side of the Chamber. I had noticed a page placing one of the small mahogany speaker's podiums on his desk; one of Kennedy's legislative aides was standing in the back of the Senate Chamber. Obviously, something was up. I turned to Conrad and asked him whether he had any idea what position Robert Kennedy was going to take on the Dirksen amendment. He replied that, although he had been in touch with Senator Kennedy's office, his staff had been able to tell us nothing. A little later, Lesher came up to us. "The word is that Senator Kennedy has a nine-page speech prepared, and it won't be much to our liking."

"Where did you hear that?" I asked sharply.

"I don't know, boss," he replied. "It's just the rumor that's going around."

I shifted uneasily in my chair. Senator Kennedy had been Attorney General at the time his assistant, Nicholas Katzenbach, had testified in support of S.J. Res. 35, so that Katzenbach must have given the testimony with his superior's knowledge and consent. Perhaps the new senator was going to follow in his predecessor's footsteps and come out for the old Keating approach, much of which was embodied in the Dirksen amendment. If so, we would be in really bad trouble. Bob Kennedy might be only a freshman senator, but he had the great respect of many of his colleagues and, because of his past experience, would have considerable influence over them. I wanted to kick myself for not discussing our efforts with him before that point. I had, of course, thought about doing so; but it was a delicate subject. Robert Kennedy had suffered greatly over the death of his brother; and it would have been in exceedingly poor taste to discuss with him a legislative problem which could not help but reawaken the horrible memories of Dallas. Now I wondered if perhaps I had erred.

Glancing up, I noticed that Ethel Kennedy was sitting in the gallery above. I called her presence to Conrad's attention. It looked as if the rumor Lesher had brought us had some substance to it. Opposition from Bob Kennedy would hurt, but I was at a loss as to how to deal with the situation.

Meanwhile Senator Frank Carlson of Kansas had taken the floor to deliver a strong statement in support of S.J. Res. 1, thereby dispelling a little of the gloom I felt hanging over the Chamber. Another Republican, I thought, was not going along with the Minority Leader.

When Senator Dirksen returned, he looked a little better than he had before, but he was still far from being his usual vigorous self. As he came down the center aisle, I stopped him. "Everett, are you really sure you're up to this?" I asked. "I don't want to be a part of anything that's going to put you through torture. If you feel as bad as you look, we can wait and do it another day." But the Minority Leader's years of legislative service had trained him not to let himself be slowed down by pain.

"I'm all right, Birch," he said. A moment later he rose to address the chair.

> I am sensible of the urgency that is involved in connection with the proposal to amend the Constitution. Events in history such as what happened on the 22nd of November 1963, the assassination of President

Garfield, who signed only a single extradition paper while he lay in a virtual coma for 90 days, and the difficulty that the country encountered at the time President Woodrow Wilson was stricken, have from time to time reenergized this issue. I am quite aware of the desire to have something done and to have it done as quickly as possible.

However, I am rather sensible of an old line in the Book of Exodus: 'Thou shalt not follow a multitude to do evil.'

The word "evil" might mean "error," and it can be used in its broadest sense. I believe it has been pretty much of a rule in our constitutional history that we do not legislate in the Constitution. We try to keep the language simple. We try to keep it at a high level, and we offer some latitude for statutory implementation thereafter, depending upon the events and circumstances that might arise. For that reason I have submitted a substitute . . . which I believe would encompass the problem that confronts us, would meet virtually every exigency, and would leave in the hands of the Congress whatever legislation might be necessary.

The Minority Leader went on to point out what he considered to be the shortcomings of S.J. Res. 1 as it was now drafted. He noted that it provided for the eventuality of a disabled President, but failed to provide for circumstances under which the Vice President was also disabled. Next he questioned whether the wording of our resolution would actually permit us to fill a Vice-Presidential vacancy—a doubt which, to my knowledge, no one had voiced before. Then the Minority Leader turned, as we had thought he might, to some excerpts from Attorney General Katzenbach's testimony before our subcommittee; I realized he was stating the questions the Attorney General had raised but was skipping over the passages in which Nicholas Katzenbach himself had answered those questions. Would we require a quorum of the House and Senate before action could be taken? What about the meaning of the word "immediately"? Could Congress convene itself in special session to deal with Presidential disability if it was not in session when the disability occurred?

But the most telling part of the Minority Leader's statement came when he asserted that the general philosophy of his amendment had the support of Attorney General Katzenbach and all of his predecessors, as well as the American Bar Association. He did not seem concerned with the fact that all of these—with the exception of Senator Kennedy, whose position I still did not know—had subsequently thrown their unqualified support behind the provisions of S.J. Res. 1. As Everett Dirksen went on to use Attorney General Katzenbach's testimony to undermine our position, I whispered to Conrad, "Thank God we have that letter. It will really help us to shoot down that part of Everett's argument, at least."

Next, Senator Hruska again expressed his disapproval of our "placing too many detailed procedural provisions in the Constitution" and our purported violation of the principle of separation of powers.

In the back of the Senate chamber, Sam Ervin could sit still no longer.

> Mr. President, I rise in opposition to the Dirksen amendment. The Dirksen amendment totally ignores one of the crucial questions which has brought this matter to the floor of the Senate. That is the fact that vacancies occur in the office of Vice President.
>
> The Dirksen amendment makes no attempt to provide for the election of a Vice President in case a Vice President succeeds to the Office of President, or is removed from office by impeachment. It ignores one of the things which has made this question so crucial. . . .

The senator from North Carolina continued his attack.

> . . . There is another fatal flaw in the Dirksen Amendment. That is the provision that "the commencement and termination of any inability shall be determined by such method as Congress may by law provide."
>
> I thank God that was not placed in the Constitution when the Constitution was adopted. If it had been placed in the Constitution, we would have seen, in the most tragic period of our history, the total blackout of government of the people, by the people, and for the people in this Nation. I refer to the tragic days when a congressional group was trying to take complete power in this Nation. The group was led by the then Senator Ben Wade, who was President pro tempore of the Senate and who wanted to be President. At that time there was no Vice President. Lincoln had been assassinated and had been succeeded in the office of President by Vice President Andrew Johnson. . . .
>
> . . . Power-hungry men headed by a man who aspired above everything else to become President of the United States, and who was in line for the Presidency if Andrew Johnson had been removed from office, were prevented from taking control by a provision of our Constitution which required a two-thirds vote for impeachment, and then by only one vote short of the two-thirds majority.
>
> If the provision referred to had been in the Constitution at that

time—"The commencement and termination of any inability shall be determined by such method as Congress may by law provide"—Andrew Johnson would have been removed from office. The group would have set up a medical commission and had President Johnson declared mentally disabled. But they did not have the power under the Constitution. The only way that they could have removed him would have been by impeachment, and only by impeachment by a two-thirds majority.

Mr. President, someone has very wisely said that a nation which does not remember the history of the past is doomed to repeat its mistakes. . . .

The senator from North Carolina had eloquently driven home the concern which both he and I had expressed almost two years earlier when the subject of disability had first been brought before the Judiciary Committee. Senator Ervin then turned to Senator Hruska's argument about the separation of powers and the inadvisability of including specifics within the Constitution.

. . . I am not disturbed about the doctrine of the separation of powers here, because the powers of government are not always separated. The Constitution provides a good many things that must be done by the President and the Congress. The Constitution provides that the President may make treaties, but they must be ratified by the Senate. It provides that the President shall appoint heads of departments of the Federal Government, judges, ambassadors, and other officers of the United States; but the nominations are subject to confirmation by the Senate, under the Constitution.

. . . I agree with my good friend from Nebraska, in that I do not like to have too many specific things written into the Constitution, but when we try to protect somebody, we had better write specifics into the Constitution if we do not want to run the risk of converting the United States into what I would call a banana republic. We had better provide for a two-thirds vote by the Congress, such as the joint resolution reported by the committee provides, to remove the President from office, where he risks the charge of disability.

I rose in an attempt to reinforce Senator Ervin's telling argument.

I am glad the Senator from North Carolina has pointed out the time when our forefathers determined that there should be a commingling of the various branches which in most cases we keep separate. I am also glad he pointed out the need for specifics under certain circumstances.

While the Constitution was a "wonderful, broad, general plan for a wonderful society," I continued, it did contain many specific details: how elections are to be conducted and qualifications for public offices, for example. Sam Ervin documented this point further.

> As the Senator knows, in the Bill of Rights specifics are provided for the protection of the individual against governmental tyranny. There are specifics protecting the individual against unreasonable searches and seizures of his papers, effects, and home. The Constitution contains specifics to protect many rights.
>
> That is the reason why the amendment proposed by the committee was prepared in the form it is in. It was necessary to protect a President against a power-hungry Congress. . . .

As we continued to answer the questions which had been raised by the distinguished Minority Leader, Senator Saltonstall gave us some assistance. "If Congress were not in session," he asked me, "would the fact that the transmission is to be to the President of the Senate and the Speaker of the House automatically call Congress into session?" I replied that the words "immediately proceed to decide" were, in our opinion, sufficient to enable the President of the Senate or Speaker of the House to call a special session. Senator Ervin interjected that the entire matter had been discussed in committee and that the language had specifically been chosen to provide for the contingency of Congress not being in session.

"That is why the wording was changed," he said. "But it is implied that Congress shall meet, because Section 5 contains the language 'Congress shall immediately proceed.' "

We still had to set the record straight as to the damaging implication that the present Attorney General did not support the terminology of S.J. Res. 1. I thought the time had come to introduce the full text of Attorney General Katzenbach's letter into the record. In doing so, I emphasized the strong closing sentence, "In view of the above, there should be no question that I support Senate Joint Resolution 1."

"Mr. President," Senator Ervin said with his characteristic North Carolinian wit, "my opinion is that the present Attorney General can now claim something which all of us would like to be able to claim; namely, that we are wiser today than we were yesterday."

In my point-by-point rebuttal, I tried to answer the doubts raised by Senator Dirksen, concluding with the practical argument that our version was more likely to be accepted by state legislatures.

> . . . We are making a general policy determination . . . as to whether we are going to open a Pandora's box to permit a blanket provision to be given to Congress to provide laws in these vital areas at some later date.
>
> There has been a trend of thinking that if we have a loosely drawn, nonspecific constitutional amendment, the legislative bodies might be more inclined to accept it. I am satisfied that several Members of this body who have had legislative experience at the State level can speak with more authority than I. But my eight years in the Indiana General Assembly have led me to believe that this is a false assumption. With this in mind, we sent copies of Joint Resolution 35, which was merely an enabling act giving Congress power to act, and Joint Resolution 139 of the previous year, which is almost identical with Senate Joint Resolution 1, to the president of the senate and the speaker of the house of all the States.
>
> The preponderance of evidence—I believe we received only three letters to the contrary—was that State legislative bodies would prefer to enact the ratification resolution, that State legislatures should deal with a specific proposal and not give Congress a blank check to take away the safeguards to which the Senator from North Carolina has so adequately directed our attention.

Senator Saltonstall again spoke out to substantiate my conclusion. After so many years' discussion of the subject, he asked, if we were to send it back to the state legislatures in only a general form, saying that Congress would do something if the amendment were adopted, was it not true that "the average legislator, the average citizen will say, 'Pshaw. Congress is putting the thing off further, and this is not definite'?"

"The Senator is absolutely correct," I replied, adding that if an enabling constitutional amendment were passed by both Houses of Congress and sent to and subsequently ratified by the legislatures, "we would still have to enact a law, which we have not done in 170 years."

By this time we had done the best we could to accentuate the advantages of our approach. Little could be gained by delaying the vote on the Dirksen amendment. As the roll call of senators began, I slouched back in the Majority Leader's chair and glanced at Conrad.

We both crossed our fingers. When the presiding officer announced the results, it was twelve yeas, sixty nays. The Dirksen amendment had been soundly defeated. We had won the first round.

Senator Strom Thurmond of South Carolina now called down his amendment, which required that the electoral college be convened to fill a vacancy in the office of Vice President. After he spoke in behalf of his proposal, I briefly stated my opposition to it. I had repeatedly consulted with people, I said, concerning their knowledge of the electoral college and to date had found only one person who knew the name of even one member of that body. Since one of the main criteria for the orderly transition of authority was acceptance by the people, surely the people would be far more likely to accept a decision made by Congress than "if we brought in members of the electoral college whom they did not know from Adam." The amendment of the senator from South Carolina was rejected on a voice vote.

Next Senator Hruska proposed an amendment to our resolution. The original wording of S.J. Res. 1 provided two days for the Vice President and the Cabinet to consider whether or not it would be advisable to disagree with the President at such time that a disabled President declared himself ready to reassume his powers and duties. The senator from Nebraska believed this period was far too short and proposed to lengthen it to ten days. In my judgment that was far too much time. In a hurried consultation on the floor, I asked him if he would consider shortening the period to seven days, which seemed fair for the determination of such a critical question, even though I personally would have preferred less time. It seemed wise to give a little here. The senator from Nebraska could, I knew, be a great asset to us during the floor debate; and if we could secure his wholehearted cooperation by accepting this relatively minor amendment, it seemed a good trade. Senator Hruska agreed to seven days, and the amendment was accepted without further debate.

Next Senators Stennis and McClellan rose to make statements supporting the provisions of our amendment. During Senator McClellan's remarks, a page advised me that Senator Mansfield wanted to see me in the cloakroom. As I pushed my way through the large swinging doors and into the cloakroom, I saw Senators Robert Kennedy, Phil Hart, John Pastore, and Ross Bass clustered around the Majority Leader. All were engaged in a heated discussion which ceased temporarily as I entered.

"Birch," said the Majority Leader, "there seems to be a feeling on the part of some of our colleagues that we shouldn't try to push this amendment to a vote this evening. It's late in the afternoon, and some people feel that there are still some serious questions to be answered concerning the impact of the amendment. I've said that I'll abide by your decision. What do you think?"

I was badly shaken by this news. After a moment's thought I said, "Mike, I can't see what we'll gain by putting this off until tomorrow. This is the second time the measure has been before the Senate. As far as I'm concerned, I'd rather go ahead and argue it out this evening." We began to discuss some of the provisions of the amendment. Senators Kennedy and Hart were alarmed about the possibility that the Cabinet and Vice President might precipitate a coup and depose the President, under the pretext that he was disabled.

"What do you think, Birch?" asked John Pastore. The situation struck me as unlikely; I reminded the group that the hypothetical Cabinet would have been appointed by the very President they would be seeking to depose.

"Birch," said Bob Kennedy, who was obviously deeply concerned over this possibility, "do you know how many members of the Cabinet President Kennedy knew personally before he appointed them?" I shook my head. "Well, he didn't know a single one."

"Still," I replied, "even if the Cabinet and Vice President are part of a conspiracy, they wouldn't be able to get around the Congress. The Congress makes the final determination; the Cabinet and Vice President haven't a chance of succeeding unless they've got two-thirds of Congress behind them."

Just then John Graves, of the Senate staff, came in to advise me that Senator McClellan had finished speaking. I had the floor yet wasn't present in the Chamber. As I turned to follow Graves back into the Chamber, I suggested that if anyone had questions that needed clarification, he could ask them on the floor of the Senate and we could straighten things out there, thus writing our intentions and interpretations into the legislative record.

I hurried back into the Senate, wondering if I looked as deflated as I felt. Ross Bass, of Tennessee, who had also returned to the Chamber, wanted to make some personal observations about the resolution. I yielded the floor to him.

"Well, Counselor," I said to Conrad as Bass was speaking, "our playhouse is about to tumble down." I told him of the brief but hectic session in the cloakroom. "I just don't know who has the ball now." When Senator Bass finished, I rose to reply to the concern he had expressed over the possibility of a Congress controlled by one party dragging its feet and not selecting someone to fill a Vice-Presidential vacancy.

"I have more faith in Congress acting in an emergency under the white heat of publicity with the American people looking on," I said. "The last thing Congress would dare do would be to become involved in a purely political move."

"The election of the President is just as political as anything can be under our American system," Senator Bass countered. "With the next man in line sitting in the Speaker's Chair, this becomes a political bomb. We are very political in choosing our Presidents. I hope that situation will always remain."

Next, Senator Pastore zeroed in on the meaning of the word "immediately" in the disability provisions.

> . . . If we are talking about restoring the Presidency, it would occur to me that there should be a mandate upon the Congress that once such an issue came before it involving the chief elective office of the United States, the man who has the trigger on the atomic bomb, Congress should not indulge in any other business until it has decided that issue.

I told my friend from Rhode Island of the long discussions over the term during our committee hearings, during which it had been decided that "immediately proceed to decide the issue" was the best we could accomplish. But Senator Pastore was not persuaded, and Senator Bass expressed his support of Senator Pastore's position.

Senator Ervin came to my defense. "Does not the Senator from Indiana agree with me that the word 'immediately' does exactly that?" he asked. "The words 'immediately proceed' mean that we are going to do that and nothing will occur in between."

But that was not the interpretation of Senator Pastore, who proposed an amendment which would add "and no other business shall be transacted until such issue is decided" to the existing language of S.J. Res. 1. Now it seemed that Senators Bass and Pastore were arguing different points. The former wanted to see that a new Vice President was elected "immediately," while the latter felt that a greater sense of urgency ought to be contained in the language providing for Presidential disability—the question of the President's disability should be settled immediately.

Senator Fred Harris of Oklahoma expressed a concern similar to that of Senator Bass. At this point our foundation of support appeared to be extremely shaky. A number of senators were present and many of them were criticizing specific wording here and there in the amendment. "Boy, oh boy," I said to Conrad, "if we had to take a vote right now, I don't think we'd even get a majority." Still the debate went on. Senator Phil Hart of Michigan suggested that a time limit not to exceed seventy-two hours be placed upon any congressional deliberation of disability.

"What we are talking about," he said, "is a situation in which the Senate, in the event of a cruel national crisis, might find two men contending that each is the President of the United States. . . . Why do we not pin down precisely when we shall vote on the question?"

At that moment, my inclination was to accept Senator Pastore's amendment—to accept the wording "Congress shall immediately proceed to decide the issue and no other business shall be transacted until such issue is decided." It seemed this would not actually do much to change the intention of the resolution; and it might allay some of the fears that had been expressed, picking up a vote or two here and there in support of our resolution. Just as I began to say this, Sam Ervin came rushing down the aisle toward me and said, "No, no, no, don't do it." Simultaneously, Roman Hruska hurried into the well from the opposite side. "Birch, Birch, no! no!" I paused a moment. "Don't do it, Birch," said Sam Ervin, "we have the votes."

At this point Roman Hruska interposed: "If we get into the process of amending a proposed constitutional amendment on the floor of the Senate," he said, "we shall be treading on dangerous ground. I say that the proposed amendment is difficult, and probably unnecessary, although I shall not oppose the amendment for the purpose of taking it to conference so that the conferees may consider it."

Yet Senator Pastore persisted in his argument.

> . . . All I am saying is that while such an important question—the most important question that could beset the people of our country—as determining who is the President in a moment of crisis is pending, we ought to determine that and nothing else.
>
> We should include a restriction in the joint resolution that we would do nothing else but determine that question, and we would do so expeditiously. But if we should permit Senators to talk about what color the rose in the State of Rhode Island should be, or what flower we should adopt as our national flower, and have a morning hour to talk about pansies in the spring while we are trying to determine who the President of the United States should be—and there is sometimes a tendency to indulge in such things in moments of capriciousness—we might face serious consequences. I say let us avoid that. Let us act correctly. We desire to amend the Constitution. I say that when there is a question as to who should be the President of the United States, we should do nothing else until we make a decision on that question. Such a provision ought to be in the law.

I questioned Senator Pastore in return. Did he feel, I asked, that we would decide a different question in relation to Section 5 of our resolution from what would be decided under the provisions of the Twelfth Amendment to the Constitution? Under that amendment, I pointed out, the House must decide who is President in the event that no candidate gets a majority of the electoral votes. The Constitution there said that the House shall "immediately" decide the issue. "It means 'immediately,' 'get going,' 'dispense with everything else,' " I said.

"I agreed with everything the Senator from Indiana said," replied Senator Pastore, ". . . but I am being very explicit about it—by saying 'Write a provision in the joint resolution to the effect that we could not transact any other business until the question discussed had been decided.' "

As Senator Hart proceeded to repeat his suggestion that a specific limitation—for example, three days—be included in the amendment, Senator Ervin rose to his feet and addressed the chair in a loud voice. The face of the solon from North Carolina was flushed

with exasperation at the tenor of the debate which had been raging
in the Chamber. He took one deep breath and thrashed out against
the logic of any time limit.

> If we cannot trust Members of the Senate and House to exercise
> intelligence and patriotism in a time of national crisis, we might as
> well not do anything. We might as well not try to improve the situa-
> tion. I think we should pass a constitutional amendment and leave the
> action to be taken under that constitutional amendment to those who
> are in office at the time such action must be taken. I think we shall have
> to indulge the assumption that those persons will love their country as
> much as we do; that they will not jeopardize their country by holding
> up the consideration of matters of that kind.
>
> This is essentially a subject, as I said before, which will require the
> taking of testimony.

Then, pausing for a moment, he lifted his face to the gallery, and
raised both arms as if he were delivering a sermon from the pulpit.
"We cannot put a time limit on the search for truth," he exclaimed,
"especially when it concerns the intelligence of the President." Then
he continued,

> The amendment offered by the Senator from Rhode Island would
> not jeopardize the situation in that way. I see no objection to his
> amendment. But to try to set a time limit because it is feared that the
> action of those who would be controlled by this condition would be
> delaying, requires us to assume that they would not be patriotic and
> intelligent and would not act reasonably.

The debate continued heatedly between Senators Ervin and
Hart. At one point I put in a few words, trying to clarify matters:

> May I suggest . . . that before the situation which concerns the
> Senator from Michigan would exist, namely, before a small group of
> Senators could tie up the Senate in debate and thus prevent a decision
> restoring the President. . . . the Vice President, the majority of the
> President's cabinet, and two-thirds of the House of Representatives,
> which does not have unlimited debate, would have to support the con-
> tention of the Vice President. As soon as one less than two-thirds of
> the House casts their votes, the issue would become moot, the question
> would be "out of court."

Would not the Senate have a voice in that decision, the senator
from Michigan inquired. It would take both two-thirds of the Senate and two-thirds of the House to sustain the Vice President's posi-

tion, I explained. Thus once one house votes and disagrees with the Vice President and Cabinet, the President would be back in office. Then Senator Pastore returned to the fray, pressing for the adoption of his amendment. At the same time Senator Hart continued to urge that there be an additional restriction on Senate debate.

My own feeling, at that moment, was that the best parliamentary move might be to accept the Pastore amendment. Senators Ervin and Hruska were not enthusiastic about the amendment, but they were not as violently opposed to it, as they were to the specific day-or-hour limitation that Senator Hart was advocating.

"Do I correctly understand that the Senator from Indiana will accept my amendment?" Senator Pastore asked.

"I was under the impression that the Senator from Rhode Island did not think it was necessary," I replied, sparring for time.

"I did not say that at all. I never said that," he answered.

I was beginning to give way. Questions were being fired from all sides. During the last few frantic seconds I felt as if the roof of the Chamber were caving in upon my head. Events seemed to be propelling us in a direction over which I had no control. It seemed to be us against the world, and just then I definitely felt that the cards were stacked against us.

"I see no objection to taking the amendment with one proviso," I said. "I should like to drop the last word; I do not think it necessary."

But Senator Saltonstall's next words were like a chill breeze in comparison with the heat of the moments before. Standing in the center aisle next to his seat two rows behind me, the senator from Massachusetts said in his quiet voice, "I hope we shall not adopt this amendment or any additional amendments of this character. We are trying to amend the Constitution with respect to an important question. If an amendment is offered on the floor of the Senate, I believe the bill should be returned to committee for a limited time, to make possible a careful discussion of what the amendments are."

"Mr. President," Senator Pastore concurred, "if the Senator from Massachusetts will make a motion to send the measure back to committee, I shall second the motion."

What had I been thinking of? I suddenly saw where we were heading and what it would mean for me to give way on this amend-

ment. Senator McClellan had been right earlier. After all our deliberation, it would be folly to allow such amendments to be made
on the Senate floor. The horrible panorama of all our work going
for nothing flashed before my eyes as Senator McClellan's next
words made the gravity of the situation even clearer.

"Mr. President," he said, "if the amendment is accepted, I hope
it will be referred back to committee for further study."

I made a snap judgment. Our support seemed to be breaking
up; the Senate was growing restless. It was already after six on a
Friday evening, and many of our colleagues were waiting around
for the vote but wanted badly to get out of town. Bill Fulbright,
next to me, kept looking at his watch; I knew he had a 6:30 plane to
catch. Just behind me, Senator Magnuson had been saying "Vote!
vote!" into my ear. It was now or never.

"Mr. President," I said,

> . . . a moment ago, hoping we would accomplish what we wanted
> to accomplish, I said I was willing to accept the Senator's amendment.
> I acted hastily.
>
> I feel wisdom requires us to proceed on the measure presented by
> the committee, as the committee carefully studied the measure. I cannot
> see a more firm determination made by the Congress than the deter-
> mination which it makes under the 12th amendment. . . .
>
> Frankly, this question has been discussed in committee. It has been
> discussed on the public platform. I do not think we can come closer to
> resolving this question than by using the terminology in the joint
> resolution before us.
>
> If the Senator from Rhode Island wishes to proceed, wisdom
> would cause me, with great reluctance, to vote against his amendment.
> I think it is wrong. I think the wording in the joint resolution is tight.
> The urgency is clear. The record is written. No Member of this body
> does not share the feeling that this is a matter which the U. S. Senate
> should decide immediately.

Later, thinking it over, I was to see that moment as a turning
point. If I had given ground on the Pastore amendment, all would
have been lost: the resolution would have gone back to committee
and might never have seen the light of the Senate Chamber again.
Just as surely as I had felt our support beginning to crumble a few
minutes ago, I now sensed that the tide had turned in our direction.
I didn't even dare say so to Conrad, but I began to think that if we
just let them talk themselves out, if we held out for the way our

amendment was written and answered all their arguments, the support we had slowly and painfully won through staff lobbying and innumerable personal contacts would surely not fail us. The important thing at that moment was not to lose the courage of our conviction that we had the best solution that could be achieved.

Subsequently, Senator Bass changed the focus of the argument, moving from Presidential disability back to his original contention that more stringent provisions needed to be incorporated into Section 2, dealing with the choice of a Vice President. I was unequivocally opposed to his suggestion; Senator Ervin once more rushed to my aid.

"Mr. President," he said, "I wish to reply to the Senator from Tennessee."

> . . . There is a precedent involved in the language which the Senator from Rhode Island wishes to amend. The Senator from Tennessee wants to amend the provision relating to the nomination of the Vice President. He says he is afraid that, when the Vice President's office is vacant, Members of the House who are anxious to get their Speaker in the Presidency will "sit still" on the nomination until the President dies.

Sam Ervin's voice was rising. "God help this nation," he said, raising his left arm high in the air and tilting back his head, "if we ever get a House of Representatives, or a Senate, which will wait for a President to die so someone they love more than their country will succeed to the Presidency."

Finally the time allotted for the debate of the Pastore and Bass amendments ran out. No roll call had been requested; it would be a voice vote. The chair put the question on the Bass motion first. "All in favor of the amendment of the Senator from Tennessee, say aye." There were a few isolated responses. "All opposed to the amendment, say nay." A chorus of nays rose from the Senate. I breathed a sigh of relief. Next came the vote on Senator Pastore's amendment; again, the nays were vastly stronger than the ayes. I felt that we had won a major victory—one that I had almost allowed to slip through our fingers.

Senator Pastore walked over to the desk at which I was sitting. Smiling, he put his elbow on the desk top and leaned his chin on the palm of his hand. "I'd have won that amendment," he said, "if the others hadn't tried to help me." He might very well have, I thought to myself.

As the debate continued, one of Senator Robert Kennedy's assistants came over to me to ask if I would include in the debate a certain definition of the term "inability." I knew from the conversation in the Senate cloakroom that Senator Kennedy felt it to be extremely important to have an absolute definition of when and under what circumstances a President would be considered disabled. In some future time of controversy or debate, the Court might well look to the record to determine what Congress meant by the term. As a principal sponsor of the measure, my own definition of "inability" would have particular significance. Because Kennedy's suggestion had merit, I took the slip of paper the senator from New York had sent over, and I told the Senate, "Let the record show that as the Senator in charge of the bill, I am fully aware of the complexity of the terms with which we are dealing." Then I read Bob Kennedy's handwritten definition which had hastily been penciled on a slip of Senate note paper: "The word 'inability' and the word 'unable,' as used in sections 4 and 5 of this article, which refer to an impairment of the President's faculties, mean that he is unable either to make or communicate his decisions as to his own competency to execute the powers and duties of his office. I should like for the record to include that as my definition of the words 'inability' and 'unable.' "

Senator Hart sought further clarification. "The Senator has just stated a definition of 'inability,' dealing with the impairment of the President so as not to be able to make or communicate a decision as to his own competency. Is it clear that this means far more than disagreement with respect to a judgment he may make?"

I replied that I agreed with the senator from Michigan: ". . . we are not dealing with an unpopular decision that might be made in time of trial and which might render the President unpopular. We are talking about a President who is unable to perform the powers and duties of his office."

The senator from Michigan sought clarification of another point which had been discussed at some length in both the House and the Senate committees. "With reference to the heads of the executive departments," he asked, "is it clear that we are talking about those whom we regard as comprising the Cabinet. . . ?"

"The Senator is correct," I answered. Then, I inserted into the record a report I had asked the Library of Congress to prepare dealing with the thorough interpretation of the provisions of that passage of the U.S. Code upon which our definition was based. This should remove all doubt as far is the Cabinet was concerned.

Senators Bob Kennedy and Phil Hart, sitting together in the back row of the Senate, had obviously been going over many of the points we had discussed earlier in the cloakroom. I was glad that these were being brought into the open on the floor of the Senate, making it as clear as possible what Congress had meant when it passed our resolution. Senator Hart now asked what could be done to prevent a usurping Vice President from consolidating his position by firing the President's Cabinet.

"The Committee in its hearings discussed this subject at some length, because we must tread a very narrow line," I replied. "On one side, we do not want a Vice President who is acting in good cause, say, for example, in a three-year term of office, to be unable to re-appoint Cabinet members who may have died or resigned." As I saw it, I continued, the main protection against a power-hungry Vice President's firing his Cabinet lay in the fact that "unless the Vice President could be sustained by a two-thirds vote of Congress, he would be 'out.' "

Senator Hruska agreed. "Does not the real protection against that kind of situation," he inquired, "lie in the good judgment of Congress?" If a Vice President's ambitions were that transparent, he continued, "the good judgment of the House and Senate would assert itself"; on the other hand, if two-thirds of Congress voted with him, "that would be the democratic process in action."

Senator Frank Lausche of Ohio brought to our attention another difficult point: Who, he asked, would continue to act as President during the period when there was uncertainty about the President's disability? We had considered this touchy question in committee, and the committee had concurred with my own judgment that from the time the Vice President assumed the powers and duties of the President until Congress decided the issue, the Vice

President should continue to act. We wanted to keep to a minimum the amount of uncertainty that would exist here and abroad
over where the Presidential power lay. We also wanted to be as sure
as we could that a President gone berserk could not reclaim his
powers and duties even for a few hours, thus doing irreparable
damage before Congress was able to decide on his inability.

We were drawing near a vote. The senator from Nebraska
took the floor and delivered an eloquent statement of his support of
our resolution, concluding,

> It is apparent that Senate Joint Resolution 1 does have aspects
> which alleviate the dangers attendant to a crisis in Presidential inability.
> Nevertheless, it is felt by this member of the Committee that caution
> and restraint will be demanded should this inability measure be called
> into application.
>
> A time does arrive, however, when we must fill the vacuum. The
> points which I have emphasized and previously insisted upon are im-
> portant; but having a solution at this point is more than important, it
> is urgent. For this reason I support Senate Joint Resolution 1 and urge
> its passage. I hope that it will be given expeditious approval by the
> other body and early ratification by the required number of States.

This was it. The day and the hour had arrived. We would
know in a matter of minutes if all our efforts would be crowned
with success or doomed to failure. Senator Hruska and I yielded
back all the time remaining to us for debate.

I leaned over and whispered to Larry, "Roman really gave us a
hand. I guess it was well worth accepting his amendment, at that."

There was a momentary silence in the Chamber. The tension
was so thick you could cut it. I again rose to my feet and suggested
that I was prepared to vote if none of my colleagues objected. There
was no objection.

"The question is," said the presiding officer, "shall the joint
resolution pass?" The legislative clerk called the roll. There were
seventy-two yeas and no nays.

"Two-thirds of the Senators present and voting having voted
in the affirmative," the presiding officer said, "the joint resolution
is passed."

Conrad and I looked at each other. We had done it. Senate
Joint Resolution 1 had passed without a single dissenting vote. Ju-

bilant as I was, I did not forget the parliamentary lesson I had learned from the morning-after reconsideration during the last session. This time I remembered to move that the vote be reconsidered; Senator Hruska countered with the standard motion that it be laid on the table, thus making it final with no future possibility of reconsideration.

I felt great exhaustion and great satisfaction. We had had to fight hard, but in the process we had written a good record. As I left the Senate Chamber amid the congratulatory words of my colleagues, I heard, as if from very far off, the last words on the subject before the Senate moved to another matter. They were uttered by Senator Magnuson:

"Mr. President," he said, "I believe it is apropos now, after all the discussion today, that the Senate should wish the President and Vice President good luck and good health."

CHAPTER 11

Irresistible Force—
Immovable Object

On February 22, S.J. Res. 1 was delivered to the House of Representatives; from there it was promptly referred to the House Judiciary Committee, whose hearings on its own H.J. Res. 1 had ended only the week before. A few minor amendments in terminology had been made in the House resolution. Only two of these struck me as being possible sources of concern to my Senate colleagues. The first was the ten-day limit the House had imposed upon congressional consideration of a Presidential disability; if the Congress did not declare within ten days that the President was disabled, he would resume his office. Second, the House had restored the original provision that the Vice President and Cabinet be given forty-eight hours in which to consider whether or not they wanted to overrule the President's declaration that he was able to resume the powers and duties of his office. On the Senate floor I had accepted

Senator Hruska's amendment which lengthened this period to seven days.

On April 13, the House of Representatives considered S.J. Res. 1. Senate business kept me from attending much of the debate; but Larry Conrad was there, as were Don Channell and Lowell Beck of the American Bar Association. They sent occasional word to me of what was happening during the lively session.

One of the strongest reservations to the measure was expressed by Congressman Clarence Brown of Ohio, who felt that

> It takes away from the House a constitutional right it now has to select a President. How can anyone justify the idea. . . ?
>
> We have the complete constitutional right and authority . . . to fix by statute the line of succession and to provide for filling any vacancies that may occur because of disability, temporary or otherwise, of the President and the Vice President of the United States. I say to you it is simply a foolish thing to consider, enact, and approve legislation like this.

Congressman Brown was disturbed about the powers the resolution would give the President. Using the example of Lyndon Johnson's succession to the Presidency, he pointed out that if our measure had been in effect at that time President Johnson could have appointed anyone at all to fill the vacancy in the Vice Presidency, subject to the final approval of the Congress. "The Congress could disapprove, but do you think they would have under such circumstances?" he asked. "That individual would not have needed to have any qualifications or background as a public official. He could have been any neighbor or friend of the President. . . ." Congressman Brown's concern was then echoed by Roman Pucinski of Illinois, whose strong opposition to our measure I knew of from a discussion we had had a week or so before during a late evening flight from Chicago to Washington.

Congressman Joe D. Waggonner, Jr., of Louisiana and Basil Whitener of North Carolina again questioned the phrase "principal officers of the executive departments." Here Chairman Celler came on strong: "We are talking about the President's Cabinet, nothing more and nothing less!"

Next, Chairman Celler and Congressmen McCulloch and Poff —all of whom were members of the House Judiciary Committee

—continued in the House Chamber their argument stressing the advantages of the House version of S.J. Res. 1. Poff and Mc-Culloch both felt strongly that the time available for congressional consideration ought to be subject to specific limitation; indeed, McCulloch introduced a bill to this effect.

During the debate, both argued that a Senate filibuster, or for that matter any such dilatory tactic in either House, could prevent a legally elected President from reassuming the powers and duties of his office.

Congressman John Lindsay of New York, another member of the House Judiciary Committee, then restated his dissatisfaction with the provisions which permitted the President's power to be taken away before the Congress had decided he was disabled. But Lindsay stated his concern had been greatly lessened by the acceptance of the 10-day limitation upon congressional deliberation prescribed by Congressman Poff. Nonetheless, Lindsay said, he would much have preferred a provision that the President always retain his powers unless Congress should decide otherwise.

Congressman Charles Mathias of Maryland spoke next, expressing his concern about Section 2, which permitted the President to nominate a Vice President who would then be elected by a majority vote of both Houses. "I question whether a proposal of this sort is in harmony with principles which have guided the Republic for almost two centuries," he said. "From its very inception, the Vice Presidency has been considered to be an elective office." Under our measure, said Mathias, "neither the people nor their direct representatives will be choosing the Vice President, the heir apparent to the most powerful office in all the world." (Apparently, Conrad noted as he recounted this to me, Congressman Mathias did not consider senators and congressmen, who under our resolution would make the final determination of who would be Vice President, to be the direct representatives of the people.) Toward the end of the debate, Congressman Pucinski offered an amendment which would strike from the resolution this provision of Section 2, thus removing the means provided for filling Vice-Presidential vacancies. But Pucinski's opposition to the measure went much deeper than that. "It seems to me," he said at one point, "we are inviting a great deal of trouble when we propose this change by way of a constitutional amendment." Thus the House, too, had those who questioned the advisability of following the amendment route.

At that point the House debate became very spirited indeed. Congressman Celler offered a forceful rebuttal of the Pucinski amendment. He began with an anecdote: One day during the Lincoln administration, he told the House, someone ran into the President's office saying "Mr. Lincoln, Mr. Lincoln! Senator Sumner on the floor of the Senate this morning said he does not believe in the Bible." And President Lincoln said: "Of course he doesn't; he didn't write it." "I fear," the Judiciary Committee Chairman had remarked, "that the gentleman who just spoke did not write this bill and is offering this amendment to a section which is one of the keystones thereof." Chairman Celler had gone on to present a telling counterargument to the substance of the Pucinski amendment. The effect of his rebuttal could be seen in the vote—44 ayes to 140 nays. The Pucinski amendment failed.

After that, amendment after amendment was proposed. Congressman Mathias, also sought, in effect, to do away with Section 2, but was defeated after a short debate. Next, Congressman Arch Moore offered an amendment shifting the burden of proof in the event of Presidential disability. Instead of the Vice President having to prove to Congress that he was justified in replacing the President, the President would have to argue his case in order to be reinstated. This amendment, too, was defeated, by a vote of 122 to 58. The next amendment, offered by Congressman H. R. Gross of Iowa, would have added to Section 2 language from Jefferson's manual requiring a roll call on bills and resolutions—requirements which by most standards were already inferentially included within the wording of the resolution. This, too, was voted down.

Throughout the entire House debate, the only amendment that had been accepted was that of Congressman Poff, which required Congress to assemble within forty-eight hours after being confronted with the need to deliberate upon the problem of Presidential disability. This proposal originally had been suggested by Speaker McCormack. During much of the afternoon, he moved about the Chamber talking to members of the House, urging that they support the forty-eight-hour amendment. In addition, he also left the presiding officer's chair to make a forceful statement in support of the resolution as a whole.

As a man who had been personally involved in the Presidential succession, Speaker McCormack had made a very telling statement about the necessity of an amendment. "I have lived for 14 months," he said, "in the position of a man who, in the event an unfortunate event happened to the occupant of the White House, under the law would have assumed the Office of Chief Executive of our country. I can assure you, my friends and colleagues, that a matter of great concern to me was the vacuum which existed in the subject of determining inability of the occupant of the White House, if and when that should arise." For this reason, he said, he was especially glad to support Section 4, which allowed the Vice President and the Cabinet to determine Presidential disability. "I know I could never have made the decision."

"As Speaker," he concluded, "I am proud of the debate that took place today." Then Congressman Celler accepted the Poff amendment, and the resolution moved toward its final passage.

After the Senate adjourned, I walked over to the House Chamber and took a seat in the rear. The voting was in progress when I arrived. The roll call on the resolution seemed interminable, but when it was announced there were 368 yeas and 29 nays. The joint resolution had passed.

On April 22, S.J. Res. 1, as amended by the House, was returned to the Senate. Although the differences between the House measure and ours did not really seem great, I knew that the feathers of some of my Senate colleagues would be ruffled by the imposition of time limits within which Congress had to decide the President's disability. Many would feel that such limitation violated the Senate tradition of free debate. Thus, after discussing the strategy with Senators Mansfield and Eastland, as well as with members of my own subcommittee, I moved that the Senate disagree with the House amendments and requested a conference.

I wanted very much to be appointed to the conference committee and told Chairman Eastland so. From the standpoint of seniority, of course, I was low on the list; but as an active participant and the major Senate sponsor of the measure, I felt that the knowledge which I had gained, as well as my determination to have S.J. Res. 1 passed, could be used to advantage in the conference. Chairman Eastland agreed, and, in fact, charged me with the responsibility of heading the Senate delegation to the conference, which, besides myself, consisted of Senators Eastland, Ervin, Dirksen, and Hruska.

On April 28, the House insisted on its amendments and agreed to the conference; its appointees were Congressmen Celler, Rogers of Colorado, Corman of California, McCulloch, and Poff. Mannie Celler was chairman of the House conferees. He and I decided, by telephone, to hold the first conference meeting on May 11, at two o'clock in the afternoon. Minority Leader Dirksen volunteered the use of his office, which was located between the House and the Senate Chambers and, therefore, was strategically handy to members of both bodies.

The eve of our first meeting with the House delegation, I invited all the Senate conferees to meet in my office late in the afternoon of May 10. If we were to have any measure of success in pressing the Senate version as the final form of our amendment, all five of the Senate conferees would have to be in complete accord beforehand. Senator Dirksen had strenuously disagreed with the form of S.J. Res. 1; Senator Hruska, too, had had serious reservations about it. Now, I felt, it was imperative that we forget our differences and enter the conference with a solid common ground.

Over cups of warmed-over coffee from the Senate cafeteria, I opened our informal meeting by saying that this was the first time I had been appointed to a conference committee, let alone headed the Senate group. I solicited my colleagues' advice as to how we could best deal with our House counterparts. The feeling of everyone was that we should try to be firm and hold fast in our efforts to accomplish what the Senate wanted. Chairman Eastland, puffing on his traditional long cigar, told me that the business of the full Judiciary Committee on the following afternoon would prevent him from attending. "You take my proxy, Birch, and use it any way you want."

Senator Dirksen began to reminisce about some of the experiences he had had on earlier conference committees. Once, he told us, Congressman Earl Wilson of Indiana, chairman of the House delegation, had come over to Senator Dirksen's office to tell him, "You senators have been getting your way on all these things too often. You might as well know you're not going to get your way on this one, and we're not having any report coming out of the conference unless you give in to the House position."

"At that," the Minority Leader recalled, "I jumped up from behind my desk, slammed my hand down as hard as I could on the desk top, and said, 'Listen here, Wilson, you just get the hell out of here and don't come back! I don't care whether we have a conference on this bill or not, and as far as I'm concerned, we won't have!' With that," Senator Dirksen continued, "Wilson disappeared through my door. That was the last I heard about a conference meeting on that bill—until," he chuckled, "he called a month later, meek as a lamb, asking whether the conferees could please meet together. Needless to say, it was a very amicable and conciliatory meeting." We all laughed heartily at the Illinois stateman's handling of the situation. Making himself more comfortable in his easy chair, Senator Dirksen mellowly continued to reminisce.

"You know, Birch," he said with a mischievous twinkle in his eye, "when I think of how you should deal with those House members tomorrow, I recall the story of the stranger traveling through Arkansas who ran across a man having trouble with a balky mule. 'Can I help you, friend?' asked the stranger, stopping and getting down. The man replied, 'I don't think anything can be done; I just can't make this jackass move.' At that the stranger went over to the roadside ditch and found a two-by-four, about eight feet long, lying there. He grasped it firmly and walked over to the mule; and then he reared back and clubbed the helpless beast a mighty blow right between the eyes. Throwing the two-by-four back into the ditch, he put his mouth close to the donkey's ears and whispered a few words. Much to the owner's surprise, the mule got right up off his hindquarters and was ready to go back to work once again. As the stranger started to leave, the owner grasped him by the arm. 'Wait a minute, stranger,' he said. 'Tell me what you said to that damn mule to make him move.' 'Friend, what I said really doesn't make a bit of difference,' replied the stranger. 'The two-by-four was what did it. First you have to get his attention before he'll listen to anything you say.' "

"So, Birch," said the Minority Leader when our laughter had subsided, "when it comes to dealing with those House members, make sure you get their attention—then they'll listen to you." That broke up our meeting. My mind was at ease, more from the atmosphere that had been created than from any specific strategy that had been outlined. Despite the earlier dissension that had existed among the Senate ranks, I knew we would present a solid front to our counterparts in the House the next day.

At two the next afternoon, the Senate and House delegations met in Senator Dirksen's office. The usual niceties were exchanged. Both sides were well aware of the importance of reconciling their differences, and some of the minor discrepancies between the two versions of the bill did get worked out. But it became clear that, as I had feared, the main bone of contention was going to be the time limitation the House had added to its version of the bill. Fearing a filibuster in the Senate, they had limited congressional debate over Presidential disability to ten days; the Senate conferees, on the other hand, did not want to put any limitation whatever on such debate. After all, no one could tell for certain what type of disability might strike a President or how long a reasoned judgment about it might take. After an hour and a half of discussion on this point, it became apparent that we were not going to reach agreement during that sitting. We decided to adjourn temporarily and to meet at a later time to be agreed upon by Chairman Celler and myself.

Staff members Conrad, Lesher, and Norton had been present, and it was the first conference for them as well as for me. The four of us walked down the front steps of the Senate entrance to the Capitol and across the street toward the Old Senate Office Building.

"Well, boys," I said, thinking out loud to them, "we have our work cut out for us here. It's plain as the nose on my face that the Senate conferees aren't going to get all they want in this conference."

"What do you think we should shoot for, Senator?" Conrad asked.

I thought a minute. "As I see it, we have only three real differences, and all of them involve time. Each member of the Congress wants this problem to be dealt with immediately—only some want it dealt with more immediately than others; and, furthermore, no one is quite sure how that word 'immediately' might someday be

interpreted. Our first difference is the period of time during which
the Vice President and Cabinet must decide whether they're going
to disagree with the President's declaration that he is well and able
to perform the powers and duties of his office. You know, fellows,"
I said, turning to them as we waited for the light to change, "we've
talked about this problem a hundred times. The only time it would
present itself—the only time the President would say 'I'm well and
able' and the Vice President and Cabinet would disagree—would be
if the President was as nutty as a fruit cake. Mental illness, pure and
simple, is the only time this provision would be used. The House
says the Vice President's and Cabinet's deliberation should be limited to two days. That was what we originally said ourselves until
Senator Hruska came out for ten and we compromised on seven.
Now if we're going to get anywhere, we'll have to compromise
between seven and two. I think we ought to try for four and find
some way to convince Roman that that will be enough time. He
feels strongly about this, and we need his agreement.

"The second difference is the requirement that Congress convene within forty-eight hours to discuss the President's disability,
once it becomes an issue between him and the Vice President and
Cabinet. We've written an abundant record on this, both in committee and in floor debate; I don't see any real need for the provision because it's what we intended all along. On the other hand, it
is a definite safeguard. The only danger of including it," I went on,
"is the danger inherent in the inclusion of any time limit in the
Constitution. Who knows what contingencies might arise? If we're
hit by an atomic attack and the Capitol building is destroyed, it
might take more than forty-eight hours for Congress to convene.
Who knows what shape our transportation system would be in?
Yet there it would be, written into the Constitution, that we had to
meet within forty-eight hours."

The light changed and we crossed the street. "From a practical
standpoint," I continued. "the forty-eight hour provision is a special
amendment that's close to Speaker McCormack's heart. It would be
like pulling teeth to try to get it out of there. I personally see no
objection to accepting it as it is." As we went through the revolving
doors of the office building and into the dimmer light of the interior,
Clark Norton said, "Senator, you haven't mentioned the ten-day
time limit. That's McCulloch's and Poff's favorite. It seems to me

this is the real bone in our throat, and I don't think you can over-look it."

"You're right, Clark," I answered. "Frankly, I think the first two problems will take care of themselves, but this is an entirely different matter. It's not that I've overlooked it—I was just hoping that if I saved it till last, either it would have disappeared by then or one of you fellows would have worked out some way of solving it." But they were obviously as much at a loss as I.

"What makes it particularly bad," Conrad interjected, "is the fact that McCulloch and Poff are both committed to that ten-day provision. And Chairman Celler works very closely with McCul-loch, since he's the ranking minority member. I just can't see how we're going to blast them loose."

"On the other hand, Larry," Lesher argued, "can you ever see two-thirds of the United States Senate accepting any provision that would write into the Constitution a time limit on debate? Why, that would be destroying a hundred and fifty years of tradition. Some of the old boys on our side of the Capitol would never buy that kind of arrangement. Almost every time there's a new Congress, Sam Ervin and his fellow southerners fight that battle on Senate Rule 22 and the filibuster. Senator," Lesher concluded, "you might get a majority of senators to support some kind of a time limit, but you'll never get two-thirds."

"You boys have hit the nail on the head," I agreed. "This ten-day limit is really going to be a can of worms. If we're not careful, it could blow things sky high."

We climbed the stairs to the third floor of the office building (with the usual grumbles from my able-bodied staff about having a boss who refuses to use the elevator) and walked down the dimly lit corridor to the door marked "Mr. Bayh, Indiana." I paused out-side for a moment, looking at the seal of the state of Indiana which had been given me when I first arrived in Washington. A woods-man, clearing forest land, was painted upon it; and I thought to myself that we had a lot of chopping to do ourselves before we could clear the thicket that had grown up around our efforts to solve the succession-disability problem. With my hand on the door-knob, I turned around to my staff members, who had worked so many hours on the problem.

"You know, boys, I don't like that time-limit business. I think our wording conveys the proper urgency—'immediately' means *immediately*, and there's no other way to describe it. If we write a time limit into the Constitution, we can't possibly foresee what we might face at some later time when its provisions have to be implemented. I'm no medical expert, but I'll bet there are some illnesses which can't even be diagnosed in ten days, let alone permitting enough time for congressional discussion. Yet if we let the House have its way, at the end of that period, if all those facts haven't been gathered and discussed and decided upon, then we might have a President who could be completely off his rocker reassuming his powers and duties, even if it meant he could blow us all to kingdom come in an hour's time."

"Senator," said Lesher, "You're right. *We're* right, and we've got the ABA behind us. You'll just have to go to the mat with them on this."

I thought for a moment. "Maybe so, Steve—and yet the net result of getting into a knockdown, drag-out fight might be that we'd just beat each other's brains out. If neither side gives, then we've all wasted one heck of a lot of work and worry."

"Senator," said Conrad, who was obviously deeply distressed by this possibility, "do you think there actually might be some middle ground—some agreement that both sides will buy?"

"I just don't know, Larry. Frankly, I'm as down in the mouth about this as you are. We have to strive for some reasonable agreement. First of all, what's the maximum time limit we can get the House conferees to buy? Second, what's the minimum amount of time we feel would be necessary under most circumstances for Congress to solve this problem? And then, of course, there's the really tough question: Can we get the Senate to agree to any time limit at all? What do you fellows think?" I asked. "What should we realistically try for in our own minds?"

As the four of us stood there in the long, dim, marble corridor, two years' work seemed to hinge on the answer to the question I had just posed. Conrad, Lesher, and Norton all hesitated, unwilling to venture a guess. Finally Conrad broke the silence: "What do *you* think, Senator? Have you arrived at a decision about it?"

"I don't mind admitting that I've mulled over this problem a lot, Larry," I replied. "Last night I thought I'd wear out my mattress wrestling with this one sticky little problem. Your guess is as good as mine as to what we can get either side to accept—but, when you come right down to it, I think that twenty-one days would come pretty close to answering all three requirements."

"Twenty-one days?" they responded in unison. They seemed disbelieving.

"Yes," I replied rather defensively, "twenty-one days. Look at it this way. In three weeks' time, most problems about Presidential disability ought to have been decided—under most circumstances that should be enough time to do the job. Both McCulloch and Poff said that ten days wasn't any magic number—in the hearings they both talked about twenty or thirty or even sixty days. Now I agree that once the House has actually passed a measure that says ten days, they're a lot more committed than they were before. But still, I think they'd eventually buy a twenty-one-day limitation. Of course," I added, "we'd be fools to suggest that at the outset. From the old bargaining standpoint, we ought to argue for a thirty- or forty-day limitation, then diplomatically let them whittle us down to twenty-one."

"But boss," Lesher blurted out, "the Senate will never buy a twenty-one-day time limitation."

"Steve, that's the toughest thing to answer," I replied. "You may very well be right. What, if anything, will the Senate buy as a limit on debate? I have the feeling that the one to look to on this is Sam Ervin. Sam doesn't want any time limit on debate in the Senate, and for that matter I don't think we should write anything like that into the Constitution either. But when you come right down to it, Sam's a reasonable man, and if both of us see that the only way we can get any amendment, any solution to this problem, is by accepting a time limit—well, then, we might both be willing to accept it. I'd be willing, even though I'm reluctant as the devil about it. I'm going to try this idea on Sam for size."

"Well, boys," I concluded as I finally opened the heavy mahogany door to my office, "I've got work to do." As Conrad, Lesher, and Norton turned away, Conrad said, "Senator, I'll keep my fingers crossed for you." I had the feeling that none of them would have given very good odds, at that moment, on our coming to some solution. Frankly, I wasn't too certain myself.

Early the next morning, before the Senate went into session, I was knocking on the door of the senior senator from North Carolina. Sam Ervin was just about to leave to preside over his subcommittee on constitutional rights. In order not to delay him, I walked with him toward the meeting room. "Sam," I said, wasting no time, "what can we do to break the logjam that's holding up our constitutional amendment in conference?"

"I don't know what to advise you, Birch," my friend from North Carolina replied. "Those House fellows certainly are a stubborn bunch."

I went straight to the point. "Sam, you've had a lot more experience than I have at this conference committee business, so check me if I'm wrong. But as I see it, it's far too early for us to begin making major concessions. If we did it would just be used as a starting point when the really hard bargaining begins later."

"I expect you're right, Birch," the southern statesman nodded.

"But I wonder," I continued, "whether we shouldn't start planning now for the time when we do have to reach some agreement. You and I are both strongly opposed to any time limit—that floor statement of yours that there should never be a time limit placed on the search for truth was a real masterpiece. There's no question that much of the Senate would be opposed to any time limit." Sam Ervin was watching me attentively as we walked along, no doubt wondering where my conversation was heading. "But, Sam," I continued, "we've worked at this problem for almost two years now; and the time might come when we have to decide whether we're going to sit still and let it all go for nothing or whether we're going to attempt some reasonable reconciliation which will give us a final solution to the problem. Which do you think we ought to do?"

"I know how you feel thinking about all your work going right out the window," Sam Ervin said sympathetically. "I guess if that time arrives, we'll just have to act like reasonable men and come up with some sort of compromise."

We were approaching the committee room, where I knew that Senator Ervin soon would be deluged with witnesses, staff members, and the press. I hastened to finish our conversation. "Sam, I know it will seem like taking medicine to both of us. I couldn't sleep last night and I gave this matter a lot of thought. I think there's an outside possibility we could get the House conferees to up their time limit from ten to twenty-one days. I think *they* could be sold on that, but frankly I don't know whether we could ever sell the Senate."

"It certainly would be giving in a lot to the House," Sam Ervin replied.

"Of course, I don't know if we'll ever get to that point," I went on. "It seems to me that we'd be fools to start bargaining for twenty-one days. I think we ought to ask for sixty or forty—certainly no less than thirty. Then, at the propitious moment, we could concede and meet the House group halfway. Well," I concluded, "I know you're in a hurry. I just wondered if you'd kick this around in your mind for a day or two. I'll get back to you as soon as I contact Mannie Celler and arrange for the conferees to meet again. Would the afternoon of Tuesday, May 26, be all right with you?"

"Sounds all right to me," said my colleague from North Carolina as he went into the committee room, "but why don't you have your secretary check with mine before you firm something up?"

"All right, Sam," I said, turning to walk down the hall. "And thanks a lot for letting me cry on your shoulder." Going back to Room 304, I thought about the conversation we had just had. I hadn't pushed Sam Ervin to give me a definite answer. In fact, I wasn't looking forward to the time when that answer was forthcoming. Would the Senator from North Carolina, to whom, as a southerner, the tradition of free debate was even more precious than to other senators, buy the twenty-one-day period? I was afraid not.

It was due to our good luck and the skill of Larry Conrad and House Judiciary Counsel Bill Foley that the May 26 date held. Getting a quorum for a Senate subcommittee meeting is difficult enough, but finding a convenient time for five senators and five members of the House to get together is like playing musical chairs. And there is always the possibility, after painfully working it down to a day and hour convenient for everybody, that one house or the other will have a vote or quorum call, thereby making it necessary to start all over again from scratch. Perhaps I should have been satisfied to get all the conferees together that day; perhaps it was too much to have hoped that we could conclude anything as well.

We met once again in Senator Dirksen's office. The meeting

was very much a replay of the first. Congressman Celler led the House delegation and was on that occasion joined by Congressmen McCulloch, Corman, and Poff; on the opposite side of the conference table were Roman Hruska, Sam Ervin, Everett Dirksen, and myself.

The discussion moved back and forth for more than an hour.

"The Senate just won't buy a time limit on debate! And why should it? You can't tell how long it might take to determine whether the President is really disabled."

"But, Senator," one of the House delegates said, "we've just witnessed in the Senate an extended debate—some have even impolitely called it a filibuster—which indicates the necessity of some time limit on the solution to a problem as important as who has the powers of the Presidency." He was referring, of course, to the long debate on the 1964 Civil Rights Act.

"My colleagues in the House," said another congressman, "feel very strongly that the Vice President and Cabinet should be given only forty-eight hours to make their determination. If they're going to buck the President's return to office, the country should know about it and the President should know about it, too.

"But what if some of the Cabinet members are off traveling on missions or performing duties in some far-off corner of the world?" I asked. "It might take them most of the forty-eight hours just to get back to the country. Remember Dallas? Half of the Cabinet was on its way to Japan and had to be summoned back."

As the argument went on, voices began to rise. Looking directly at Congressman McCulloch, who seemed to be chief among those who insisted on the ten-day provision, I said, "Bill, we have to reach some agreement. Why don't you fellows in the House accept a thirty-day debate provision? That seems like more than a fair compromise between ten days and no limit at all."

But after a few minutes of the House conferees' thrashing this suggestion about, it was obvious that neither McCulloch nor Poff would buy thirty days. Suddenly, and to my great surprise, the deep southern voice of Sam Ervin, who had remained quiet through the hectic give-and-take of the last hour, boomed out.

"Well, it would seem to me that we've wasted entirely too much time trying to resolve our differences. Our distinguished colleagues from the House won't accept the Senate language 'immediately proceed to decide.' This language is abundantly clear. The Senate feels strongly about this provision. Now the Senate sponsor of the amendment, my colleague Senator Bayh, has made the concession of accepting a thirty-day time limitation. He has leaned over backwards to meet the objections of our illustrious colleagues from the other body.

I was listening in amazement. Sam Ervin turned to address me directly. "Now, Mr. Chairman, I hesitate to make this proposal in light of your strong feelings to the contrary, but I suggest we all agree on a twenty-one day time limitation to congressional debate. I personally am opposed to such a limitation, but I am willing to consent to it out of the feeling of necessity that we reach an accord on such an important matter."

I nearly fell off my chair. Sam Ervin, who had been one of the strongest opponents of any time limitation at all, had taken me entirely by surprise. I had not talked to him since that day we had walked to his committee room together, and from that conversation I had not the slightest inkling that he would take this stand.

The senator from North Carolina leaned back, folded his arms, and waited for a response. It was not long in coming. The House members were as intransigent as ever. Another half hour went by; there was sporadic fruitless argument, with each side simply restating its case. Some members fiddled with pencils or shifted in their chairs; and occasionally there would be a long period of unbroken silence. Each side knew its own position and that of the other. The Senate conferees had, I felt, given more than enough; the other side not at all.

"It appears," I said finally, "that we have reached an impasse. I would be happy to hear any suggestion anyone might have on how to break it." No one spoke. "We have come such a long way toward solving this critical problem," I said to the group, almost pleading, but feeling some anger as well. "How can we be so close yet so far apart?"

"Well, you know, that's mighty nice," one of the House members said rather witheringly, "but we in the House are committed to this position, and we can't just pick up and go along with yours." Obviously the House delegates all felt that if they could just stand pat they might wring the last concession out of us. But we had conceded much already—I still had not gotten over my surprise that Senator Ervin had taken it upon himself to go as far as suggesting the twenty-one-day limit, which still would have been difficult to sell the Senate. Naturally, all of us were committed to defending our positions; but if our amendment were to survive at all, some concessions would have to be made. I knew good and well, however, that if the House was going to give even a little, it wouldn't do so that afternoon. There seemed no reason for the meeting to go on any longer.

When we adjourned there were as many differences between the two sides as there were when we had begun. I came back to my office in a foul mood. I buzzed Larry Conrad, and together we called Don Channell at the American Bar Association.

"Don, isn't there any way you folks can bring pressure on those House members? We can't get them to budge an inch."

"At the moment I just don't know how," Channell replied. "But let me think about it a little. I may be able to come up with something."

"What we need is a small miracle," I replied. "I'm going to sit tight for the rest of the week; then I'm going over to see Mannie Celler myself. Maybe the two of us can work out some agreement."

There is much congressional folklore concerning who should take the initiative in reaching a compromise in disputes between House and Senate members. One of the most striking tales concerns one occasion where the entire Congress was tied in knots because the House and Senate Appropriations Committee chairmen were unable to agree upon a meeting place for the conference committee which was to discuss disagreements over a critical bill. In the same tradition, perhaps some of my Senate colleagues would have felt it a breach of dignity for a senator to walk from his office over to that of a House member to discuss something. But I have never been a stickler for protocol, and such distinctions seemed ridiculous to me. I was a newcomer to the Senate, whereas Mannie Celler had been in the Congress for forty-two years and was chairman of an important House committee. And apart from questions of seniority and protocol, I thought the atmosphere would be more conducive to reaching an agreement if I made the first move. I had nothing to lose by it; and the game of cat-and-mouse that the conferees on both sides had been playing was a risky business. The stakes were just too high.

The next Tuesday, I telephoned Mannie Celler just as he was about to leave for a Judiciary Committee meeting. "Mannie," I said, "can I come over and talk to you about our differences on the amendment? It seems to me that you and I together ought to be able to work something out."

"Surely, Birch," he replied. "When do you want to come?"

"The sooner the better, Mr. Chairman."

"Well," he said, "what about half-past twelve today? I should be back from the committee meeting by then. Would that be all right?"

"That's fine with me," I replied. "I've been looking for an excuse to see those fancy new suites you fellows have in the Rayburn Building."

At half-past twelve on the dot, Larry Conrad and I were ushered into the spacious office of the House Judiciary Committee Chairman. After ordering coffee, Congressman Celler gave us a quick tour of his new quarters; then we took seats across from his big desk and got down to business.

"Mannie," I said, "isn't there some way we can resolve our differences? It really troubles me to see us bogged down this way, especially since both sides have put in so much work getting this amendment into shape."

"I think surely there must be, Birch. I'm as anxious to get this settled as you are—not only because of its importance, but because I've also got some pressing business in the Rules Committee to worry about."

"This is how I see it, Mannie," I said. "It seems to me that all our problems have to do with time. If the Senate conferees go ahead and accept Speaker McCormack's amendment requiring Congress to convene within forty-eight hours to discuss Presidential disability, do you think that we could come to some compromise on the period within which the Vice President and Cabinet have to decide whether or not they want to overrule the President's decision to reassume his powers and duties? The House says two days, and we went along with Roman Hruska on seven. It seems to me that four days would be a fair compromise."

"Birch, I think that sounds like a good bargain," the Judiciary Committee chairman replied. "But that leaves the really tough one —the period within which Congress has to make its decision."

"Well, as you know, we'd rather not see any limitation at all," I told him. "It's going to be hard to get the Senate to go along on any time limit, and frankly I was surprised when Senator Ervin went as far as he did the other day. But if we give in on your forty-eight hours, don't you really think that you could get your side to compromise here on twenty-one days?"

Congressman Celler thought for a moment while Larry and I sat there in tense anticipation. "Birch," he said finally, "that seems pretty reasonable to me. I think we can arrange it that way. I'll tell you what," he said, turning to Larry, "let me talk to Bill Foley about this, and you and he can get together and work out some specific language. Then we'll propose that language at the next conference meeting." Looking down at his desk calendar he asked, "What about June 10? Is that convenient for everyone?" I nodded, and Congressman Celler continued, "I can't say for sure what the other committee members will think of this, but I'm pretty certain that they'll go along with what I say."

"That sounds mighty good to me, Mannie," I replied, standing up to go. "I knew if we just sat down and talked things over, we could work out something." We concluded our visit with a handshake and a pat on the back for good luck. Conrad and I had been in that office less than ten minutes—we left our coffee only half finished—but I felt that we had accomplished a good day's work.

We were elated as we left the Rayburn Building. It was a long walk in the hot sun back to my office, but we couldn't have cared less. It looked as if our problems were solved.

"There's just one thing that bothers me," I said to Larry, "and that's whether or not we can get my Senate colleagues to go along on this. That's going to be tough. You know the story of the man who had the bear by the tail?"

Conrad nodded. "How's that fit in here, Senator?"

"Well, he couldn't hang on any longer," I said, "but he was going to be in a bad fix if he let go!" Conrad chuckled wryly.

"I guess only time will tell, Senator," he said.

The date of June 10 was verified for what I hoped would be

the final conference meeting on the joint resolution. During the intervening time, Conrad had been working closely with Bill Foley to perfect the language that would soon become part of the Constitution. Congressman Celler and I had been consulted on each word, comma, and period; and Foley had repeatedly reassured us that the House conferees "would be all right."

In the meantime, I had my work cut out for me in my dealings with the Senate. Judiciary Chairman Eastland had given me his proxy and would accept any agreement that was acceptable to me. Minority Leader Dirksen had said that he would be willing to accept the twenty-one-day time limitation, if that was the best we could get. As for Senator Ervin, he had already surprised me by suggesting that limit during our last conference. Still, I telephoned him to be sure he was still willing to make what I felt to be, for him especially, a highly significant compromise.

"Birch," he said, "perhaps I did give in a little too early the other day—that might have been the wrong time to make any concessions. But I was tired of all that fooling around, and I thought the least they could do was to give us the twenty-one-day period. I'll admit," he went on, "as I left that meeting I was angry with the so-and-so's for being a bunch of stubborn asses. But in the cold light of sober reflection, and for the sake of getting an answer to this problem, I'll reluctantly go along with the agreement you and Congressman Celler have reached. I think it's the best you can get out of them." I thanked Sam profusely and we said good-bye.

Now the only remaining question mark was the senator from Nebraska. Roman Hruska's office was just across the corridor from my own. On an impulse, even though by then it was seven o'clock in the evening, I looked out into the hall and saw that the light was still burning under his office door. I went into his reception room and was told by his receptionist that indeed Senator Hruska was still at work. In just a moment I was warmly greeted by my Judiciary Committee colleague. This was the first time I had been into the inner office of my neighbor from Nebraska. Neatly framed and displayed on the wall were numerous political cartoons and caricatures. The editorial comment, both friendly and critical, graphically told the story of the twenty-one years he had served the people of Nebraska.

"Well, Birch, my friend," said Roman, "what brings you visiting your poor neighbor from Nebraska at this hour of the night?"

"Roman, I know it's late," I said, "but I wanted to keep you posted on our negotiations with the House on Senate Joint Resolution 1." I informed him of the conversation that had taken place between Chairman Celler and me and of my conversations with Senators Dirksen, Ervin, and Eastland. It seemed important that Senator Hruska know the positions of his fellow Senate conferees on the subject. Finally, I ventured my own thoughts on the inadvisability of further delay in reconciling our differences with the House.

The junior senator from Nebraska wrinkled his brow in thought. "Well, well, well," he muttered, more to himself than to me.

I offered one further comment. "Roman, I know that you feel very strongly about the seven-day meditation period for the Vice President and the Cabinet. I was glad to accept your amendment on the floor. Now, frankly, it looks to me that four days is the best we're going to be able to get. I'd hate to see the whole thing come falling down because of this one disagreement."

Roman Hruska minced no words. "Birch, I'd be most reluctant to give ground to the House on this. It won't be an easy matter to sell the Senate on any type of time limitation. Are you sure this is the best we can do?"

"Well, Roman, you've sat there beside me during those last two sessions. We didn't accomplish a thing. Their heads are harder than this desk." I pounded the large mahogany surface, piled high with papers. "I'm afraid we're at an impasse."

He pursed his lips. After a moment or two of silence, he said, "Well, if that's the best we can get, it'll have to do. Surely it's better than no answer at all to the problem we've been working with. But, Birch, it may be quite a job selling our colleagues in the Senate." How well I knew—it could, indeed, be quite a job.

The hour was late, and I saw no need to take up any more of Roman's time. I thanked him for all of his efforts and took my leave. I remember as I drove home that evening, across the Potomac toward McLean, Virginia, the lights along the river seemed to twinkle more brightly than usual. The sky was dark overhead, but over Lee's Mansion and the hill beyond it to the west, a vivid stream of scarlet still lingered, suspended in the darkness. I began to hope that things were, indeed, that rosy and that we were nearing the end of a long, hard journey.

By half-past two on June 10, the conferees were again gathered in Senator Dirksen's office. I was feeling optimistic. Having informed each of my Senate colleagues about the agreement we had reached with Chairman Celler, I anticipated that the meeting would be a mere formality which would put the finishing touches on months of effort.

Congressman Celler opened the meeting by stating the terms of our agreement. In his judgment, he told us, we should proceed to finish our work along those lines. He paused for a moment, and Congressman McCulloch spoke out.

"Mr. Chairman," he said, "with all due respect, I think this would be extremely dangerous. Of course I am willing to forego my own very definite personal opinions on the matter; but the House feels very strongly about the ten-day time limitation, and I feel duty-bound to support the provisions of the House bill. I think that the ten-day time limitation is sufficient, and thus I would be compelled to vote against such an agreement as the distinguished Chairman outlines."

Before I could fully assimilate what had just been said, Congressman Poff, on McCulloch's right, reinforced this argument. He, too, had been one of the original authors of the ten-day provision, and he felt that the utmost care should be taken to prevent dilatory congressional tactics from keeping a duly elected President out of office.

I had been sitting dumbfounded as the two congressmen spoke. At first I could not believe my ears. As I began to realize what was happening, I turned to look at Larry Conrad, who was sitting behind me; I knew he could read in my glance thoughts that could never have been printed. As I was recovering from the initial shock of realizing that our differences apparently had not, after all, been reconciled, Senator Hruska joined the argument.

"Mr. Chairman," he said to me, "I was led to believe—in fact, I think the Senate conferees were led to believe—that this matter had been settled and an agreement had been reached. The Senate conferees have leaned over backwards to make an accommodation.

I, too, have been the author of an amendment in the Senate bill. Yet I was willing to see its provisions drastically reduced in an effort to come to some agreement with our colleagues in the House." He paused for a moment. "Well, Mr. Chairman," he continued in his sternest manner—and Roman Hruska can be very stern indeed— "if the House conferees are going to continue to be arbitrary about this matter, then I suggest there is little reason for us to be here." He pushed his chair back from the table as if to get up. By that time, I had calmed down at least enough to speak coherently.

Looking squarely across the table at Congressman Celler, I said, "I, too, was of the opinion expressed by my colleague from Nebraska. In fact, if that is not the case, I apologize to my Senate conferees for having asked them to come here under false pretenses. We are all busy men and have much to do with our time. I see no reason for wasting it further on this needless bickering back and forth."

I thought for a moment and then continued. "This is my first conference. I was of the opinion that a conference committee met to reconcile differences and to reach agreement. With all due respect, it appears to me that there has been little effort on the part of some of our colleagues in the House to reach an agreement. Rather, they seem determined to have their own way on all disputed provisions."

Congressman Celler stepped in here, a little defensively. "Well, now, I think it's important for the House conferees to consider the opinion of our minority members. Mr. McCulloch has been very helpful to me as chairman of the committee, and I have always been willing to listen to his advice and counsel." I realized that I had probably been a little hard on Mannie Celler when I addressed my angry remarks to him. From the way he was defending McCulloch's action, I sensed that he was as much taken by surprise as I was. At this point the congressman from Ohio, thanking his chairman, proceeded again to expound the same old arguments he had voiced before at the House hearings, during the House debate, and what seemed like a hundred times during our conference dispute. We were getting further and further from the agreement we had been seeking.

Things went on this way for about three quarters of an hour.

I was boiling inside, but at the same time I was desperately trying to think of some last-ditch strategy which might reconcile our differences. The Senate side had made most of the concessions, and I did not think they would make any more; I was surprised that many of them had been willing to yield as much as they had. Nor was I certain that two-thirds of the Senate would accept such a severe limitation. Certainly it had never done so before. How could I convey to our House colleagues on the opposite side of the table that this was it—this was as far as we could go? The distance between the two sides seemed to be getting wider with every passing minute. Each side was becoming progressively more hostile. Something had to be done.

At the next pause in the discussion, I raised my voice to interrupt. "Well, gentlemen, it seems to me there is little to be gained from wasting any more of our time here." Glancing at the solemn faces of my Senate colleagues to the right and left of me, I continued. "I think I speak for my fellow Senate conferees. We have gone as far as we can on this matter. The country has been searching for a solution to the problems of disability and succession for over a hundred years. We, sitting at this table this afternoon, are closer to finding such a solution than ever before in the history of our country. A lot of people have put in long hours to get us where we are now. The American Bar Association and its officials all across the country have pledged their support. The President of the United States has endorsed our program. Both Houses of the Congress have given us the necessary two-thirds votes. I thought we had reached an agreement which would reconcile our differences."

I shoved my chair back from the table. "As much as it grieves me," I went on, "if the House conferees are determined to proceed in this arbitrary manner, then they will have to accept the responsibility for scuttling all the efforts which have been made by so many." I stood up, scooped together the papers in front of me, and turned to leave. The other conferees, caught by surprise by this intemperate outburst, were watching me in silence. Suddenly I turned once again to the conference table and slammed my fist down hard enough to make a resounding crash. "Gentlemen," I said, looking hard at the House conferees, "we have gone as far as we can go. We have gone as far as the Senate will let us go. You will have to accept the burden of responsibility for our failure." I turned away once more. "Let's get out of here," I told the startled Conrad and Lesher.

By the time I strode out the door, the other senators were on their feet. The meeting had ended precipitously.

As I turned down the hallway, walking at double time toward the Senate Chamber, I heard steps running to catch up with me. I slowed my pace and looked over my shoulder to see Lesher and Conrad. When they had caught up, without slowing my pace I asked, "Did I overdo it?"

"Did you overdo it?" Conrad said. "You mean you—?"

"Overdo it? You convinced *me*, Senator, I thought you were really burning," said Lesher.

Just then I had another thought. Turning on my heel and leaving Lesher and Conrad, who still were not sure what was happening, I hastily retraced the steps I had taken from the Minority Leader's office and walked brusquely back through the outer reception room and into the private office with the large conference table. By that time the House members were picking up their papers. Congressman Celler was at the near end of the table, about to leave, with McCulloch and Poff immediately behind him. I went straight to the House Judiciary Committee Chairman.

"Mannie," I said, "if I acted hastily, I want to apologize." The conferees who remained in the room were looking at me, as startled by my return as they must have been by my leaving. "I just wanted —" But the Judiciary Committee Chairman interrupted me.

"Now, Birch," he said, putting a paternal arm on my shoulder, "there's no need to get excited. A long time ago, an elderly friend of mine cautioned me about the danger of getting angry. Just remember, my young friend, 'he who riseth in anger sitteth down to defeat'; and 'he who the devil would conquer, he first maketh angry.'" Congressman Celler's message came through loud and clear. My intemperate anger was, to him, a sign of immaturity. Still, I had become convinced that something was necessary to jolt our conference committee out of the futile House-Senate bickering into which it had fallen. I had hoped that a little well-controlled "anger" could serve that purpose. Now I was worried that I had overplayed my hand.

"I wasn't angry, Mr. Chairman," I replied, somewhat on the defensive. "I was just trying to remind the conference of the size of the stakes with which we are dealing. You and I could sit down at this table and reach agreement on the wording in sixty seconds' time, but our agreement would be useless unless it was ratified by two-thirds of our colleagues in the House and Senate. The message I was trying to convey is this: The most difficult problem standing in the way of our consummating weeks and months of hard work is getting two-thirds of the United States Senate to ratify our agreement. Mannie," I said, looking him in the eye, "I don't need to tell you that the Senate has a strong aversion to any limitation whatever being placed on debate. You limit debate every day in the House and no one thinks anything about it; but over on our side, we don't follow this procedure once in twenty-five years."

Congressman McCulloch and Poff were restless. I had effectively blocked the exit, and undoubtedly they had commitments to attend to. The time had come to complete my argument.

"Frankly, Mannie, I'm not sure I can sell the Senate on any limitation on debate; but I'm willing to gamble that we can persuade them to accept a reasonable limitation of twenty-one days— at least I'm willing to give it the old college try. But it would be a waste of the Senate's time to try and talk them into a greater restriction. I'd be laughed out of the Chamber. You fellows think about that, won't you, please?" I left the Minority Leader's office without waiting for an answer. Nothing could be gained by continued arguing among the conferees. The House had to understand that the Senate had gone as far as it could go; until they realized that, we were at an impasse.

Out in the corridor, Conrad and Lesher were waiting in a state of total amazement. They did not say a word, but I could tell by their faces that they were wondering what sort of crazy stunt I had been up to now. At a fast pace, without saying a word, the three of us went back toward the office—around the Senate Chamber, past the elevators, out the revolving doors, and down the steps which front the Senate wing of the Capitol. My anger, which in part had been very real, was beginning to give way to a deep depression. "The Congress has been trying to deal with this problem for over a century," an inner voice mocked me. "What makes you think you're any better than those who have come before you?" Yet, I reflected, we had not for a moment thought we were any better than our many predecessors who had tried to safeguard their country against a disabled President or a Vice-Presidential vacancy. It was just that we had dared to hope that the circumstances, the national awareness of the problem, would help us accomplish our goal.

Waiting to cross Constitution Avenue, I finally broke the silence. "Well, boys, it looks as if our efforts are in the hands of the Lord." The light changed and we started across the street. "We've done all I know how to do," I said. "Do either of you have any suggestions?" They shook their heads despondently. "Our only hope," I went on, "is to try and convince those House conferees they have to move. I know the Senate will never buy McCulloch's ten days. We're perilously close to forcing the House conferees to defend a position that some of them don't even want to defend. Once we get to that stage, then the ball game's over."

By then we had entered the Old Senate Office Building and had started up the stairway to the third floor. As we got to the landing, I turned to Conrad, "Larry, what about our friends at the Bar? Do you think they might be our court of last resort? When we get back to the office, why don't you give Don Channell a buzz and lay your cards on the table. Ask him if there's any way his people can persuade the House conferees." Conrad accompanied me into the office and tried to contact Channell. He wasn't in Washington. Finally, we managed to reach him in San Juan, Puerto Rico, where he was attending a regional meeting of the American Bar Association. Conrad discussed the discouraging news with him, and I joined in on an extension phone to confirm what Conrad had been saying.

"What do we do now, Senator?" the southern accent of our co-worker came from so many miles away. There was a long period of silence; I remember thinking that it was going to be an expensive phone call.

"Frankly, Don, I don't know," I finally said. "Is there any way your people at the Bar can get the message through to Mannie and his colleagues in the House?"

"I'm just not sure, Senator. Maybe we can think of something. They're meeting downstairs right now. As soon as I hang up, I'll go down and talk to Lewis Powell; maybe he can think of something."

Twenty-four hours later Lewis Powell was sitting in my car

as we rushed through Washington on the way to the airport, where I had to catch a plane to make a speaking engagement in Indiana. Don Channell had called us back to ask whether we thought it would help for Powell to serve as an intermediary. I had said yes, never dreaming that he would leave immediately, forsaking the conference and Puerto Rican sun to bring his personal influence to bear in straightening out our problem. I had been out of the office when he called from the airport to say that he was in town. Conrad, who spoke with him, suggested that he see Chairman Celler first. After having done so, he came over to my office. By that time it was so late that we all decided to talk over our problem on the way to the airport.

"Birch," said the Richmond attorney in his slow drawl, "why don't you go over and see Mannie Celler?"

"Lewis, I've already walked over there once to see him, as a conciliatory gesture. I thought we'd reached an agreement, then Bill McCulloch pulled the rug out from under our feet." I paused for a moment and then continued, "Still, if that's what it takes, I don't mind walking over there again. I'm just worried that any further argument between the two of us could end up making Mannie and the House conferees even more intransigent than they are now. That's why I thought it was important for you or some of the Bar people to do the persuading. I think further insistence on my part would only increase the tension."

We got out of the car at National Airport. While Conrad parked, Lewis and I continued our conversation on the way to the TWA counter. Then something happened which defied all the rules of probability. Conrad had rejoined us, and Powell and I were deep in conversation with our backs to the airport entrance. Suddenly Conrad, who was facing the doorway, looked beyond us unbelievingly. Instinctively I turned around; there, coming through the hordes of milling travelers, was none other than Congressman Emanuel Celler, walking toward us. "Hi, Birch," he said.

Obviously he was as surprised as I, although having spotted me first he had a second or two of advance notice. It was Lewis Powell who must have been in the strangest position of all. Having just concluded a conference with the Chairman of the House Judiciary Committee, pleading for his cooperation in solving the conference problem, he was now caught red handed in the company of Celler's main Senate opponent, the junior senator from Indiana. There was not a moment to spare before I had to dash to make my plane for Indianapolis and Congressman Celler undoubtedly had the same problem getting to New York. I said hello, and the Judiciary Committee Chairman proceeded on through the crowds toward his plane. I looked at Lewis Powell; he looked back at me. Then, as if both of us had been thinking on the same wave length, I turned and pursued the illustrious New Yorker, who had by that time almost been swallowed up by the swirling crowd of travelers.

I caught Congressman Celler shortly and stopped him only long enough to ask one important question. "Mannie," I said, "do you suppose there is any chance of us ironing out our differences over the amendment?"

The experienced lawmaker from New York turned with a cherubic grin on his face. Looking out over the top of his glasses like a wise old owl, he said, "That would be fine with me, Birch. Why don't we get together the first of the week? Would you want to come by the office? Just give my secretary a call and let her know if it's all right. Surely we can work something out." With that we went our separate ways through the airport crowds. In a matter of minutes each of us would be among his own constituents. Left behind in the mob, Lewis Powell must have been filled with satisfaction as well as amazement at the fortuitous encounter which had brought his emergency mission to its successful conclusion.

Shortly before noon the following Tuesday morning, I was once again in the large blue-carpeted office in the Rayburn Building. In less than thirty minutes, Mannie Celler and I had agreed on what were to be the final provisions of the Twenty-fifth Amendment. As I had thought, he had been sincere in his belief that Congressman McCulloch would go along with his decision. But, by the time Celler realized that he was mistaken, he could not go ahead and overrule the ranking Republican's position. Again, Larry Conrad, who accompanied me, was to work out the final details with Bill Foley. We agreed to poll our respective conferees on the final language rather than have another conference meeting. Within forty-eight hours, the final wording had been worked out and all of the conferees had affixed their signatures to the report. Both Chairman Celler and I were glad that the report was unanimous. Even though the Demo-crats were in the majority on both sides, and that majority alone could have reached an agreement, neither chairman wanted to see his delegation vote break down along party lines. We were glad to have Congressman McCulloch and Poff aboard. On the only remain-ing subject of controversy, the conference had agreed to limit con-gressional debate on Presidential disability to twenty-one days.

"Well, Senator," Conrad said to me when it was signed, sealed, and delivered, "we made it after all. But I must confess that when you stomped out of that conference, I wouldn't have given you a plugged nickel for our chances. What was that all about, anyway?"

"Remember Senator Dirksen's story about the man with the mule?" I said. "I'm beginning to think he was right. All you have to do is get them to listen."

"Yes," said Conrad, "but it wasn't just hitting them over the head. There was a lot of hard work, and patience, in there too."

He was right. Much of it had been a question of patience, of sitting still and not allowing ourselves to give way. Some, I thought with a chuckle, might even call it mulishness.

CHAPTER 12

Success at Last

By eleven o'clock on June 30, 1965, when the long buzzer sounded and Senator Donald Russell of South Carolina declared the Senate to be in session, Conrad and I were already in the Senate Chamber. This was to be the day. We fidgeted through the morning hour. Physically we were there in the Senate, but our minds were on the other side of the Capitol in the House Chamber, where we knew Congressman Celler was submitting the conference report on Senate Joint Resolution 1 to the House for its approval. I had every reason to believe that the House action would be only perfunctory, a quick approval of the conference report. Then it would be carried over to the Senate, which would, I hoped, act on it with equal dispatch. Nevertheless, I was pacing up and down in the back of the Senate Chamber with all the nervousness of an expectant father, eager for the final action which would once and for all deal with the problem we had been working on for so long.

Meanwhile, in the House, Chairman Celler was submitting the conference report and discussing its contents. He was followed by Congressman Poff, who explained his own interpretation of the report and urged its adoption. The question was ordered and the vote taken. Two-thirds of the House voted in its favor, and the conference report was passed. The Reading Clerk, Joseph Bartlett, was assigned to carry it over to the Senate.

I had been listening with something less than rapt attention to the pending order of Senate business, the discussion of a bill to alleviate the national shortage of boxcars. Finally Bartlett arrived with the message from the House. I gained recognition from the presiding officer and submitted the conference report to the Senate for its approval.

> . . . At long last the Senate and House conferees have completed their studies of the proposed amendment. A short while ago the conference report was approved by the House of Representatives. All that remains is for this body to approve the conference report, and then the measure will be sent to the States for ratification.
>
> If the Senate acts affirmatively, it will be the 11th time in the past 90 years that Congress has submitted a proposed amendment to the Constitution to the several States. Of the last 10 that have been submitted, 9 have been ratified.
>
> We have every reason to believe that the States will look with favor upon the proposed amendment, which is not designed really to alter the Constitution, but rather to fill a void in that great document which has existed for 178 years.

In a few short sentences, I outlined the main purpose of the bill, then moved quickly to the changes which had been made since the Senate passed it. It was imperative, I thought, that the record contain a full statement of the intentions of the conference committee. In the Senate version, I said, we had prescribed that all declarations of Presidential ability or inability be transmitted to the Speaker of the House and the President of the Senate. For the latter, the conference committee had substituted the President pro tempore of the Senate, since the Vice President, who serves as President of the Senate, would otherwise be transmitting his own declaration to himself.

The committee had further added specific language to the effect that if the President were to surrender his powers and duties voluntarily, he would resume them immediately upon declaring that his inability no longer existed. This, I said, had been implicit in the

Senate version; by being more specific, we had wanted to encourage the President to make a voluntary declaration, if such a declaration were necessary.

I then told the Senate of the change in the amount of time permitted for the Vice President and Cabinet to decide whether or not the President was disabled, from seven days to four—a compromise between our version and the two-day limit the House had desired. "I urge the Senate to accept that as a reasonable compromise between the time limits imposed by the two bodies." We had also added language to make it quite clear that the Vice President must be a party to any action declaring the President unable to perform his powers and duties; I cited President Eisenhower's statement that "it is a constitutional obligation of the Vice President to help make these decisions." The Senate conferees, I continued, had accepted the House amendment requiring Congress to convene within forty-eight hours if the Vice President and Cabinet challenged the President's declaration that his inability no longer existed.

Then I arrived at the last change I wished to outline—the one that had nearly killed the entire amendment in conference. This was the twenty-one-day time limitation imposed upon Congress to settle a dispute between the President and his challengers. I sketched the circumstances under which we had compromised between a ten-day limitation and none at all and made it clear that if during the twenty-one-day limit either the House or the Senate voted on the issue but failed to obtain the necessary two-thirds majority to sustain the position of the Vice President and the Cabinet, the issue would then and there be decided in the President's favor. The other House would be precluded from using the twenty-one days, and the President would immediately reassume the powers and duties of his office. I concluded, "I feel that further remarks are unnecessary. I thank all who have made it possible for us to bring the amendment to this stage, especially the distinguished Senator from Nebraska."

Senator Hruska was on the floor and immediately commented on the importance of our efforts: "I join the Senator from Indiana in urging the Senate to adopt the conference report and to do whatever any of us can do toward urging the legislatures of the several states to ratify the amendment to our organic law, so that it may be duly promulgated and given force and effect."

Senator Robert Kennedy, who was still concerned about the

inclusion of the Cabinet in the decision concerning the President's disability, now spoke to this point, relating the example of President Wilson's Secretary of State, Robert Lansing, who had called about twenty-five meetings of the Cabinet during Wilson's illness in late 1919. Learning of these, Wilson had charged Lansing with usurpation of the Presidential powers and had asked for his resignation, which Lansing eventually tendered. The point, said Senator Kennedy,

> . . . is that, even though no procedure there existed for declaring a President to be disabled and even though there was no evidence of any overt attempt to usurp the powers of the President, the ailing President nevertheless decided to dispose of any Cabinet member who seemed to present a threat. More serious conflict might follow, in a comparable situation, now that a procedure for determining disability is established. Indeed, a President might fire his entire Cabinet.

The junior senator from New York continued.

> . . . The question that might arise is whether the President had, in fact, fired the Cabinet at the time they had met and decided to put in a new President. What we could end up with, in effect, would be the spectacle of having two Presidents both claiming the right to exercise the powers and duties of the Presidency, and perhaps two sets of Cabinet officers both claiming the right to act.

Despite these factors which Senator Kennedy saw as inherent dangers, he went on to say,

> . . . Nevertheless, I believe we should go forward, since the dangers involved in not enacting Senate Joint Resolution 1 are greater still and we do not know whether a procedure better than Cabinet determination can be found. Certainly if one were now possible, I believe the Senator from Indiana would have found it.

Then, in an exchange with me, Senator Kennedy sought to clarify other points of the wording of the resolution. As previously during the debate on the Senate floor, he was still concerned about the definition of "inability." Was it not true, he asked, that "the inability to which we are referring . . . is total inability to exercise the powers and duties of the office?" I concurred, pointing out that a President might, for example, be able to walk, and thus in one sense be physically able, but still not possess the mental capacity to perform his powers and duties. "We are talking about inability to perform the constitutional duties of the office of President." However, I went on, in answer to another question of Bob Kennedy's, the term should not be limited to mental disability. "It is conceivable that the President might fall into the hands of the enemy, for example."

Senator Kennedy summarized, "It involves physical or mental inability to make or communicate his decision regarding his capacity and physical or mental inability to exercise the powers and duties of his office." Was it not true, he continued, that "the inability referred to must be expected to be of long duration, or at least one whose duration is uncertain and might persist?"

"Here again," I replied, "I think one of the advantages of this particular amendment is the leeway it gives us. We are not talking about the kind of inability in which the President went to the dentist and was under anesthesia. . . . The Cabinet, as well as the Vice President and Congress, are going to have to judge the severity of the disability and the problems that face our country. . . ." The sort of disability we were discussing, I continued, was "one that would seriously impair the President's ability to perform the powers and duties of his office." The junior senator from New York inquired whether such a disability could last only a short period of time. I pointed out that "a President who was unconscious for 30 minutes when missiles were flying over this country might only be disabled temporarily, but it would be of severe consequence when viewed in the light of the problems facing the country."

Thus, I continued, "even for that short duration, someone would have to make decisions. . . . If a President were unable to make an executive decision which might have severe consequences for the country, I think we would be better off under the conditions of the amendment." Such circumstances would pose complications for the nation and the world, Senator Kennedy observed; I replied that the complications would be much worse with no amendment at all.

Just then, Senator Eugene McCarthy, who earlier had joined with Senator Dirksen in an effort to make drastic amendments in the resolution, was recognized. He was as dubious as ever over the provisions of the amendment.

> If it were not for the fact that the amendment provides that the Congress of the United States has a right to designate some body other than the Cabinet to pass upon the question of Presidential disability I

could not support the amendment. . . . History shows that it is better to have one sane king rather than two who are not, each one of them claiming to be the right king. There is the possibility of a situation in which one man, having been elected President, claims he was capable of exercising the duties of his office, and the other person, the Vice President, engages in a letter-writing contest as to which is the appropriate man. There could be a body other than the Cabinet which should have the ability to make a decision which would have the effect of giving the American public confidence in the person they had approved and a disposition not to accept the authority of someone who would be disapproved.

It is my judgment that it would have been better to follow the recommendations made by the Senator from Illinois and not try to be so specific as provided in the present amendment.

Senator Kennedy backed him up with another example:

A Cabinet decides that a President was disabled. The President fires the Cabinet. The members of the Cabinet say they did not receive notice that they were fired until after they had declared the President disabled. The President says he fired them first. If the Congress is in recess, the President appoints another Cabinet. . . . There would be two Presidents and two Cabinets. There would be a conflict as to which ones were the members of the Cabinet and as to whether the members of the first Cabinet had made the decision before or after they were fired by the President.

Such a situation, commented Eugene McCarthy, would be "something like the old days in Avignon, when there were two Popes, which created a great deal of trouble, the same kind of trouble which was created for many, many years in England when two Kings claimed the crown."

While Senators McCarthy and Kennedy were discussing the confusion that might arise from S.J. Res. 1, Senator Albert Gore of Tennessee came into the Chamber. From his seat toward the back, our colleague from Tennessee, who during the past year's debate on the problem had not once been heard from, listened intently to the discussion for a few minutes. Then he sought recognition. When Senator McCarthy yielded to him, he said:

The Senator from Minnesota finds some consolation in the fact that, if I have understood him correctly, the amendment provides that Congress could designate another body by law. I invite his attention to the possibility that this could compound the question, because the amendment reads:

> *Whenever the Vice President and a majority of either officers of the executive departments or of such other body as Congress may by law provide.*
>
> I should like to inquire of the Senator, if, in addition . . . there would be a possibility of a contest or controversy between the Cabinet that may or may not have been dismissed, and one which may or may not have been confirmed by the Senate. Might there not be the probability of a contest between the two groups which, by the conjunction "or" are permitted to perform the same function?

This, replied Senator McCarthy, seemed to him to be an open question. He referred it to me, and I tried to answer the Tennessee senator's doubts.

> First, let me go into a brief explanation of why this provision was included. . . .
>
> It was felt that if there was an arbitrary Cabinet that completely refused to go along with the fact that the President, who was obviously disabled, was disabled—the condition referred to by the Senator from New York—the President might get wind of it and, although he might be in extremely bad condition, he might manage to have issued a document firing the Cabinet. This would not preclude Congress, in its wisdom, from establishing another panel, perhaps, of the majority and minority leaders of both Houses, the Chief Justice of the Supreme Court. . . . This body, in conjunction with the Vice President, could make its determination.

"In the meantime," asked Senator McCarthy, "who would control the Army, Navy, and Air Force?"

"The President of the United States," I replied. But who, asked the senator from Minnesota, would be President at that time?

"The President would serve as President until a declaration from the Vice President and a majority of the Cabinet or the other body had been made and received by the Speaker," I answered. At this point Senator Gore stepped in again.

> The answer of the Senator from Indiana indicates that he is thinking of the possibility of action by Congress at such time, and after such time as there may be an obstinate, non-existent, or otherwise inactive Cabinet.
>
> As I read the proposed amendment, Congress could, by law, provide now, subsequent to approval of this amendment. . . . for such a body. Or, to add still further to the uncertainty, it could await such time as the Senator has foreseen when, because of uncertainties . . . which are not now unforeseen, Congress could act at that time. . . .

This is done specifically for the purpose of giving Congress a certain amount of leeway which the Senator from Minnesota feels it should have?

I responded that Congress could establish another body at any time it thought such an action was necessary.

"Do I correctly understand the able Senator to say," asked Senator Gore, "that Congress could . . . provide by law such a body as herein specified and that, then, either a majority of this body created by law or a majority of the Cabinet could perform this function?"

"No," I replied. "The Cabinet has the primary responsibility. If it is replaced by Congress with another body, the Cabinet loses the responsibility, and it rests solely in the other body."

"But the amendment does not so provide," said the senator from Tennessee.

"Yes, it does." I began. "It states—"

"The word is 'or.' "

"It says 'or.' It does not say 'both.' " I quoted the passage: " 'Or such other body as Congress may by law prescribe.' I wish the record to be abundantly clear," I continued, "that that is the case. I am glad the Senator brought up that point. . . . The Cabinet, upon enactment and ratification, has the responsibility, unless Congress chooses another body, at which time that other body, and that other body alone, working in conjunction with the Vice President, has the responsibility. Indeed, Congress may choose a third body." I did not see how I could be clearer, but the senator from Tennessee was still not convinced that this was the meaning. I tried again: ". . . when there is an 'either/or' solution, it nails it down to one or the other."

"It seems to me," said Senator Gore, "that if it is 'either/or' it places the two on a par. . . ."

"I do not see how that would be the case at all," I broke in. "The Cabinet has the responsibility. What if Congress by law should provide for another body that it feels should have the responsibility?"

"Then it has such a responsibility, too," said Senator Gore. This had hardly been my point, and I suddenly realized that our amendment was not going to sail through the Senate as smoothly as I had hoped.

"Could we not have both?" Senator McCarthy chimed in.

"If we have one or the other, we do not have both," I repeated. "If I have apples or pears, I do not have both." Just as I was beginning to despair of finding some way of expressing what seemed to me a self-explanatory concept, my colleague from across the Ohio River, Senator John Sherman Cooper of Kentucky, stepped in seeking to clarify the matter. Senator Cooper, who was widely respected by Democrats and Republicans alike, was indeed a welcome ally at the moment.

> . . . Is it the intention of Congress, as interpreted by the Senator from Indiana, who is in charge of the conference report, that the Vice President and a majority of the principal officers of the executive departments would transmit the information of the President's inability to perform his duties to Congress, unless Congress has by legislative action provided for the establishment of another body to perform this function?

I replied by setting up a hypothetical example: the President becomes disabled, the Vice President convenes the Cabinet to announce the Presidential disability, and the Cabinet refuses to concur in the Vice President's judgment. At that time, if Congress judged the Vice President to be correct, it might by law set up another body which, "upon agreeing with the Vice President, again might declare that the President was unable to perform his duties. At this time the Vice President would assume the office of Acting President."

"Then it is the intention," asked Senator Cooper, "that this function and duty shall be that of the Vice President and the Cabinet unless the Congress provides that it shall be performed by another body. . . ?" I replied in the affirmative. "The question of the Senator from Tennessee," Senator Cooper continued, "expressed concern that the words 'either' and 'or' might give rise to a situation in which . . . a majority of the Cabinet, and a body which Congress might establish, would both claim the authority to exercise the function. Is there any problem about the use of those words that troubles the Senator from Indiana?"

"That is a good point to clarify for the record," I replied gratefully. "However, in my mind it is perfectly clear that if I said I would go to the office of either the senator from Kentucky or the senator from Tennessee, my statement would not reasonably be interpreted to indicate that I would go to both. It would be either one or the other."

"Then," the senator from Kentucky summarized, "the intent of the conference committee was that the language meant that unless another body were established by law, the Vice President and the Cabinet would perform the function; but in the event that Congress should establish another body by law, that body alone would have the authority to exercise the function, and in that event, the Vice President and the Cabinet would be without authority to exercise the function."

"It would then be exercised by the Vice President and the other body. The Cabinet would be out of the picture at that time."

But the senator from Tennessee was still not persuaded. He felt that, if that was our meaning, it ought to be written into the amendment itself—which to my own mind, it was. "We are not passing on conversations held between the conferees," he said. "Undoubtedly there have been many conferences and colloquies, but the language should be explicit when it becomes a part of the United States Constitution." Senator Cooper tried to convince him that my answers to these questions, since I was the senator in charge of the bill, were important to the amendment's interpretation. I concurred, pointing out that

> The language to which the Senator has referred has not been changed one iota from the specific language which was passed by this body. The conference report does not alter that language. Any interpretation of the Constitution, as the Senator knows, includes reference to the record of the debate, the record of the hearings, and specific interpretations placed upon the measure by the Senator in charge of the bill. Those who have been in particularly intimate touch with it are those whose statements are considered in an interpretation of the measure. . . .

Still Senator Gore maintained that the language of the proposed constitutional amendment was ambiguous. "Why cannot the conferees return to their labors and prepare language that is explicit?"

he asked. I suppressed a shudder at the thought of sitting down once again to that conference table where all our work had almost gone down the drain. Surely, I thought, we would not have to go through that again. I tried to end the debate on this matter once and for all.

> The Senator from Tennessee has been in the halls of this great body much longer than has the junior Senator from Indiana. I do not believe that it is necessary for his extremely junior colleague to point out that we have been 178 years getting a measure on this subject even voted upon in either House of Congress. I do not need to point out that it has been 18 months and more the subject of deliberation by both Houses of Congress to get it thus far. It took us almost 2 months in the conference committee alone. I would seriously doubt the wisdom of going back to the conferees and risk undoing everything that has been done—the House already adopted the conference report this afternoon at a quarter after twelve—on the premise that we cannot understand what is in the measure. The Senator from Indiana, with all respect, feels that we have written a very good record as to what that language means, if, indeed, there is any doubt of its proper interpretation. The Senator from Tennessee is a student of law and has expressed doubt. For that reason, we have gone to some length to explain what the interpretation of the language is.

The white-maned senator from Tennessee persisted; I was growing increasingly nervous. "The Senator from Tennessee knows," I almost pleaded, "that if there were to be a conference for every little misinterpretation that might be involved among 100 Senators, we would never obtain a conference report. The Senator from Tennessee is more aware of this than I, because he was serving on conference committees before I was out of knee pants."

"I appreciate all the nice compliments," he answered wryly, "but I doubt if that is a compliment." Obviously my attempt at flattery had misfired. I had certainly intended it as a compliment, I replied, "because the Senator from Tennessee knows how much respect the Senator from Indiana has for him."

"I appreciate the respect," replied Senator Gore, "but do not put too much longevity on me." I seemed to be getting in deeper and deeper. To my relief, Senator Javits of New York stepped in to try to bail me out.

> ... In a situation in which the Congress has conferred, and enacted legislation providing for a new body, ... it would be my judgment, if

I were a judge sitting on a case involving the constitutionality of that legislation that if that power of Congress were exercised, it was exercised to give exclusivity to the other body. I believe that the court would construe this amendment to most feasibly accomplish the purpose of Congress. As the purpose of Congress is to settle this kind of issue, rather than leave it in a great area of uncertainty and controversy would it not be completely contrary to the purpose of Congress to create two bodies which could compete with one another?

I believe that the construction which the courts would give to what we are doing is that if the Congress were to exercise the authority that the amendment would give, the courts would hold that that body has exclusivity as to its action.

That is my opinion as a lawyer, and I have submitted my reasons to the Senator.

I was becoming more concerned with each passing minute. We seemed to be in real trouble. It was a Wednesday afternoon, just before the long Fourth-of-July weekend. The Majority Leader had given his consent to our considering the conference report that day only because we had all thought it would be accepted without controversy. Now the hour was growing late and many senators were anxious to leave town for the weekend; some, in fact, had already departed. When Senator Gore and others suggested the possibility of delaying final consideration, I became increasingly impatient.

I tried to express the urgency of my feeling that we should have no further delay.

> Of course, the Senate of the United States is the world's greatest deliberative body. If my colleagues feel it should be debated more, I believe we should do so. I have tried, and will continue, to listen to every argument. However, I have studied this measure enough to know —and I say this from the bottom of my heart—that if we ever expect to have a constitutional amendment on this important question, the most complicated and intricate issue that we have ever tried to put into the Constitution, because of all the medical ramifications and power struggles that might exist—if we ever intend to get a measure with respect to which there will not be a scintilla of controversy, with very specific wording, we might as well terminate the debate and throw this year and a half's work in the ashcan, because we are not going to do it.
>
> I have never pretended to the Senate or to my colleagues that this measure is noncontroversial or that it would cover every possible, con-

ceivable contingency that the mind of man could contrive. I have suggested that it is the best thing we have been able to come up with, and it is so much better than anything we have ever had before— namely, nothing—that I dislike to see us, by delay, jeopardize the great protection we would get by this constitutional amendment.

But my words were to no avail. Clearly, if things went on this way, there would be no possibility of bringing the matter to a vote.

As the discussion became more heated, Senator McCarthy, walking down the center aisle, paused briefly at my desk. "Gene," I challenged, "why don't you get off our backs and stop trying to kill this amendment?"

The senator from Minnesota, taken back by the sharpness of my voice, replied, "Birch, I'm not trying to kill your amendment. I just think we need to have some questions answered and the language clarified."

But my patience had worn thin, and McCarthy's answer sounded like a hollow excuse. "Come off it, Gene, you've been opposed to our way of amending the Constitution since we first introduced it. You opposed our approach originally. You joined with Ev Dirksen in trying to cut the guts out of our amendment, and now you're trying to talk it to death at the very last minute. Why don't you let up on us? After three years' work, do you want this whole thing to fall apart on us so that we end up with nothing?"

Senator McCarthy turned away and walked off without answering. Probably he was wise in ignoring my outburst. In retrospect, I was not proud of myself, but the developing tension and the possibility that all our efforts might be blocked so close to the goal line had worked on my better judgment. Little was to be gained by such a confrontation with my Minnesota colleague, for whom I had great admiration as a legislator.

As the senator from Tennessee continued to point out the inadequacies he felt were present in the wording of our amendment, I noticed, out of the corner of my eye, the Majority Leader coming out of the Senate cloakroom. He, too, was worried about the way things were going. We had a quick, whispered conversation.

"Birch, Albert and Gene want this to be postponed. My own feeling is that if we don't put it off, Albert's just going to go on talking; and we won't come to a vote on it today anyway. What do you say?"

"I hate like the very devil to delay this thing further," I answered. By then Senator Dirksen had ambled in and sat down on the minority side in the front row. We went over to him and filled him in on the situation. For a while the Minority Leader held out for trying to bring it to a vote that day, but at that point even I did not think this was possible. "At this particular moment, Albert has us over a barrel," I told Everett Dirksen.

In the meantime, Senator Gore had suggested the absence of a quorum; as the clerk was calling the roll, Senator Mansfield and I had a hasty conference with Senators Gore and McCarthy. I saw no choice but to agree that the matter be put over until after the holiday, until Tuesday, July 6. But I thought it was important to try to get everyone to agree to a definite time for taking the vote. Senator Mansfield sought recognition and asked that the matter be laid aside temporarily. Then we secured a unanimous consent agreement limiting further debate on the conference report:

> *Ordered.* That effective on Tuesday, July 6, 1965, at the conclusion of the routine morning business, further consideration of the conference report on S.J. Res. 1, proposing an amendment to the Constitution of the United States relating to succession to the Presidency and Vice-Presidency and to cases where the President is unable to discharge the powers and duties of his office, be limited to 2 hours of debate to be equally divided and controlled by the Senator from Indiana (Mr. Bayh) and the Senator from Tennessee (Mr. Gore).

Although I was very much upset about the delay, it was a partial relief to be guaranteed a day and hour on which a final vote could be taken. I had begun to have visions of a filibuster which would prevent us from ever coming to such a vote.

I spent the Fourth-of-July weekend calling my Senate colleagues, who had previously indicated strong support for our amendment, to tell them of the latest unexpected turn of events and solicit their support on the floor during the final two hours of debate. Congressional weekends being what they sometimes are, I was afraid that some of our supporters might yield to the temptation to spend an extra day or two with their families, and thus be absent when the final roll call was taken. We called our Bar Association friends, too, urging them to use their good offices to remind our supporters of the importance of this final effort.

During those five days, we also did extensive research into the "either/or" question, which had been central to the entire dispute during the last session. Conrad spent the Fourth of July with Vince Doyle of the American Law Division of the Library of Congress, researching the subject. He and Doyle were almost alone in the entire Library of Congress building during that national holiday. Conrad tracked down another prominent lawyer, our ABA friend John Feerick, who also went to work on the problem. We were desperately searching for legal precedent for our usage, knowing that whatever ammunition we could bring to bear on this point would be useful next Tuesday. I still felt that the wording of that section was perfectly adequate; moreover, we had thoroughly defined, explained, and interpreted it during the course of the floor debate. But if it was legal precedent we needed, then legal precedent we would have—anything rather than take it back to conference as Albert Gore wished us to.

Early in the morning of Tuesday, July 6, Conrad, Lesher, Norton, Keefe, and I gathered in my office to plan our final strategy. We intended to make the most of the hour that had been allotted to us. By the time we arrived on the Senate floor, shortly after noon, our plans had been carefully laid out.

Although I was nervous, I felt that our position was basically a strong one. We had general support in the Senate; our primary responsibility, as I saw it, was to maintain this support. Senator Gore and his colleagues, on the other hand, had the burden of reversing and delaying all the progress that had already been made—not, I hoped and believed, an easy task; yet our opponents could succeed by persuading one-third plus one of those voting. I was not yet sure how many of my supporters would be present; thus it would not be wise to take anything for granted.

Our strategy was for me, as chief sponsor of the amendment, to go first with an extremely brief summary of the measure, saving most of the time allotted to us for rebuttal of the points Senator Gore would raise. Then we would yield the floor to our opposition who, we hoped, would use up the bulk of their time in explaining their position. After Senators Gore and McCarthy had finished their closing argument, it was my plan to call up our big guns—Senator Ervin, who was back from North Carolina, and Senators Dirksen and Cooper.

My opening remarks lasted far less than the ten minutes I had originally planned.

> Mr. President . . . this has been a much discussed subject over the 187 years of our history. The record of the past 187 years is replete with studies by the Congress, the Senate, and individuals concerned.
>
> The purpose of the constitutional amendment, the conference report upon which we are now called to approve, is to provide a means by which the Vice President will be able to perform the powers and duties of the Office of President if the President is unable to do so.
>
> . . . In my estimation, it is impossible to devise a bill or a constitutional amendment which can cover all the contingencies in this particular, complicated field, but this Congress has gone farther than any of its predecessors toward meeting the problem.
>
> On the last day of the debate I went into some detail to specify the details of the report. I do not believe it is necessary to do so again today, unless some of my colleagues wish to question me or engage in colloquy.

Before I could take my seat, Senator Javits of New York sought recognition to insert into the record a *New York Herald Tribune* editorial that echoed his own support of our amendment. "The argument that not everything is 'buttoned down' by the proposed amendment is not, in my judgment, persuasive," he said. "We should not 'monkey around' with the amendment to provide for something which could be taken care of by legislation later in Congress."

By now the two minutes I had originally yielded to myself had expired; two more minutes had been used up as I yielded them, one by one, to the senior senator from New York. As Senator Javits completed his brief statement, Senator Gore was on his feet to request a quorum call. I was afraid that a quorum would not be present, and held my breath as the roll was called by the reading clerk. At the end of the first roll call, only forty senators had answered to their names—eleven short of the required number to do business. The Sergeant at Arms was ordered to request the absent senators' attendance. As the minutes ticked by, one by one, our colleagues drifted into the Senate Chamber.

Finally Senator Edward Kennedy, who had assumed the presiding officer's chair, announced that a quorum was present. Senator Gore yielded fifteen minutes to Senator McCarthy, the lead-off batter for the opposition. As had been the case from the beginning, the senator from Minnesota's reservations about the amendment rested on a broader base than the verbal ambiguity which troubled Senator Gore.

> I have serious reservations about more than the language of the amendment. I have very serious reservations about the substance of the amendment itself. It was my view when the question of presidential disability and vice-presidential succession was raised that there was sufficient authority in the Constitution to permit Congress to proceed by statute.

Unable to secure a statute, Senator McCarthy had joined Minority Leader Dirksen in seeking to obtain approval of a brief nonspecific constitutional amendment, enabling Congress to provide the missing details later by law. He had failed to persuade the Senate of the wisdom of either course of action. Now he reminded the Senate that in 1963, Nicholas deB. Katzenbach, who was then the Deputy Attorney General, had supported his position. At this point I once again inserted into the record the letter we had received from the Attorney General on just this point—a letter stating unequivocal support of S.J. Res. 1.

At that point Senator Gore entered the fray, yielding to himself "such time as I may desire." He quickly outlined his major objection to the provisions of our resolution.

> . . . Clarity and certainty are the essential characteristics of any constitutional provision. . . .
>
> The basic objectives of an amendment such as we now consider should be the provision of a procedure certain for the declaration of disability of a President of the United States, but I submit that the provision now before the Senate provides an uncertain procedure.

The senator from Tennessee then proceeded in a detailed discussion of the "either/or" provision which had so concerned him previously.

> To me, it . . . seems clear, under the language of the provision, that if Congress should "by law provide" some "other body," the Vice President might then be authorized to act in concert with either the Cabinet or such other body. . . .

> ... The Senator from Indiana says that the Cabinet would have
> the primary responsibility. The amendment does not so provide. . . .
> ... I do not know how the words "either" and "or" can be inter-
> preted to mean that if the other body is created, the first body has no
> responsibility and no power to act. . . . The words . . . established the
> possibility of two coequal bodies—coequal in responsibility under the
> Constitution—coequal in authority to act in concert with the Vice
> President to declare the disability of a President of the United States.
> ... If my interpretation of the language is correct . . . the Vice
> President would be free to choose to ally himself with either of the
> groups, depending upon which included individuals sympathetic with
> his view of the then current situation. . . . a Vice President would be
> in a position to "shop around" for support of his view that the Presi-
> dent is not able to discharge the duties of his office. . . .

Senator Ervin, who had been observing Senator Gore's presentation from the rear of the Chamber, now rose to challenge his
argument.

> What is the harm in providing alternatives in making the determi-
> nation? Would that not improve the amendment? It would make it
> more flexible. If the Senator from Tennessee is correct in his interpre-
> tation—and he is making a very fine argument—that the Vice Presi-
> dent, either acting with the majority of the Cabinet or acting with the
> majority of an alternative body established by Congress, could declare
> a President to be disabled, would that not be an advantage? I feel that
> it would, in that it provides some flexibility instead of only one inflex-
> ible procedure.

Although Sam Ervin was proceeding in his usual effective manner,
I thought it important not to lend credence to the Tennessee senator's claim that the wording was ambiguous. The constitutional
provision should, I thought, have one meaning, not two. I left my
post behind the Majority Leader's desk and hastily headed up the side
aisle for a whispered consultation with my colleague from North
Carolina. Meanwhile, Albert Gore was arguing, as I had feared, that
there was disagreement even among those who supported S.J. Res.
1 concerning its actual meaning.

> Mr. President, an anomalous situation has just been revealed. The
> distinguished senior senator from North Carolina, formerly a justice of
> the Supreme Court of North Carolina, has agreed with my interpre-
> tation and has said that the language improves the amendment. The
> distinguished Senator from Indiana disagrees with my interpretation.

> I submit that when there is a disagreement as to interpretation be-
> tween two of the authors of an amendment, this is the time to restudy,
> to redefine, and to clarify, before we submit the constitutional amend-
> ment to the States for their ratification or rejection. We are about to
> write into the Constitution of the United States an amendment that
> could be the most important amendment ever written.

Senator Ervin sought to clarify his earlier remarks, but the senator
from Tennessee refused to yield; only four minutes remained of the
time allotted to him. Senator Ervin protested briefly that he had only
been operating on the assumption that the Tennessee senator's interpretation was correct.

Without restating, Senator Gore proceeded to his concluding
argument.

> In a situation involving the passing of the power of the Presidency
> from the hands of one individual to another it is equally important
> that the law be certain as that it be just or wise. . . .
> Unfortunately, under the existing parliamentary situation, there is
> no way in which language revision can be considered other than by
> rejection of the conference report. Once this step has been taken, a
> further conference with the House can be requested—that is what I
> propose—and the conferees would then have an opportunity to pre-
> sent language free of uncertainty. We should establish a procedure
> with certainty for the declaration of the disability of the President of
> the United States. . . .
> For the reason I have stated, I urge Senators to vote to reject the
> conference report and give the conferees an opportunity to bring us
> an amendment having precise, clear meaning.

The senator from Tennessee reserved the few minutes remaining
to him.

At the close of Senator Gore's presentation, I was recognized
by the chair and immediately yielded to Senator Ervin, enabling
him to clarify his position. After expressing his strong support for
the proposed amendment, Senator Ervin pointed out the real difficulty we had encountered in reaching our present stage of consensus.

> The Senator from Indiana, the Senator from Tennessee or I could
> have drawn a better resolution if we had uncontrolled authority to do
> so. I have worked on this problem. If I were allowed to draft a resolu-
> tion by myself, I think I could draw a better one. As a matter of fact,
> I drew what I believe to be a better one.
> . . . However, the measure before us reflects an amalgamation of

views. As such, it represents a consensus which may not satisfy any of its proponents entirely. It may not be perfect. Indeed, in my view, it is not perfect but I feel that it is the best resolution that is attainable.

... I am not at all disturbed by the interpretation which my good friend, the Senator from Tennessee, places on the document. If it is a correct interpretation, in my judgment, it would make the resolution better. ...

Many provisions of law provide alternative means. For example, in virtually every State of the Union, a prosecution for a felony can be started either by an individual in the court of a justice of the peace or by the indictment of a grand jury. ...

As the senator from North Carolina continued his remarks, he and Senator Gore became involved in an eloquent debate over the procedural details contained in the amendment. I had been checking with the parliamentarian and, at the end of the Ervin-Gore discussion, fifteen minutes of our time had elapsed. From the standpoint of time, things were going as we had hoped; we had used only one quarter of our own time, while Senator Gore's time had nearly expired.

Again I sought recognition and yielded ten minutes to Senator Dirksen. I had counted strongly on the persuasiveness of the Minority Leader to put forth our argument. Despite his earlier opposition to the form of S.J. Res. 1, he came out strongly for us now; and his expression of support exceeded our fondest expectations.

I presume that the first thing we discover is that language is not absolute. The only word I can think of that is absolute is the word "zero." However, interpretations of all kinds can be placed upon language, and all the diversities of judicial decisions that are presumed since the beginning of the Republic, if placed in a pile, would reach up to the sky. Consequently, in dealing with the language before us, we have the same problem that we had in the subcommittee and in the conference.

Fashioning language to do what we have in mind, particularly when we are subject to the requirement of compression for constitutional amendment purposes, is certainly not an easy undertaking. However, I believe that a reading of the resolution will speak for itself.

From there the Minority Leader proceeded to a section-by-section analysis of S.J. Res. 1. When his allotted ten minutes expired he was still going strong, and I yielded him five minutes more. During this time, the senator from Tennessee expressed his continued dissatisfaction with the wording of our resolution, arguing that the likelihood of two bodies—the Cabinet and some other—between which the Vice President could choose would present an insurmountable temptation for the Vice President to indulge in self-serving and dangerous activity. Senator Dirksen replied,

> I doubt the substance of my friend's premise. I should not like to be around to enjoy the furor if ever the Vice President undertook, for venal purposes, or motivations of his own, to pursue that kind of course.

The Minority Leader's deep resonant voice boomed louder in the Senate Chamber as he continued:

> . . . After all, the people of this country will have something to say about that. Where would it lead? They would not exactly run him out on a rail, but his whole political future, such as it might be, would come to an end at that point.
>
> Let us always remember that we are dealing with human beings and human motivations, and also with the sense of fidelity and affection that people bear, one for another, when they are thrown into a common labor, such as that of a President and Vice President, and the principal executive officers under those circumstances.

The Minority Leader moved toward the conclusion of his argument.

> There are some fundamentals we must remember in dealing with a matter of this kind. The first is that we do not strive for the eternal. . . . Second, we know that there will always be change, but . . . the Constitution in its interpretation itself indicates that we would take it in our stride.

He paused for a moment and gazed about him, before putting the finishing touches on his argument. An unusual hush hung over the Senate as each member hung on his words.

> There was once a professor at Johns Hopkins University who had fashioned a thesis and a postulate that he thought would stand up under every circumstance. Then he sat down with his fellow faculty members to discuss it. When the discussion was ended, his thesis and postulate were torn apart with suppositions and other arguments to the point that he gave out a frantic cry, "In God's name, is there nothing eternal?"
>
> One of his fellow professors answered, "Yes, one thing, and that is change."
>
> . . . Mr. President, I believe we have done a reasonably worthwhile job insofar as the feeble attributes of the language can accomplish it. . . .

I rose to my feet. "Mr. President, I thank the Senator from Illinois and the other senators who have labored tirelessly to help us get this far down the road." The time was growing short. It was my responsibility, as principal sponsor, to conclude the debate for the proponents of S.J. Res. 1—answering any last-minute questions, shoring up any last-minute doubts which might linger in the minds of my colleagues who, as the debate had gone on, had been filling the Chamber in increasing numbers. I yielded to myself all the time I needed. There was not too much remaining.

> . . . I have no prepared speech. I have made some notes on one or two points that I wish to discuss. I shall . . . try to clarify the question of intent in the consideration of this subject. However, I emphasize that the Senator from Tennessee and I share one intention, among others, and this is we seek to clarify any ambiguity which may exist.
>
> Reference has been made to the position of the Attorney General of the United States. . . . Mr. President, I . . . quote one sentence from his testimony before the subcommittee. He said:
>
> *I want to reaffirm my prior position that the only satisfactory method of settling the problem of Presidential inability is by constitutional amendment, as Senate Joint Resolution 1 proposes.*
>
> In this position, he was joined by a rather long list of Attorneys General of the United States, going back to Biddle and Brownell. He was also joined by such constitutional experts as Paul Freund. They felt that if there was any doubt, the Congress should propose an amendment to the Constitution.

I paused for a moment to catch my breath, glancing upward at the eagle, embossed in glass, which adorned the ceiling of the chamber which housed the world's greatest deliberative body. Could it possibly be that in the next few minutes I, a neophyte in this council of veteran statesmen, would actually have helped play a part in amending the Constitution of the United States? But there was no time to think about that now; the remaining loose ends had to be pinned down.

> The question has been raised as to why we have put the Vice President in the position of acting in the capacity he would have under the amendment. Former President Eisenhower dramatically made this point in his presentation before the conference of the American Bar Association last June. President Eisenhower said he felt it was the responsibility of the Vice President to assume the authority of the Presidential office in the event that the President was unable to per-

form his duties, and that the Vice President could not escape that authority and obligation.

Therefore, I believe that we have done the right thing in placing the Vice President in the position of participating in the determination of Presidential disability.

Next I turned to a discussion of the most controversial part of the entire amendment.

> There has been a great deal of discussion about the last section, the most controversial section, of the proposed amendment. I point out, based upon my judgment, that this most controversial part of the amendment rarely if ever would be brought into play.
>
> As the Senator from Illinois has pointed out, the amendment provides for the voluntary declaration of disability by the President. Let us assume, for example, that he is undergoing a serious operation, and that he does not want to take the chance of having the enemy take advantage of the situation.
>
> The amendment also deals with the kind of crisis which President Eisenhower described, such as a President suffering from a heart attack. For example, at the time he might lie helpless in an oxygen tent the Russians might begin to move missiles into Cuba. At that moment, no person in the United States would have the power to make those critical decisions that would have to be made.
>
> The amendment would take care of these points.
>
> Now we get to the point to which the Senator from Tennessee has correctly alluded; namely, the question of a President who, although physically able, is not the man . . . who was previously elected to that office. Thus arises the difficult problem of mental disability.
>
> The Senator from Tennessee bases his argument on the fact that changes were made in the conference committee. I point out that in referring to the "either/or" change, the Senator from Tennessee overlooks the fact that several other changes were made in conference. . . .
>
> . . . With respect to "either/or," it is clear to me—and I invite the attention of Senators to the definition of this phrase in Black's Legal Dictionary and to most legal cases on the point—that when we talk about "either/or" it is interpreted in the disjunctive. It does not refer to two, but to either one or the other.
>
> Reference was made—not by the Senator from Tennessee but by another Senator—to the fact that the Vice President could in effect at one time go to either one of these bodies and use them simultaneously. I do not see how it is possible to do that.

At this point Senator Gore asked if I would yield; but I felt it important to continue my presentation without interruption. Time was running out.

> . . . Certainly it is the intention of the conference committee and
> it is my contention . . . that Congress should have some flexibility, and
> that we do not wish to nail down a plan which may not work. It is
> our intention for the plan, as it is enacted, to have the Vice President
> and a majority of the Cabinet make the decision, unless Congress, in
> its wisdom, at some later time, determines by statute to establish some
> other body to act with the Vice President. . . . It is our intention that
> at that time this other body shall supersede the Cabinet.

I yielded briefly to Senator Lausche, who asked whether we
had ever contemplated using the conjunctive rather than the dis-
junctive—"having both a majority of the members of the Cabinet
and a majority of the members of the body created by Congress act"
on the disability problem? We had never considered that, I replied.
Then I moved into the documentation of our interpretation of
"either/or." The search of our staff and that of the American Bar
Association over the hot Fourth-of-July weekend for legal precedent relating to the question had borne fruit.

> Since the Senator from Tennessee raised the question I have tried
> my best to look for cases which might soothe his concern about the
> ambiguity which he believes exists and which I believe does not exist.
> Mr. President, I have uncovered three or four cases dealing with
> article V of the Constitution. They are Hawke v. Smith, 253 U.S. 221;
> Dillon v. Gloss, 256 U.S. 368; the National Prohibition cases, 253 U.S.
> 350; and United States v. Sprague, 282 U.S. 716.
> As the Senate knows, article V deals with the means to amend
> the Constitution itself. Congress is given the authority to use either
> the means of legislative ratification or State convention ratification.
> Either one or the other may be used. In dealing with the fifth article,
> the courts have held in those cases to which I have referred—which
> are as close to being on the point as any I have been able to find—
> that Congress has full and plenary power to decide which method
> should be used, and once the choice is made, the other method is
> precluded. . . .
> These cases substantiate our feeling—at least our intention—as to
> what we desire to accomplish in the wording which has been placed
> in the conference report.
> I should like to go one step further. In the debate I do not wish
> to concede ambiguity. But out of friendship for the Senator from
> Tennessee, I should like to suppose, for only a moment, that there
> might be ambiguity in the use of the words "either/or". What then
> would be the result? In the event of ambiguity there is no question

that the Court would then look to the legislative intent. As a result of the insight and the perseverance of the Senator from Tennessee, we have now written a record of legislative intent, as long as our arms, to the effect that we desire only one body to act on the subject. In the event that an ambiguity is construed, I suggest that there is one last safeguard. I am certain that Congress under the enabling provision which would permit another body to act with the Vice President, would in its wisdom at that time specify that, pursuant to section 4 of the 25th amendment to the Constitution, the other body is designated to supplant and replace the Cabinet and act in concert with the Vice President. So I am not concerned that there might be a vexatious ambiguity present.

Again I was briefly interrupted, this time by Senator Long of Louisiana, who pointed out that whichever body made the declaration of Presidential inability, what was important was that Congress should be the final judge of the question. I agreed that the two-thirds vote of both Houses of Congress was the greatest safeguard we could give the President; then I moved on to the one final point Senator Gore's presentation had made. The Senator from Tennessee, I said, was of the opinion that if there was any doubt, we should wait. But

> I doubt very much that there have been many pieces of proposed legislation, certainly none related to constitutional amendments, that have passed this body in which there has not been considerable and heated debate as to whether some of the proposed language was right or wrong. . . . I think we have to determine two questions. Is the conference report the best piece of proposed legislation we can get and is it needed? As loudly as I can, I say that we must answer both of these questions in the affirmative.
>
> Some Senators might say, "What is the rush? We are not ready to adjourn yet. We can send the measure back to the conference committee and have it reworked."
>
> To those who are students of history I do not have to document again and again the fact that we have labored for 187 years as a country and we have not yet been able to get sufficient support for any type of proposed legislation in this area. In 38 of those years we had no Vice President. We have had three serious presidential disabilities. . . . Can Senators imagine what would happen to the United States and the world today if the United States were without a President? For all intents and purposes, we would be involved in world chaos from which we could not recover.

For more than 18 months the Senate has studied the proposed legislation. Two sets of hearings have been held. I appreciate the support that Senators have given us in this effort.

In the last session of Congress, the Senate passed the proposed legislation by a vote of 65 to 0. In the present session of the Congress, the Senate passed the measure by a vote of 72 to 0.

This measure is not something which we have arrived at on the spur of the moment. We have had controversy and differences of opinion over individual words. I should like to remind all of my colleagues that during the past few years we have received over 100 different proposals. Since I have been chairman of the Subcommittee on Constitutional Amendments, during the past few months, 26 different proposals have been submitted.

I point out that if those who had the foresight to introduce proposed legislation on the subject—the Senator from North Carolina, the Senator from Illinois, the Senator from Kentucky, the Senator from Idaho, and others—had not been willing to agree and had not been willing to try to reach a consensus, and if it had not been for the guiding hand of the American Bar Association to try to get those with differing views together, we would not be as far along as we are now. I do not believe that we should let two words separate us.

Again Senator Long asked if I would yield. When I did so, he spoke briefly on the urgency of coming to some decision now. He himself was not convinced that our form of amendment was perfect, he said; but, "if we start all over again, not only will the junior Senator from Louisiana have two or three additional suggestions that he would like to urge, but other senators will also have suggestions to make, and we shall be 100 years getting to the point which we have now reached."

Senator Ervin then spoke for a moment.

When we started to consider the proposal, the Senator from Indiana and I had a discussion. We were convinced of the old adage that too many cooks spoil the broth. We had more cooks with more zeal concerned with preparing this "broth" than any piece of proposed legislation I have ever seen in the time I have been in the Senate. If it had not been for the perseverance, the patience, and the willingness to compromise which was manifested on a multitude of occasions by the junior Senator from Indiana, we would never have gotten the resolution out of the subcommittee, much less through the full Judiciary Committee and then through the conference with the House. I am of the opinion that the conference report which the Senator from Indiana is seeking to have approved would submit to the States the very best possible resolution on the subject obtainable in the Congress of the United States as it is now constituted. The Senator from Indiana deserves the thanks of the American people for the fact that he was willing to change the ingredients of the broth in order to appease a multitude of different cooks who had different recipes for it, including myself.

I thanked my friend from North Carolina, saying that we were "greatly indebted to him for his 'seasoning' and his willingness to compromise. Although there were many cooks, we had a paddle large enough so that we could all get our hands on it and stir."

I paused a moment and looked down at the notes I had made on the points Senator Gore had raised. They had all been covered. Glancing at Conrad, on my left, I saw him drawing his index finger across his throat in a cutting motion: my allotted time was close to expiration. I took a deep breath and hoped I could end my presentation on the right note.

I should like to conclude with one last thought. We know that over the great Archives Building downtown there is a statement engraved in stone. Standing out in bold letters is the statement: "What is past is prologue."

I cannot help but feel that history has been trying to tell us something.

There was a time in the history of this great Nation when carrier pigeons were the fastest means of communication and the Army was rolling on horse-drawn caissons. Perhaps it did not make any difference then whether the Nation had a President who was able at all times to fulfill all the duties and powers of his office. But today, with the awesome power at our disposal, when armies can be moved half way around the world in a matter of hours, and when it is possible actually to destroy civilization in a matter of minutes, it is high time that we listened to history and make absolutely certain that there will be a President of the United States at all times, a President who has complete control and will be able to perform all the powers and duties of his office.

I slumped to my seat. We had had enough time—there was even a little to spare, during which Senators Javits and Cooper briefly expressed their support of our amendment. Then our time expired.

Senator Gore had three minutes left in which to close his presentation. He proceeded to do so in his usual eloquent manner, contending that there was still doubt over the language. "Let us return the report to conference; let it be clarified."

Fred Harris, the capable new senator from Oklahoma, was presiding at that moment. "All time has expired," he stated. "The question is on agreeing to the conference report."

It had been previously agreed that there would be a yea and nay vote on final passage. The clerk began to call the vote. "Well, Counselor," I said, "it's all over but the shouting." Conrad glanced up from the three-foot-long card listing the senators in alphabetical order with which he was trying to keep track of the voting. "Good luck, Senator," he said.

The next ten minutes seemed the longest of my life. "Mr. Aiken." Not present. "Mr. Allott."—"Aye." "Mr. Bass." I thought of the exception he had taken earlier to the use of the word "immediately," and wondered whether he would come with us now or support his colleague from Tennessee. — "Aye." "Mr. Bayh." I shouted my affirmative vote. Down through the C's. "Mr. Dirksen." —"Aye." Mentally I thanked the Minority Leader for his support, despite his previous strong feelings about his own version of the amendment. Down through the E's. "Mr. Ervin." — "Aye." Where would we have been without Sam Ervin's constitutional wisdom, his sympathy and stalwart support, his flexibility in the conference committee? The F's. "Mr. Gore."—"Nay." It was, I suddenly realized, the first negative vote. "Mr. Kennedy of Massachusetts." — "Aye." "Mr. Kennedy of New York." — "Aye." What terrible memories this whole issue must have raised for them, I reflected. It was the tragic assassination of President Kennedy which shocked the country and Congress into the realization that our amendment was necessary. "Mr. Lausche." — "Nay." "Mr. McCarthy." — "Nay." "Mr. Mondale." — "Nay." I thought that Fritz Mondale must be in an extremely embarrassing position; newly come to the Senate, he was obviously reluctant to oppose his senior colleague, Gene McCarthy.

It was impossible to say precisely who cast the sixty-sixth vote. The Senate acoustics are not the best. There was noise in the Chamber, making matters worse. Conrad was frantically trying to keep track, but by the time the clerk had gone through the alphabet once, then started over for latecomers, Conrad's unofficial count was no longer certain, despite the help of Bill Fulbright, sitting next to him and pointing out senators he had missed on his list. There was a "nay" vote here and there, and I realized that some of our supporters were absent. At last the roll call was completed.

"On this vote the yeas are 68, the nays 5," announced the Presiding Officer. "Two-thirds of the senators present and voting have voted in the affirmative; the conference report is agreed to."

What followed was a blur to me: the congratulations of colleagues who had worked along with us; the exchange of looks with Don Channell and Lowell Beck of the ABA, who had been sitting in the visitor's gallery hanging on to every word; a smile from Marvella, who was also sitting above; the exuberant walk back to the Senate Office Building with those who had helped guide the amendment to its final passage pummeling me on the back. We had experienced success and failure during the many months as we labored through the legislative thicket. But this was a new feeling. Hard as it might be to believe, once and for all the job was done. The final outcome, of course, was in the hands of the state legislators, but for the moment I could relax and enjoy the exhilaration of victory. It had not always been that way.

A Nation Speaks

At last the Congress had spoken. But the United States Constitution is not so lightly amended. The final determination had to come, not from the federal government, but from the 7,741 senators and representatives who made up the state legislatures throughout the nation. Three-quarters of these legislatures—thirty-eight out of fifty—would have to concur that our amendment should become a part of the Constitution.

We knew that the process of state ratification would be the most long and drawn out, if not the most difficult, stage of the journey. How long it would take was anyone's guess. The Twenty-second Amendment, which allowed the President a maximum of two terms in office, had taken forty-seven months to secure approval. On the other hand, the Twelfth Amendment, which altered the electoral college, had spent only seven months in the limbo between congressional passage and state ratification.

Moreover, we were not merely uncertain how long it would take to pass; the question of whether it would pass at all was a very real one. Of the first twelve amendments proposed to the Constitution, only ten now make up the Bill of Rights. The other two failed to receive approval from the thirteen states. Since that time, three additional amendments have failed to obtain state ratification after having received the necessary two-thirds vote in each house of Congress.

At the moment of congressional passage, the intricate mechanism of the American Bar Association went into high gear. The state bar associations, which had long been directing their advocacy of S.J. Res. 1 toward the members of Congress, shifted their target and began to bombard the state legislators with information about our amendment, preparing and distributing to them a comprehensive critique of the provisions of S.J. Res. 1. A local member of each state bar association had been assigned the individual responsibility for mobilizing support within his state. In addition, numerous junior bar associations had formed state speaker's bureaus to disseminate the message.

My staff and I did what we could to hasten the process. I addressed letters to each of the state governors, soliciting their assistance in obtaining ratification in their state legislatures. We also sent masses of detailed correspondence to the state legislative leaders— the men who would direct the flow of legislation within their own states.

Before noon on Wednesday, July 7, less than twenty-four hours after final congressional passage of S.J. Res. 1, I received a call from Senator Tom McIntyre of New Hampshire. The legislature of his state was anxious to be the first to ratify the proposed amendment; but it was due to adjourn at midnight on Friday, July 9. Could we, he asked, speed things up so that the Granite State could have first crack at ratification? All day long we were in touch with Senator McIntyre's office. The New Hampshire legislator was more than willing to fly to Washington, obtain the necessary papers, then return and present them to the governor prior to adjournment. Conrad made a series of calls to the General Services Administration and the National Archives, finally to be informed by the GSA that it would be impossible to prepare the necessary documents in time. The New Hampshire legislature's valiant effort came to nothing, and they adjourned sine die without considering the proposed amendment.

The next week ratification began in earnest. Nebraska and Wisconsin were both eager to be the first state to ratify. Nebraska notified the Archives that its unicameral legislature had ratified the amendment on July 12; Wisconsin's final action came the next day. Yet it is still unclear which of the two states actually ratified first. The proposed amendment, introduced in Nebraska by state Senator Marvin E. Stromer as Legislative Resolution 72, was cosponsored by almost the entire legislature. The Resolution was passed July 12, the same day it was introduced. It was quickly signed by the president of the legislature, Kenneth Bowen, and by Hugo F. Srb, the clerk of the legislature. There was some dispute over whether a resolution ratifying a constitutional amendment required the signature of the governor,[1] Frank B. Morrison, who was out of town that day. Finally, acting as governor, Lieutenant Governor Phillip C. Sorenson approved the measure at 10:19 A.M. on July 13—after the Wisconsin State Assembly had officially ratified. In all probability the argument will never be solved to the satisfaction of conscientious Wisconsin and Nebraska legislators. In any case, the Wisconsin State Assembly ratified by a vote of 84 to 11, and the senate followed suit by 28 to 0. The first two states had ratified what was to be the Twenty-fifth Amendment.

The next state to ratify was Oklahoma, on July 16, 1965; Massachusetts was fourth, on August 9.

Two weeks later, we heard that the resolution had been passed by the Pennsylvania state senate, but that it had become logjammed in the house of representatives. The chairman of the house committee to which it had been referred was dissatisfied with the form of the amendment. We heard he said he intended to sit on it and hold it in committee. However, after many telephone calls between Washington and Harrisburg, the Pennsylvania legislature ratified on August 18.

Kentucky was the sixth state to ratify. The governor, Edward

---

[1] Research disclosed substantial evidence to the effect that the Constitution does not require the state governor's signature after the legislature has passed it. In their capacity of ratification, state legislatures are performing a federal function entirely different from that of state lawmaking which, under most circumstances, does require the approval of the state's chief executive.

Breathitt, had called a special session of the state legislature, partially for the consideration of the proposed amendment. It was ratified on September 16.

Arizona ratified on September 22 and Michigan on October 5, bringing the number to eight.

My home state of Indiana was the ninth to ratify. Governor Roger Branigin called a special session of Hoosier State legislators —mainly for the purpose of considering legislative reapportionment. Our amendment was on the agenda as well. I had been invited to address a joint session of the state legislature, in which I had served for eight years. It was a pleasure to "come home," so to speak, and our amendment was ratified that same day, October 20, by an overwhelming vote of both houses.

California was tenth to ratify, on October 21.

There was some difficulty in Arkansas. As the Arkansas legislature was preparing to consider the amendment, Representative Paul Van Dalsen distributed to each member a copy of a *South Carolina Law Review* article which was extremely critical of some aspects of the amendment. He was finally able to convince the Arkansas speaker, J. H. Cottrell, that the amendment was undesirable, and Cottrell committed himself not to bring it up for the vote. Thereupon the members of the state bar association went to work, vigorously arguing the amendment's merits before Speaker Cottrell, who promised that he would reconsider his stand. In addition the ABA asked Governor Orval Faubus to use his good offices to help secure ratification. On November 4, the goal was accomplished; Arkansas was the eleventh state to ratify.

New Jersey followed on November 29. Delaware ratified our amendment on December 7, the 178th anniversary of its being the first state to ratify the original Constitution. Utah followed on January 17, 1966.

West Virginia was fifteenth to ratify, on January 20th. Some days before, Conrad had received a call from the floor leader of the West Virginia senate. His legislature, we discovered, was very much concerned about the disability provision. Would it be possible for them to ratify one part of the amendment and not the other? Conrad told them that this was impossible, and referred the problem to me. The next morning, I had a long telephone conversation with the West Virginia floor leader and the chairman of the state senate judiciary committee, in which I attempted to explain the reasoning behind the disability provisions of the amendment. Whether or not these conversations were helpful, West Virginia finally came through.

Four days later, Maine ratified, followed by Rhode Island on January 28. This brought us up to seventeen.

In Colorado, too, there were problems. Back in July 1965, the Governor had called the Colorado legislature into special session to deal with the problems created by the disastrous floods which had hit Colorado and many other areas of the country in the spring of 1965. This session was to be limited to three days and although it was not included on the agenda the Governor presented, the amendment was introduced. A severely critical article in the *Denver Post* maintained that although there was nothing to be said against the amendment itself, it was inappropriate to consider it during a special session. Nevertheless, the matter came to a vote at that time. The amendment passed, but not by the two-thirds vote required by a peculiarity of the Colorado constitution relating to ratification of constitutional amendments. This provision is required by neither the United States Constitution nor any other state constitution. We hastily abandoned our efforts in Colorado for the time being. We did not want the black mark of an outright defeat by any legislature if it could be avoided and had, early in the ratification process, taken great care to avoid such blemishes on our record of ratification.[2]

But, with the clearing of the calendar in the New Year, the Colorado legislature went back into regular session. This time, an editorial in the *Denver Post* criticized not the timing but the wisdom of the amendment itself, with the result that a young Democratic legislator, John S. Carroll, began a crusade against it. The Colorado legislators felt no real sense of urgency. As State Senator L.T. Skiff-

[2] In Alabama, for example, we had discussed with the state bar association the advisability of trying for ratification when the legislature was in session. My own feeling was that no one could be certain what would happen in Alabama. I could imagine Governor George Wallace seizing on the criticism contained in the *South Carolina Law Review*, and making opposition of the amendment into a states' rights issue. This could hurt us not only in Alabama, but elsewhere as well. We delayed our efforts there, and the Alabama state legislature never got around to considering the Twenty-fifth Amendment.

ington said, "We got along without it for a hundred and fifty years, and we could get along without it now." The weekend of January 30, Lesher, Conrad, and I worked desperately preparing a careful analysis of the amendment and a rebuttal to the arguments raised against it. This analysis was sent over my signature to the speaker of the Colorado house, Alan Dines. Early Monday morning, we mimeographed it in quantity, planning to send a copy to each member of the Colorado legislature. The material was carefully bundled and rushed to National Airport to be flown to Denver, where the legislature was to debate and vote on the amendment the next day. To our distress, all planes were grounded by a raging blizzard. In desperation, Conrad and Lesher called the bar representatives in Denver, and spent almost an hour dictating the entire critique over the telephone. It was mimeographed in Denver and distributed to each member of the legislature, as we originally planned. This joint effort must have won us some of the support we thought we might lose there, for on February 3 Colorado became the eighteenth state to ratify.

New Mexico ratified on February 3, bringing us to the halfway point. Kansas followed on February 9, Vermont on February 10, Alaska on February 18.[3]

We made steady progress through the first half of 1966. Idaho ratified on March 2, Hawaii on March 3, Virginia—reacting to the strong leadership of its native son, ABA president Lewis Powell— on March 8. Mississippi, New York, Maryland, and Missouri followed during the month of March. That brought us to twenty-nine —nine states away from our goal.

By the end of March, we realized that few of the remaining states would be holding regular legislative sessions during 1966. Thus, we began to concentrate on the handful of states that were holding special sessions in response to the Supreme Court decision on reapportionment. In this way, New Hampshire, which had tried

[3] On February 18, too, Georgia was on the verge of becoming the twenty-third state to ratify, but they never quite made it. It was late in the evening of the session's final day; both houses had gone through the procedure required for ratification, but somewhere along the line a relatively insignificant procedural step necessary for finalizing the process never was taken. We never discovered what actually took place, but it appeared that, in the rush which surrounds adjournment in 99 per cent of state legislatures, the necessary papers had been lost or mislaid.

to be the first state to ratify, became the thirtieth on June 13. Louisiana—the last state to ratify in 1966—followed suit in a regular
session on July 5. We resigned ourselves to the fact that further
legislative efforts in the states that had not yet ratified would have
to await the convening of regular sessions the following year. Preparation continued on the necessary groundwork to do battle then.

When the new year arrived, we were only seven states away
from the thirty-eight required for final ratification. Early in January, we wrote the governors of all the remaining states whose
legislatures would be in session, urging them to use their influence
in helping to complete the task. We were coming into the home
stretch now: Tennessee ratified at the end of the second week in
January, Wyoming followed on January 25, and Washington and
Iowa the day after. We had only three states to go; then two, as
Oregon ratified on February 2.

It is considered quite an honor to be the state responsible for
actually incorporating an amendment into the Constitution. The
last state to ratify plays this role. Therefore, North Dakota's two
houses passed the resolution on February 9, with the understanding
that they were the thirty-eighth state to ratify—only to be informed by the Archives in Washington that someone had mis-
counted and they were only the thirty-seventh. The Flickertail
State legislative leaders decided to declare the ratification illegal, on
the technicality that there had been only a voice vote in one house.
They hoped to pass the measure after one more state had ratified
and thus make their niche in history. But before they could bring the
amendment to ratification again, both Minnesota and Nevada ratified
on February 10. The amendment was now a part of the Constitution.

Technically, no Presidential signature is necessary after a constitutional amendment has been ratified by three-quarters of the
state legislatures. But President Lyndon Johnson, desiring to give
recognition to the importance of our accomplishment, held a formal
ceremony in the East Room of the White House. There, after GSA
administrator Lawson Knott officially signed the proclamation, the
President of the United States affixed his signature to it as well—
not as an official part of the amending process but as a witness to
the GSA proclamation. The television cameras whirred away as the
document was signed by the President and Knott, flanked by Vice

President Humphrey, Senate President pro tempore Carl Hayden, Speaker of the House John McCormack, Congressmen Celler and McCulloch, and the junior senator from Indiana.

In 1787, John Dickenson of Delaware, a delegate to the Constitutional Convention meeting in Philadelphia, had asked, "What is meant by the term disability and who shall be the judge of it?" On February 23, 1966, at 1:18 P.M., 179 years later, in the East Room of the White House, John Dickenson received his answer.

Appendix

Chronology

January 20, 1961	John F. Kennedy inaugurated as President of the United States; Lyndon B. Johnson inaugurated as Vice President
November 6, 1962	Birch Bayh elected United States Senator
June 11, 1963	Subcommittee on Constitutional Amendments, under chairmanship of Senator Estes Kefauver, begins hearings on presidential succession and disability
June 25, 1963	S.J. Res. 35, initially proposed by a special subcommittee of the New York State Bar Association (Martin Taylor, chairman), and sponsored by Senators Kefauver and Keating, favorably reported to full Committee on the Judiciary
August 10, 1963	Senator Kefauver dies of a heart attack
September 30, 1963	Judiciary Committee ratifies appointment of Senator Birch Bayh as Chairman of the Subcommittee on Constitutional Amendments
November 22, 1963	President Kennedy assassinated in Dallas, Texas; Lyndon B. Johnson becomes President of the United States
December 12, 1963	Senator Bayh introduces S.J. Res. 139 in Senate
January 17, 1964	S.J. Res. 139 referred to Subcommittee on Constitutional Amendments

January 20–21, 1964	American Bar Association Conference on Presidential Inability and Succession held in Mayflower Hotel, Washington; consensus of conference supports S.J. Res. 139
January 22, 1964– March 5, 1964	Subcommittee on Constitutional Amendments holds hearings on joint resolutions relating to the problem of presidential inability and filling of vacancies in the office of the vice president
May 25, 1964	ABA holds Conference on Presidential Inability and Vice-Presidential Vacancy
May 27, 1964	S.J. Res. 139, revised to conform with ABA consensus, favorably reported to Judiciary Committee
August 4, 1964	Revised S.J. Res. 139 unanimously approved by Senate Judiciary Committee
September 28, 1964	S.J. Res. 139 passed by voice vote in Senate
September 29, 1964	Senate reconsiders vote on S.J. Res. 139; resolution is passed again in Senate, by roll call vote of 65 to 0
October 3, 1964	Congress adjourns sine die with no further action on S. J. Res. 139
November 2, 1964	Lyndon B. Johnson re-elected President of the United States; Hubert H. Humphrey elected Vice President; Senator Kenneth Keating, author of S.J. Res. 35, defeated in New York senatorial election
January 4, 1965	H.J. Res. 1, the House equivalent of S.J. Res. 1, introduced by Congressman Emanuel Celler in House of Representatives
January 6, 1965	S.J. Res. 1 introduced by Senator Bayh in Senate
January 28, 1965	Presidential message to the Senate supports S.J. Res. 1
January 29, 1965	Senate Subcommittee on Constitutional Amendments holds hearings on S.J. Res. 1 and other measures relating to the problem of presidential inability and filling of vacancies in the office of vice president
February 1, 1965	S.J. Res. 1 favorably reported to Judiciary Committee by Subcommittee on Constitutional Amendments
February 4, 1965	S.J. Res. 1 favorably reported to Senate by Judiciary Committee
February 7–17, 1965	House Judiciary Committee holds hearings on H.J. Res. 1 and other proposals relating to presidential inability
February 19, 1965	Senate Joint Resolution 1 passes Senate 72–0
February 22, 1965	S.J. Res. 1 delivered to House of Representatives
February 25, 1965	Senator Roman Hruska officially appointed to the Subcommittee on Constitutional Amendments

April 13, 1965   House of Representatives passes S.J. Res. 1, in modified form, by vote of 368–29

April 22, 1965   S.J. Res. 1 returned to Senate, which disagrees with House amendments and requests conference

April 28, 1965   House insists on its amendments and agrees to conference

May 11, 1965–   Conference committee, headed by Senator Bayh and
June 10, 1965   Representative Celler, considers S.J. Res. 1

June 30, 1965   Joint conference report on S.J. Res. 1 passed by House of Representatives and delivered to Senate

July 6, 1965   Senate passes joint conference report on S.J. Res. 1, by roll call vote of 68–5

February 10, 1967   Minnesota and Nevada become the 37th and 38th states to ratify the Twenty-fifth Amendment

February 23, 1967   White House ceremony at which time the Twenty-fifth Amendment to the United States Constitution is signed by General Services Administrator Lawson Knott and witnessed by President Lyndon B. Johnson

Texts

CONSENSUS ON PRESIDENTIAL INABILITY AND SUCCESSION

January 20 and 21, 1964

The Conference on Presidential Inability and Succession was convened by the American Bar Association at the Mayflower Hotel, Washington, D.C., on January 20 and 21, 1964. The conferees were Walter E. Craig, president, American Bar Association; Herbert Brownell, president, Association of the Bar of the City of New York, and a former Attorney General of the United States; John D. Feerick, attorney, New York; Paul A. Freund, professor of law, Harvard University; Jonathan C. Gibson, chairman, Standing Committee on Jurisprudence and Law Reform, American Bar Association; Richard H. Hansen, attorney, Lincoln, Nebr.; James C. Kirby, Jr., associate professor of law, Vanderbilt University, and a former chief counsel to the Subcommittee on Constitutional Amendments, Senate Judiciary Committee; Ross L. Malone, past president of the American Bar Association, and a former Deputy Attorney General of the United States; Charles B. Nutting, dean of the National Law Center; Lewis F. Powell, Jr., president-elect, American Bar Association; Sylvester C. Smith, Jr., past president, American Bar Association; Martin Taylor, chairman, Committee on Federal Constitution, New York State Bar Association; and Edward L. Wright, chairman, house of delegates, American Bar Association.

The members of the conference reviewed as a group the following statement at the close of their discussions. Although there was general agreement on the statement, the members of the conference were not asked to affix their signatures; and it should not be assumed that every member necessarily subscribes to every recommendation included in the statement.

The conference considered the question of action to be taken in the event of inability of the President to perform the duties of his office. It was the consensus of the conference that:

1. Agreements between the President and Vice President or person next in the line of succession provide a partial solution, but not an acceptable permanent solution of the problem.

2. An amendment to the Constitution of the United States should be adopted to resolve the problems which would arise in the event of the inability of the President to discharge the powers and duties of his office.

3. The amendment should provide that in the event of the inability of the President the powers and duties, but not the office, shall devolve upon the Vice President or person next in line of succession for the duration of the inability of the President or until expiration of his term of office.

4. The amendment should provide that the inability of the President may be established by declaration in writing of the President. In the event that the President does not make known his inability, it may be established by action of the Vice President or person next in line of succession with the concurrence of a majority of the Cabinet or by action of such other body as the Congress may by law provide.

5. The amendment should provide that the ability of the President to resume the powers and duties of his office shall be established by his declaration in writing. In the event that the Vice President and a majority of the Cabinet or such other body as Congress may by law provide shall not concur in the declaration of the President, the continuing inability of the President may then be determined by the vote of two-thirds of the elected Members of each House of the Congress.

The conference also considered the related question of Presidential succession. It was the consensus that:

1. The Constitution should be amended to provide that in the event of the death, resignation, or removal of the President, the Vice President or the person next in line of succession shall succeed to the office for the unexpired term.

2. It is highly desirable that the office of Vice President be filled at all times. An amendment to the Constitution should be adopted providing that when a vacancy occurs in the office of Vice President, the President shall nominate a person who, upon approval by a majority of the elected Mem-

bers of Congress meeting in joint session, shall then become Vice President for the unexpired term.

SENATE JOINT RESOLUTION 35

JOINT RESOLUTION Proposing an amendment to the Constitution of the United States relating to cases where the President is unable to discharge the powers and duties of his office

Resolved by the Senate and House of Representatives of the United States of America in Congress assembled (two-thirds of each House concurring therein), That the following article is proposed as an amendment to the Constitution of the United States, which shall be valid to all intents and purposes as part of the Constitution only if ratified by the legislatures of three-fourths of the several States within seven years from the date of its submission by the Congress:

"ARTICLE ——

"In case of the removal of the President from office or of his death or resignation, the said office shall devolve on the Vice President. In case of the inability of the President to discharge the powers and duties of the said office, the said powers and duties shall devolve on the Vice President, until the inability be removed. The Congress may by law provide for the case of removal, death, resignation or inability, both of the President and Vice President, declaring what officer shall then be President, or, in case of inability, act as President, and such officer shall be or act as President accordingly, until a President shall be elected or, in case of inability, until the inability shall be earlier removed. The commencement and termination of any inability shall be determined by such method as Congress shall by law provide."

SENATE JOINT RESOLUTION 139

(original form)

JOINT RESOLUTION Proposing an amendment to the Constitution of the United States relating to succession to the Presidency and Vice Presidency and to cases where the President is unable to discharge the powers and duties of his office

Resolved by the Senate and House of Representatives of the United States of America in Congress assembled (two-thirds of each House concurring therein), That the following article is proposed as an amendment to the Constitution of the United States, which shall be valid to all intents and purposes as part of the Constitution when ratified by the legislatures of three-fourths of the several States:

"ARTICLE ——

"*Section 1.* In case of the removal of the President from office, or of his death or resignation, the Vice President shall become President for the unexpired portion of the then current term. Within a period of thirty days thereafter, the new President shall nominate a Vice President who shall take office upon confirmation by both Houses of Congress by a majority of those present and voting.

"*Sec. 2.* In case of the removal of the Vice President from office, or of his death or resignation, the President, within a period of thirty days thereafter, shall nominate a Vice President who shall take office upon confirmation by both Houses of Congress by a majority vote of those present and voting.

"*Sec. 3.* If the President shall declare in writing that he is unable to discharge the powers and duties of his office, such powers and duties shall be discharged by the Vice President as Acting President.

"*Sec. 4.* If the President does not so declare, the Vice President, if satisfied that such inability exists, shall, upon the written approval of a majority of the heads of the executive departments in office, assume the discharge of the powers and duties of the office as Acting President.

"*Sec. 5.* Whenever the President makes public announcement in writing that his inability has terminated, he shall resume the discharge of the powers and duties of his office on the seventh day after making such announcement, or at such earlier time after such announcement as he and the Vice President may determine. But if the Vice President, with the written approval of a majority of the heads of executive departments in office at the time of such announcement, transmits to the Congress his written declaration that in his opinion the President's inability has not terminated, the Congress shall thereupon consider the issue. If the Congress is not then in session, it shall assemble in special session on the call of the Vice President. If the Congress determines by concurrent resolution, adopted with the approval of two-thirds of the Members present in each House, that the inability of the President has not terminated, thereupon, notwithstanding any further announcement by the President, the Vice President shall discharge such powers and duties as Acting President until the occurrence of the earliest of the following events: (1) the Acting President proclaims that the President's inability has ended, (2) the Congress determines by concurrent resolution, adopted with the approval of a majority of the Members present in each House, that the President's inability has ended, or (3) the President's term ends.

"*Sec. 6.* (a) (1) If, by reason of death, resignation, removal from office, inability, or failure to qualify, there is neither a President nor Vice President to discharge the powers and duties of the office of President, then the officer of the United States who is highest on the following list, and who is not under disability to discharge the powers and duties of the office of President, shall act as President: Secretary of State, Secretary of Treasury, Secretary of Defense, Attorney General, Postmaster General, Secretary of

Interior, Secretary of Agriculture, Secretary of Commerce, Secretary of Labor, Secretary of Health, Education, and Welfare, and such other heads of executive departments as may be established hereafter and in order of their establishment.

"(2) The same rule shall apply in the case of the death, resignation, removal from office, or inability of an individual acting as President under this section.

"(3) To qualify under this section, an individual must have been appointed, by and with the advice and consent of the Senate, prior to the time of the death, resignation, removal from office, or inability of the President and Vice President, and must not be under impeachment by the House of Representatives at the time the powers and duties of the office of President devolve upon him.

"(b) In case of the death, resignation, or removal of both the President and Vice President, his successor shall be President until the expiration of the then current Presidential term. In case of the inability of the President and Vice President to discharge the powers and duties of the office of President, his successor, as designated in this section, shall be subject to the provisions of sections 3, 4, and 5 of this article as if he were a Vice President acting in case of disability of the President.

"(c) The taking of the oath of office by an individual specified in the list of paragraph (1) of subsection (a) shall be held to constitute his resignation from the office by virtue of the holding of which he qualifies to act as President.

"(d) During the period that any individual acts as President under this section, his compensation shall be at the rate then provided by law in the case of the President.

"*Sec.* 7. This article shall be inoperative unless it shall have been ratified as an amendment to the Constitution by the legislatures of three-fourths of the several States within seven years from the date of its submission."

SENATE JOINT RESOLUTION 139

*(as reported out of committee and
passed by the Senate)*

JOINT RESOLUTION Proposing an amendment to the Constitution of the United States relating to succession to the Presidency and Vice Presidency and to cases where the President is unable to discharge the powers and duties of his office

Resolved by the Senate and House of Representatives of the United States of America in Congress assembled (two-thirds of each House concurring therein), That the following article is proposed as an amendment to the Constitution of the United States, which shall be valid to all intents and purposes as part of the Constitution when ratified by the legislatures of three-fourths of the several States within seven years from the date of its submission by the Congress:

"ARTICLE ——"

"*Section 1.* In case of the removal of the President from office or of his death or resignation, the Vice President shall become President.

"*Sec. 2.* Whenever there is a vacancy in the office of the Vice President, the President shall nominate a Vice President who shall take office upon confirmation by a majority of both Houses of Congress.

"*Sec. 3.* If the President declares in writing that he is unable to discharge the powers and duties of his office, such powers and duties shall be discharged by the Vice President as Acting President.

"*Sec. 4.* If the President does not so declare, and the Vice President with the written concurrence of a majority of the heads of the executive departments or such other body as Congress may by law provide, transmits to the Congress his written declaration that the President is unable to discharge the powers and duties of his office, the Vice President shall immediately assume the powers and duties of the office as Acting President.

"*Sec. 5.* Whenever the President transmits to the Congress his written declaration that no inability exists, he shall resume the powers and duties of his office unless the Vice President, with the written concurrence of a majority of the heads of the executive departments or such other body as Congress may by law provide, transmits within two days to the Congress his written declaration that the President is unable to discharge the powers and duties of his office. Thereupon Congress shall immediately decide the issue. If the Congress determines by two-thirds vote of both Houses that the President is unable to discharge the powers and duties of the office, the Vice President shall continue to discharge the same as Acting President; otherwise the President shall resume the powers and duties of his office."

SENATE JOINT RESOLUTION 1[1]

(original form)

JOINT RESOLUTION Proposing an amendment to the Constitution of the United States relating to succession to the Presidency and Vice Presidency and to cases where the President is unable to discharge the powers and duties of his office

Resolved by the Senate and House of Representatives of the United States of America in Congress assembled (two-thirds of each House concurring therein), That the following article is proposed as an amendment to the Constitution of the United States, which shall be valid to all intents and purposes as part of the Constitution when ratified by the legislatures of

[1] The text of House Joint Resolution 1 is identical to this.

three-fourths of the several States within seven years from the date of its submission by the Congress:

"ARTICLE ——

"*Section 1.* In case of the removal of the President from office or of his death or resignation, the Vice President shall become President.

"*Sec. 2.* Whenever there is a vacancy in the office of the Vice President, the President shall nominate a Vice President who shall take office upon confirmation by a majority vote of both Houses of Congress.

"*Sec. 3.* If the President declares in writing that he is unable to discharge the powers and duties of his office, such powers and duties shall be discharged by the Vice President as Acting President.

"*Sec. 4.* If the President does not so declare, and the Vice President with the written concurrence of a majority of the heads of the executive departments or such other body as Congress may by law provide, transmits to the Congress his written declaration that the President is unable to discharge the powers and duties of his office, the Vice President shall immediately assume the powers and duties of the office as Acting President.

"*Sec. 5.* Whenever the President transmits to the Congress his written declaration that no inability exists, he shall resume the powers and duties of his office unless the Vice President, with the written concurrence of a majority of the heads of the executive departments or such other body as Congress may by law provide, transmits within two days to the Congress his written declaration that the President is unable to discharge the powers and duties of his office. Thereupon Congress will immediately decide the issue. If the Congress determines by two-thirds vote of both Houses that the President is unable to discharge the powers and duties of the office, the Vice President shall continue to discharge the same as Acting President; otherwise the President shall resume the powers and duties of his office."

SENATE JOINT RESOLUTION 1

(as passed by the United States Senate)

JOINT RESOLUTION Proposing an amendment to the Constitution of the United States relating to succession to the Presidency and Vice Presidency and to cases where the President is unable to discharge the powers and duties of his office

Resolved by the Senate and House of Representatives of the United States of America in Congress assembled (two-thirds of each House concurring therein), That the following article is proposed as an amendment to the Constitution of the United States, which shall be valid to all intents and purposes as part of the Constitution when ratified by the legislatures of three-fourths of the several States within seven years from the date of its submission by the Congress:

"ARTICLE ——

"*Section 1.* In case of the removal of the President from office or of his death or resignation, the Vice President shall become President.

"*Sec. 2.* Whenever there is a vacancy in the office of the Vice President, the President shall nominate a Vice President who shall take office upon confirmation by a majority vote of both Houses of Congress.

"*Sec. 3.* Whenever the President transmits to the President of the Senate and the Speaker of the House of Representatives his written declaration that he is unable to discharge the powers and duties of his office, such powers and duties shall be discharged by the Vice President as Acting President.

"*Sec. 4.* Whenever the Vice President, and a majority of the principal officers of the executive departments or such other body as Congress may by law provide, transmit to the President of the Senate and the Speaker of the House of Representatives their written declaration that the President is unable to discharge the powers and duties of his office, the Vice President shall immediately assume the powers and duties of the office as Acting President.

"*Sec. 5.* Whenever the President transmits to the President of the Senate and the Speaker of the House of Representatives his written declaration that no inability exists, he shall resume the powers and duties of his office unless the Vice President, and a majority of the principal officers of the executive departments or such other body as Congress shall by law provide, transmit within seven days to the President of the Senate and the Speaker of the House of Representatives their written declaration that the President is unable to discharge the powers and duties of his office. Thereupon Congress shall immediately proceed to decide the issue. If the Congress determines by two-thirds vote of both Houses that the President is unable to discharge the powers and duties of the office, the Vice President shall continue to discharge the same as Acting President; otherwise the President shall resume the powers and duties of his office."

SENATE JOINT RESOLUTION 1

(as passed by the House of Representatives)

JOINT RESOLUTION Proposing an amendment to the Constitution of the United States relating to succession to the Presidency and Vice Presidency and to cases where the President is unable to discharge the powers and duties of his office

Resolved by the Senate and House of Representatives of the United States of America in Congress assembled (two-thirds of each House concurring therein), That the following article is proposed as an amendment to the Constitution of the United States, which shall be valid to all intents and purposes as part of the Constitution, when ratified by the legislatures of three-fourths of the several States within seven years from the date of its submission by the Congress:

"ARTICLE ——

"*Section 1.* In case of the removal of the President from office or of his death or resignation, the Vice President shall become President.

"*Sec. 2.* Whenever there is a vacancy in the office of the Vice President, the President shall nominate a Vice President who shall take office upon confirmation by a majority vote of both Houses of Congress.

"*Sec. 3.* Whenever the President transmits to the President pro tempore of the Senate and the Speaker of the House of Representatives his written declaration that he is unable to discharge the powers and duties of his office, and until he transmits a written declaration to the contrary, such powers and duties shall be discharged by the Vice President as Acting President.

"*Sec. 4.* Whenever the Vice President and a majority of the principal officers of the executive departments, or such other body as Congress may by law provide, transmit to the President pro tempore of the Senate and the Speaker of the House of Representatives their written declaration that the President is unable to discharge the powers and duties of his office, the Vice President shall immediately assume the powers and duties of the office as Acting President.

"Thereafter, when the President transmits to the President pro tempore of the Senate and the Speaker of the House of Representatives his written declaration that no inability exists, he shall resume the powers and duties of his office unless the Vice President and a majority of the principal officers of the executive departments, or such other body as Congress may by law provide, transmit within two days to the President pro tempore of the Senate and the Speaker of the House of Representatives their written declaration that the President is unable to discharge the powers and duties of his office. Thereupon Congress shall decide the issue, assembling within forty-eight hours for that purpose if not in session. If the Congress, within ten days after the receipt of the written declaration of the Vice President and a majority of the principal officers of the executive departments, or such other body as Congress may by law provide, determines by two-thirds vote of both Houses that the President is unable to discharge the powers and duties of the office, the Vice President shall continue to discharge the same as Acting President; otherwise, the President shall resume the powers and duties of his office."

CONFERENCE REPORT ON SENATE JOINT RESOLUTION 1

The committee of conference on the disagreeing votes of the two Houses on the amendment of the House to the joint resolution (S.J. Res. 1) proposing an amendment to the Constitution of the United States relating to succession to the Presidency and Vice Presidency and to cases where the President is unable to discharge the powers and duties of his office, having met, after full and free conference, have agreed to recommend and do recommend to their respective Houses as follows:

That the Senate recede from its disagreement to the amendment of the House and agree to the same with an amendment as follows: In lieu of the matter proposed to be inserted by the House amendment insert the following:

"That the following article is proposed as an amendment to the Constitution of the United States, which shall be valid to all intents and purposes as part of the Constitution when ratified by the legislatures of three-fourths of the several States within seven years from the date of its submission by the Congress:

" 'ARTICLE ——*

" '*Section 1*. In case of the removal of the President from office or of his death or resignation, the Vice President shall become President.

" '*Sec. 2*. Whenever there is a vacancy in the office of the Vice President, the President shall nominate a Vice President who shall take office upon confirmation by a majority vote of both Houses of Congress.

" '*Sec. 3*. Whenever the President transmits to the President pro tempore of the Senate and the Speaker of the House of Representatives his written declaration that he is unable to discharge the powers and duties of his office, and until he transmits to them a written declaration to the contrary, such powers and duties shall be discharged by the Vice President as Acting President.

" '*Sec. 4*. Whenever the Vice President and a majority of either the principal officers of the executive departments or of such other body as Congress may by law provide, transmit to the President pro tempore of the Senate and the Speaker of the House of Representatives their written declaration that the President is unable to discharge the powers and duties of his office, the Vice President shall immediately assume the powers and duties of the office as Acting President.

" 'Thereafter, when the President transmits to the President pro tempore of the Senate and the Speaker of the House of Representatives his written declaration that no inability exists, he shall resume the powers and duties of his office unless the Vice President and a majority of either the principal officers of the executive department or such other body as Congress may by law provide, transmit within four days to the President pro tempore of the Senate and the Speaker of the House of Representatives their written declaration that the President is unable to discharge the powers and duties of his office. Thereupon Congress shall decide the issue, assembling within forty-eight hours for that purpose if not in session. If the Congress, within twenty-one days after receipt of the latter written declaration, or, if Congress is not in session, within twenty-one days after Congress is required to assemble,

---

* The Twenty-fifth Amendment as it appears in the Constitution.

determines by two-thirds vote of both Houses that the President is unable to discharge the powers and duties of his office, the Vice President shall continue to discharge the same as Acting President; otherwise, the President shall resume the powers and duties of his office.' "

And the House agree to the same.

EMANUEL CELLER,
BYRON G. ROGERS,
JAMES C. CORMAN,
WILLIAM M. McCULLOCH,
RICHARD H. POFF,
Managers on the Part of the House.

BIRCH E. BAYH, Jr.,
JAMES O. EASTLAND,
SAM J. ERVIN, Jr.,
EVERETT M. DIRKSEN,
ROMAN L. HRUSKA,
Managers on the Part of the Senate.

The Subcommittee
Hearings

EIGHTY-EIGHTH CONGRESS, SECOND SESSION

SENATE COMMITTEE ON THE JUDICIARY

James O. Eastland, *Mississippi*, CHAIRMAN

Olin D. Johnston, *South Carolina*
John L. McClellan, *Arkansas*
Sam J. Ervin, Jr., *North Carolina*
Thomas J. Dodd, *Connecticut*
Philip A. Hart, *Michigan*
Edward V. Long, *Missouri*
Edward M. Kennedy, *Massachusetts*
Birch Bayh, *Indiana*
Quentin N. Burdick, *North Dakota*

Everett McKinley Dirksen, *Illinois*
Roman L. Hruska, *Nebraska*
Kenneth B. Keating, *New York*
Hiram L. Fong, *Hawaii*
Hugh Scott, *Pennsylvania*

SUBCOMMITTEE ON CONSTITUTIONAL AMENDMENTS

Birch Bayh, *Indiana*, CHAIRMAN

James O. Eastland, *Mississippi*
Thomas J. Dodd, *Connecticut*

Everett McKinley Dirksen, *Illinois*
Kenneth B. Keating, *New York*
Hiram L. Fong, *Hawaii*

Larry A. Conrad, CHIEF COUNSEL
Clyde Flynn, MINORITY COUNSEL

HEARINGS BEFORE THE SUBCOMMITTEE ON CONSTITUTIONAL AMENDMENTS

Eighty-eighth Congress, Second Session

on S.J. Res. 13, S.J. Res. 28, S.J. Res. 35, S.J. Res. 84, S.J. Res. 138, S.J. Res. 139, S.J. Res. 140, S.J. Res. 143, S.J. Res. 147

January 22, 23; February 24, 25, 28; March 5, 1964

STATEMENTS

Bayh, Hon. Birch, a U.S. Senator from the State of Indiana, chairman of the Subcommittee on Constitutional Amendments

Biddle, Francis, former Attorney General of the United States, Washington, D.C.

Brownell, Herbert, former Attorney General of the United States, New York, N.Y.

Burns, James MacGregor, chairman, Political Science Department, Williams College, Williamston, Mass.

Church, Hon. Frank, a U.S. Senator from the State of Idaho

Craig, Walter, president, American Bar Association, Phoenix, Ariz.

Ervin, Hon. Sam J., Jr., a U.S. Senator from the State of North Carolina

Feerick, John, attorney at law, New York, N.Y.

Fong, Hon. Hiram, a U.S. Senator from the State of Hawaii

Freund, Paul A., professor of law, Harvard University, New York, N.Y.

Hamilton, Laurens, Warrenton, Va.

Hruska, Hon. Roman L., a U.S. Senator from the State of Nebraska

Hyman, Sidney, author, Washington, D.C.

Javits, Hon. Jacob K., a U.S. Senator from the State of New York

Keating, Hon. Kenneth B., a U.S. Senator from the State of New York

Kirby, James A., Jr., associate professor of law, Vanderbilt University

Long, Hon. Edward V., a U.S. Senator from the State of Missouri

Monroney, Hon. A. S. Mike, a U.S. Senator from the State of Oklahoma

Moss, Hon. Frank E., a U.S. Senator from the State of Utah

Neustadt, Richard, professor, Columbia University

Nixon, Hon. Richard M., former Vice President of the United States

Powell, Lewis F., Jr., president-elect, American Bar Association

Rossiter, Clinton, professor of American institutions, Cornell University

Silva, Ruth A., professor, Pennsylvania State University

Taylor, Martin, chairman of the Committee on Constitutional Law, New York Bar Association

STATEMENTS SUBMITTED FOR THE RECORD

American Bar Association, consensus report

American Bar Association, house of delegates report

Albaugh, William A., Mount Rainier, Md.

Ayres, Hon. William H., a Congressman from the State of Ohio

Brown, Hon. Edmund G., Governor of the State of California

Cardozo, Michael H., executive director, Association of American Law Schools

Church, Hon. Frank, a U.S. Senator from the State of Ohio

Crown, Joseph H., attorney at law, New York, N.Y.

Dinnes, Jacob M., New York Bar Association

Eisenhower, Hon. Dwight D., former President of the United States

Ervin, Hon. Sam J., Jr., a U.S. Senator from the State of North Carolina

Hofstadter, Samuel H., Justice, Supreme Court of New York

Indiana State Bar Association, resolution

Katzenbach, Nicholas deB., Deputy Attorney General of the United States

McKeage, Everett D., San Francisco, Calif.

McCarthy, Hon. Eugene J., a U.S. Senator from the State of Minnesota

Michigan State Bar Association, resolution

Miller, William E., chairman, Republican National Committee

Miner, Ruth, professor, Wisconsin State College

Pearson, Hon. James B., a U.S. Senator from the State of Kansas

Pell, Hon. Claiborne, a U.S. Senator from the State of Rhode Island

Rockefeller, Hon. Nelson, Governor of the State of New York

Saltonstall, Hon. Leverett, a U.S. Senator from the State of Massachusetts

Wyman, Hon. Louis C., a Congressman from the State of New Hampshire

EIGHTY-NINTH CONGRESS, FIRST SESSION

SENATE COMMITTEE ON THE JUDICIARY

James O. Eastland, *Mississippi*, CHAIRMAN

Olin D. Johnston, *South Carolina*

John L. McClellan, *Arkansas*

Sam J. Ervin, Jr., *North Carolina*

Thomas J. Dodd, *Connecticut*

Philip A. Hart, *Michigan*

Edward V. Long, *Missouri*

Edward M. Kennedy, *Massachusetts*

Birch Bayh, *Indiana*

Quentin N. Burdick, *North Dakota*

Joseph D. Tydings, *Maryland*

Everett McKinley Dirksen, *Illinois*

Roman L. Hruska, *Nebraska*

Hiram L. Fong, *Hawaii*

Hugh Scott, *Pennsylvania*

Jacob K. Javits, *New York*

SUBCOMMITTEE ON CONSTITUTIONAL AMENDMENTS

Birch Bayh, *Indiana*, CHAIRMAN
James O. Eastland, *Mississippi*   ***George A. Smathers, *Florida*
Thomas J. Dodd, *Connecticut*   Everett McKinley Dirksen, *Illinois*
*Sam J. Ervin, Jr., *North Carolina*   †Roman L. Hruska, *Nebraska*
**Joseph D. Tydings, *Maryland*   Hiram L. Fong, *Hawaii*

Larry A. *Conrad*, CHIEF COUNSEL
Clyde *Flynn*, MINORITY COUNSEL

HEARING BEFORE THE SUBCOMMITTEE ON CONSTITUTIONAL AMENDMENTS

Eighty-ninth Congress, First Session

on S.J. Res. 1, S.J. Res. 6, S.J. Res. 15, S.J. Res. 25, S.J. Res. 28

January 29, 1965

STATEMENTS

Bayh, Hon. Birch, a U.S. Senator from the State of Indiana, chairman of the Subcommittee on Constitutional Amendments

Brownell, Herbert, former Attorney General of the United States, New York, N.Y.

Curtin, Hon. Williard S., a Representative in Congress from the Eighth Congressional District of the State of Pennsylvania

Deasy, Robert J., Providence College

Dodd, Hon. Thomas J., a U.S. Senator from the State of Connecticut, as presented by Dean Sharp

Folsom, Hon. Marion B., Chairman, Committee for Improvement of Management in Government, Committee for Economic Development

Fong, Hon. Hiram L., a U.S. Senator from the State of Hawaii

Hruska, Hon. Roman L., a U.S. Senator from the State of Nebraska

Katzenbach, Nicholas deB., Acting Attorney General of the United States

* On February 4, 1965, Hon. Sam J. Ervin, Jr., was appointed to serve on the Subcommittee on Constitutional Amendments.

** On February 4, 1965, Hon. Joseph D. Tydings was appointed to serve on the Subcommittee on Constitutional Amendments.

*** On April 30, 1965, Hon. George A. Smathers was appointed to serve on the Subcommittee on Constitutional Amendments.

† On February 25, 1965, Hon. Roman L. Hruska was appointed to serve on the Subcommittee on Constitutional Amendments.

Miller, Hon. Jack, a U.S. Senator from the State of Iowa
Musmanno, Hon. Judge Michael, justice, Supreme Court of Pennsylvania
Powell, Lewis F., Jr., president-elect, American Bar Association
Taylor, Martin, chairman of the Committee on Constitutional Law, New
    York Bar Association

STATEMENTS SUBMITTED FOR THE RECORD
American Bar Association, consensus report
American Bar Association, house of delegates report
Ervin, Hon. Sam J., Jr., a U.S. Senator from the State of North Carolina
Javits, Hon. Jacob K., a U.S. Senator from the State of New York
Kraus, Lawrence G.
Mundt, Hon. Karl E., a U.S. Senator from the State of South Dakota
Pearson, Hon. James B., a U.S. Senator from the State of Kansas
Saltonstall, Hon. Leverett, a U.S. Senator from the State of Massachusetts
Thurmond, Hon. Strom, a U.S. Senator from the State of South Carolina

Senate Action

COSPONSORS OF S.J. RES. 139

Bayh	Edmondson	Moss
Bartlett	Ervin	Nelson
Bible	Fong	Pearson
Burdick	Hartke	Pell
Case	Inouye	Randolph
Clark	Javits	Saltonstall
Dodd	Long, Missouri	Scott
Dominick	McGovern	Simpson
Douglas	McIntyre	Young, Ohio
	Metcalf	

COSPONSORS OF S.J. RES. 1

Bayh
Allott
Anderson
Bartlett
Bible
Boggs
Brewster
Burdick
Byrd, Virginia
Carlson
Case
Church
Clark
Cooper
Curtis
Dirksen
Dodd
Dominick
Douglas
Eastland
Ervin
Fannin
Fong
Gruening
Hart

Hartke
Hickenlooper
Inouye
Jackson
Javits
Johnston
Jordan, North Carolina
Jordan, Idaho
Kennedy, Massachusetts
Kennedy, New York
Kuchel
Lausche
Long, Louisiana
Long, Missouri
Magnuson
Mansfield
McCarthy
McClellen
McGee
McGovern
McIntyre
Metcalf
Mondale
Monroney
Morse

Morton
Moss
Murphy
Muskie
Nelson
Neuberger
Pastore
Pearson
Pell
Prouty
Proxmire
Randolph
Ribicoff
Robertson
Saltonstall
Scott
Simpson
Smathers
Sparkman
Stennis
Symington
Tydings
Williams, New Jersey
Yarborough
Young, North Dakota
Young, Ohio

ROLL CALL VOTE ON CONFERENCE REPORT

July 6, 1965

YEAS—68

Allott	Hill	Pastore
Bass	Holland	Pearson
Bayh	Inouye	Pell
Boggs	Jackson	Prouty
Brewster	Javits	Proxmire
Burdick	Jordan, Idaho	Ribicoff
Byrd, West Virginia	Kennedy, Massachusetts	Robertson
Case	Kennedy, New York	Russell, South Carolina
Church	Kuchel	Russell, Georgia
Clark	Long, Louisiana	Scott
Cooper	McClellan	Smathers
Curtis	McGee	Smith
Dirksen	McGovern	Sparkman
Dodd	McIntyre	Stennis
Douglas	McNamara	Symington
Ervin	Metcalf	Talmadge
Fannin	Miller	Thurmond
Gruening	Monroney	Tydings
Harris	Morton	Williams, New Jersey
Hart	Moss	Williams, Delaware
Hayden	Mundt	Yarborough
Hickenlooper	Muskie	Young, North Dakota
	Nelson	Young, Ohio

NAYS—5

Gore	McCarthy	Tower
Lausche	Mondale	

NOT VOTING—27

Aiken	Dominick	Magnuson
Anderson	Eastland	Mansfield
Bartlett	Ellender	Montoya
Bennett	Fong	Morse
Bible	Fulbright	Murphy
Byrd, Virginia	Hartke	Neuberger
Cannon	Hruska	Randolph
Carlson	Jordan, North Carolina	Saltonstall
Cotton	Long, Missouri	Simpson

Index

DATE DUE